VOLUME I: THE WAY OF THE ANIMAL POWERS

PART 2

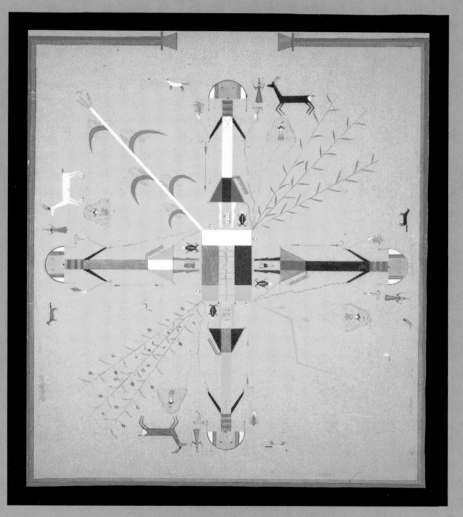

MYTHOLOGIES
OF THE
GREAT HUNT

1. The God and his animal messengers. The god's feet rest on the beaks of a pair of birds portrayed upside down. Bronze plaque known as the Lafone luevedo Disk. Diameter, 4¼ inches; thickness, about ⅛ inch. La Aguada culture, Catamarca, northwest Argentina, C. A.D. 650 to 750. Thought by some to represent the pre-Incan divinity Viracocha with his servants, Imaymana and Tocapu.

JOSEPH CAMPBELL

HISTORICAL ATLAS OF WORLD MYTHOLOGY

VOLUME I

THE WAY OF
THE ANIMAL POWERS

PART 2

MYTHOLOGIES
OF THE
GREAT HUNT

PERENNIAL LIBRARY
HARPER & ROW, PUBLISHERS NEW YORK

CAMBRIDGE, PHILADELPHIA, SAN FRANCISCO, LONDON
MEXICO CITY, SAO PAULO, SINGAPORE, SYDNEY

TABLE OF CONTENTS

Library of Congress Cataloging-in-Publication Data: Campbell, Joseph, 1904–1987. Historical atlas of world mythology. Includes bibliographical references and indexes. Contents: v.1. The way of the animal powers. pt.1. Mythologies of the primitive hunters and gatherers. pt.2. Mythologies of the great hunt. 1. Mythology. I. Title. BL311.C26 1988 291.1'3 87-40007
ISBN 0-06-055149-6 (v.1, pt.2)   88 89 90 91 92 10 9 8 7 6 5 4 3 2 1
ISBN 0-06-096349-2 (v.1, pt.2) (pbk.) 88 89 90 91 92 10 9 8 7 6 5 4 3 2 1

MYTHOLOGIES
OF THE
GREAT HUNT

Paleolithic Rock Paintings

That an abrupt expansion of human consciousness occurred toward the close of the last glacial age, some 30,000 years ago, is evident in the appearance at that time in southwestern France and northern Spain of the earliest known works of visual art—both the rock paintings of the vast temple caves of the men's hunting ceremonials, and the numerous nude female figurines that have been found associated chiefly with dwelling sites (see I.1:58–79). Evidence of the skulls suggests that an evolutionary advance from the mentality of Neanderthal to that of Cro-Magnon Man ("archaic" to "modern" *Homo sapiens*, see I.1: Figures 16 and 17) is what unleashed this *creative explosion*—to borrow a term from a recent study of the period by John E. Pfeiffer.[1]

According to Pfeiffer's interpretation of the phenomenon: There had been at that time an increase in population density with an associated social problem of conflict control, to which (in Pfeiffer's words) impressive institutions and occasions had to be addressed incorporating symbolic figurations, through which the regulations of a corpus of socially constructive rituals were pictorially encoded for storage and transmission through generations—which may be all very well as far, at least, as the sociological aspect of the remarkable occasion is concerned. The question remains, however, as to the originating source and sense of those affective symbolic figurations, which, when thus socially encoded by way of a "creative explosion" of literally thousands of magnificent masterworks of an unprecedented form of human expression, remained for some 20,000 years in force (c. 30,000 to 10,000 B.C.) as the founding mythological revelation for unnumbered generations of hunting tribes, whose lives and way of life were utterly dependent, not only on the physical support, but also on the spiritual instruction, of the animals thus displayed and celebrated in their subterranean chambers of initiation and invocation.

A Note on cross-references: The Foreword makes use of an internal cross-referencing system that is a condensation of, but consistent with, the system used elsewhere in the book. Hence, "(see Volume I, Part 1, page 112)" has been shortened to "(see I.1: 112)." References to illustrations read the same as before, i.e., "(see I.1: Figure 74)."

André Leroi-Gourhan, the present leading authority on the cavern art of Paleolithic Europe, has found through a comparative study and computerized count of the animals depicted in the caves (see I.1: 58–62), that the number of species represented is much lower than the number of species known to have existed at the time. "Paleolithic artists," he writes, "did not portray just any animal, but animals of certain species, and these did not necessarily play a part in their daily life....The main actors," he discovered, "are the horse and the bison, the animals next in importance being the hinds, the mammoths, the oxen, the ibexes, and the stags....Bears, lions, and rhinoceroces play an important part, but as a rule there is only one representation of each per cave, and they are by no means represented in every cave."[2]

Such, then, were the animals selected by the Paleolithic master artists from the bounty of their environment for depiction in the galleries of their subterranean corridors and chambers, as being in some way significant of a mystic dimension of their landscape perceived by the eye of the mind, not the eyes of the physical look of things. One may compare their number to that of the masquerade of metaphorical birds and beasts selected by the Kwakiutl of the North American North Pacific Coast from the bounty of their environment, as shown in the photograph by Edward Curtis here reproduced (see below: 188–189), to be evoked to life in seasonal dances.

As Leroi-Gourhan discovered further in this comparative study of the painted caves (see I.1:62), certain animals turned up next to each other "too often for such associations to be explained only as chance": oxen or bison next to horses, for example, or bisons next to mammoths. "The fundamental principle," he concluded, "is that of pairing....Starting with the earliest figures, one has the impression of being faced with a system polished in the course of time—not unlike the older religions of our world, wherein there are male and female divinities whose actions do not overtly allude to sexual reproduction, but whose male and female qualities are indispensably complementary."[3]

Moreover, as he also found, there is an architectural order in the distribution of the symbolic beasts and signs throughout the geographical as well as historical range of this earliest known, recorded testament to a system of ideas. "What constituted for Paleolithic men the special heart and core of the caves," he discovered, "is clearly the panels in the central part, dominated by animals from the male category and male signs. The entrance to the sanctuary, usually a narrow part of the cave, is decorated with male symbols, either animals or signs; the back of the cave, often a narrow tunnel, is decorated with the same signs, reinforced by horned men and the rarer animals (cave lion or rhinoceros). Although crowded with images this framework is quite simple; yet it leaves us completely in the dark concerning what we should like to know about the rites, and let us say, about an underlying metaphysics. However, it rules out any simplistic idea concerning the religious system of Paleolithic men."[4]

This important statement from an unimpeachable authority confirms and validates the impression which immediately overtakes even the ill prepared visitor to such a sanctuary of Stone Age faith and hope as, say, the magnificently conceived grotto of Lascaux: which is, namely, of an ordered system of metaphorical reflections preserved from an age beyond our horizon of time in the pictorial script of this truly amazing Stone Age testament. It is certainly not a mere mindless arrangement of accurately observed animal forms, expertly delineated by a school of accomplished artists striving for decorative optical effects. The sense of an intelligible metaphorical statement is incontestable.

Comparably, on entering such a relatively modern sacred space as, for example, the cathedral of Notre Dame de Paris, or the temple in Nara, Japan, of the Great Sun Buddha, Vairochana, the visitor, the stranger from afar, will immediately know that he has entered an area where everything is not only metaphorical, but intelligibly related to everything else. And the reader of the present volume, likewise, on viewing the photograph by Edward Curtis (see below: 188–189), will surely have realized that the array of bizarre physical shapes there brought together and arranged for the camera's eye adumbrates a mythological order visible only to the eye of the informed mind, signifying a way of understanding and relating to the universe.

The universe viewed by the physical

eye alone is but an array of shapes, some alive, some not, all changing either rapidly or slowly, which though linked along chains of cause and effect, are seen as distinct and separate from each other. In this phenomenal field, an Aristotelian logic prevails: *a* is not *not-a*. Morever, except for the miracle of fire (and today, the electric bulb), the observed forms are not self-luminous. They are visible only by daylight to the daylight mind, when awake and outwardly cognitive, attentive to objects apprehended as apart from, and other than itself. As quoted by Ananda K. Coomaraswamy from a sermon by the medieval Rhineland mystic and theologian Meister Eckhart: "Subtract the mind, and the eye is open to no purpose."[5]

By night, however, when the sun has set, the mind turns inward and, together with its universe, which is now a reflex of itself, "doth change Into something rich and strange." The forms now beheld are self-luminous and in definition ambiguous, unsubstantial yet insuppressibly affective. For *not-a* is now indistinguishable from *a*. The beholding mind and the objects beheld are of the same, non-dual, dreaming consciousness and of an intimately suggestive yet elusive import of some kind.

As defined, classified and described in the Indian Upanishads (first millennium B.C.), these contrasting states of consciousness in waking and in dream are known, respectively, as *Vaiśvānara*, meaning "Common to all Men," and *Taijasa*, "Originating from and consisting of *tejas* ('light')." They are identified, furthermore, with the first and second elements of the sacred syllable AUM or OM (*a* and *u* being in Sanskrit pronounced together as *o*), the concluding element, M, being then identified with the state of deep dreamless sleep.

As described in the *Māṇḍūkya Upanishad*:

1. "OM! This perishable sound is all. As further explained: it is the Past, the Present, the Future, all that has become, is becoming, and is yet to be. Moreover, whatever transcends this three-fold Time: that also is OM.

2. "For verily, this all is *brahman* (the Imperishable). One's Self, too, is *brahman*. The Self (*ātman*) is of four conditions:

3. "The Waking State (*jāgarita-sthāna*), outwardly cognitive, experiencing the gross enjoyments common to all men (*sthūlabhug-vaiśvānara*) by way of the body, its senses, organs of action, vital energies, and aspects of mind: this is the first condition of the Self.

4. "The Dreaming State (*svapna-sthāna*), inwardly cognitive, experiencing in exquisite solitude luminous enjoyments (*praviviktabhuk-taijasa*) by way of the body, its senses, organs of action, vital energies, and aspects of mind. This is the second condition.

5. "Where one asleep has no desires whatsoever, sees no dream whatsoever: that is deep sleep. The Deep Sleep State (*sushupta-sthāna*) is at one with itself (*ekībhūta*), an involuted cognitional mass (*prajñānaghana*), alone (*eva*), ensheathed in bliss (*ānandamaya*), enjoying bliss (*ānandabhuj*), the portal to knowledge [of the other two states]. Of the Knower (*prājña*) this is the third condition.

6. "This, verily, is the all-knowing Lord of all, Indweller and Controller; the Matrix (*yoni*) of all; the Beginning and End (*prabhavāpyayau*) of all beings.

7. "What is thought of as the fourth condition of the Self — cognitive neither inward, outward, nor of the intermediate state; not a uniform cognitional mass; neither knowing nor unknowing (*naprajñam-nāprajñam*); unseen (*adṛṣṭa*); detached (*avyavahārya*); incomprehensible (*agrāhya*); without characteristics (*alakṣaṇa*); beyond thought (*acintya*); indescribable (*avyapadeśya*); the essence of the assurance of a state of identity with the Self (*ekātmya-pratyaya-sāra*); the cessation of manifestation (*prapañcopaśama*); at peace (*śānta*); felicitous (*śiva*) and non-dual (*advaita*) — that is the Self (*ātman*) to be realized.

8. "This then is the Self (*ātman*) in the sense of the elements of the imperishable syllable. The elements are the four conditions and the four conditions are the elements: namely, A, U, M [and the Fourth, the Silence before, after, and supporting the sounding of the syllable OM].

9. "The Waking State, the Common to all Men, is the A-sound, the first element, for its comprehensiveness and priority. He who knows this obtains verily all his desires and becomes preeminent.

10. "The Dreaming State, Self-Luminous, is the U sound, the second element, for its eminence and intermediacy. He who knows this becomes verily a fountain of knowledge equal to any. In his family no one is born ignorant of *brahman*.

11. "The Deep Sleep State, of Intuitive Wisdom (*prājña*), is the M sound, the third element, as being the measure (*miti*), the termination or quenching (*apīti*) wherein all become one. He who knows this measures and comprehends all in himself.

12. "Transcendent, unsounded, beyond action (*avyavahārya*), is the Fourth, of no phenomenal existence, supremely blissful and without a second. Thus OM is indeed *ātman*, the Self. He who knows this enters through the Self into the Self— yea, he who know this."[6]

Sigmund Freud, treating of the dreaming state in the early masterwork by which his reputation was established, *Die Traumdeutung* (*The Interpretation of Dreams*, published 1899 but dated 1900), distinguishes two sources of the impulses contributing to the instigation of dreams:

(1) wish-impulses originating in waking consciousness (*Cs.*) but carried into the dream state by way of what he termed the "Preconscious" (*Pcs.*), and then

(2) wish-impulses arising from the Unconscious (*Ucs.*) system.

"In general, I am of the opinion," he states, "that unfulfilled wishes of the day are insufficient to produce a dream in adults. I will readily admit that the wish-impulses originating in consciousness contribute to the instigation of dreams, but they probably do no more. The dream would not occur if the preconscious wish were not reinforced from another source.

"That source is the unconscious. I believe that *the conscious wish becomes effective in exciting a dream only when it succeeds in arousing a similar unconscious wish which reinforces it....* I believe that these unconscious wishes are always active and ready to express themselves whenever they find an opportunity of allying themselves with an impulse from consciousness, and transferring their own greater intensity to the lesser intensity of the latter. It must, therefore, seem that the conscious wish alone has been realized in the dream; but a slight peculiarity in the form of the dream will put us on the track of the powerful ally from the unconscious....

"The thought-impulses continued into sleep may be divided into the following groups:

1. Those which have not been completed during the day owing to some accidental cause.

2. Those which have been left uncompleted because our mental powers have failed us, i.e. unsolved problems.

3. Those which have been turned back and suppressed during the day. This is reinforced by a powerful fourth group:

4. Those which have been excited in our *Ucs.* during the day by the workings of the *Pcs.*; and finally we may add a fifth, consisting of:

5. The indifferent impressions of the day, which have therefore been left unsettled.

"We need not underrate the psychic intensities introduced into sleep by these residues of the day's waking life, especially those emanating from the group of the unsolved issues....I cannot say what change is produced in the *Pcs.* system by the state of sleep, but there is no doubt that the psychological characteristics of sleep are to be sought mainly in the cathectic changes occuring in just this system....On the other hand, I have found nothing in the psychology of dreams to warrant the assumption that sleep produces any but secondary changes in the conditions of the *Ucs.* system. Hence, for the nocturnal excitations in the *Pcs.* there remains no other path than that taken by the wish-excitations from the *Ucs.*; they must seek reinforcement from the *Ucs.*, and follow the detours of the unconscious excitations.

"But what is the relation of the preconscious day-residues to the dream? There is no doubt that they penetrate abundantly into the dream; that they utilize the dream-content to obtrude themselves upon consciousness even during the night; indeed, they sometimes even dominate the dream-content, and compel it to continue the work of the day; it is also certain that the day-residues may just as well have any other character as that of wishes."[7]

And so, returning to India with this 19th-century European insight into the nature of what Freud called the "dream work" in mind, we find that the Vedantic theologian Sankara (c. A.D. 700–750), treating, in his commentary on *Māṇḍūkya Upanishad* verse 4, of the intermediate Dream State between Waking and Deep Dreamless Sleep, was already fully aware of the interplay there of (1) the preconscious day-residues, and (2) what in India is recognized as the "inner light" (*taijasa*) of the Self.

"Waking consciousness," we read in Sankara's discussion, "being associated with many manners of relationship and seemingly conscious of objects as external (although in reality they are nothing but states of mind), leaves in the mind corresponding impressions. That the mind in dream, maintaining none of the external connections, yet possessed of these impressions left upon it by the waking consciousness, like a piece of canvas with pictures painted upon it, should experience the dream state as though it were a waking state, is due to its being under the influence of ignorance (*avidyā*), desire (*kāma*), and impulse to action (*karma*). Thus it is said in the *Bṛihadāraṇyaka Upanishad* (c. ninth century B.C.):

"'When, on falling asleep, one takes along the material (*mātrā*) of this all-containing world, tears it apart and builds it up, oneself, and by one's own light dreams: that person becomes self-illuminated.

"'There are no chariots there, no spans, no roads. Yet he projects from himself chariots, spans, and roads. There are no blisses there, no pleasures, no delights. Yet he projects from himself, blisses, pleasures, and delights. There are no tanks there, no lotus-pools, no streams. Yet he projects from himself tanks, lotus-pools, and streams. For he is a creator.

"'To this point there are the following verses:

"'*Striking down in sleep what is bodily,*
Sleepless, he looks down upon the sleeping senses.
Having taken to himself light, he has returned to his own place:
That Golden Person (hiraṇmaya purusha), *the Lone Wild Gander* (ekahaṁsa).

Guarding with his breath his low nest,
Out of that nest the Immortal goes forth.
He goes wherever he pleases, that Immortal,
The Golden Person, the Unique Wild Gander.

In the State of Sleep, soaring high and low,
A god, he puts forth for himself innumerable forms:
Now, as it were, enjoying pleasure with women;
Now, as it were, laughing, or beholding even terrifying sights.

People see his pleasure ground;
Him no one sees at all.'"[8]

Just what overpowering transpersonal experiences and associated thoughts informed the minds and moved the practiced hands of the artists of the Late Paleolithic, we shall of course never directly know, since no word of whatever speech may have been theirs has come down to us. From the Bushmen of the South African Kalahari Desert, however, whose rock art has been practiced (apparently without interruption) since the close of the last glacial age (see I.1:42–43 and 81–101), verbal accounts have been recorded, not only of the mythology, but also of the out-of-body experiences in trance state, from which their spirited representations have been taken of an intelligible sphere, known to the eye of the mind, unseen by the light of day.

Certainly one of the most vivid accounts of such a visionary adventure yet recorded from any quarter of the globe is that from the report of an experienced Kung trance dancer, as delivered to Marguerite Anne Biesele scarcely more than a decade ago (see I.1:96). Bearing in mind the image of the Self as the Lone Wild Gander in flight, let us here recall the circumstances of that remarkable out-of-body adventure, which is such, apparently, as occurs nearly every night among the Bushmen of the Kalahari.

A little cluster of women, who have lighted a large fire and are seated on the ground, has begun intoning a wordless chant while steadily clapping time. Eventually, a few of the men stray in behind them, to circle with short heavy stamps in a single line, which turns about, from time to time, to circle the other way. Their rhythms are complex, built into 5- and 7-beat phrases, and their body postures tight, hunched forward, arms close to the sides, slightly flexed. Others join the round, and as the night runs on, those approaching trance begin to concentrate intently. A climax strikes when one or another of them breaks and passes into the state known as half-death, while his spirit flies and climbs along threads of spider silk to the sky.

"When people sing," declared Marguerite Biesele's trance dancer, "I dance. I enter the earth. I go in at a place like a place where people drink water. I travel a long way, very far. When I emerge, I am already climbing. I'm climbing threads, the threads that lie over there in the south. I climb one and leave it, then I climb another one. Then I leave it and climb another.... And when you arrive at God's place you make yourself small. You have become small. You come in small to God's place. You do what you have to do there. Then you return to where everyone is, and you hide your face. You hide your face so you won't see anything. You come and come and come and finally you enter your body again. All the people who have stayed behind are waiting for you—they fear you. You enter, enter the earth, and you return to enter the skin of your body...And you say 'he-e-e-e!' That is the sound of your return to your body. Then you begin to sing. The *ntum*-masters are there around. They take powder and blow it—Phew! Phew!—in your face. They take hold of your head and blow about the sides of your face. This is how you manage to be alive again. Friends, if they don't do that to you, you die.... You just die and are dead. Friend, this is what it does, this *ntum* that I do, this *ntum* here that I dance."[9]

The term *ntum* has been explained (see I.1:94–95) as a supernatural power that in the Mythological Age of the Beginning was put by the creator god into a number of things: medicine songs, ostrich eggs, certain plants and fruits, the sun, falling stars, rain, bees, honey, giraffes, aardvarks, blood, redwing partridges, and fires made in certain situations; also into certain persons, who may function as medicine men and healers.

Ntum varies in force in the various things it informs: beneficent in some, always strong, but in some things dangerously so. *Ntum* is so strong in the great god Gauwa that should he approach an ordinary mortal, like a lightning bolt his *ntum* would kill the man. The Kung call *ntum* a "death thing"; also, a "fight."

As discussed at length in my chapter on the Bushman trance dance and its mythic ground (see I.1:90–101, from which pages I have here been quoting), the supreme occasion for the activation of *ntum* is the trance dance. The exertion of the tirelessly circling dancers heats their medicine power, which, as reported in the writings of Lorna Marshall and Richard B. Lee,[10] they experience as a physical substance in the pit of the stomach. The women's singing, the men say, "awakens their hearts," and eventually their portion of *ntum* becomes so hot that it boils. "The men say it boils up their spinal columns into their heads, and is so strong when it does this," Lorna Marshall reports, "that it overcomes them and they lose their senses."[11]

One of the very greatest Indian God-men of the last century, Sri Ramakrishna (1836–1886), once described to a circle of his devotees the physical sensation of the unfolding ascent up his spine of the charge of psychic energy known in India as the *Kuṇḍalinī*, the "Coiled Serpent Power." In Ramakrishna's words:

"Sometimes the Spiritual Current rises through the spine, crawling like an ant. Sometimes, in *samādhi* [ecstasy in full trance], the soul swims joyfully in the ocean of divine ecstasy, like a fish. Sometimes, when I lie down on my side, I feel the Spiritual Current pushing me like a monkey and playing with me joyfully. I remain still. The Current, like a monkey, suddenly with one jump reaches the *Sahasrāra* [the supreme spiritual center, envisioned as a thousand-petalled lotus at the crown of the head]. That is why you see me jump with a start. Sometimes, again, the Spiritual Current rises like a bird hopping from one branch to another. The place where it rests feels like fire ….Sometimes the Spiritual Current moves up like a snake. Going in a zigzag way, at last it reaches the head and I go into samadhi. A man's spiritual consciousness is not awakened until his Kundalini is aroused."[12]

In the Indian Vedantic manner of speech, such a consummate holy man as was Ramakrishna is known as a *Paramahaṁsa*, "Paramount of Supreme Wild Gander," in recognition of his having realized in life the ultimate Vedantic goal of complete self-identification with the Self; which is to say, with that metaphorical "Lone Wild Gander" whose invisible flight throughout the world of his creation has been described in the above-quoted lines from the *Bṛihadāraṇyaka Upanishad*.

It is relevant to recall at this point, that in Bushman rock paintings the released spirits of the trance dancers, as well as of the dead, are represented as flying antelope men, called in the literature, *alites*, or "flying bucks." (See I.1:98–99.) Also to be noticed again is the shamanic figure pictured in the most sacred recess of the cavern of Lascaux, lying in trance before the vision of an eviscerated bull, wearing a bird mask, and with the figure of a bird on the top of what appears to be a shamanic staff at his side (see I.1: Figure 105.).

The image of a bird in flight is a well-nigh universal sign of the Holy Spirit, whether as in the Christian figure of the Holy Ghost descending in the form of a dove, both at the moment of Mary's conception of the Word, and again, at the time of the baptism of her Son, when the heavens opened "and he saw the Spirit of God descending like a dove and alighting on him" (Matthew 3:16); or as in the metaphorical Indian figure of the Lone Wild Gander (*ekahaṁsa*), as signifying the non-dual ground of all being (*brahman*) which is in each and every thing the one enlivening Self (*ātman*).

"Striking down in sleep what is bodily,
Sleepless, he looks down upon the sleeping senses."

Such is the experience of the knowing subject released in trance to the raptures of the untrammeled eye of vision. Suddenly unloaded of the material weight of commitments to the field of waking consciousness:

"A god, he puts forth for himself innumerable forms."

The leading reference of the Upanishad here is, of course, to the Self (*ātman*) as identical with the sole, non-dual ground of all being and becoming (*brahman*), putting forth the phenomenal universe in a continuous act of creation. Also implied, however, as recognized in Sankara's application of the passage, is a reference to the microcosmic aspect of the Self, as the indwelling immortal part of each and every living being, enjoying in each in the Dreaming State a creative life analogous to that of the macrocosmic creator. The two creations, though analogous, are not exactly comparable, since the field of manifestation of the microcosmic Self is confined to the mental sphere of the dreamer, whereas that of the macrocosmic Creator extends to the grossly visible pleasure ground of the daylight consciousness that is "Common to All Men." Moreover, the chariots, spans and roads, blisses, pleasures and delights, envisioned by the microcosmic Self are not original to its inward field of exquisite manifestations, but have been imprinted, carried and recollected from an outward field of already manifest gross phenomena. And still further, the inward eye of the mind by which those forms are beheld is not of the immortal, creative, universally indwelling Self (*ātman*), but of an intervening, historically conditioned ego (*ahaṁ-kāra*: "making the sound I"), which is not only bounded by ignorance (*avidyā*) of their true nature, but also attached to them with desires (*kāma*) and impulses to action (*karma*).

Freud's name for the same ground and source of all human willing is the *id*, the "It," which he characterized (as summarized by his authorized translator A.A. Brill), as "an unorganized chaotic mentality…the sole aim of which is the gratification of all needs, the alleviation of hunger, self-preservation and love, the preservation of the species….As the child grows older," Brill's explication continues, "that part of the id which comes in contact with the environment through the senses learns to know the inexorable reality of the outer world and becomes modified into what Freud calls the ego. This ego, possessing awareness of the environment, henceforth strives to curb the law-

less id tendencies whenever they attempt to assert themselves incompatibly." A neurosis may result from "a conflict between the ego and the id," or from "a conflict between the ego and the super-ego [the internalized parental warnings and ethical laws of a local society]." In a psychosis, the illness results from "a conflict between the ego and the outer world."[13]

"Psychoanalysis," we are informed in Freud's classic essay on *The Ego and the Id* (published 1923), "is an instrument to assist the ego in its progressive conquest of the id."[14] "The id is completely amoral, the ego is striving to become moral; the super-ego can become hypermoral and as ferocious then as the id."[15]

In contrast, according to Sankara's view and in general throughout the philosophical and yogic systems of India, no functional conflict of this kind between id and ego is recognized. Freud's id corresponds to the Indian reincarnating will to life, the so-called *jīva* (compare Latin *vīvo*, "I live, am alive, have life"; English *vivacious* and Greek *bios*, "life"), that chaotic bundle of motivating desires (*kāma*), impulses to action (*karma*), and ignorance of the true nature of being (*avidyā*) which "puts on bodies and puts them off as a man puts on and puts off clothing" (*Bhagavad Gita* 2.22). Freud's super-ego is the Indian *dharma*: the body of local laws and customs that has become internalized as constituting the dreamer's sense of his duties to society; and Freud's ego, understood as that part of the id which has become conscious of "the inexorable reality of the outer world," is known in Sanskrit, also, as "ego," *aham*—except that in India its commitment to what Freud regarded as "the inexorable reality of the outer world" is recognized as itself the maintaining cause of that state of ignorance (*avidyā*) of the *jīva* which it is the function of yoga and philosophy to illuminate and dissolve. The compulsive force of *dharma* will then also be annulled. And so, in diametric contrast to the Freudian formula of "where there is id there shall be ego," is Sankara's ideal, as stated in his Vedantic classic, "The Crest Jewel of Discrimination":

"Shedding the activities of ego and its adjuncts, abandoning all attachments in realization of the Highest Truth (*paramārtha*), be released from dualities through enjoyment of the bliss of the Self (*ātman*) and rest in *brahman*; for thou hast there attained thy full Self-Nature unqualified (*pūrṇātmanā brahmaṇi nirvikalpa*)."[16]

In contrast to this opening of ego (*aham*) to the light and force of its own larger reality in the Self (*ātman*), the psychoanalytic Freudian approach to the interpretation of dreams, and therewith of mythology and the arts, remains enclosed in a tight horizon of egocentric day-residues from both the recent and most distant past.

For not only is the Preconscious (*Pcs.*) motivated by wish-impulses from the Waking State (*jāgarita-sthāna*), but so too is the Unconscious (*Ucs.*), since, as diagnosed by Freud, this occult source of all spiritual afflictions is but a manifold of libidinous desires and fears repressed from infancy and reflecting the individual's earliest Waking-State experiences of a mother and a father (*Oedipus Complex*).[17] Freudian psychotherapy, therefore, is fixated in the past, its method being to uncover, not the zone of infinite light from which the energies of the psyche derive, but those suppressed infantile memories of specific traumatic scenes and events through which the light has been, so to say, deflected and occluded, the ideal of ego-enlightenment being of adjustment to the inexorable demands of both the local moral order (*super-ego*) and the "outer world."

Carl G. Jung, in his approach to the interpretation of dreams and the imagery of myth, recognized two distinct spheres of relevancy, as functional of two orders or levels of the unconscious: (1) a historically and biographically conditioned *personal* unconscious, corresponding to the Freudian id-to-ego-bounded system, and (2) a transpersonal, instinctive, biologically grounded *collective* unconscious, matching Sankara's understanding of the force of the Wild Gander, the macrocosmic atman, in the sphere of consciousness of Deep Dreamless Sleep (*sushupta-sthāna*).

"There are present," states Jung, "in every individual, besides his personal memories, the great 'primordial' images, as Jacob Burckhardt once aptly called them, the inherited powers of human imagination as it has been since time immemorial. The fact of this inheritance explains the truly amazing phenomenon that certain motifs from myths and legends repeat themselves the world over in identical forms. It also explains why it is that our mental patients can reproduce exactly the same images and associations that are known to us from the old texts."[18]

"The collective unconscious is a part of the psyche," he states further, "which can be negatively distinguished from a personal unconscious by the fact that it does not, like the latter, owe its existence to personal experience and consequently is not a personal acquisition. While the personal unconscious is made up essentially of contents which have at one time been conscious but which have disappeared from consciousness through having been forgotten or repressed, the contents of the collective unconscious have never been in consciousness and therefore have never been individually acquired, but owe their existence exclusively to heredity. Whereas the personal unconscious consists for the most part of *complexes*, the content of the collective unconscious is made up essentially of *archetypes*.

"The concept of the archetype, which is an indispensable correlate of the idea of the collective unconscious, indicates the existence of definite forms in the psyche which seem to be present always and everywhere. Mythological research calls them 'motifs'; in the psychology of primitives they correspond to Levy-Bruhl's concept of 'representations collectives,' and in the field of comparative religion they have been defined by Hubert and Mauss as 'categories of the imagination.' Adolf Bastian long ago called them 'elementary' or 'primordian thoughts.' From these references it should be clear enough that my idea of the archetype—literally a pre-existent form—does not stand alone but is something that is recognized and named in other fields of knowledge."[19]

And with respect, then, to the imagery specifically of the Dream State (*svapna-sthāna*): "The inner image," states Jung, "is a complex structure made up of the most varied material from the most varied sources. It is no conglomerate, however, but a homogeneous product with a meaning of its own. The image is a *condensed expression of the psychic situation as a whole,* and not merely, nor even predominantly, of unconscious content pure and simple. It undoubltedly does express unconscious contents, but not the whole of them, only those that are momentarily constellated. This constellation is the result of the spontaneous activity of the unconscious on the one hand and of the momentary conscious situation on the other, which always stimulates the activity of relevant subliminal material and at the same time inhibits the irrelevant. Accordingly the image is an expression of the unconscious as well as the conscious situation of the moment. The interpretation of its meaning, therefore, can start neither from the conscious alone nor from the unconscious alone, but only from their reciprocal relationship.

"I call the image *primordial* when it possesses an archaic character. I speak of its archaic character when the image is in striking accord with familiar mythological motifs. It then expresses material primarily derived from the *collective unconscious,* and indicates at the same time that the factors influencing the conscious situation of the moment are *collective* rather than personal. A *personal* image has neither an archaic character nor a collective significance, but expresses contents of the *personal unconscious* and a personally conditioned conscious situation.

"The primordial image, elsewhere also termed *archetype*, is always collective, i.e., it is at least common to entire peoples or epochs. In all probability the most important mythological motifs are common to all times and races; I have, in fact, been able to demonstrate a whole series of motifs from Greek mythology in the dreams and fantasies of purebred Negroes suffering from mental disorders."[20]

The transformations of consciousness that occur when the mind, disengaged from its normal state of attachment to forms of the past, is through identification with luminous apparitions of the intermediate dreaming state transported toward a realization of non-duality in infinite being, are in the Upanishad termed, respectively, A. *Viśva* or *Vaiśvānara*, "Pervasive, Prevailing," or "Common to all Men"; U. *Taijasa*, "Originating from and Consisting of *tejas*, 'Light'"; and M. *Prajña*, the "Knower." As stated by the sage Guadapada (c. A.D. seventh century): "*Viśva* is he who cognizes with the senses; *Taijasa*, he who cognizes in the mind; *Prajña*, he who constitutes the infinite space (*ākāśa*) in the heart. Thus the one Self (*ātman*) is [experienced as] threefold in the body."[21]

The condition of *Prājña* has been described in the Upanishad as "ensheathed in bliss" (*ānandamaya*), "enjoying bliss" (*ānandabhuj*). Hence, when the mind disengaged from the "gross enjoyments" of the Waking State (*jāgarita-sthāna*), transported by way of the luminous enjoyments of the Dreaming State (*svapna-sthāna*), approaches in exquisite solitude the condition of *Prājña*, in non-dual identification with the *ātman*, it is overtaken by a surpassing rapture which is of the order of a trance-revelation. And it typically is out of ecstatic transports of this kind that works of visionary arts derive.

Marguerite Anne Biesele has given us the account of a moment of revelation experienced by a South African Bushman woman, which became the inspiration of a traditional song and dance. Her account appears in Volume I. 1, (see I.1:94), in connection with a discussion there of the Bushman trance experience as a way of access to an acquisition of the supernatural power called *ntum*. We may recall the incident here for its relevance to our present question, of the origin, meaning, and essential function of a work of authentic primitive art.

"A woman named Be was alone in the bush one day in Namibia, when she saw a herd of giraffes running before an approaching thunderstorm. The rolling beat of their hooves grew louder and mingled in her head with the sound of sudden rain. Suddenly a song she had never heard before came to her, and she began to sing.

"Gauwa (the great god) told her it was a medicine song. Be went home and taught the song to her husband, Tike. They sang and danced together. And it was, indeed, a song for trancing, a medicine song. Tike taught it to others, who passed it on."[22]

The first point of importance here is the solitude of the moment when the inspiration occurred. The second is of what happened in the woman's head: two separate observations combined to suggest a common ground, the sound of the hooves of a herd of giraffes, and the sound of sudden rain. The third point is of her immediate utterance of a song never heard before, which when sung to an accompanying dance had the power (*ntum*) to induce trancing. And the fourth point is of the voice of a god letting her know that what had sprung to her mind was an incantation of supernatural power.

The experience had begun with her mind in the Waking State (*jāgarita-sthāna*). But when the two external incidents had mingled in her head to call forth from her own nature an associated response which had a power (*ntum*) that was not of her intention, she was for that moment in a state of ecstasy (Greek, *ekstasis*, "standing aside"); in other words, "beside herself." She was spellbound. The incantation which at that moment sprang to her tongue had the power, furthermore, to transport others to the state of mind from which it had been brought. And that state might culminate in the out-of-body experience of trance, which is an extreme incidence of the Dreaming State (*svapna-sthāna*), which, as we have seen, is described in the *Māṇḍūkya Upanishad* as "inwardly cognitive, experiencing in exquisite solitude luminous enjoyments." Plato in *Phaedo* 65–69 likens such an experience to that of the immortal soul at death, liberated from this mortal body which "fills us with loves and desires and fears and all sorts of fancies and a great deal of nonsense....That is why...if we are ever to have pure knowledge of anything, we must get rid of the body and contemplate things by themselves with the soul by itself."[23]

James Joyce, in his fundamental discussion of esthetics in his early novel, *A Portrait of the Artist as a Young Man*, distinguishes between what he terms "proper" and "improper" art: art which is designed to render a purely *esthetic* experience (the word is from the Greek *aisthētikos*, "perceptive"; *aisthanēsthai*, "to perceive, to feel"); and art which is in the service of interests other than the purely esthetic—for example, ethics, politics, or advertising.

Improper art is of two orders: that which excites desire for the object depicted, and that which inculcates loathing or fear of it. The former Joyce terms pornographic, and the latter, didactic art. These are of art, that is to say, in the service, either of the *id* or of the *super-ego*; either of all those "loves and desires and fears and all sorts of fancies and a great deal of nonsense" which are to be "shaken off," according to Plato, if we are ever to contemplate things as they are; or else of some kind of control system, to pull the confusion of all that bewilderment into some sort of socially tolerable formation.

Proper art, on the other hand, has nothing to do either with exciting or with controlling the impulses of the *id* by depicting objects simply as they appear to waking consciousness in various appealing, entertaining, instructive, edifying, or terrifying arrangements. Proper art does not move one either to desire or to loathing, either toward the object or away from it. One is held, on the contrary, in esthetic arrest, a moment of sensational (esthetic) contemplation, as before a recognized revelation, or in Joyce's language, an "ephiphany." "The mind," he writes, "is arrested and raised above desire and loathing."[24] The original, biological function of the eye, to seek out and identify things to eat and to alert the mind to danger, is for a moment, or (in the case of a true artist) for a lifetime suspended, and the world (beheld without judgment of its relevance to the well-being of the observer) is recognized as a revelation sufficient in itself. "If the doors of perception were cleansed," wrote Blake in *The Marriage of Heaven and Hell*, "every thing would appear to man as it is, infinite." Or, as in the words reported of Jesus in the recently discovered and translated Gnostic *Gospel According to Thomas*: "The Kingdom of the Father is spread upon the earth, and men do not see it."[25]

Writing of the art of the Paleolithic caves, Leroi-Gourhan points out, as we have already remarked, that the number of animal species represented is much lower than the number of species known to have existed at the time, and that those that do appear did not necessarily play an important part in the people's lives (see I.1:62). Patricia Vinnicombe, writing of Bushman art, has likewise noticed that the number of animal species depicted is not a fair sample of the species of the region; nor do they represent those of the Bushman diet. The paintings, she declares, are neither a menu nor a checklist, but the illustrations of a Late Stone Age mythology, in which the most prominent figure is a strikingly beautiful, large and noble antelope, the eland (see I.1:91). Harold Pager, writing of such a visionary painting as that of the magnificent Sebaaiene Cave, in the Ndedema Gorge of the Drakensberg range (see I.1:98, and Figure 176), interprets it as the Bushman's idea of their "eternal hunting grounds," the everlasting scenery to which the great *ntum* masters in their half-death states pay visits three or four times a month. Prominent in such visionary scenes brought back from the "world behind this one we see with our eyes," are "antelope men," partly eland, partly human, frequently flying.

Now in the mythic tales of the Bushmen, telling of the time of the Beginning, the first eland appears in a curiously ambiguous relationship to their creator-god and trickster-hero, Kaggen ("Mantis"). In one tale the first eland evolves from the shoe of Kaggen's son-in-law, soaked in water. Fondled and beloved of Kaggen, the beautiful animal is slain and butchered by the son-in-law and his son; whom Kaggen then attempts to slay, but the flung weapons circle back and nearly kill himself. A second shoe, flung into the sky, then becomes the moon (see I.1:91).

Another folktale has it that Kaggen's wife bore the first eland and that Kaggen tried to kill it by throwing sharpened sticks, but missed. In his absence, his own sons discovered and killed the eland and he, on returning, rebuked them furiously. Then, together with his wife he mixed fat from the animal's heart in a pot, along with some of its blood, and churned. The drops became, first eland bulls, then cows, which spread over the earth. Whereupon Kaggen sent his sons out to hunt them. And that day, game were given to men to eat (see I.1:92).

Patricia Vinnicombe has called attention to the Bushmen's use of blood and fat in the composition of their paints, and Herbert Kühn has suggested that blood and fat may have been ingredients of the paints of the Paleolithic caves (see I.1:93). The suggestion follows that the act of painting will have been a ritual act of restitution in the sense (as in the folktale) of the restitution and multiplication of Kaggen's eland. Like the art of the song that sprang to the tongue of the Bushman woman Be, that of the paintings had the power of a medium uniting the two worlds, of the outer eyes of the body and the inward eye of the mind.

The weapons, the points of the arrows and spears, of the Bushmen are anointed with a poison, the effects of which take a day or more to bring an eland down. From the moment an animal is struck, the hunter from whose hand or bow the weapon flew is bound to a sympathetic routine of ritual observances which must be followed without fault throughout the period of the stricken animal's dying. The mystical identification here implied of the slayer with the slain (the *a* with the *not-a*) is of a piece with the notion that the Bushman dead are themselves transformed into elands; also, that the "half-dead" visionaries in trance fly forth and about in the forms of antelope men. Elands seen near Bushman graves may be spirits of the dead.

There can be no doubt but that the rock paintings, whether of the Paleolithic caves or of the Kalahari Desert, served primarily a religious function relevant to the ritual lore of the hunt. The art of the caves, furthermore, was evidently of an esoteric order, hidden from general view and having to do, not only with the practice of rites to return the lives of animals slain to their source for future reappearances, but also with the initiation of youths to experiences orienting their minds to accord with the sense of these ceremonials, which from the point of view of waking consciousness would make no sense whatsoever.

The mystery of death and the mind's

requirement to come to terms with it have been everywhere the prime inspiration of spiritual inquiry and practice, from the period already of Neanderthal Man, over a hundred thousand years ago, when (as already noticed and discussed at length, see I.1:51–56) the earliest human burials appear, in graves furnished with provisions for some kind of continuing invisible existence. Also from that context have come our earliest evidences of rites addressed to the worship, appeasement, and (possibly) restitution and multiplication of the animals necessarily slain for the nourishment of their human fellow creatures: little chapels, namely, in high Alpine grottoes, containing arrangements of preserved cave-bear skulls and with associated fire-hearths suggesting some sort of relevant ceremonial.

Freud's recognition in *Totem and Tabu* (1913) of a theme of guilt, complicity in a common crime, consequent remorse and sense of a requirement for appeasement as informing the religious life, social ideas and moral requirements, not only of totemistic aboriginal societies, but of all societies, everywhere, would be difficult to refute. "Society is now based," he states, "on complicity in the common crime, religion on the sense of guilt and the consequent remorse, while morality is based partly on the necessities of society and partly on the expiation which the sense of guilt demands."[26] His invention of an actual prehistoric incident of patricidal cannibalism to explain this sense of an original sin was superfluous, however, since the killing and eating of other living beings is the one fundamental daily requirement of all human, as well as animal life. Basing his imagination on Darwin's early suggestion that the primal state of human society must have been something comparable to a scattering of small hordes of manlike apes, in each of which the jealousy of the strongest or oldest male prevented sexual promiscuity, "when the young male grows up," Freud quotes from an interpreter of this theory, "a contest takes place for mastery, and the strongest, by killing and driving out the others, establishes himself as the head of the community."[27] Freud's own completion of the fancied scenario, then, is given in the following words:

"One day the expelled brothers joined forces, slew and ate the father, and thus put an end to the father horde. Together they dared and accomplished what would have remained impossible for them singly. Perhaps some advance in culture, like the use of a new weapon, had given them the feeling of superiority. Of course these cannibalistic savages ate their victim. The violent primal father had surely been the envied and feared model for each of the brothers. Now they accomplished their identification with him by devouring him

and each acquired a part of his strength. The totem feast, which is perhaps mankind's first celebration, would be the repetition and commemoration of this memorable, criminal act with which so many things began, social organization, moral restrictions and religion."[28]

As already remarked, however: To explain the sense of guilt and necessity for expiation—which is a theme, by the way, of especial prominence and force in the established Judeo-Christian way of interpreting the universal archetypes of myth—there is no need for any such grim conjecture as this of an actual, prehistoric, patricidal cannibal feast, since already in the daily work of killing, slaughtering, cooking and eating their respected animal neighbors, the earliest human beings of *Homo sapiens* rank at least knew very well what they were doing. This we know from the evidence of those bear-skull sanctuaries of some 100,000 years B.C. or more.

For it is a grim but undeniable fact that life, in its primal character, is horrendous. There is engraved high on a wall of the American Museum of Natural History, in New York, a saying of Theodore Roosevelt to the effect—"There are no words that can tell the hidden spirit of the wilderness, that can reveal its mystery…"—that the civilized mind cannot bear to contemplate the full terror of life in the jungle. Or, as stated somewhere by Schopenhauer, "Life is something that should not have been." And yet as noticed in my chapter on "The Awakening of Awe" (see I.1:25), it seems not to have been until the period of Neanderthal Man that the human mind, in its evolution, awoke to that sense of the dread of death which is what sets man apart from the beasts. At that moment, as I there declare, the eyes which along the lines of animal life had evolved as agents of the quest for nourishment were opened to a dimension within, beyond, and behind what in India is termed "the sheath of food," the tangible, visible forms of phenomenality; and at that moment the consciousness of mankind fell in two, separated in the awakened mind from the innocence, not only of the beasts without, but also of the beast within, which through millennia had been maintaining itself without hesitation by killing, eating, and digesting other living beings.

Homo sapiens neanderthalensis was followed in Europe by the people of the great "creative explosion" of the painted temple caves. We have no art of any kind, however, from the period of *H. Neanderthalensis;* only the burials, those cave-bear skull chapels, and a few other signs bearing witness to what Leroi-Gourhan describes as an order of interests "not confined to eating and drinking": little clumps and deposits of red ocher, assembled shells, collected fossils, and a number of curious limestone slabs on which little cup marks appear (see I.1:58). "That the ex-

traordinary should have been explicitly perceived," Leroi-Gourhan comments, "warrants a strong presumption in favor of an intuition of the supernatural. …Certain facts sufficiently well authenticated suffice to show that practices not related to techniques of the material life existed…; we may call them religious, because they testify to interests beyond those of the vegetative life."[29]

We have no evidence from Neanderthal times of anything like shamanic practices, trance states, out-of-body experiences, visionary revelations, or the like. The point of view is of "waking consciousness" (*jāgarita-sthāna*), ego-maintenance in the light world "common to all men" (*vaiśvānara*), with intuitions, however, of an invisible realm beyond, with which it would be prudent to establish and maintain contact. The appearance of the mighty cave bear as the recognized representative of the power of that invisible world, to be honored in skull sanctuaries located in high mountain caves, announces already from terminal glacial times the existence of a mythology of the Animal Master, associated with a head cult, where the position of the revered master animal is analogous to that of Freud's hypothetical primal father. The bear, as we shall see (see below: 147–155), is an especially revered beast to this day among hunting peoples of the north, and among the Ainu of northern Japan a bear sacrifice and sacramental meal, during which the bear itself is given of its own flesh to eat (see below: Figure 264), is still practiced. The bear to be sacrificed has been raised as a pet, as a member of an Ainu family, and revered as a visiting mountain god, so that the whole occasion of the sacrifice is of genuine sorrow and love.

It is unlikely, of course, that the mighty cave bear could ever have been sacrificed with such affection; but the aspect of reverence is evident in the way in which the preserved skulls have been found arranged. There is even one with a longbone (its own?) placed in its mouth (see I.1: Figure 82), which suggests (to me at least) something very like the Ainu service of a bowl of its own meat to their sacrificed divinity — himself, as it were, to Himself, the self to the Self.

For this earliest known form of sacrifice was clearly an offering, not simply *to* a god, but *of* god, even as in the Christian sacrifice the offering is of God the Son to the Father with whom he is consubstantial. In the course of the Ainu ceremony the bear is told that he is being sent back with gifts to the mountain home of his original father and mother; also, that should he ever wish to return for another stay with his earthly foster family, they would gladly honor him again with a sacrificial ceremonial. What the glacial-age Neanderthalers may have thought we of course cannot know. However, we do have the testimony of those two symmetrical novelties of their time, their graves furnished for a life beyond death, and shrines furnished with the relics of animals slain for food and consumed.

Which can only mean that those glacial-age hunters and killers of the mammoth, cave lion, cave panther and huge cave bear must already have been aware of a sense of guilt, or at least anxiety, in their exercise of the fundamental method of life of man as a beast of prey. The opening of the eyes to a dimension beyond that of the "sheath of food," and with that the falling of the mind in two, had apparently already turned man the hunter against himself in a quandary of terrors and desires. For the survival of the dead beyond death, invisible to the hunter's eye, will have opened to his imagination the possibility of a horde of invisible avenging spirits. (There was at least one of the preserved bear skulls found with a longbone thrust through one of its eyes, as though to avert its menacing gaze.) And with that there was born the super-ego, or, as otherwise denominated, the sense of a moral imperative and the faculty of conscience.

What sort of otherworld can that have been, however, into which the lives of the Neanderthal dead departed and out of which there breathed such a chill of dread? The only signs remaining to us are from the light world side of the invisible threshold: furnished graves, reliquary shrines, and those enigmatic clumps of shells, red ocher and collected fossils that Leroi-Gourhan has recognized as witness to an order of interests "not confined to eating and drinking."

It was not until the appearance of a race with a skull form signifying an advance in the evolution of human consciousness from "archaic" to "modern" *Homo sapiens* rank (see I.1:20–22, Figures 16 and 17) that there was devised and developed a medium of experience and expression empowered to extend the range of human vision beyond the limits of such immediately physical sight as is "common to all men" (*vaiśvānara*). The invisible threshold was being actually crossed in shamanic flights of ecstatic trance — as appears in the oft cited figure from the cavern of Lascaux, of a shaman wearing a bird mask, "spaced out" before the vision of an eviscerated master bison (see I.1: Figure 105). As Leroi-Gourhan has demonstrated, the arrangements of the animals depicted in the caves do not reflect their perceptible relationships in the light world, but are of a symbolic order, significant of an intuited mythology of some kind, of which the entire cavern is a manifestation.

As in a dream, where the forms displayed, although reflecting the daylight world where they are experienced as separate from each other, reappear as complementary features in a unified, single statement of which the import is not apparent to waking consciousness (*jāgarita-sthāna*), but is of the dreaming state (*svapna-sthāna*), so in these selections and arrangements of the animals depicted in the dark subterranean chambers of the Paleolithic cavern artists, there is a unitary connotation to be recognized which is of an order of interests "not confined to eating and drinking," where the metaphorical relationships of the animals to each other do not correspond to the actualities which the artists themselves would have daily encountered as hunters on the great open plains above ground.

James Joyce, in his discussion of the characteristics of any achieved work of proper art, denominates three moments which he declares correspond to "the necessary phases of artistic apprehension," and which he names by way of a statement borrowed from the medieval scholastic, Thomas Aquinas. "Aquinas says," he quotes, "*ad pulcritudinem tria requiruntur, integritas, consonantia, claritas....Three things are needed for beauty, wholeness, harmony, and radiance.*"[30]

1. *Integritas* (wholeness): the object or assemblage of objects under consideration is viewed purely and simply as *one thing*, whether it be a tree, an insect, mountain landscape, battlefield of contending armies, pantheon of strange or familiar gods, condemned felon, or canonized saint. There is no such emotional or judgmental distortion as prevails in popular ("improper"), didactic and pornographic art. The "doors of perception" have been "cleansed." "Judge not, that you be not judged." "The Kingdom of the Father is spread upon the earth and men do not see it."

Accordingly, the details of the *one thing* are now viewed, not as distinct or in any way separate from each other, but as parts or members of a single harmonious system, like the leaves, roots, trunk and branches of a tree. In such a vision of the Christian pantheon, for instance, God the Father and Satan would be seen, not as eternal antagonists, but as synergic contributors to the functioning of a temporal universe. The late Buckminster Fuller has left with us a definition of this way of seeing and appreciating (italics mine):

"In order to be able to understand the great complexity of life and to understand what the universe is doing, the first word to learn is synergy. *Synergy is the behavior of whole systems, unpredicted by the behavior of their parts.* The most extraordinary example of it is what we call mass attraction. One great massive sphere and another massive sphere hung by tension members are attracted to one another. We find there is nothing in one sphere in its own right, that predicts that it's going to be attracted to another. You have to have the two. It is, then, synergy which holds our earth together with the moon; and it is synergy which holds our whole universe together....*Synergy is to energy as integration is to differentiation.* Energy studies separate out—isolating phenomena out of total nature and total universe, and studying those separate phenomena. *Synergy is associated behavior of the whole*: great complexes all the way to total universe itself."[31]

The Buddhist doctrine of "dependent origination, or mutual arising" (*pratītya samutpāda*) corresponds to this of Fuller's "synergy." When on the occasion of the Buddha's silent flower sermon (which is regarded traditionally as the founding sermon of Zen), he simply held out to his congregation a handful of flowers, the only one who understood was his foremost disciple, Mahakashyapa, who quietly smiled at him in recognition.[32] In the symbol, which is almost universal in the Orient, of the universe as a lotus and the lotus as a manifest sign on the surface of the waters of an invisible life below waves, the Buddhist doctrine is already implicit of *pratītya samutpāda*, "dependent origination, or mutual arising"; for the petals are not to be interpreted as in any way independent of each other, casual or consequential of each other. The whole system has simply arisen, "thus come" (*tath-āgata*), like the Buddha himself.

And so it is, also, in the way of vision of proper art. With the mind "raised above desire and loathing," the eye does not rest with favor, desire, revulsion, disapproval or approval on this or that detail. The object is viewed consistently as a whole, whether it be an insect, flower, historical scene, or total universe. And thus: *integritas* (wholeness), the first of those three things needed for beauty.

2. *Consonantia* (harmony): "Having first felt that it is *one* thing, you feel now that it is a *thing*," states Joyce. "You pass from point to point, led by its formal lines; you apprehend it as balanced part against part within its limits; you feel the rhythm of its structure."[33]

The critical words in this passage are "felt" and "feel": having *felt* that the object viewed is one thing, you *feel* now the rhythm of its structure. In the Upanishad, the inwardly cognitive Dreaming State (*svapna-sthāna*) is described as "experiencing in exquisite solitude luminous enjoyments" (*praviviktabhuk-taijasa*). The critical moment of *ekstasis in esthetic arrest*—such as was that of the Bushman woman Be, when the sound of the hooves of a running herd of giraffes united in her mind with a sound of sudden rain to strike her spellbound and call forth from her throat a song of trancing power (*ntum*) that had never been heard before—is of *an immediately recognized coalescence, in that part of the mind which in the Orient is called the heart, of an outward and an inward rhythm.* This is not an experience of relationships and values known to the "waking consciousness" (*jāgarita-sthāna*) "common to all men" (*vaiśvānara*). Its effects are neither of pornography (exciting and fulfilling desires) nor of didacticism (inculcating ideals). In fact, as far as practical living in a community faced with acute problems of survival is concerned, such experiencing in exquisite solitude of luminous enjoyments might be judged unconscionable or insane. And yet, when translated into such a song of rapture as was Be's, the effect of the inspiration upon those prepared to respond is of an awakening within to a sense of synergetic participation in a shared identity of some kind. The trance dancing of the Bushmen, as described by Lorna Marshall, Richard B. Lee, and Marguerite Anne Biesele (see I.1:94–96), exerts on the little family bands an essential integrating force, in relation especially to the otherwise severely separated worlds of interest of the males and females. In Lorna Marshall's words, their trance dancing "draws people of a Bushman band together as nothing else does. They stamp and clap and sing with such precision that they become like an organic being. In this close configuration—together—they face the gods. They do not plead, as they do in their individual supplications, for the favour of the divine, all powerful beings, and do not praise them for goodness. Instead, the medicine men, on behalf of the people, releasing themselves from ordinary behaviour by trance and overcoming fear and inaction, throw themselves into combat with the gods and try to force them with hurled sticks and hurled words to take away the evils they might be bringing."[34]

There is a well-known Tantric saying: *nādevo devam arcayet*, "by none but the godly may a god be worshiped." The function of a ritual, a ritual of such primal force as that of the Bushman trance dance, is to convert the prepared participant, for the duration at least of the rite, into the counterpart of a god; to effect, that is to say, a transubstantiation. The participant's state of consciousness is shifted from that of waking (*jāgarita-sthāna*), experiencing the gross enjoyments common to all men (*sthūlabhug-vaiśvānara*), to vision, which is to say of dream (*svapna-sthāna*), inwardly cognitive of luminous enjoyments (*praviviktabhuk-taijasa*). As remarked by Coomaraswamy, the participant, "rapt away from his habitual and passable personality...becomes a god for the duration of the rite, and only returns to himself when the rite is relinquished, when the ephiphany is at an end and the curtain falls."[35] But what, then, is the meaning here of the term "god"?

Unsentimentally defined, a god is an envisioned name and form metaphorical of a transpersonal state of consciousness, conceived as functioning in relation to human values locally recognized, whether actively (creating, supporting, negating) or at rest (in contemplation). Since every god is thus in name and form culturally specific, none may properly claim exclusive identity with whatever may be beyond name and form as the transcendent ground of all being and beings, i.e., as that which in the Orient is referred to as beyond and without forms, hence the "void" (*śūnya*), or as *brahman*—for which we have in our Western tongues, unfortunately, no word but "God," which has led, not only to a general idolatry of our own historically conditioned god as "God Eternal," but also to an equally improper notion of the gods of other mythologies as in this same way idolized: which they are not. Even the Bushmen recognize the temporally relevant (metaphorical) nature of their divinities.

Primal rituals, then, are works of art derived, like the Bushman trancing song, from states of ecstatic vision which, when properly performed, engage participants in a shared experience of the state of mind from which the ritual originated. Contributive to the effect of the rite is the environment in which it is rendered: the trance dance of the Bushmen, for example, at night, around a fire, the women chanting, seated, clapping time, the men circling around both them and the fire (see I.1: Figures 171–175). In mythologically grounded, traditional societies all essential activities are performed as rites, according to forms of metaphorical import. Consider, for example, the words of the Oglala Sioux holy man, keeper of the sacred pipe, Black Elk, as recorded by the poet John G. Neihardt, in May, 1931:

"After I came to live here where I am now between Wounded Knee Creek and Grass Creek...we made these little gray houses of logs that you see, and they are square. It is a bad way to live, for there can be no power in a square.

"You have noticed that everything an Indian does is in a circle, and that is because the Power of the World always works in circles, and everything tries to be round. In the old days when we were a strong and happy people, all our power came to us from the sacred hoop of the nation, and so long as the hoop was unbroken, the people flourished. The flowering tree was the living center of the hoop, and the circle of the four quarters nourished it. The east gave peace and light, the south gave warmth. The west gave rain, and the north with its cold and mighty wind gave strength and endurance. This knowledge came to us from the outer world and our religion. Everything the Power of the World does is done in a circle. The sky is round, and I have heard that the earth is round like a ball, and so are all the stars. The wind, in its greatest power, whirls. Birds make their nests in circles, for theirs is the same religion as ours. The sun comes forth and goes down again in a circle. The moon does the same, and both are round. Even the seasons form a great circle in their changing, and always come back again to where they were. The life of a man is a circle from childhood to childhood, and so it is in everything where power moves. Our teepees were round like the nests of birds, and these were always set in a circle, the nation's hoop, a nest of many nests, where the Great Spirit meant for us to hatch our children.

"But the Wasichus have put us in these square boxes. Our power is gone and we are dying, for the power is not in us any more. You can look at our boys and see how it is with us. When we were living by the power of the circle in the way we should, boys were men at twelve or thirteen years of age. But now it takes them very much longer to mature.

"Well it is as it is. We are prisoners of war while we are waiting here. But there is another world."[36]

"Art," as Cézanne has said somewhere, "is a harmony parallel to nature." But as Aristotle has pointed out, "nature" has two senses, "the matter and the form" (*Physics* II.2.194a). The harmony of nature that is imitated in proper art (and in the life of such a mythologically informed culture as the one Black Elk remembered from the decades of his youth) is not of its outward appearances, but of the principles giving life to these: nature namely, in its synergetic manner of operation, not as already become, but in its becoming. There is a valuable statement to this point by Goethe, which he let fall while in conversation with his young secretary, Johann Eckermann:

"The Godhead is effective in the living and not in the dead; in the becoming and the changing, not in the become and the set fast. Therefore Reason (*Vernunft*) is concerned only to strive toward the divine through the becoming and the changing, and Intelligence (*Verstand*), to make use of the become and set fast."[37]

In terms of the states or modes of consciousness identified in the Upanishad, the field of concern of Goethe's "Intelligence" (*Verstand*) is of "Waking Consciousness" (*jāgarita-sthāna*), which, as described, is outwardly cognitive by way of the physical senses, and by way of the organs of action makes use of objects of the physical world. These are experienced and made use of as separate from each other (*a* is not *not-a*), and although they may be modified by manipulations and will change in the course of time, they are experienced and made use of as they are, which is to say, as having already become. And in that sense they are of "the become and the set fast." Moreover, they are composed of what is known in India as "gross matter" (*sthūla-bhūtāni*) and their experience and manipulation are for the "gross enjoyments (*sthūlabhug-*) common to all men (*vaiśvānara*), which are in no way comparable or even related to any of the orders of rapture (*samādhi*) which are intended and rendered, either by the rites of a mythologically grounded civilization, or by proper art.

The state of consciousness proper both to esthetic arrest and to religious exaltation is of the "Dreaming State" (*svapna-sthāna*). It has nothing to do with either morality or immorality, pornography or didactic. It is an opening of the eye of the mind, which is of the faculty of Reason (*Vernunft*), having nothing to do with righteousness, but identification and Self-recognition in the object or universe beheld (*samādhi*); and the concomitant spiritual sentiment is of compassion (*karuṇā*).

As in a dream, where objects of the waking state (day-residues) reappear, not as material "gross bodies" (*sthūla-śarīrāni*) situated in external space and separate from each other, but as immaterial, self-luminous, "subtle bodies" (*sūkshma-śarīrāni*) of one substance with the containing mind of which they are an expression; so within the field of a mythology, the symbolic details reflect, indeed, a local material history and environment, yet they are of an order of the mind, and to be interpreted by the faculty of reason as expressions of a spiritual insight. The magnificent bulls of the painted cavern of Lascaux, the black leaping cow and herds of woolly ponies (see I.1: Figures 91–93), are related to each other not as they ever might have been on the open hunting plains, but as features of an architecturally conceived metaphorical statement of some kind, which Leroi-Gourhan has recognized, from cave to cave, as consistent in its patterning throughout the twenty-odd thousand years of history of this earliest known documentation of myth. The idea of a temple (or European cathedral) is what is here announced, an enclosure wherein every feature is metaphorical of a connoted metaphysical intuition, set apart for ritual enactments.

The heart in such an environment is at home, as it were, in its own place: removed from the chaotic spectacle of the world of waking consciousness, at rest and at peace in the recognition of a harmony (which is of one's own nature) informing the whole terrible scene of lives forever consuming lives. And the function, then, of the ritual is to bring one's manner of life into accord with this nonjudgmental perspective, in the way, not of crude ego-maintenance in a world one never made, but of synergetic participation in a phantasmagoric rapture. There is a beautiful poem by Goethe to this realization:

Wenn in Unendlichen dasselbe
Sich wiederholend ewig fliesst,
Das tausendfältige Gewölbe
Sich kräftig ineinander schliesst;
Strömt Lebenslust aus allen Dingen,
Dem kleinsten wie dem grössten Stern,

Und alles Drängen, alles Ringen
Ist ewige Ruh in Gott dem Herrn.[38]

"When in endlessness the same, ever renewing itself, flows on; The vaulting, thousandfold, powerfully interlocking, draws itself together: Life-joy streams from all things, the smallest as from the greatest star; and all striving, all struggling, is eternal rest in God the Lord."

And so we come to the realization of Aquinas's third thing needed for beauty, which is namely:

3. *Claritas* (radiance): "The word," says Joyce's alter-ego, Stephan Dedalus, in the novel, "is rather vague. Aquinas uses a term which seems to be inexact. It baffled me for a long time. It would lead you to believe that he had in mind symbolism or idealism, the supreme quality of beauty being a light from some other world, the idea of which the matter is but the shadow, the reality of which it is but the symbol. I thought he might mean that *claritas* is the artistic discovery and representation of the divine purpose in anything or a force of generalization which would make the esthetic image a universal one, make it outshine its proper conditions. But that is literary talk. I understand it so. When you have apprehended that basket as one thing and have then analysed it according to its form and apprehended it as a thing you make the only synthesis which is logically and esthetically permissible. You see that it is that thing which it is and no other thing. The radiance of which he speaks is the scholastic *quidditas*, the *whatness* of a thing. This supreme quality is felt by the artist when the esthetic image is first conceived in his imagination. The mind in that mysterious instant Shelley likened beautifully to a fading coal. The instant wherein that supreme quality of beauty, the clear radiance of the esthetic image, is apprehended luminously by the mind which has been arrested by its wholeness and fascinated by its harmony is the luminous silent stasis of esthetic pleasure, a spiritual state very like to that cardiac condition which the Italian physiologist Luigi Galvani, using a phrase almost as beautiful as Shelley's, called the enchantment of the heart."[39]

In terms again of the Upanishad, we have passed in one spellbinding instant from the Waking State of "gross enjoyments common to all men" (*sthūlabhug-vaiśvānara*), through a dreamlike, inwardly cognitive moment in "exquisite solitude," of "luminous enjoyments" (*praviviktabhuk-taijasa*), to a state of consciousness equivalent to that of Deep Sleep (*svapna-sthāna*), "enwrapped in bliss" (*ānandamaya*), but while still awake and with eyes open, fixed on the object, whether insect, landscape, basket, the heavens, the smallest or the greatest star.

Aquinas's scholastic *quidditas* corresponds here to Sankara's vedantic *ātman*; but with a difference, since in medieval scholastic thought—where Aristotle is the final philosophical authority, *a* is not *not-a*, and things are separate from each other—every "soul" is to be thought of as an individually created yet everlasting separate entity that is to continue thus (following death of the body), as judged forever to either heaven or hell by a god who is not identical with itself. This, in contrast to the Vedantic view, is a mythology of irreducible egoism locked in ethical dualism, having as its opposed final terms, an everlasting God, everlasting Devil, and ever-increasing plurality of temporally created yet also everlasting "souls." There is here no place for any such concept as that of the upanishadic state of consciousness in Deep Dreamless Sleep (*sushupta-sthāna*), where *Prajña*, the Knower fully Self-realized as constituting the "infinite space" (*ākāśa*) in the heart, "is verily the all-knowing Lord of all, Indweller and Controller, the Matrix (*yoni*) of all, and the Beginning and End of all beings" (Mandukya 6). Aquinas's *quidditas*, or "whatness of the thing," therefore, is an individuated closed circle, which the *ātman*, as we have seen, is not.

And yet, there has been in Christian thought an alternative, suppressed tradition, wherein the scholastic *quidditas* might indeed have been recognized as only provisionally enclosed, as pertaining to the mode of consciousness of the *Viśva*, *Vaiśvānara*, which is "common to all men." For there are passages in the recently discovered Gnostic *Gospel According to Thomas* in which there are sayings attributed to the historical Jesus where he appears, not only to have identified himself with the universally immanent World Dreamer (which in Christian terminology is second Person of the Trinity, namely Christ), but also to have taught that those who receive and live by his teaching will themselves realize their identity in eternity with this non-dual, universal Immortal. For example:

"Jesus said: I am the light that is above them all, I am the All, the All came forth from Me and the All attained to me. Cleave a piece of wood, I am there; lift up the stone and you will find me there" (Logion 77).

"Jesus said: Whoever drinks from My mouth shall become as I am and I myself will become he, and the hidden things will be revealed to him" (Logion 108).

"Jesus said: If those who lead you say to you: 'See, the Kingdom is in heaven,' then the birds of the heaven will precede you. If they say to you: 'It is in the sea,' then the fish will precede you. But the Kingdom is within you and it is without you. If you will know yourselves, then you will be known and you will know that you are the sons of the Living Father. But if you do not know yourselves, then you are in poverty and you are poverty" (Logion 3).

"His disciples said to Him: When will the Kingdom come? Jesus said: It will not come by expectation; they will not say: 'See, here,' or: 'See there.' But the Kingdom of the Father is spread upon the earth and men do not see it" (Logion 113).[40]

Or again, as told in the words of Black Elk:

"The sky is round, and I have heard that the earth is round like a ball, and so are all the stars. The wind, in its greatest power, whirls. Birds make their nests in circles, for theirs is the same religion as ours. The sun comes forth and goes down again in a circle. The moon does the same, and both are round. Even the seasons form a great circle in their changing, and always come back again to where they were. The life of man is a circle from childhood to childhood, and so it is in everything where power moves....Everything the Power of the World does is done in a circle....This knowledge came to us from the outer world and our religion."

For in every mythologically grounded traditional society the mind, which is open by nature to the recognition of synergic affinities, is in such recognitions reenforced and confirmed by whatever local system of metaphorical ceremonials the infant is taken into the tribe and the tribe or civilization held to accord with the perceived natural order of the universe. Such lesser and greater institutions and occasions may indeed be described (to return to the vocabulary of John E. Pfeiffer in his discussion of cavern art: see above, page viii) as a "corpus of socially constructive rituals...for conflict control...pictorially encoded for storage and transmission through generations." However, the potential conflicts comprehended in the symbolic range of a ritualized traditional order of art are not only, or even principally, of the claims of clans or individuals against each other, but of ego interests, *aham-kāra*, against the universal *ātman*, or will in nature: in sociological terms, urban economic interests against the biosphere of a local ecology, or in Freudian psychological terms, ego-interests against the super-ego and the id.

The address and appeal of any traditional art is of two degrees or ranges, an exoteric or popular range, addressed to the well-being and harmonious organization of the community, and an esoteric or recondite range, made known only to initiates through trials and transformative revelations.

That the paintings of the Paleolithic caves cannot have been created to serve an exoteric function is obvious from the fact of their inaccessibility to general view. They are hidden, deeply hidden, to be approached only by way of dangerous, often very difficult passages (see I.1:73–79). Moreover, as the findings of Leroi-Gourhan have revealed, the order of their appearances on the walls and along the corridors of the caves suggests a metaphorical connotation of some kind. This subterranean domain, that is to say, is to be entered and experienced in a different state of consciousness from that of the daylight mind informed on the hunting plains above through the physical senses. Down here the state is of myth, of dream, the same of mind that is evoked in exoteric ceremonials by theatrical means, masked dances, mimetic enactments of mythic scenes, ceremonial chanting and the like. Such theatrical arts are addressed to people in the Waking State (*jāgarita-sthāna*), where things are experienced as separate from each other and *a* is not *not-a*. The psychological transformation that is by such arts effected for the period at least of the ceremonial, however, is to the Dreaming State (*svapna-sthāna*), where what is beheld is a unified, synergetically integrated field in which the viewer himself is participating as a member.

For as Buckminster Fuller has stated, "Synergy is the behavior of whole systems, unpredicted by the behavior of their parts." And as James Joyce has stated of the experience of a proper work of proper art, "three things are needed for beauty," which are, namely, *integritas* (wholeness), *consonantia* (harmony), and *claritas* (radiance); the last following from a revelation (epiphany) of the *quidditas* or "whatness" of the one thing or whole system beheld — which, as we have recognized, is equivalent finally to the non-dual *ātman/brahman*, as experienced in the state of Deep Dreamless Sleep (*sushupta-sthāna*) by the Knower (*Prajña*), the singular Wild Gander (*ekahaṁsa*)—Christ of the Thomas gospel—the all-knowing Lord (*sarveśvara*), the Matrix (*yoni*), Beginning and End, Indweller and Controller of all beings.

The social function of conflict control which is served by the exoteric institutions and occasions of a corpus of socially maintained rites is in primal cultures an effect, not of any sort of applied force, but of a people's spontaneous enjoyment in the synergetic experience of their common identity as of one state of being. Nor is it population density that occasions the need for such ceremonials. As Lorna Marshall has reported: the nightly trance-dancing of the Kalahari Bushman camps "draws people of a Bushman band together as nothing else does...they become like an organic being."[41]

In contrast, the ceremonials performed in esoteric sanctuaries—the men's rites, for example, of painful, terrifying trials and revelations which in many hunting cultures are applied to the initiation of youths to manhood (see below: 143–146 and 226–231)—have rather to do with the spiritual transformation of elected individuals than with communal solidarity, which is a condition already presupposed. Such rites begin where the exoteric end, with consciousness in the Dreaming State (*svapna-sthāna*); and the passage is rather from Dreaming to Deep Dreamless Sleep (*sushupta-sthāna*), than from the Waking State to Dream.

Undoubtedly, the rituals of the painted caves were of this order (see I.1:73–79). Already on entering the absolute dark beyond the craggy facings of these rock sanctuaries, the imagination is awakened and runs wild. Today the passages and great chambers are electrically illuminated. From c. 30,000 to 10,000 B.C., only fires and flickering torches can have served to reveal to the neophyte the paintings on the ceilings and rock walls; and their effect, surely, will have been rather to increase than to diminish the sense of sanctity and mystery of these dark, unmeasured recesses of the living earth. In Volume I.1, some of the interiors have been described. We need here remind the reader only of the actual dangers and difficulties of the rocky ways; the long tunnel, for example, in the cavern known as Les Trois Frères, not much broader than a man's shoulders, nor higher, through which it was necessary to worm and crawl for a distance of some 50 yards before abruptly opening to the revelation of an immense hall, from top to bottom covered with engravings of all the beasts that lived at that time in southern France: the mammoth, rhinoceros, bison and wild horse, bear, wild ass, reindeer, wolverine and musk-ox; snowy owls, also, hares and fish (see I.1:73–76).

The Abbé Henri Breuil (1877–1961)—to whose years of devotion to the study, recording, and interpretation of the engravings and paintings of the French and Spanish caves we owe most of what we know today of their contents — having spent a season of several weeks in this same ornamented chamber, alone, perched high in a hidden niche in the wall, making copies with a practiced hand of its whole incredible tangle of animal forms, in one of his discussions of his own experience of the passages of the cave suggests a possible scenario for the rites of initiation to which the provocative atmosphere of this labyrinthine underworld will surely have contributed (see I.1: 76).

"All these complicated hidden passages lent themselves," he wrote, "to extraordinary effects which would be inexplicable to uninitiated novices, who must have been deeply impressed....The effect of songs, cries, or other noises, or mysterious objects thrown from no one knows where, was easy to arrange in such a place."[42]

The great chamber itself, as we have already told (see I.1: 75), is an apse with a floor sloping steeply toward the back, the walls converging at the end, where, at the right, there is a steep, two-fold recess. One of these conducts the visitor to a small rotunda ending in a well, and this again, through turning, winds to a point where, at a height of about 13 feet, there is an opening, a sort of window, beyond which there looms a composite, part animal, part human figure that has become known to science as the *Sorcerer of Les Trois Frères,* and which, by its prominence and position in relation to the tangle of engravings of animal forms, must have been the cardinal culminating revelation (epiphany) of the whole initiation ordeal.

The figure appears (in the copy rendered by the Abbé Breuil) as a man-lion rampant, to whose head antlers have been added. The head is turned to face the hall, the round staring eyes suggesting those either of a lion or of an owl; the pricked ears suggest those of a stag. There is a man's full beard descending to the great chest, which is evidently of a lion. The tail is of a wolf or wild horse, but the position beneath the tail of the prominent sexual organ, is of the feline. The hands are the paws of a lion. The torso might also be of this beast; but the legs, which seem to be dancing, are of a man. The figure is 2½ feet high, 15 inches across, and the only figure in the gallery rendered full-face, *en face,* and in paint, black paint (see I.1: Figure 132). All the others are in profile and engraved.

Leo Frobenius has recognized on a rock high in the Sahara-Atlas mountain range of northwest Africa an engraving of a lion, *en face,* with round, staring eyes, in a posture very like that of the *Sorcerer of Les Trois Frères* (see I.1:78–79). It, too, is situated above, as though dominating, a number of engravings of game animals, all in profile—elephants and giraffes, a buffalo and an antelope. Moreover, its situation is such that the first rays of the rising sun fall upon it; and when we now return to study again the Abbé Breuil's rendition of the great animal scene over which the *Sorcerer* presides in the chamber of Les Trois Frères (see I.1: Figure 131), we now notice that there is a face in the upper left corner, full face, with round staring eyes, which may well represent a rising sun. These two manifestations of the mythic figure known as the Animal Master date from the last millenia of Paleolithic art, the *Sorcerer,* c. 12,000 B.C., and the lion of the Atlas range, c. 7000 B.C. A solar mythology associated with the rituals of the hunt had by that time, as it here would seem, become established.

But now, in hunting mythologies generally the sun appears ambiguously as both the protector of the game animals and the archetypal hunter. Likewise in the Bushman tales of Kaggen (Mantis) as a kind of trickster-clown creator, in one story he appears as the lover and cherisher of the beautiful first eland, but in another he tries to kill it. In a third, when he flings darts at his own son-in-law discovered butchering the eland, the weapons circle back and nearly kill himself. He and his wife invent a means to multiply the species, and when the bulls and cows have spread over the earth, he sends his sons out to hunt them, "and that day," we are told, "game were given to men to eat." (See above: xiii; also I.1:92–93).

Almost certainly, the essential revelation delivered in the inspiring animal-chamber of the cavern of Les Trois Frères to the companies of boy initiates at the conclusion of their underworld ordeal was of the symbiosis of the animal and the human in the striking figure of the Animal Master glaring down at them from his place of prominence and dominance over the pictured herds of animals already known to them from the hunting plains of the world of light, far above. Such an organic symbiosis of the animal and the human is a fundamental theme of the mythologies and ritual lore of hunting tribes. Totemic societies attribute common ancestry to the human members of the denominated clan and the animal species of its totem. An immemorial covenant, in understanding of the order of nature as requiring daily acts of killing and slaughtering by the two-legged tribes of their four-legged relatives and neighbors, underlies the entire system of those hunting-culture ceremonials through which game animals are invoked to be slain as willing sacrifices, knowing that through restorative rites their lives will be returned to the source for a return next season. (See again the Bushman stories of Kaggen inventing restorative rites and sending his sons out to hunt: I.1:91–93; also, the Blackfoot Indian legend, *The Buffalo's Wife;* see below: 234). It is significant that in many of their invocative rites the hunters themselves are costumed and masked to simulate the animals invoked (as in the Blackfoot legend of *The Buffalo's Wife;* and see again the Curtis photograph below: 188–189); while in the Bushman order of tabus placed on the hunter whose poisoned arrow or dart has struck an eland—that he may identify himself as completely as possible with the agony of the stricken beast until it succumbs to the poison in death—we have as immediate an example as could possibly occur in the field of Waking Consciousness (*jāgarita-sthāna*), where things are separate from each other and *a* is not *not-a,* of a reconstruction of the symbiotic identity of the animal and its hunter, which in the Paleolithic animal chamber of the cavern of Les Trois Frères is metaphorically connoted in the unforgettable form of its Animal Master.

As expressed in the Upanishad, the quality of the Dreaming State (*svapna-sthāna*) is of light (*tejas*) revealed through "luminous enjoyments experienced in exquisite solitude" (*praviviktabhuk-taijasa*). The effect of the rites of any valid initiation ceremonial is to bring about in the mind of the individual under treatment an awakening of his inward life to identification with this light. And the aim of the art of the ceremonial is, so to reorganize in the way of an apprehensible rhythm of beauty and sublimity the day residues of the initiate's own immediate past that they should be experienced in a context, now, of unforeseen possibilities, concluding in the revelation (epiphany) of a life-transforming total insight.

The architecturally conceived organization in sequence of the animal forms that come to view as one moves into and through the labyrinths of these dark, uncanny caves remained essentially the same, as Leroi-Gourhan has recognized, throughout both the geographical range and the almost incredible span of 300 centuries of this manner of art as a revelation. In Volume I.1(see I.1: 76–77), a suggestion has been hazarded, marking the archetypal encounters that do seem to have been intentionally arranged for in the composition of the paintings of these temple caves. "If we cannot assume," as Ananda K. Coomaraswamy has remarked, "that a language is not understood by those who speak it, we must assume that a doctrine is coeval with the symbolic formulae in which it is expressed." "Primitive art depicts not what the artist sees, but what he knows."[43]

As already reviewed, (see I.1:77), the sequence of initiatory experiences that appears to have been deliberately arranged to lead to a culminating revelation opens with a compulsory separation of the initiate from his boyhood way of experiencing the world in the state of waking consciousness (*jāgarita-sthāna*) "common to all men" (*vaiśvānara*). A difficult, scary adventure follows through dimly illuminated subterranean passages, along the course of which animal forms already known from the lightworld are revealed in unforeseen relationships, not only as to the initiate himself, but also to each other. As told in the words of Sankara, "When, on falling asleep, one takes along the material (*mātrā*) of this all-containing world, tears it apart and builds it up, oneself, and by one's own light dreams: that person becomes self-illuminated" (see above: x). In the context of a tribal initiation, the tearing apart and building up will be according to the force and sense of a local tribal or larger, more general cultural mythology. The day-residues are not, as in a psychoanalytic session, read back to their context of origination in the past, but forward to new insights. We do not know, of course, what words or signs of interpretation may have accompanied these revelations as they unfolded along the trailway of this visionary journey; but since the youth in consideration was being prepared to hunt and kill in a sacred manner the animals appearing to view, the instruction can have been only to his proper understanding of the way of life to which he was here being introduced.

An essential effect of the experience of

these caves, perceptible even to the mind today, is of the world of light above as secondary to this interior dark, which with its synergic appeal to one's own most inward darkness, here is felt to be prime. The herd animals on the plains above were but reflections of the archetypes of these wondrously illuminated corridors and great chambers. The mind of the young hunter was being thus mystagogically prepared for his culminating realization of the mystical, as opposed to the practical economic sense of the acts of killing to which his whole adult career was from this moment to be dedicated.

As described in the Upanishad: the quality of wisdom of *Prajña,* the Knower in the state of Deep Dreamless Sleep (*sushupta-sthāna*), is of being at rest in the Imperishable (*brahman*), at one with itself (*ekibhūta*) as the universal Lord (*sarveśvara*), which is the Matrix (*yoni*) wherein all become one, the Beginning and End (*prabhavāpyayau*) of all beings.

The symbiotic image of the *Sorcerer of Les Trois Frères* suggests an intuition of this kind, as does very much more strongly the Bushman rites of identification of the hunter with his stricken prey. Kaggen's darts, in flight returning and nearly killing himself speak also to this theme. And again we may turn to that most mysterious scene in what appears to be the holy of holies of the cavern of Lascaux, of a shaman in trance, phallus erect and wearing a bird mask, confronted by a standing, great, eviscerated bison, struck from behind by a lance from an invisible hand. As suggested in my earlier consideration of this material (see I.1:76), the essential effect upon the young initiates subjected to the intense experiences of the terrors and revelations of these eerie passages cannot but have been of an opening of their minds to the knowledge of a world behind, beyond, or below this seen with the eyes, and of which both the beasts that they were being prepared to hunt and kill and themselves as those who were to kill the beasts were in some way but secondary effects. The hidden truth is of what has been revealed to them down here, which is of a life-maintaining order of being whereby in the slaughter of the hunting grounds the mystery of life which lives on lives is in a sacred manner celebrated. And the hunter aiming at his quarry in this same sacred manner, in the order not of service to himself but of life in accord with itself, is enacting a ritual of reverence for life in the act of taking it. In Eugen Herrigel's valuable little volume on *Zen in the Art of Archery* a mystic discipline of this kind is indicated. "The contest consists," he declares, "in the archer aiming at himself—yet not at himself, in hitting himself—yet not himself, and thus becoming simultaneously, the aimer and the aim, the hitter and the hit."[44] And in the Indian *Muṇḍaka Upanishad,* of about the sixth century B.C. the same principle is enunciated in relation to the syllable AUM.

"AUM," we read [i.e., the ritual, the meditation], "is the bow, the arrow verily is *ātman,* and *brahman* is said to be the mark. Calmly that mark is to be hit, and oneself absorbed in It with the arrow."[45]

The Second Art: Rock Sculpture

The infinitely enduring prehistoric era of the European, Late Paleolithic "Great Hunt," from c. 30,000 to 10,000 B.C., has been classified by prehistorians as the following succession of cultures foraging over gradually changing landscapes, from tundra to grassy plains, to forest: Lower Perigordian (c. 32,000 to 28,000 B.C.), Aurignacian (c. 28,000 to 22,000 B.C.), Upper Perigordian (c. 22,000 to 18,000 B.C.), Solutrean (c. 18,000 to 15,000 B.C.), and Magdalenian (c. 15,000 to 10,000 B.C.). The earliest signs of art appeared in the Aurignacian age, and were not impressive: macaroni-like finger tracings and meanders dragged along the wet clay of tunnel walls; but also, little line engravings of animals, stiff and hardly more than a foot long, yet remarkably true to life. There is nothing of the majesty of the great Magdalenian sanctuaries about these earliest galleries. They cannot possibly have been used for such theatrical initiations as the Abbé Breuil surmised for the cavern chamber of Les Trois Frères. The quality of the engravings improved, however, through the centuries. Lines which had been originally of uniform thickness were retouched, details of pelt and muscles were introduced.

One of the clearest testimonials to the very gradual development from engraving to painting is the art of the cavern known as Les Combarelles, first entered and explored by the Abbé Breuil on September 8, 1901.

"It was by the light of a single candle and after painfully progressing for 100 meters with no result," he tells, "that the long series of engravings, forming a frieze on both walls, rose before us....The decorated gallery of Combarelles has no side branches, it is a very narrow corridor 237 meters long in its upper section, which was the only part accessible at the time of its discovery and, probably, during the Paleolithic epoch. The height varies from 4 meters at the entrance, falling soon to 2 meters or less and thence continuing with a width of 1½ to 2 meters. The monotonous shape of this long gallery is broken by bends at almost right angles. At long intervals, and mostly at these bends, the gallery widens into very small rooms, and the roof...rises in a little cupola. In some parts of the gallery where the roof is lower and smoother, it too is adorned with engravings....

"The number of figures deciphered at Combarelles is almost 300 (291 to be exact); to these may be added the remains of about a hundred other figures, too poorly preserved to be identified. Among the best we see 116 horses or equine animals, 37 bison, 19 bears, 14 reindeer, 13 mammoths, 9 ibexes, 7 oxen, 5 stags, 3 hinds, 1 fallow-deer, 5 lions, 4 wolves (3 of these are doubtful), 1 fox, 1 rhinoceros, another uncertain, 1 human hand, stencilled in black, 4 tectiforms, 19 human or semi-human figures, some of which seem to be masked, and a few signs that may represent sexual organs. There are also some signs that are like darts or javelins....

"The figures in Combarelles are mostly of medium size; the smallest have a length of only 10 cms. and the largest, scarcely more than a meter. The technique varies. Engraving predominates everywhere.... There are many superimpositions. Painting is not much used, perhaps it has been partly destroyed. Except in a few instances, it was never put on in flat wash or used to fill in, but replaced or accentuated the outlines of engravings....

"The style of these few remains of painting can help to disentangle the different periods in the art of Combarelles. The pretty little horses painted in black and slightly shaded, and the shallow engravings associated with them, must belong to the Middle Magdalenian epoch. The other, incomplete black drawings, often associated with deeply engraved figures or even sculptures, all date from an older Magdalenian. Now in every case, these deep engravings cut across thin blue-black, very ancient lines, which are seldom decipherable and therefore older....

"Few decorated caves give more of an impression than Combarelles of the artists having pursued a definite aim other than the decoration of a place where they lived. This low narrow corridor 237 meters long was not convenient to live in and this persistent covering of the walls with figures cannot be explained as designed to please the eye. We must also say that in no case could it have been used as a meeting place; only a very small number of people could have occupied it at the same time, unlike the vast caverns of Pech Merle, Niaux, etc."[46]

No explanation of the possible function of such a tangle of engravings superimposed upon each other along the walls of a narrow tunnel has been proposed, however, beyond the obvious one of "sympathetic magic," to multiply the animal species represented. The Bushman legend of Kaggen's conjuring, together with his wife, to regenerate and multiply the elands that were then to be hunted (see above: xiii) is an example of this way of thought. It is, however, difficult to interpret in this simple light the sense of the masked anthropoid appearances scattered here and there among the animal forms. In the words of the Abbé Breuil:

"We have spoken of the influence born of the talent which Paleolithic artists had for painting animals. This influence is undeniable, but if certain errors in the shapes of human bodies and limbs and the clumsiness of certain heads can be explained by this greater aptitude for drawing animals, we cannot attribute to it such precise details as the man with the horse's tail at Lourdes, the Sorcerer at Pech Merle, etc., and the 39 anthropoid figures at Combarelles.

"These are hunting or ceremonial masks, or either ghostly or mythical beings. The man with a mammoth's head, the one with a bird's head, and all the other masked beings, here or elsewhere, are perhaps hunters in disguise, ready to start on their expeditions. More probably they are members of the tribe performing some magic rite, or mythical beings from whom favors must be requested and who must be conciliated. As for the scenes with a sexual trend, which are rather rare, they seem to spring from a different source, and we hardly see any connection with the other works of art, if not on the side of fertility magic. We must also mention that, on the left wall, there is the presentation of a human skull seen full face."[47]

In striking contrast to the development, gradually through millennia, of the art of the magic of the hunt, from crudest beginnings in the Aurignacian era to fulfillment in the great dream-temples of the Magdalenian masters, is the art of the earliest rock sculptures, and of the numerous little female statuettes carved in ivory and bone, which first appear, likewise, in the Aurignacian era, but already fully realized in form and with a clearly defined mythological association. Leo Frobenius is the only authority I know who has addressed himself to this remarkable enigma. As already quoted in our general Prologue (see I.1:40–41):

"Is it not singular," he asks, "that in the Late Paleolithic of Europe, as also in the Neolithic of Egypt, sculptured representations of the human form should have appeared already fully realized and stylistically secure? May it not be that the stone sculpture of the north was born of an art of wood sculpture from the south, and led thereby to a blade culture as well? May it not be that in primeval times the cultural trend was from south to north, as later, from north to south?…It is obvious that everything of wood must have returned, since those times, to the earth, and that only by chance can any specimen have survived—as in arid Egypt. Such disappearances could explain the gap that separates the distributions of southern European and central African assemblages. It is worth keeping this possibility in mind."[48]

The key figure to this whole complex of relationships is the justly celebrated and admired *Venus of Laussel, The Woman with the Horn,* carved in bas-relief, some 17 inches high, on the surface of a rock located in a kind of sanctuary at the end of a limestone overhang which for millennia served as a domestic site. The figure has been already discussed at length (see I.1:66–68; and Figures 66, 109). To be noted as of special interest here are, first, the surprisingly early date, c. 20,000 to 18,000 B.C.; next the sculptural mastery already achieved (the figure was carved, it must be understood, with tools not of metal but of stone); and finally, the realization metaphorically represented, of an affinity of some kind, synergetically coordinating the celestial mysteries of the waxing and waning moon and the earthly of the female body and womb.

Of the same Aurignacian-Upper Perigordian era are the numerous female statuettes carved in stone, mammoth ivory and bone, which have been found distributed from southwestern France (none south of the Pyrenees), eastward across Asia, as far as to Siberian Lake Baikal (see I.1:70–73). Some 130 examples are now known, all showing remarkable consistency in their accent on breasts and buttocks, lack of definition of facial features (except for one tiny ivory head, 1⅜ inches high, which may be the earliest portrait head in the history of art: see I.1: Figure 114), and every one of these figurines, without exception, is without feet. They were evidently intended to be stood up in the soil of little household shrines; and indeed, in a number of excavated encampment sites of mammoth hunters in European Russia, on the rivers Desna and Don, examples have been discovered still standing in just this way in special niches built into the hut walls (see I.1:70–71).

The fact that it was in neighboring Asia Minor and southeastern Europe that the earliest and most abundant appearances of Early Neolithic figurines of the Great Goddess of Many Names appeared speaks for a continuity of tradition from the truly primordial Aurignacian-Upper Perigordian statuettes, even to, let us say, the image of the Virgin in the Lady Chapel of the St. Patrick's Cathedral in New York. See Marija Gimbutas, *Goddesses and Gods of Old Europe: 7000–3500 B.C.*[49]

In the Aurignacian-Upper Perigordian dwelling site at Laussel, where *The Woman with the Horn* was discovered, there was found another sculptured panel, showing a male and female in coitus, female above, male below (see I.1: Figure 110), which Frobenius, in his discussion of the possible influence of African wood carving on the Late Paleolithic arts of Europe compares with a series of three symbolic figures on the decorated facade of a priestly dwelling in the western Sudan, at Kane Kombole, south of Hombori, in Mali. Here

the male is above; but in two of the figures the little forked chin-beard of the male is the same as on the panel at Laussel. "I have frequently found such reliefs, clearly representing coitus," Frobenius declares, "among the nearby Mossi [of the present Republic of Upper Volta]. They were displayed on the mud walls of granaries and temples, and the chaste, ingenuous minds of these people saw in them a likeness, as well, to the fertilization embodied in the union of heaven and earth."[50]

Undoubtedly, the panel at Laussel, in what now appears to have been some kind of domestic chapel at one end of the long limestone overhang, had for the inhabitants of the ledge a like connotation. The posture of *The Woman with the Horn,* left hand upon pregnant belly and regard turned toward the lunar horn elevated in her right, already associates the burden of earthly womanhood with the celestial mystery of the waxing and waning moon. The superior position in the coitus scene then carries this statement to conclusion.

Mythologically, the heaven-earth polarity was in Egypt symbolized in the image of the star-spangled body of the sky-goddess Nut overarching the plane of earth, whereon the earth-god Geb reclines. Frobenius's suggestion of a common, Late Paleolithic wood tradition antecendent to the stone of both the Aurignacian and very much later, ancient Egyptian monuments, would seem to imply that a shared mythological tradition of symbolic forms might have been carried in this context as well. In any case, the coitus panel at Laussel is certainly not to be interpreted with reference only to the human act, since, as Coomaraswamy has remarked, "Primitive art depicts not what the artist sees, but what he knows." The connotation is simultaneously of the human and celestial as the one event, the micro- and macrocosmic mystery as of equivalent dignity and import.

And so we find that in the two, emergent, original arts of the Aurignacian Old Stone Age, the respective mysteries addressed were of the animal herds, ever-renewed, as the source of the nourishment of mankind, and the female body, inexhaustible of life, as the source of the race itself. The painter's art, translating into two-dimensional forms optical experiences of three, was, like the art of the hunt, to which it was applied, an intensely outward-directed exercise of the analytical mind, whereas the sculptural approach and regard were in the way rather of an acclamation and metakinetic interpretation of the forms as they were, in being. Frobenius has characterized the former as in essence a magical art, directed to control and mastery, and the latter as finally mystical, recognizing in every form in being an everlasting life to be fostered.

Accordingly, as it would now seem,

there were two distinct mythologies brought together and represented in the ritual arts of the European, Late Paleolithic era. That of the men's rites and disciplines of the hunt had originated, apparently, on the hunting grounds themselves; whereas the other, of the domestic hearth, appears to have entered the region from some forested area to the south, of a landscape rich in wood. The dominant figure of the hunting mythology was the Animal Master, semi-animal, semi-human. Identification of the hunter, when in the act of killing, with the will of this overlord of life placed him in accord with the natural order of the universe. The dominant figure of the domestic cult, in contrast, was the living female body, which was not, like the animal master, an intuited figment of the imagination, but a formidable physical presence (if we may judge from its representations in contemporary art), mysteriously overtaken monthly, in accord somehow with the lunar cycle. And the significant act was of sexual union, understood as a rite in sympathic mystical accord with the continuing creative act, now and forever in process, of the world becoming.

This is an ancient mythology, widely known and fundamental in India, where the symbol of the yoni, penetrated from below by the lingam, is the prime, ubiquitous sign of the mystery of the continuing creation of the universe. In Egypt, as already remarked, in the mythology of the sky-goddess Nut and her earthly consort Geb—out of which the whole great cosmogonic legend of the death and resurrection of Osiris unfolds (early model of the resurrection of Jesus)—the dignity, as well as antiquity, of the metaphor of earthly parenthood as a reflex of the cosmic process received its most elegantly documented representation. The appearance in France of an explicit image of the mystery as early as c. 20,000 B.C., adds millennia to the antiquity of this already all but ageless myth. And if Frobenius's suggestion of a tradition of wood carving antecendent to that of the carved stones of both Europe and Egypt is to be credited, then no one knows or shall ever know to what era this myth should be assigned. Let me quote here from Frobenius's remarks on the vitality of the art of carving in wood:

"A group of rock carvings stands in durable stone, elevated, permanently there. Storm, flood, animals and the rank growth of plants avail against it nothing through generations. The artist's hand has long since decomposed. The works, however, live on; and if their presence lacks the power to inspire further works of the kind, there they remain, alone, sufficient to themselves, for generations. Indeed, their monumentality itself is enough to preserve them in isolation. Since they suffice as they are, there is no need for anyone to chisel in additional rock figures beside

them. The stronger, more durable the material, the less reason for renewal, the less their influence on younger generations in the fashioning of art, and the weaker the prospects for survival of a technique.

"Otherwise is the case with such a perishable material as wood. The forest, the tree, the wood, grow most abundantly just there where their greatest enemies live and are at work: animals and rain. Also, it is there that man is most inspired to turn his hand to woodwork. Such works, however, are extremely short lived. They are fragile, subject to fire, and eaten away by worms. Things of wood require constant renewal and thus give cause and occasion for technical education over long terms and in extended contexts. A group of monumental stoneworks can suffice to serve large communities for many generations, and even remain there standing long after their reason for being has faded from the mind of man, and the last craftsmen capable of creating anything of their kind have crumbled to dust. Work in wood requires renewal and when practiced by many, conduces to the development of an inherited tradition of manifold applicability. Stone moves art to monumentality, and its own durability tends to a passing away of the art. Wood, on the contrary, conduces to continued practice and an enduring, many sided development of the craft. Hundreds of years after the first carving of a certain mask, after the mask itself has turned to rot, there may still be people alive who carve and make use of identical masks for the instruction of their children—and this precisely because the individual masks are so perishable. And so it comes to pass that a figure in wood that was fashioned only yesterday may be older than a work in stone that was completed hundreds of years ago.

"In all work in wood there is reflected the nature of the forest and of the tree. The individual dies, but its life continues in the species. The separate object crumbles; the work itself, however, is a formed idea (*Gestalt gewordene Idee*); and this idea endures. The form lives, not as a singular shape, but as expression of an idea, the influence of which may be unbounded. And that in the course of the development of this influence tendencies of differing kind, degeneration and regeneration, impoverishment and enrichment, should come to view—that too is homologous of the nature of the tree, of wood, and of the forest."[51]

The Mythic and the Mystical Modes of Religious Art

The magnificent rock-carved chapel at Angles-sur-Anglin to the triune or Triple Goddess (see I.1: Figure 111) is a monu-

ment of the Magdalenian era, dated c. 13,000 to 11,000 B.C., and about contemporary with the painted caves of Lascaux and Les Trois Frères. The appearance in this majestic panel, lower right, of the head or mask of a bull suggests very strongly a continuation of the mythology already illustrated in the Aurignacian-Upper Perigordian *Venus of Laussel, The Woman with the Horn,* where the elevated bison horn, symbolic of the moon, and left hand on the pregnant belly give notice of an already recognized correspondence of the lunar and menstrual cycles. A persistent association throughout the Early Neolithic of Old Europe, from c. 7000 B.C. of a bull with the imagery of the Great Goddess of that age has been noticed by Marija Gimbutas. Also to be recognized is an association throughout antiquity of the horns of the bull with the radiant crescent moon, which dies to be resurrected and reborn. The bull, consequently, throughout the ancient world was the principal animal of sacrifice. (Compare in the cavern of Lascaux the mysterious scene of a shaman in trance before the presence of an eviscerated bull.) On the printed ceramic wares of Greece, seventh to fifth centuries B.C., the classic triad of supreme goddesses, Hera, Athene, and Aphrodite, at the scene of the Judgment of Paris, are normally shown led or accompanied by the god Hermes, patron of the hermetic arts and mysteries, and guide of souls to the knowledge of eternal life, the head of whose symbolic wand is topped by a horned disk. And finally, as illustrated (see I.1: Figure 112), there is in the basement of the Musée de Cluny in Paris, a large stone altar of the Gallo-Roman period, from the site of the present Cathedral of Notre Dame, whereon there is carved a scene of three cranes perched above the figure of a bull, which duplicates exactly the message of the great Magdalenian panel at Angles-sur-Anglin. There can be no doubt that a single, enduring mythology of a supreme Great Goddess in her transformations is what we have illustrated in these precious monuments, from c. 20,000 B.C. to the triumph of Christianity in the fourth century A.D. or so. And in the light of Frobenius's suggestion of an art of woodcarving from the South (i.e. from Africa), antecedent to that of the rock-carved panels of Laussel, the antiquity of this mythology of the Great Goddess is beyond calculation. What is represented, apparently, is a truly primordial mythology and associated art in recognition and celebration of the Female Power as the giver and sustainer of all life, transported at the opening of the Late Paleolithic era, c. 30,000 B.C., from some forested region.

If a judgment may be ventured on the evidence of hardly more than a half-dozen masterworks of the art of rockcarving remaining to us from the vastly distant periods of the Aurignacian-Upper Perigordian *Woman with the Horn* (c. 20,000 to 8,000 B.C.), and the Magdalenian sanctuary at Angles-sur-Anglin to the Triple Goddess (c. 13,000 to 11,000 B.C.), there will have taken place a development in the art about equivalent to that which transformed the animal art from the period of the earliest engravings in the tunnels of Les Combarelles to that of the great painted temples of initiation and revelation of Lascaux, Les Trois Frères, Niaux, Tuc d'Audoubert, Altamira, El Castillo and the rest. *The Woman with the Horn* is clearly a figure in illustration of a myth already known. It is addressed to the mind in the waking state (*jāgarita-sthāna*) as common to all men (*vaiśvānara*), its function being to bring the society into accord with the rhythm of Nature by means of the mythic image here illustrated in an art that maintains the separate forms of moon and female (*a* is not *not-a*), yet enhances the significance of the female role and provides access to the magic of creation through her. In the later Magdalenian sanctuary at Angles-sur-Anglin, the three powerful female presences made manifest above the figure of a bull immediately transform the perspective of the viewer, for it is clearly a visionary image, (*a* = *not-a*), derived from the eye of the mind and addressed to the inwardly cognitive Dreaming state (*svapna-sthāna*). This art, expressing what the artist knows, not what he sees with his physical eyes, brings about the experience of an epiphany. The Triple Goddess and the Bull, two image-ideas become one in the connotation of the import of their relationship. Both are arts of revelation but addressed to different levels of consciousness. The Aurignacian *Woman with the Horn*, an example of the mythic mode, brings the tribe/community into social harmony in accord with the natural order of the universe. The later Magdalenian Triple Goddess, an art in the mystical mode, opens to a deeper mystery of synergetic nature.

These two modes of religious art are found in the Neolithic period and throughout Historical Antiquity. One can see in Michelangelo's, *The Creation*, painted on the ceiling of the Vatican Sistine Chapel, (see I.1: Figure 2), that the Creator is given a human form bursting through a heavenly cloud with a powerful gesture of his arm. Larger-than-life in its expression but understood by the physical eye, in the way of exoteric art as an illustration of the myth. A twelfth-century European mosaic (see I.1: Figure 4), of God sitting before the perfect sphere of the Universe He creates, thus maintaining the separateness of subject and object as is proper to the Waking state, (*jāgarita-sthāna*), common to all men, (*vaiśvānara*) is, also, an exoteric art of religious instruction.

In contrast, the "flying bucks" or *alites* of the Paleolithic Sebaaniene Cave (see I.1: Figure 176); the sculptured, wooden figure of Polynesian Tangaroa generating Gods and men from his own body (see I.1: Figure 7); the visionary, African, Ancestral image of the "living dead," as an Intermediary between the Tribe and the Invisibles (see I.1: Figure 6); and, finally, the Indian Great Lord, Shiva Maheshvara (see I.1: Figure 5), carved in high relief against the back wall of a great hand-hewn cave, a sublime triadic image symbolic of the imminent ground of all being and becoming, although beheld externally, are to be known internally. These are esoteric arts in the mystical mode expressing not cause and effect as in the natural world but rather a synergy, a "mutual arising" or emanation; out of the One, the Many.

It is evident that "Primitive Art," both in the mythic and mystical modes, is eloquent of the experience of an intelligible dimension beyond the sight of the physical eye. Pfeiffer's "conflict control," therefore, is a term not correctly applied to the "creative explosion" which is not a popular explosion but the *first* revelation of Nature-in-its-manner-of-operation to the inner eye of the mind of *Homo sapiens sapiens*, c. 40,000 B.C.

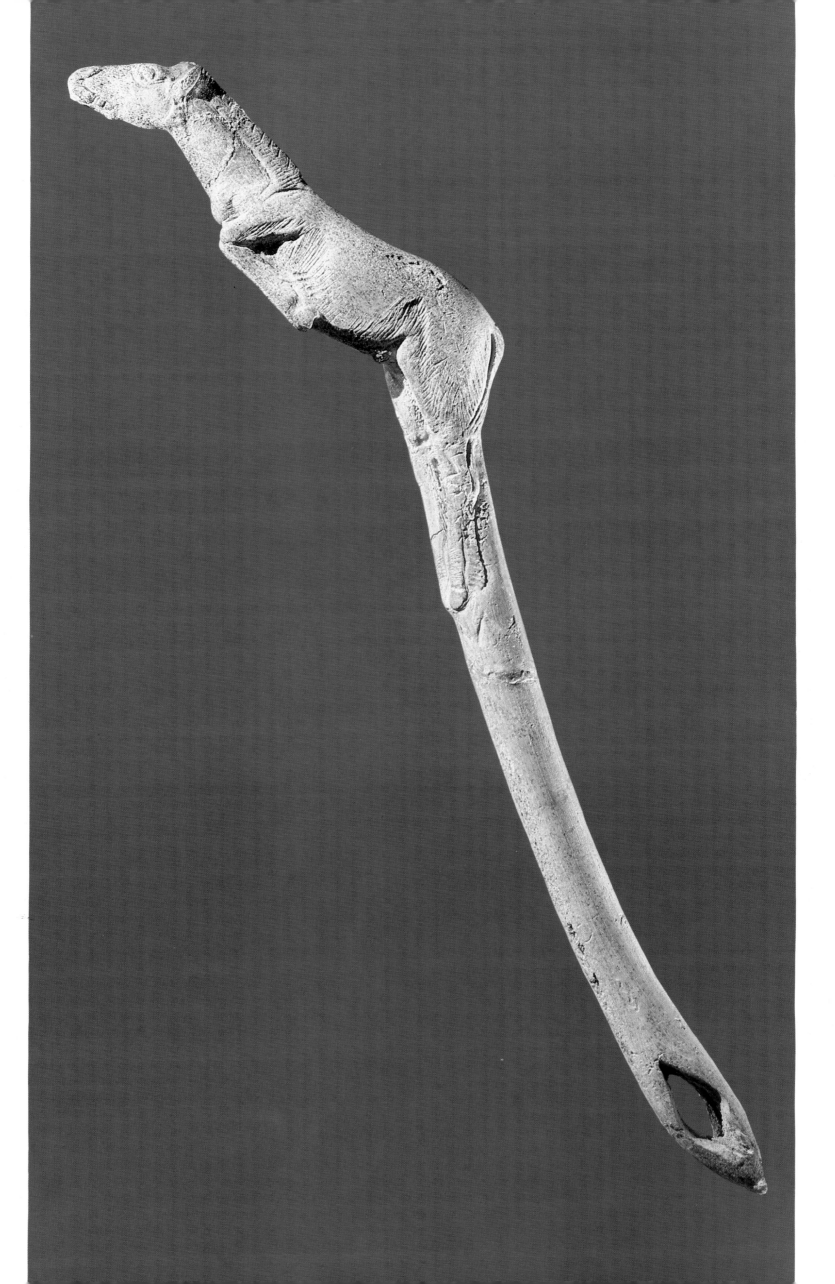

That a fundamental transformation of human consciousness occurred toward the close of the last great glacial age, some 40,000 years ago, is evident in the sudden appearances in Europe at about that time of the two symbolic visual arts of rock painting and stone sculpture; respectively, in the painted temple caves of the men's hunting rites and in the "Venus" figurines and reliefs associated both with dwelling sites and with sanctuaries in veneration of the female power (see Vol. I.1: pages 58–79).

Evidence of the skulls suggests that an advance, at just that time, from "archaic" to "modern" Homo sapiens must have been an essential determinant in the production of this sudden beginning of the history of the visual arts, which has been termed by John E. Pfeiffer, the "creative explosion."[1] Simultaneously there was an increase, as Pfeiffer points out, in population density, with an associated social problem of conflict control, to which formidable institutions and occasions had to be addressed, incorporating affective symbolic figurations through which the regulations of a corpus of socially constructive rituals became pictorially encoded for storage and transmission through generations. A third factor (and this, the one from which the symbolic forms derived) was the inspiration of the abundant herds of a happy hunting ground, which were being unremittingly slaughtered for the nourishment of the two-legged tribes. The necessity to kill the magnificent beasts and the inevitable Oedipal conflicts engendered by this requirement, with the compensatory mythology, then, of a bonding covenant between the animal and human communities—such as had already been recognized in the earlier cave-bear-skull sanctuaries of "archaic" Homo sapiens (see

pages 54–56) supplied the moral motivation of this art. The animals were willing victims and the paintings an essential constituent of the system of rites of gratitude and increase by which the mythology of the covenant was not only realized (see pages 73–79), but also maintained and taught through generations—for a season of some 20,000 years, which is a longer period than has elapsed since the end of the Magdalenian era, c. 10,000 B.C. A fourth determinant was the local landscape and especially the experiences of religious awe inspired by its deep caverns—of which there were hundreds, and within the greatest of which the "creative explosion" itself occurred, immortalizing the animals as messengers of occult powers, as well as required food. And finally, a fifth essential factor was the contribution of shamanic visionary trance-seizures, out of which the otherwise unconscious psychological realities of the contemporary *condition humaine* were brought to consciousness and delivered to the tribes through healing rites and initiations.

The inspiration of the female figurines was of another context, namely, the recognition of the identity of the lunar and female cycles and their relevance to the generation of life. The possibility noted by Frobenius (see page 82) of a prehistoric extension of the three-dimensional art of sculpture northward into Europe from equatorial West Africa, where a characteristic three-dimensional art of woodcarving (in contrast to the two-dimensional arts of painting and engraving) has been practiced for as long as anyone knows, suggests that the two mythological contexts implied in the two orders of art may have, originally, been of two distinct and geographically separate populations. The interest of Paleolithic sculpture, whether in the round or in relief, is almost exclusively in the *human* form (and that, female), whereas the paintings and engravings are of *animals* (with here and there a dancing or tranced-out shaman). The animal art was unquestionably a product of the experiences and intentions of the Great Hunt on the open plains.

224. God of the Center, with an atlatl (spear-thrower) and handful of spears. Detail from an illuminated page of the Pre-Columbian Codex Fejérváry-Mayer. Nahua-Mixtec Culture, Mexico. A.D. 15th century.

That of the figurines, on the other hand—if it actually represents, as Frobenius believed and argued, the translation of an art of wood into stone—must have originated in a region where wood was available, as it surely was in equatorial West Africa. The arts of engraving and painting, Frobenius points out, are analytical, in that their secret lies in the reduction of three-dimensional forms to illusions on a two-dimensional surface; their purpose, moreover, is magical: atonement with the animals slain and increase of their number. Sculpture in wood, however, is synthetic and in a sense mystical, in that it identifies the object visualized with the material: the female form, for example, with the wood and the tree, or in stone sculpture, with the living stone.[2] In the image of the Woman with the Horn the identification is fourfold: the woman, the stone, the horn, and the moon. Contrast the scene in the crypt of Lascaux of the tranced-out shaman and eviscerated master bison! The two distinct arts are, in any case, of very different styles. They obviously represent two distinct traditions. A sixth determinant of the constitution of the Paleolithic "creative explosion" may well have been, therefore, the coming together and amalgamation of two mythologies.

223. Spear-thrower (atlatl), length 13 inches, from Bruniquel (Tarn-et-Garonne), France. Dated Middle Magdalenian, c. 13,000 B.C. Regarded by André Leroi-Gourhan as "one of the greatest Stone Age masterpieces."

THE GREAT
WEST-TO-EAST
DISPERSAL

As the glaciers retreated and forests from the south overgrew in Europe what had formerly been tundra, then grassland, the great herds moved gradually northward and eastward, followed by their Paleolithic hunters. The way of this dispersal is marked by four unmistakable trace-elements: (1) ceremonials associated with worship of the bear; (2) shamanic practices; (3) an art style, associated with shamanism, in which skeletal and other internal features appear, as if by x-ray; and (4) the Great Hunt with spear and spear-thrower (the atlatl). All four of these items can be followed into America: *atlatl* is an Aztec noun; x-ray features are conspicuous in native North American art; and the elegant, redstone pipe bowl of

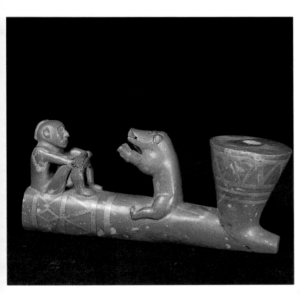

the Sioux that shows a bear instructing a shaman (**226**) speaks for the safe arrival of these two trace-elements from across the Bering landbridge. In Australia, as illustrated in the bark painting opposite (**225**), x-ray art and the atlatl are recognized features of the culture. There are no bears, of course, in Australia; but there are shamans.

225. Kangaroo hunt with spear and atlatl. Bark painting in x-ray style. Alligator River region, Northern Territory, Australia.

The Migration of X-Ray Style Art

We have already traced the course of the appearance of rock paintings and engravings (without the figurines, however) through Spain and across what once was a populated Sahara, south to the Cape of Good Hope, where the course terminates in the rock paintings and associated myths of the Bushmen (see pages 90–101). Between the life-ways of these little hunters on the open plain and the ways of the forest-dwelling, West-African Pygmies (see pages 102–112) there is today, as we have seen, a radical contrast. Both groups are but vestigial, however, of earlier, greater days: refugees who through the centuries were pressed by the stronger peoples of later cultures into ever remoter retreats, the Pygmies into the deepest jungle and the Bushmen into a desert.

As Carleton Coon has remarked of the Pygmies (see page 108, Figures 190–194), "we know nothing about these little people, except that they have lived in the equatorial forests of Africa for as long a time as is covered by the records of history."[3] "There is some historical evidence," he states further, "that the western Pygmies once extended along the entire coast of Africa as far as Liberia, and that

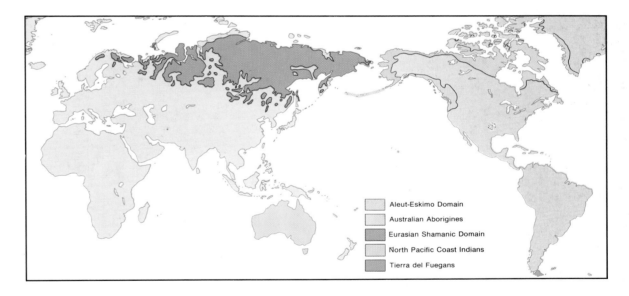

Map 30. The mythologies and rituals of the Great Hunt treated in this chapter are chiefly of: (1) the Aleut-Eskimo Domain, (2) the Australian Aborigines, (3) the Eurasian Shamanic Domain, and (4) the Tierra del Fuegans. Particular note is taken of the dispersal of bear ceremonials, shamanic practices, x-ray-style art, and the atlatl, as suggesting and marking ways by which early and later mythological traditions were diffused.

as late as the sixteenth century the Pygmies were the principal if not the only inhabitants of the forest between Lakes Albert and Edward."[4]

The forest-dwelling Tasaday of Mindanao in the Philippines also are refugees. John Nance has suggested that they may be the descendants of town-dwellers from the coast who in the sixteenth century fled deep into the jungle from a raid and pursuit by slave-collecting pirates, there to remain, both lost and afraid.[5] Likewise, the culture of the Andamanese (who are now extinct) was vestigial of more developed systems (see pages 118–119).

None of the cultures considered thus far, therefore, can be regarded as properly representing what Jamake Highwater has suggested should be termed the "primal mind."[6] The Congoid Pygmies have the best claim and may actually represent,

227. Earliest known intimation of x-ray style in Paleolithic art. Mammoth (or elephant, *Elephas antiquus*), from corridor-cave El Pindal, Oviedo, Spain. Early Magdalenian, c. 15,000 B.C.

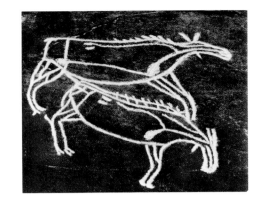

228. Fish (sole) in x-ray style (eyes on opposite side). Bone; length, 1¾ inches. Lespugue (Haute-Garonne), France. Late Magdalenian, c. 10,000 B.C.

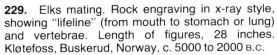

229. Elks mating. Rock engraving in x-ray style, showing "lifeline" (from mouth to stomach or lung) and vertebrae. Length of figures, 28 inches. Kløtefoss, Buskerud, Norway, c. 5000 to 2000 B.C.

230. Seal. Contemporary Eskimo drawing in x-ray style, showing "lifeline" and ribs. Alaska.

231. Reindeer. Rock engraving in x-ray style, showing ribs. Sakachi, Amur-Ussuri region, Maritime Territory, U.S.S.R.

though in regressed condition, practicing no arts but of music and dance, the type of forest-nurtured living out of which the Paleolithic "Venus" figurines derived. One thinks of the Pygmy dance observed by Colin Turnbull in which an old woman tied up and immobilized all the men and then released them to their duties (see page 111). The Bushmen, however, are clearly on the two-dimensional, painting and engraving side of the contrast recognized by Frobenius.

The Bushmen are the last inheritors of the southerly extension of the great creative explosion of c. 30,000 B.C. There were also extensions northward and eastward that passed across Siberia and not only into America, but also through India and into Australia, together probably with the dingo (see page 33). Map 31 (adapted from Andreas Lommel) traces the course of this great west-to-east dispersal, as marked by the occurrences of the Late Paleolithic, shamanic, so-called x-ray style of art, where the skeletal structure and interior organs of the animal are represented, with special accent, occasionally, on the "lifeline" leading from the animal's mouth or neck to its heart, stomach, or lung. This motif is a prominent feature in the decorative arts of the North American Pueblos and Plains tribes but does not appear in South America below Venezuela. Another feature characteristic of the culture wave that rolled northward and eastward out of Europe across Siberia, was the atlatl, or spear-thrower, the earliest examples of which are from Magdalenian sites in France (Figure 223). The word *atlatl* itself is a noun from the language (Nahuatl) of the Aztecs. Figure 224 shows an Aztec atlatl, and in Figure 225 is one represented in a recent bark painting from Australia.

The earliest west-to-east movement out of Europe into Siberia took place during the last of the four glacial ages, c. 70,000

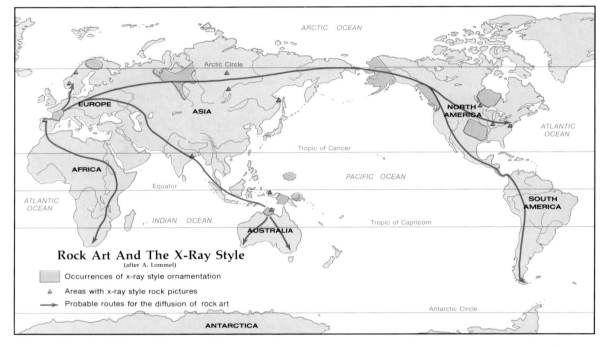

Rock Art And The X-Ray Style
(after A. Lommel)

Occurrences of x-ray style ornamentation

▲ Areas with x-ray style rock pictures

→ Probable routes for the diffusion of rock art

Map 31. West-to-east dispersal of x-ray (shamanic) art style. "It is curious," states Andreas Lommel, "that the x-ray style does not seem to have spread from its place of origin to any other part of Spain or to northern Africa."[1]

232. Pregnant cow in x-ray style from India.

233. Wallaby in x-ray style from Marind-anim, Western New Guinea. Paint on palm leaf, contemporary.

234. Fish in x-ray style. Bark painting by Mijaumi-jau, Gunwinggu people, Western Arnhem Land. Painted in 1965.

to 40,000 B.C., when Neanderthal Man ("archaic" *Homo sapiens*) was fashioning Mousterian flints. Beyond the Ural Mountains at that time, on the West Siberian Plain, game animals were proliferating, and in the farthest northeast, beyond the Central Siberian Plateau, they were crossing Beringland into America, possibly followed by straggling hunting-and-gathering bands. For as Chester S. Chard has observed: "The possibility cannot be dismissed of a move during early Zyrianka times [i.e. during the early Riss-Würm] from the general North China area to the New World. . . . Another possibility toward the very end of Zyrianka times," he adds, "is the movement of plains-adapted hunters across Siberia from the South Russian Plain into Alaska."[7]

Actually, there is little evidence from those times of early man in any part of Siberia. In the Altai ranges, among the headwaters and upper tributaries of the long, northward-flowing Ob and Yenisey rivers, a few scattered sites have been discovered in the neighborhoods of Rubtsvosk, Gorno Altaysk, and Irkutsk. Farther east, on the Amur River (which flows into the Sea of Japan), possible artifacts have been found in basic gravels at Filomoshki. Mongolia, just to the south, was apparently uninhabited during those years; but Japan, with mixed forests in the north and subtropical in the south, linked by landbridges to Siberia in the north and Korea in the south, was being entered from both regions. Sites in northern Konto have yielded implements of Mousterian type, and from a couple of caves in Kyushu have come choppers and the like.

During the relatively warmer season of the so-called Aurignacian Oscillations, from c. 40,000 to 30,000 B.C. (see Map 9, page 34), the rising waters of the Pacific submerged the landbridges, and both America and Australia, as well as Japan, were for a time cut off. However, with the return of the cold, c. 30,000 to 20,000 B.C. (see Map 10, page 34), the ocean levels dropped again and the landbridges reappeared. The oldest known site in northeastern Siberia, Ust'Nil' (59°45' N, 133°00' E), in central Yakutia, is radiocarbon-dated to this period (c. 33,400 to 28,000 B.C.). And it was then that tools of Mousteroid type were carried to America. But at the maximum of this increasing freeze, c. 18,000 B.C. (Map 11, page 35), the American glaciers closed the corridor from Alaska to the Plains; and it was only with the mounting temperatures of the terminal Pleistocene, c. 11,000 to 8,000 B.C. (Map 12, page 35), that the passage opened again and an advanced Aurignacoid industry was brought in, presently to be followed by the creators of rock engravings in the x-ray style.

Thus there were two distinct tool traditions carried across northern Asia and through Beringland to the Americas during and immediately following the long course of the Riss-Würm glaciation: the first, a Mousteroid tradition, and the second, Aurignacoid. With the first there must have traveled knowledge of the Neanderthal cult of the Master Bear, for it has left its unmistakable traces the entire length of the way. And with the second, we must assume, there traveled not only an interest in the x-ray style of animal art, but also knowledge (or at least some portion of knowledge) of the shamanistic myths and rites of the great French and Spanish caves out of which that art style took its rise. For like the bear cult, shamanism is an essential constituent of the lore of the Hyperboreans—those Dwellers beyond the North Wind who remained

235. Polychrome ceramic vessel. Zuni, western New Mexico. Animals in x-ray style, showing "lifeline." Contemporary.

settled along the Arctic way from Lapland, Norway, and Finland to Kamchatka and Alaska.

Thus, of the two Paleolithic traditions, that of the bear cult was the older by many centuries, having originated in Neanderthal Man's veneration of the cave bear as the Animal Master; whereas shamanism, as far as we know, developed as a tradition only in the period of the temple caves and the creative explosion of symbolic forms. Passing eastward across Siberia into America, as well as southeasterly to Australia, shamanism traveled as but one element of a living compound that included— besides the x-ray style of animal painting and engraving, the atlatl, and the bull roarer—an elaborate complex of social regulations, ceremonials, and associated mythological ideas, which scholars have designated by the very broad term *totemism*. The word is from the Algonquian (Cree, *ototama;* Ojibway, *ototeman)* and signified originally a

brother-sister blood relationship. As used by anthropologists, it may denote any one or all of a number of related concepts and associated customs stemming from the nuclear idea of a blood covenant between the human and the animal species. Primarily, the anthropological term denotes (1) a mythological identification of the ancestor of a given human family, clan, or tribe with the ancestor of some local animal species; but it has also been used to signify either (2) the identification of some particular animal or plant (or animal or plant species) with the guardianship or heraldic sign of some social group or class or (3) the recognition of some particular animal (or animal species) as the guardian, servant, or alter ego of an individual—which is more properly known as *nagualism*, from the Nahuatl noun *nahualli* ("sorcerer").

In 1851, Lewis Henry Morgan published an important study of the Iroquois *The League of the Ho-dé-no-sau-nee, or People of the Longhouse,*[8] in which it was shown that the clans of all the Iroquois tribes, or nations, not only bore animal names, but also were paired, with the requirement that marriages should be contracted only between couples of matched totems. In 1910, Sir James George Frazer (author of *The Golden Bough*) published *Totemism and Exogamy,*[9] in which a worldwide survey is presented of totemic systems and the related social requirement of marriage outside the clan (exogamy). In 1912, Émile Durkheim, founder of the French school of sociology, published *Les Formes élémentaires de la vie religieuse,*[10] wherein the reported totemism of the tribes of central Australia (which he mistook for the earliest form of the religious life) is interpreted as grounded in the experience of social solidarity. And in 1913, Sigmund Freud, in *Totem und Tabu,*[11] attributing the same symbolic and social phenomena to a psychological guilt reaction, explained this as a consequence of the actual group murder by his sons, in some primeval era, of the domineering father of a horde of hominids.

But the killing can have been, rather, of the animals of the hunt, and the guilt, something such as that reported of the Bushmen slayers of the eland. The social solidarity can have been that hypothesized by Pfeiffer (see page 129) as deliberately enforced in the period of the temple caves for the control of conflict. And the rites, while indeed symptomatic of guilt, are universally—whether in the Australian desert or in any one of the landscapes anywhere in the Americas—in their intention representative, and in their enactments revelatory, of a life-validating identity of the merely temporal individual with the everlasting ground of being made known through participation in the mysteries of the tribe.

Myths of the Australian "Dream Time"

A company of youths and older men of the North Aranda tribe of Central Australia is about to set off on a day's pilgrimage to their totemic center: a cave in the Ulamba region, several miles northeast of the highest peaks of the Western MacDonnell range. As described by T. G. H. Strehlow (who, as he tells, "by reason of his birth and upbringing, is able to think in Aranda as well as English"[12]), the mythological adventure proceeds as follows:

"Spears and all other chattels are left behind at a small soak near the edge of the plain and the men move off in silence towards the steep peak on whose slopes the cave is situated. There is only one correct track by which it may be approached, a track which through long disuse has become almost invisible; hence the oldest and most experienced man of the totemic group leads the way, while the remainder follow in single file. All are silent; for the cave must be approached with awe and reverence.

"From time to time the leader halts, points out rocks and trees which figure in the legend of the Ulamba ancestor, and neatly explains their significance by means of sign language. No questions may be asked, the young men must be content with such explanatory remarks as the leader is prepared to give them. If these are insufficient for a complete grasp of the myth, the young men must wait respectfully until another of these rare opportunities presents itself.

"After half an hour's steep climbing the leader stops. He points towards a huge round boulder which is resting on a smooth ledge of rock above them. The boulder has an opening in it; and the leader signals that it was from this rock and through this very opening that the Ulamba ancestor first burst into life. Still higher up another rock represents the body of a bird-totem ancestor who used to hide there, afraid lest the Ulamba chief should kill him. A little further on, the party comes upon a confused heap of rocks which marks one of the night camps of the Ulamba ancestor: the fallen rocks are the bodies of his human victims whom he had killed with his spears in order to make a meal of their 'sweet' flesh. A magnificent view can be gained from here of Mount Hay, whose blue mass dominates the dark sea of mulga in the east; of Mount Sonder and Mount Zeil, the two highest peaks in Central Australia, which raise their pale blue summits on the western horizon; and of the long line of massed parallel ranges to the south which constitute the Western MacDonnells. The leader explains that, in the beginning, the Ulamba ancestor often used to stand here on cold mornings, and scan the horizon around with his keen eyes for human victims. Finally he had set out over the low pass in the first range to the south towards the territory now held by the Western Aranda; but before plunging down to the

236. Ancestral figure crowned with the sun, emanating apparently from a swung bull-roarer. He carries, besides two boomerangs, a harpoon and a throwing-stick, inventions from the period of the European Paleolithic caves. This rock painting is of an earlier tradition than that of today's aborigines. Kimberly, Northwestern Australia.

237. Following in the footsteps of their forefather in his wanderings when spearing Emu, aborigines from the Guambone Station, near the Macquarie Reed Beds, New South Wales.

238. The MacDonnell Ranges, west-southwest of Alice Springs, rise from a plateau 2000 feet above sea level to a maximum of 4955 feet. The "footsteps of the Ancestors" here lead through marvelous rock gorges that change in coloration with changing positions of the sun.

"The leader raises himself to the level of the cave by climbing up on three little stone steps in the lower of the two great boulders. He removes the stones with which the narrow opening has been skillfully blocked up to keep out rain-storms from the south, and also to prevent animals from entering the cave. These stones, it should be added, also serve the purpose of hiding the cave from the eyes of strangers and robbers. He takes out several bundles of *tjurunga*, closely wrapped around with hair-string, and hands them to the men waiting below, who place them on a bed of grass and leaves so that they shall not touch the ground.

"Then the leader steps down, takes up each bundle in turn, unwinds the string, and chants the song which relates the wanderings of the Ulamba ancestor. Gradually the party takes up the verses of the chant; and in low, hushed voices their

239. A tribal elder maintains a silent and solitary vigil before the sacred soak from which both the sun and the Ancestor once arose (see 241).

240. At Guri-Guri, a cluster of elders contemplates a ground painting of the Emu ancestor. The tracks are of the mythological Emu himself.

basin of the Upper Ormiston on the other side, he had paused on the saddle of the mountain for a brief moment and looked back regretfully towards his native Ulamba. Finally, the leader directs the gaze of his followers to a prominent conical hill just below the narrow pass: this represents the body of the ancestor when he returned to his home from his last trail.

"The party is now close to the cave. At a signal from the leader every man stoops down and picks up a handful of sticks, stones, or pine needles. They turn around a sharp corner; the cave suddenly bursts into view; stones and sticks and pine needles are flung towards it: the spirits of the ancestors must be warned of the approach of human visitors, for to disturb them rudely means to court their displeasure, and this may result in a sudden death in the near future.

"The cave itself consists of two huge boulders piled high upon each other. The

dark bottom mass is the body of the Ulamba ancestor himself: thus had he stretched himself out for his final sleep when he returned home from his last venture. Mortally wounded by his victim, he had struggled back to his own home; nowhere else would he close his death-dim eyes. His father had awaited him here and had cast himself down in grief over the prostrate body of his son. They had changed into great rocks, filled with the seeds of life.

"The party halts. In the narrow cleft between the two boulders rest the sacred *tjurunga*. At a signal from the leader, the party sits down in a half-circle on a convenient ledge of rock at the base of the cave. Two hundred feet below them, at the bottom of a steep ravine, several slender white-barked gums are to be seen pointing upwards towards the cave: they represent spears which the Ulamba ancestor had once hurled at his victims.

241. Three North Aranda tribesmen, ceremonially attired, sit before a sacred ground-painting representing the Ilbalintja Soak, on the Burt Plain, some thirty miles northeast of Alice Springs.

The ground of this painting has been hardened with men's blood. The white circles are of down. The kneeling celebrants have just performed in three separate ceremonies. The central figure is Karora, with the decorated pole above his head. The other two, from two different sun ceremonies, are wearing the headgear of those rites. For Ilbalintja is revered as the soak out of which the sun, as well as the Bandicoot forefather, first arose.

There, in the beginning, when all was darkness, the Ancestor of the Bandicoot totem, Karora, lay asleep below ground. Above him the earth was red with flowers, overgrown with many grasses, and from the midst of a patch of purple flowers just above his head there rose as to the sky a decorated sacred pole that swayed to and fro and was a living creature. Its skin was smooth, like that of a man. Though asleep, the Ancestor was thinking. As desires flashed through his mind, Bandicoots began coming out of his navel and from his armpits. They burst through the sod above, and at that instant the first dawn appeared. The sun rose, flooding all with light, whereupon Karora himself burst through the crust that had been covering him, and the great gaping hole that he left behind became Ilbalintja Soak, filled with the sweet juice of honeysuckle buds.

Having waked, Karora felt hungry, for the magic had gone out of him. Fluttering his eyelids and groping about in a dazed state, he felt a moving mass of Bandicoots all around him and, seizing two, roasted them in the white, hot sand.

Evening approached. The sun hid its face behind a veil of hair-string pendants, and Karora, with his thoughts turning toward a helpmate, again fell asleep, stretching his arms out to both sides. Then there emerged from beneath one armpit something in the shape of a bull-roarer. It assumed human form and increased in one night to the stature of a young man. Feeling something heavy on his arm, Karora woke and saw at his side his first-born son, whose hand was resting on his shoulder.

Again dawn broke. Karora rose; and when he sounded a loud, vibrating call, his son stirred with life, got up, and danced a ceremonial dance around him. Karora was sitting adorned with ceremonial designs worked in blood and white feather-down. His son, only half awake, stumbled. Karora's body quivered violently. His son placed his hands upon him, and when this had been done, the first ceremony of the Bandicoot clan came to an end.[2]

song bursts upon the silence that has enfolded the cave up to this moment. The *tjurunga* have now been unwrapped. They are spread out side by side; each represents the ancestor at a different stage of his career, and hence has a special verse of the chant assigned to it. The leader takes up each *tjurunga* in turn, chants the words appropriate to it, and hands it around for inspection. Each man presses the *tjurunga* affectionately to his body, and then passes it on to his neighbour.

"All the while the traditional song re-echoes from the steep mountain wall. It requires much explanation. It contains a great number of obsolete and obscure words, which, furthermore, have been dismembered and had their component parts re-grouped in the chant-verses for metrical purposes. This re-grouping of the dismembered parts effectively prevents the uninitiated from being able to understand any portion whatever of the chant when it is being sung. Yet it is upon this old traditional chant, the words of which are jealously guarded by the old men of the group, that the whole of the Ulamba myth is based. Accordingly, the leader, while teaching the younger men the sacred chant in its traditional form, has to spend much time in explaining each verse of the song after it has been memorized. Again, no questions must be asked. The leader explains the general meaning of each verse, mainly by means of sign language. If anything remains unclear, the leaders have to wait for another opportunity for getting further informa-

tion unasked from their teacher. This chance is usually afforded to them during the elaborate decorations which follow that evening, decorations for the sacred ceremonies in honour of the Ulamba ancestor.

"But the afternoon is waning rapidly. The last *tjurunga* has been rubbed clean of dust, and the last verse has been chanted. No man must be here at nightfall. The leader wraps up the sacred objects with hair-string, replaces them in the cave, blocks up the opening with stones as before; and the party returns to the camp near the soak below.

"The shadows of Ulamba lengthen out across the mulga plain, the sun sinks behind the western peaks. Fires begin to gleam brightly; and the men of the party share at a leisurely meal the meat which they had obtained by hunting earlier in the day. Then they gather around the old leader once more, and begin to decorate themselves under his guidance for a ceremony in remembrance of the Ulamba ancestor, whose life story they have heard that afternoon. The ceremony which is now enacted is intimately connected with the chant and the myth: it is, in short, the dramatic representation of one of the many memorable events in the myth centering around the person of the ancestor. The actors wear a traditional ceremonial pattern in conformity with the scene of the dramatized incident; for the Ulamba chief is stated to have worn a different decorative pattern at each of the many places which he visited on his travels."[13]

242. Stone *tjurunga* of the Central Australian Aranda tribe, showing footprints of the Emu ancestor as he walked around the soak out of which he had emerged. *Tjurungas* may be of stone or of wood, oval, circular (as here), or as long as some 8 to 10 feet.

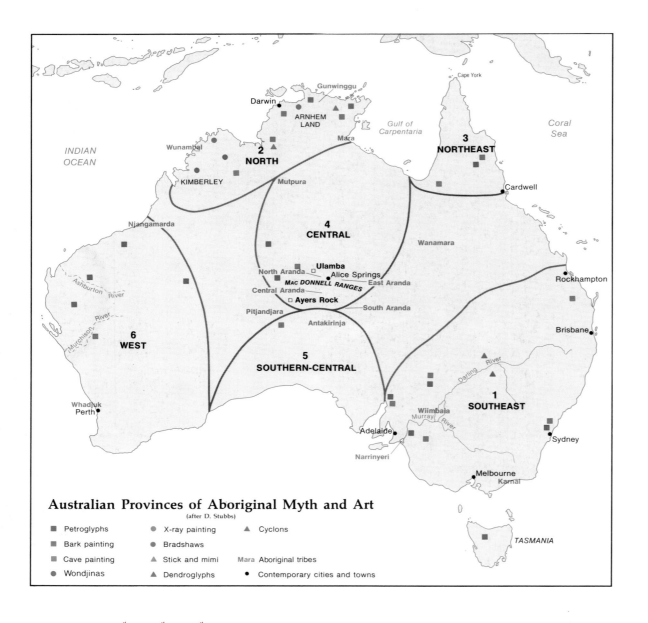

Map 32.
1.   Southeast: early Negritic-Tasmanian tribal survivals; All-Father (High God) mythologies; oldest rock arts in Australia; also, dendroglyphs (designs carved into living tree trunks) and cyclons (conical stones ritually scarred).
2.   North: Indonesian and West Papuan influences; World Mother mythologies; bisexual gods and powers; in Kimberley: Wondjina and "Bradshaw" rock paintings (named for Joseph Bradshaw, their discoverer, 1840); in Arnhem Land: "stick" and "mimi" figures; rock and bark paintings in x-ray styles.
3.   Northeast: area of entry of East Papuan influences, which then passed to areas 4, 5, and 6.
4.   Central: vast desert with rock art in isolated cult sites, such as Ayers Rock and Alice Springs; emphatically patrilineal "tribal ancestor" mythologies.
5.   Southern Central: arid, no caves or rock masses; art restricted to ornamentation of portable objects and the body (for ceremonies).
6.   West: isolated rock galleries; no extended cult sites.[3]

Also delineated are the territorial ranges of the major aboriginal tribes.

Myths of the ancestral Dream Time are known to all of aboriginal Australia. The powers therein recognized are not the same, however, in the southeast and in the north as among the Aranda in the central region. For the aborigines of these three areas are of three distinct orders of culture.[14] Those of the southeast, today all but extinct, represent an early Negritic-Tasmanian race for whom the chief mythic power was a unique, creative All-Father, not recognized by other peoples of the Australian continent. In the north and northwest, where a later, West Papuan strain covered and pressed back the Negritic, the dominant presence, not only in the myths but also in the rock paintings of the area, is a power, truly dreamlike, which may appear as one or as many; as male or as female; in human form or as the rainbow. While for the Central Australian Aranda and their neighbors, who represent an East Papuan influence, the dominant powers are the ancestors of their patrilineal totemic clans.

According to A. W. Howitt, whose reports on the southeastern tribes caused a considerable stir in the first years of this century, not only among ethnologists but also in theological and literary circles, the older women of the very primitive Kurnai tribe of Victoria speak of a supernatural

243.   A hunter with spear and spear-thrower on the western desert.

being above, whom they refer to as *Mungan-ngaua* (Our Father); but it is only in the most secret part of the male initiation ceremonies that the novices are introduced to the strictly hidden teachings concerning this figure. They are then told

that he once lived on earth and taught the Kurnai everything they know.

Mungan-ngaua's son, Tundun, and his wife were the first parents of the Kurnai. Tundun conducted the ceremonies instituted by his

244. The making of string figures, one of the oldest of art forms, flourishes at Yirrkala, an Aboriginal township in northeastern Arnhem Land. The figure here displayed is a stylized, almost abstract, canoe. (Compare **181** on page 101 and **311** on page 185.)

father; but when someone revealed their secrets to the women, Mungan-ngaua became furious and sent a fire [the Aurora Australis] that filled the space between sky and earth. Men then went mad with fear and speared one another, fathers killing their children, brothers their brothers, husbands their wives. The sea rushed over the land and most of the people drowned. Those surviving became the Ancestors of the legends, many as birds, animals, and fish. Tundun and his wife became porpoises. And it was then that Mungan-ngaua left the earth, ascending to the sky, where he remains.[15]

Many other peoples of the southeast told of such an All-Father, now living in the sky. The Narrinyeri, along the Coorong coast, believed that before departing with his family, he gave the people weapons and instituted their rites. The nearby Wiimbaio declared that he had two wives, carried two spears, and ascended from a site on Lake Victoria to which they could point.[16] His name in southwest Victoria was Bunjil, and there his two wives were said to have been sisters with a single name, Black Swan. His son was the rainbow, Binbeal, whose wife was the second

rainbow that is sometimes seen. And all were now living beyond the sky in a place that the medicine men described as a mountain. When the medicine men arrived there, they were met by an entrance guardian named Gargomitch, who took

their questions to Bunjil and returned with the answers.[17]

While on earth, Bunjil one day held his hand out toward the sun. The sun then became hot and warmed the earth, which opened and emitted the aborigines, who danced the ceremonial known as Gayip.

"It is a striking phase in the legends about him," Howitt states of Bunjil, "that the human element preponderates over the animal element." Other characters of the legends appear as the kangaroo, crane, spiny anteater, and so on, but Bunjil (to quote Howitt again) "is in all cases the old blackfellow, and not the eagle-hawk, which his name denotes." Moreover, he is the only mythic figure to be referred to as Our Father.[18] "Bunjil was the maker of the earth, trees and man," states Howitt, "and his name exists in the language as a term for wisdom and knowledge."[19] His names among other tribes are Baiame, Maamba, Birral, Tharamulun, and Kohin. The domain of his cult can be defined on the map by a line drawn from the mouth of the Murray River to Cardwell on the Queensland coast.[20]

Now the general resemblance of this figure's days on earth to what we have learned of the African Pygmy "creators" surely is obvious. Also evident is a certain resemblance to the Bible stories of that other "dream time" when Yahweh, too, walked on the earth "in the cool of the

day" in the garden that he had planted (Genesis 3:8). In fact, it was this latter resemblance that caused the stir when Howitt's publications appeared. Father Wilhelm Schmidt, in his ethnological treatise *Der Ursprung der Gottesidee*,[21] argued for an "original monotheism," evident in the lore not only of the Kurnai, but also of all the most primitive peoples known; among others, the African Pygmies and Bushmen, Southeast Asian Negritos, and Ona of Tierra del Fuego. Andrew Lang crossed swords with Herbert Spencer, Frazer, Tylor, and Howitt himself, arguing for such a primitive All-Father as "the germ of, or rough draft of, the highest of religious conceptions";[22] namely, the High God of his own and Father Schmidt's Judeo-Christian belief. Whether either Bunjil of the Kurnai or the Yahweh specifically of Genesis 2 and 3 is actually equivalent to the "idea of God" of any respectable metaphysician today is a nice question for theologians; but in any case, the recognized sharing of such mythic themes by the simplest known religions with some of those we think of as the most advanced would seem, at least, to say something about the constancy of mythological archetypes. Whether interpreted theologically as supernatural revelations, or naturally as effects of the mind, they exist, endure, and undergo significant transformations on a plane little affected, apparently, by any readily identifiable sociological or philosophical influences. And yet they *have* undergone changes, as the myths from other parts of Australia clearly show.

In contrast with the mythological All-Father of the south, the Gunwinngu of Arnhem Land, in the north, tell of a creator known as the Old Woman, who came to Australia underground from a region called Macassar, somewhere to the northeast. According to a version of the legend given to Ronald and Catherine Berndt by a woman of the tribe, this All-Mother arrived in the form of the Rainbow Serpent, Ngalijod, with children inside her—people, who later made more people. "She made us talk like people," the woman said; "she gave us understanding. She made our feet, cut fingers for us, made our eyes for seeing, made our heads, made anger and peace for us, made our belly and intestines, gave us energy to move about—made us *people.*"[23] Another female figure, Ngalgulerg, then gave to women their digging stick and the basket they hang from their foreheads and carry on their backs. Kangaroo gave to the men their spear-thrower. And all would have died of thirst had the Rainbow Serpent not made water for them by urinating. "She showed us how to dig for food and how to eat it," the woman said.

245. All-Mother, the "Old Woman" of the Northern Australian myths, who in the form of a serpent arrived in Arnhem Land from the sea and gave birth to the Ancestors. Rock painting of the birth scene, Arnhem Land (Map 32, Province 2).

246. Where the Wondjina sank into the ground, leaving his image behind, "child germs," by which women conceive, appear as a row of ancestral heads. Rock painting, Kimberley (Map 32, Province 2).

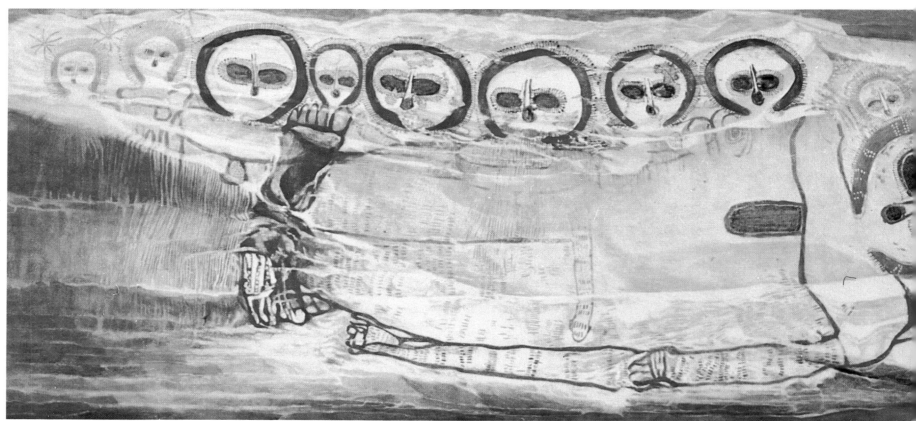

"Those First People, she scraped them with a mussel shell when they were born, until she saw that their skins were lighter, and she licked them all over. And now, when we are inside our mothers she gives us breath and shapes our bodies."[24]

Andreas Lommel has published a specimen of Great Serpent lore from the Unumbal of northern Kimberley, in which the All-Mother appears, not simply as ancestress, but also in a cosmogonic role.

In the Beginning there were only Sky and Earth: dwelling in the earth was Ungud, in the form of a great snake; and in the sky, Wallanganda, the Milky Way. Wallanganda threw water on the earth; Ungud made it deep. And in the night, as Ungud and Wallanganda dreamed, life arose from the watered earth in the forms of their dreams.

From Wallanganda's dreaming a spiritual force went forth as images that he projected onto rocks and into caves, where they can still be seen, painted red and white and black. [Or, according to another version, it was the bird Kujon who did the painting, as he grasped the images of Wallanganda's dream in his own dreaming.] And when these had been painted, Wallanganda multiplied their forms in the shape of living beings, which he sent forth over the land.

The paintings are the spiritual centers of those beings. They are the Fathers; and the living beings of each kind are Brothers. The Fathers were painted without mouths or eyes: these were given by the great serpent Ungud, who is both female and male, dwelling and dreaming in the earth. Wallanganda, too, is dreaming, sending spiritual germs to the earth, and he will not let his creatures die.[25]

On the rocks and cave walls of northern Kimberley there are painted forms, not only of plants and animals, but also of

247. Waramurungundi, the "First Woman" of the Gunwinggu people of northern Arnhem Land. Feathered ornaments hang from her head, a net bag is on her back, a dillybag dangles from her elbow, and she holds a digging stick. Her heart is shown above the center of her body. She came underground from "Macassar," bringing children inside her, and for a time wandered with her husband, Wuragog, and his relatives. But when he once rebuked her for being shameless, she and her daughter left him.

248. Wuragog, Waramurungundi's husband, with his spear, a feather in his hair, and a hair belt. He found the bottle that is on his head while wandering about after Waramurungundi left him. When she later went in search of him, she found that he had turned into the cliff now known as Tor Rock. She and her daughter continued on their way, but when they reached the caves at Banewilngugngug, they too became rocks.[4]

anthropomorphic beings without mouths that personify rain (Figure 231). They are called Wondjina. They are said to have been first discovered by Ungud at the bottom of the waters.

Immediately upon coming into being, the Wondjina went forth over the earth, fashioning hills and plains. Wherever they went they brought rain, and while the rocks were still wet, they lay down upon them here and there and sank into the earth, leaving impressions behind that remain today as rock paintings.

Every lake, river, and natural spring

belongs to the specific Wondjina whose image was left in the neighborhood and who dwells beneath the painting in the waters under the earth, creating childgerms, each of which is a particle of the Wondjina, and also, therefore, of Ungud. In dream, a father will find one of these child-germs, and in a second dream, project it into his wife, in whom it assumes a human form. And this germ is that portion of the soul which at death goes back to the waterhole, there to await reincarnation.

All those descended in this way from the same Wondjina source are the rightful owners of the region, the oldest among them being recognized as the incarnate Wondjina itself. When telling of the Wondjina, this one will speak in the first person: "As I came along in the Dream Time," he will say, "I left my impression on this rock." It is his duty to repaint the image before each rainy season, and when about to begin, he will say aloud: "I am now going to refresh and invigorate myself." When finished, he fills his mouth with water, which he blows on the painting, and when the rain comes, it is received as at once his, the Wondjina's, and Ungud's gift.[26]

We have here broken into a mythological space where all things perceived are but the reflexes of an order instituted in the Dream Time. The logic is not of daylight but of dream, where things melt into one another and their apparent separateness no longer holds. "The name *Ungud*," states A. P. Elkin, writing of the rock paintings of this region, "is sometimes used as though it referred to a person, sometimes as though it referred to a far-

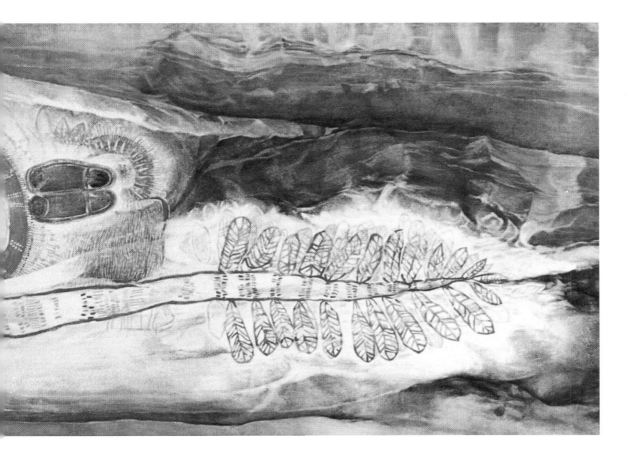

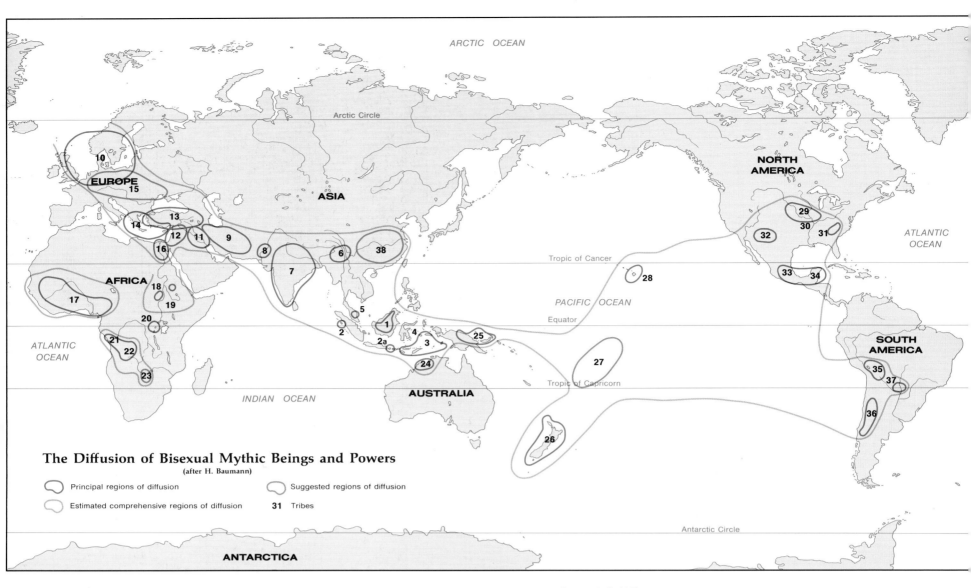

The Diffusion of Bisexual Mythic Beings and Powers
(after H. Baumann)

◯ Principal regions of diffusion   ◯ Suggested regions of diffusion

◯ Estimated comprehensive regions of diffusion   **31** Tribes

Map 33. The appearance in North Australia of such a bisexual creator as Ungud (see page 141) links the heritage of that region to a mythological context that did not originate among hunters, but among planters. There are three major centers out of which early planting traditions arose: Middle America, Southeast Asia, and the Near East (see Volume 2). Mythologies of a bisexual generation either of the universe or of humankind are found only within the zones of influence of these matrices. Hermann Baumann enumerates the regions so influenced as follows:

Indonesia: (1) Borneo [Dayak]; (2) Nias; (2a) Bali; (3) Islands from Sumba to Aru; (4) Ambon [and Ceram?]. *South Asia:* (5) Central Malaysia [Ple-Sakai]; (6) North Burma [Kochin] and Assam [Naga, Abor, Khasi]; (7) India [Vedic Aryan, Hindu, Buddhist, Tantric, and Shakti elements; Bondo, Musahar, and other native tribes]. *Antiquity and the West:* (8) Indus Valley Civilization; (9) Ancient Iran; (10) Old Germanic Zone [and the Balts]; (11) Sumer-Babylonia; (12) Western Semitic Zone [Phoenicians and others]; (13) Asia Minor; (14) Greek-Aegean Zone [in-

cluding Orphism, Gnosticism, and other cults]; (15) Europe [area roughly indicated: Kabbalah, Talmud, Alchemy, Mysticism; survivals of bisexual themes in European folklore]; (16) Ancient Egypt. *Africa:* (17) West Sudan [Dogon-Bambara], Upper Volta [Senuto? Bobo], Ghana [Akan], Dahomey, Nigeria [Yoruba, Ibo, Etik, Jukun], Saharan Moors; (18) Nubia; (19) Eastern Sudan [Kunama]; (20) Northeast Zaire [Hunde]; (21) Lower Congo [Vili-Kongo]; (22) Southwest Angola, Southwest Zaire [Luba, Lulua, Chokwe]; (23) Rhodesia [Tonga-Lala?]. *Australia:* (24) Kimberley [Wunambal, Ungarinyin]. *Oceania:* (25) North New Guinea and Bismarck Archipelago [Widaro, Mbowamb, Yatmul, and so on], New Ireland, Admiralties, and other islands]; (26) New Zealand [Maori]; (27) West and Central Polynesia [Tongens, Tahitians, Raiateans]; (28) Hawaii. *North America:* (29) Sauk and Fox; (30) Dakotas [= Sioux] and Omaha; (31) Cherokee; (32) Zuni and Navaho; (33) Aztecs; (34) Maya [Quiché, Tlapanec]. *South America:* (35) Aymaras; (36) Araucanians; (37) Lenguas. *Far East:* (38) China [Yang-Yin philosophies].

Baumann writes of this culture field: "We have here to do with a great number of manifoldly independent centers of development, which, however, have been so bound together through innumerable folk and culture movements that something like a single culture province has become defined, which we can best appreciate as such, not by comparing only the specific elements and complexes of the multitude of aboriginal cultures involved, but by including also those of our modern occidental culture province. Parts of this complex have long since disappeared. . . . Other members of the ancient complex came under its spell only after long delay and with strong resistance. There are primitive groups that, centuries ago, adopted certain more or less essential elements of the context and have held onto them with rare fidelity, often in grotesque contrast to other aspects of their life ways. Indeed, we know how late by many millennia it was that our own European forefathers submitted to the spell of urban civilization. Similarly, it has been only within the last two thousand years that city life has developed in the Sudan.[5]

off time, and sometimes, too, for the rainbow-serpent water spirit. It is also given as the ultimate explanation of such significant things as an obviously artificial arrangement of stones. To the question, 'What is that?' the answer given is simply, 'Ungud'." [27]

*   *   *

Hermann Baumann has shown in a comprehensive work that the mythological archetype of such a bisexual primordial being is not common to all mankind, but confined in its distribution to areas

either formerly of the early high civilizations or affected by influences from those centers (Map 33).[28] We have already remarked that in northwestern Australia there was a West Papuan culture strain that covered and pressed back the Negritic, and that the Gunwinngu, indeed, now claim that their All-Mother came to them from somewhere known as Macassar. "The aborigines of north-eastern Arnhem Land," states Ronald Berndt, "have for several centuries been in almost consistent contact with Indonesian voyagers to the mainland of Australia. The first phase of this alien contact seems to

have been the pre-Macassan or Baijini, while later (possibly in the sixteenth century) came the Malay and Macassans, who have left evidence of their occupation in the way of numerous old camp sites, archeological remains, old graves, tamarind trees, and so on."[29] Ungud and the Old Woman are thus reflections, on the northern margin of the continent, of a mythology that came originally from southeast Eurasia. Whereas in other parts of Australia the Rainbow Serpent is masculine, here it has become identified with a mother goddess who arrived by way of Indonesia and Western New Guinea.

* * *

The influences from eastward of New Guinea that penetrated through Queensland to the center of the Australian continent must have lacked such agriculturally related mother-goddess features as reached Arnhem Land from the northwest, for the myths and rites of the Aranda and their neighbors are of an emphatically patrilineal heritage. And yet, here too, in the final stages of initiation, symbolic forms are revealed that in a silent way point beyond the enacted myths to mysteries such as those that, in the southeast, seem to have been rendered through All-Father figures, and in Arnhem Land, through the great serpent Ungud.

When a boy is about ten or twelve, he and the other members of his age group are told that from now on they will not camp with the women, but with the men. They will not go with the women to grub for roots, but with the men will hunt the kangaroo. They are tossed into the air while the women, dancing around them, wave and shout, and each is then painted on chest and back by a man of the social group from which his wife is to come. As they paint, the men sing: "May he reach to the stomach of the sky!" Each boy is told that he now has upon him the mark of the ancestor of whom he is the living counterpart, who lived in the Dream Time—here known as the *altjurunga*.[30]

The second stage of initiation begins in the men's camp one evening, after three strong fellows have pounced upon the lad and borne him, struggling and frightened, to the ceremonial ground. There the whole camp greets him, women as well as men, the men singing while the women dance. They are now the people of the *altjurunga*. When the boy has watched and listened for some time, fur strings are wound around his head to make a tightly fitting cap, and a girdle of twisted hair is tied around his waist. Three men then lead him through the dancing women to a brake of bushes, where he is painted and warned that he must never disclose to any woman or boy anything of what he is to learn. And he must remain where he is until called.

The next day, his mother comes, together with his father's sisters and the mother of the girl who has been assigned to be his wife. All night his mother has kept a fire burning, and she now brings two sticks from that fire. While the men sing a fire song, she hands one stick to the future mother-in-law, who, passing it to the boy, ties fur strings around his neck and tells him to hold fast to his own fire; that is, never to interfere with the women assigned to other men. The boy returns to his brake, and the women depart with the second fire stick.

The youngster is next brought into the forest to sit alone for three days with little

to eat, after which his season begins of instruction in the mythic lore of his tribe. Blindfolded, he is led from his brake at midnight and made to lie face down at the edge of the men's danceground. When told to sit up and look, he sees lying before him a decorated man who represents, he is told, a wild dog. Another is standing, legs apart, at the other end of the danceground, holding up twigs of eucalyptus in each hand. He utters the call of the kangaroo and moves his head as though watching for something. The dog barks, gets up, and runs on all fours between the other's legs. When he turns and comes through from behind, he is caught, shaken, dashed to the ground, and lies still, pretending to be dead; but then, suddenly, on all fours, he comes running at the boy and lies on top of him. The kangaroo hops over and lies on both. The boy has to bear their weight for about two minutes, after which he is told that what he has just witnessed is an event of the *altjurunga*, when a wild-dog–man attacked a kangaroo-man and was killed.

249. In New South Wales (Map 32, Province 1), at the Guambone Station (see 237, page 135), four novices are being conducted along a symbolic way to the ceremonial high master waiting to receive them. Like the engravings on bull-roarers, the figures on the ground are abstractions condensing ancestral legends.

Six days and nights of such visionary mimes culminate in the ceremony of his circumcision. He is again seated behind his brake with a design in white pipe clay painted on his back. On the danceground, a performance is taking place in which the women are participating. Suddenly, the sound of the approaching bullroarers is heard. The women flee, and the boy is made to lie on his back while the men pile poles on top of him, lifting and slamming them down to the rhythm of a song they sing:

Night, twilight, a great clear light;
A cluster of trees, skylike,
*   rising red as the sun*

At the western end of the ground, in

143

250. The dreadful seriousness of some of the ordeals of these rites is grimly illustrated in these historic photographs from Arnhem Land (Map 32, Province 2). Having been exposed both to a broiling sun and to a torment of stinging insects sprinkled over them, those with short white sticks at their heads have expired.

the firelight, appear the two men who are to perform the operation. With their beards thrust into their mouths (signifying wrath), and with their arms stretched forward, they stand perfectly still, the actual operator in front, holding the small flint knife in his extended right hand, and the assistant pressing close behind. The instant they appear, the boy's future father-in-law comes down the line, carrying a shield on his head and snapping the fingers of both hands. Dropping to one knee before the operator, he elevates the shield above his head. The sound of the bull-roarers can be heard in the camp of the women, who are to think it is the voice of the great spirit Twanyirika, who has come to take the boy away. He, on his back beneath the slamming and rising poles, can hear it too.

Abruptly, the poles are removed. He is lifted and carried feet foremost to the shield, upon which he is placed. The assistant circumciser immediately grasps the foreskin, pulls it out as far as possible, and the operator cuts it off.

Instantly, like the images of a dream upon one's waking, all the functionaries of the ceremony disappear, and the boy is told by the two who carried him: "You did

well, you did not cry out." He is returned to the place where the brake once stood. It is now gone, and the men who are there congratulate him. The blood from his wound is let flow onto a shield. Bull-roarers are pressed against the wound and he is told that it was they that made the sound: they are *tjurunga,* from the Dream Time. Standing over a fire whose smoke is supposed to be healing the wound, he is introduced to the functionaries by their ceremonial names and given a packet of *tjurungas* by the oldest. As a child is smoked at birth, to be purified, so now is this boy, who has just attained his second birth.[31]

During the weeks of the healing of the wound, another series of mythic mimes is shown, culminating in the planting of a sacred pole, banded with alternate rings of red and white bird down and topped with a tuft of eagle-hawk feathers. The boy is told to embrace the pole, it will keep the next operation from hurting. One of the men has lain face downward on the ground; a second on top of him. The initiate, conducted from the pole, is placed face upward on this living altar, and while the company sets up a great shout, a third man, mounting astride the

boy, grasps and holds his penis ready for the knife, at which moment, a fourth, suddenly appearing, slits the length of it from below.

In the women's camp, meanwhile, at the sound of the men's shout, the initiate's female relatives are being slashed across belly and shoulders by his mother.

He is lifted from the altar, and while he squats over a shield into which the blood flows, one or two of the younger men, who have been subincised before, stand up and voluntarily undergo a second operation to increase the length of their incisions. Standing close to the sacred pole, hands behind their backs and legs wide apart, they shout, "Come and slit mine to the root!" They are pinioned from behind, and the work is done.[32]

There has been considerable discussion of the sense of this operation, the best testified and most obvious suggestion being in the likening of the subincision to the vulva and the blood from the wound to menstrual blood.[33] During certain periods of their long ordeal, the boys have been given nothing to eat or drink but the men's blood—in bowls, either in liquid form or coagulated, to be carved like cake. Blood has also been poured over them, so that they have been soaked, inside and out, in the men's blood. And the men have been obtaining it in great quantities by jabbing their subincision wounds and slashing the insides of their arms, the blood being then used, not only to initiate the boys, but also as paint for the ceremonials and as glue to fix bird down to their bodies when they assume the forms of the Ancestors. The blood is thus the natal blood of the boys' "second birth" from the father into life in the myths, as that of the vulva had been of their first birth from the mother into life in the world. And by virtue of their own subincision wounds, the initiates have now become eligible to give ceremonial birth to spiritual sons.

The terminating ceremony of this whole sensational season is a celebration, symbolically of the mystery of the two sexes. Known as the Engwura, it is solemnized only by a number of tribes together, with eighteen or twenty initiates, its central event being the elevation of a double *tjurunga*, supposed to have been fashioned by a supernatural being called Numbakulla, the Eternal. The name suggests an esoteric reference to some such transcendent power as was represented in Bunjil of the southeastern tribes; while in the double *tjurunga* of this supernatural's creation—obviously symbolizing the principle of duality that is manifest through all things, and most transparently in the sexes—a relationship is indicated to the tradition of a bisexual ground of creation, as in Ungud of the northwest. Again, in the sacred pole, the pivot of the universe, the feathers fastened to the top are of the eagle-hawk, and, as we have heard, the name Bunjil means "eagle-hawk." Further, the alternating bands of the pole, red and white like the double *tjurunga*, a duality. The first song sung to the young initiate—"May he reach to the stomach of the sky!"—suggests, in the context of this symbolic order of the second birth, not the stomach exactly, but the womb of the power on high; while the advice, finally, to embrace the bicolored pole before submitting to the operation, points to the requirement of a spiritual identification with the androgynous ground as prerequisite to its realization in the flesh.

Throughout the four months of the ceremonials, the men's camp has been divided from the women's by the dry bed of a stream. During the first day of the culminating double *tjurunga* ceremony, the young men are sent away on various distant assignments, so that the camp should be empty; and while they are gone, the leader of the festival prepares in secret two large wooden *tjurungas*, each about 3 feet long, which he binds together carefully with a string made of human hair, hiding them completely. The upper three-quarters of the combined symbol is encir-

251. Fathers of the Aranda tribe of Central Australia (Map 32, Province 4) donating blood for ceremonials. As menstrual blood is the medium of natural birth, so this blood from the men's arms and reopened subincision wounds will be the ceremonial medium of their sons' second, tribal or social, birth to manhood.

252. The three high celebrants of the Engwura, the most solemn mystery of the Aranda of Central Australia (Map 32, Province 4). All night the leading master of this culminating ceremonial of the season of initiations has been silently elevating and lowering the double *tjurunga*, the *ambilyerikirra*, symbolic of Numbakulla, the Eternal.

cled with rings of white down. The top is given an owl-feather tuft. When finished, it is known as the *ambilyerikirra*, and taken to be buried in the dry bed of the separating stream.[34]

The young men return at the end of the day and are made to lie on their backs in a row. Night falls, and an old man, their guardian, along the line, walks back and forth. There is perfect silence. The youths are lying still. And the leader of the festival, who has now secretly retrieved the *ambilyerikirra* from its symbolic place between the separated camps, is seated, holding it upright before his face by its undecorated lower end. Beside him, at

either elbow, is an assistant, supporting his arms. And the man is lifting and lowering the sacred object slowly before his face. All night the old man, with his two assistants supporting his arms, slowly lifts and lowers the symbol.

At a certain moment of the night all the older men begin chanting. The boys remain as they are, with the guardian silently pacing, until dawn, when they are roused and the old leader stops lifting and lowering the *ambilyerikirra*, gets up, with his two aides still at his elbows, and proceeds to the northern end of the ceremonial ground. The candidates are directed to a line of sacred bushes, where they take boughs and form a solid square behind the three with the *ambilyerikirra*. The formation moves out from the ceremonial ground to the stream bed, goes across it and up the opposite bank to the camp where the women are standing, grouped together. Each, with her arms bent at the elbow, is moving her open hands up and down at the wrist, palms upward, inviting, while calling out, "*Kutta, kutta, kutta!*", keeping one leg stiff while bending the other to a gentle sway of the body.

The formation approaches slowly in silence; and then, within five yards of the women's front rank, the men bearing the *ambilyerikirra* throw themselves to the ground hiding the double *tjurunga* from view. The initiates throw themselves on top, so that all that can be seen of the three are their heads projecting from the pile; and when all have remained so for about two minutes, the young men get up and, turning their backs on the women, reconstruct the square. The leaders, quickly coming to their feet, also turn their backs, and are hustled through the square. They lead the group back to the Engwura ground, and the ceremonial ends.[35]

The youths will now be delivered as men to their assigned women. The ritual of their being tossed in the air marked their carriage away as boys—taken by Twanyirika, the spirit of the bull-roarer; the rites of circumcision and subincision were of their transformation; and the ritual, then, of the double *tjurunga*, to the "*Kutta, kutta, kutta!*" of the women of the camp announced their eligibility to return to them from the *altjurunga* as authorized, fully fledged Aranda.

253. Celebrants of the Aranda Engwura ceremony—fathers and initiated sons—gathered about the symbolic pole of Numbakulla, the Eternal. Hanging near its top is the bull-roarer, source of the voice of the initiating spirit, Twanyirika. On the initiates' backs are their special body paintings in white clay.

Circumpolar Cults of the Master Bear

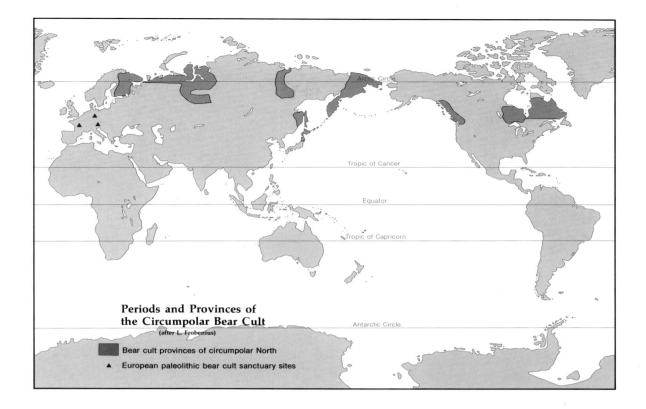

Periods and Provinces of the Circumpolar Bear Cult
(after L. Frobenius)

■ Bear cult provinces of circumpolar North
▲ European paleolithic bear cult sanctuary sites

Of the Paleolithic traditions that spread west-to-east, the bear cult is almost certainly the oldest, dating, as it does, from Neanderthal Man's veneration of the cave bear. The little black bears of the Ainu bear cult of Hokkaido, Japan, might seem to the skeptical observer hardly adequate to match, as counterparts, the gigantic cave bears of Neanderthal Man's experience, to whom they owe the origins of their worship. Yet they are apparently fulfilling the inherited role quite well; for size and ferocity are not the only, nor indeed the most important, qualifications of a divinity—as we have learned from the Bushmen's god Kaggen, the Mantis (see pages 90–93).

When the bear has come forth from his long winter sleep, he is frequently seen walking on his hind legs like a man. What sustained him during those months of his hibernation?

There is a belief, documented from Finland eastward across circumpolar Eurasia and America to Nova Scotia and Labrador, that bears in hibernation nourish themselves on a juice drawn from their paws. The eighteenth-century Danish voyager Knud Leems, in his *Account of the Laplanders of Finnmark* (1767), accepted the belief as an established fact. "It is a matter well known and ascertained through the regions of the north," he reported, "that a bear, during the winter, lies concealed in his den and is sustained by no other aliment than a certain milky juice which he sucks from his forepaws with a growling."[36] Another, earlier traveler in that period of the Enlightenment, Baron La Houton, in his *New Voyages to North America* (1703), had already accepted the belief. "Many people," he wrote, "will hardly believe that these animals can live three months in such Prisons without any other food but the Juice of their Paws which they suck continually: and yet the matter of fact is undeniably true."[37] And a third witness, P. F. X. Charlevoix, in his *Journal d'un Voyage fait par ordre du roi dans l'Amérique Septentrionale* (1744), states of the bear in hibernation: *"Il tire alors de ses Pattes, en les lèchant, une substance, qui le nourrit."*[38]

The bear hears everything, even at great distances. He also remembers and will avenge himself for every hurt. One may not talk about him when hunting; he does not allow even the mention of his name. Hence he is called by screening nicknames, such as Crooked Tail, the Chief's Son, or the Old Man in the Fur Coat, and on the hunt one employs a secret language.[39] The following are some of the pet names that have been recorded.

Among the Abnaki of Quebec: Cousin, rationalized by the observation that a skinned bear, in its proportions, looks much like a man. "These tracks," the Abnaki will say, "are our cousin's." The related Penobscot, on the Penobscot River in Maine, speak of the bear as Grandfather; he is grandfather of all the animals. And the Montagnais-Nascapi of Labrador, who likewise call the bear Grandfather, speak of him after his death, respectfully, as Short Tail, Food of the Fire, Black Food, and the One Who Owns the Chin. South of Hudson Bay, the Eastern Cree call him both Short Tail and Black

254. Amber bear, length 2¾ inches, from the Rosen Bog, Denmark. Maglemosian Culture (from the Danish *magle mose*, "great bog"), c. 9000 to 5000 B.C. Reproduced actual size.

Map 34. The earliest evidence anywhere on earth of the veneration of a divine being is in the Alpine bear-skull sanctuaries of Neanderthal Man (see pages 54–56). A second period and stage is represented in the figures of bears deliberately stabbed in the Magdalenian temple caves of Montespan (**94** on page 62) and Les Trois Frères (**133** on page 76), and a third in the epi-Paleolithic finds of Norway and Denmark (**254** below).

Across the Eurasian North, the period from 6000 to 2500 B.C. was an era of climatic optimum, warmer than today, with vegetation zones extending north of their present limits. Tlhe bear cult spread northeastward with the advancing populations and is represented in myths and customs from Finland to Labrador.

Food, as well as Crooked Tail, Old Porcupine, the Lynxlike Creature, Wrangler, and Angry One, while for the Plains Cree of Saskatchewan, he is the Four-Legged Human, Chief's Son, Crooked, and Tired. The Sauk and the Menomenee of Wisconsin refer to him as Elder Brother and as Old Man; the Blackfeet, north of the upper Missouri, as the Unmentionable One, That Big Hairy One, and Sticky Mouth. All of these tribes are Algonquian, but to the Tsimshian of the Northwest Coast the bear is again Grandfather, as he is also to the Yukaghir, the Tungus, and the Yakuts of Siberia.

The Yukaghir, a people of Paleo-Siberian speech (together with the Chukchi, Giliaks, Koryaks, and Kamchadals, all classified racially as Americanoid, and inhabiting the northeastern extreme of the Asian continent) have such names for the bear as Owner of the Earth and the Great Man. The Mongolian Tungus (related to the Manchu, and widely spread over eastern Siberia) call him the Old Man. To the Turkic Yakuts, he is known as the Worthy

255. *The Bear Kill.* Eskimo sculpture of soapstone, the knife and bear's teeth of ivory. Winnipeg, Manitoba, Canada. Contemporary.

Old Man, Beloved Uncle, Good Father, and Our Lord, while among the various Finno-Ugric peoples of western Siberia and eastern Europe, the names are of the same kind. For example, the Ostyak know him as the Beautiful One, Old Furry Father, and Old Man with the Claws; the Vogul, as the Venerable One; the Votyak, as Uncle of the Woods; and the Estonians of northeastern Europe call him Broad Foot. The Finns speak of the bear as Pride of the Woodland, Forest Apple, Light Foot, and Golden Friend of Forest and Fen; the Lapps, as King of the Woods and Old Man with the Fur Garment, while the Ainu of Hokkaido, Japan, refer to him as That Divine One Reigning in the Mountains.[40]

The likening of this animal to a man, which is already suggested by his posture—frequently upright, standing and even walking on his two hind legs—appears to be confirmed by the resemblance that has often been remarked between the human body and the body of the bear when its fur coat is removed. Karl Meuli, in an article on the funeral customs of the Greeks,[41] points out that among primitive hunting peoples, both men and animals are thought to appear now in the one form, now in the other; and that the white, soft body of a bear, stripped of its hide and lying outstretched on its back, would be a sight particularly suggestive of such a notion. Indeed, one European observer, writing of his own attendance at a bear-eating festival in Kamchatka, reported that he was at first startled on seeing the body laid out on the ground, uncertain as to whether the Kamchatkans might be on the point of making a meal of one of the members of his expedition. Emil Bächler has remarked that in the valley of the upper Yenisey around Turukhansk, the Tungas believe that a man will turn into a bear if, in the forest, he will but crawl three times around a tree stump, growling all the way.[42]

The killing of a bear is generally regarded as a ritual act, to be performed in a special way. Knives and clubs, primitive weapons, are commonly preferred even where guns are available, for they comport with the antiquity of the cult. The Ainu hunter, for example, having drawn his knife, rushes into the animal's embrace, hugs him closely, and thrusts the knife to his heart.[43] The Gilyak of the lower Amur, so as not to excite the animal's posthumous revenge, do not surprise him, but engage him in a fair stand-up fight.[44] In America, the Thompson River, Shasta, and Carrier tribes of the northwest, as well as the Montagnais-Naskapi, Penobscot, Abnaki, and Malecite of the northeast, first invite the bear to come out of his den and then inform him, with apologies, of their challenge.[45]

When the bear has been slain, it is usual to disclaim responsibility for his death. In northern Siberia today, the Ostyaks, Votyaks, Koryaks, Kamchadals, Gilyaks, Yakuts, Yukaghir, and Tungus will say: "Grandfather, it wasn't I, it was the Russians, who made use of me, who killed you. I am sorry! Very sorry! Don't be angry with *me!*" On the other hand, the general practice in North America was to praise the bear and to explain the occasion. For example, the Abnaki would tell the animal frankly: "I have killed you because I need your skin for my coat and your flesh for my food. I have nothing else to live on." The Ottawa, north of Lake Huron, would flatter him and plead: "Do not leave with an evil thought against us because we have killed you. You have intelligence and can see for yourself that our children are starving. They love you. They wish you to enter into their bodies. And is it not a glorious thing to be eaten by the children of chiefs?"[46]

The Ainu of Hokkaido have the following legend of the bear's humanity:

256. Ivory pipe with bears, seals, and walruses. Length, 4½ inches. Made by the Maritime Koryak, Kamchatka. Contemporary.

There was, once upon a time, a young woman whose custom it was to go daily to the mountains with her baby on her back to gather lily roots and other edibles. At the end of each day she would take her roots to a stream to wash them, lift the baby from her back, wrap it snugly in her clothes, and, leaving it on the bank to sleep, go into the water nude. One day, when thus washing her roots, she began to sing a beautiful song, of which the melody so enchanted her that she lost all sense of her surroundings. Coming out of the stream, continuing to sing, she set down the roots and, lost in herself, was dancing naked on the shore, when suddenly the loud crack of a stick stopped her. She looked, saw a bear, and in panic fled, leaving the child.

The bear, discovering the infant and thinking it a pity that such a helpless little thing should have been left alone, said to itself ruefully, "I came here attracted by the lovely song of that woman, approaching quietly lest she hear me and be afraid. But her singing was so beautiful that I became elated and inadvertently made a sound." The child began to cry for its mother's breast, and the bear, in pity, put his tongue into its mouth. Nursing thus, the child was kept alive for several days, during which time the bear never left its side. But then, one day, a company of hunters from the village came to the mountain, frightening the bear, which fled and left the child where it lay. When the villagers, discovering it, realized that the bear had been tending it, they were impressed. "That bear is good," they said to each other. "He has kept this lost baby alive. Surely that bear is a deity deserving of our worship." So they hunted out and shot the bear, returning with its body to their village, where they offered it food and wine along with sacred sticks, sending back its soul with praise and blessings to the other world.[47]

The Lillooet Indians of southern British Columbia had a special Bear Song that was to be chanted solemnly and with genuine emotion over the body of the bear, naming the boons of power they expected to derive from slaying him:

You were the first to die, greatest of beasts.
We respect and shall treat you accordingly;
   No woman will eat your flesh,
   No dog insult you.
May the lesser animals all follow you
   And die by our traps and arrows.
May we now kill plenty of game.

May the goods of those we gamble with
   Follow us as we leave the play,
   And come into our possession.
May the goods of those we play lehol *with*
   Become completely ours,
   Even as a beast that we have slain.[48]

257. Bear mask, Haida, Queen Charlotte Islands, British Columbia. The preeminence of the bear among the animal powers both revered and feared by northern hunting peoples—from Finland, across Siberia and America, to Labrador—has provided inspiration for many of the most impressive works of art of the masterful wood carvers of the American Northwest Coast. The dancer in this ceremonial mask might have impersonated in dance and mime the bear-husband of a favorite mystery play and legend.

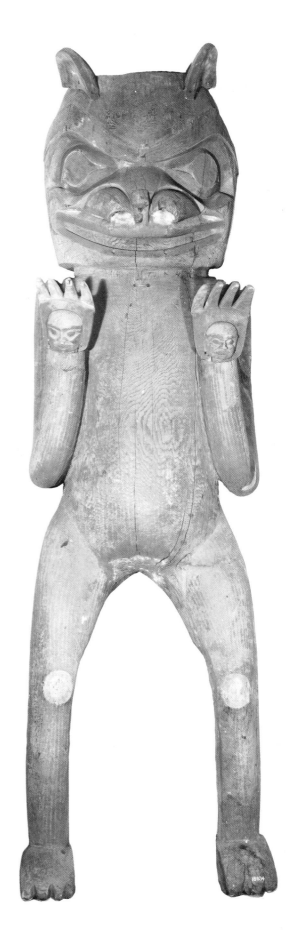

258. Heraldic grizzly bear, possibly a house guardian or totem. North Pacific Coast, Bella Coola tribe, British Columbia, Canada.

The bear hunt and sacrifice across Eurasia

259. In Lapland, bear hunters on skis with spears and crossbows close in for the sacrifice.

The nearby Shuswap chant a similar dirge of comfort, praise, and petition:

O thou greatest of animals,
Man among beasts,
Now my friend,
  Thou art dead!

May thy mystery make all the other animals
Be like women when I hunt them!
  May they follow thee,
  And fall to me
  Easy prey![49]

It is reported that when a good singer chants such a song earnestly, from the heart, those present become so moved that they weep with tears rolling down their cheeks. Singers of the Thompson River tribes, before chanting, paint their faces with alternate black and red vertical stripes. And the Western Carriers of the Mackenzie River declare that they sing so that the bear, as he dies, may say to himself: "I like that song." The hunters will then be able to kill many bears.[50]

Finally, when the body of the slain bear is brought into the village, the manner of devouring his flesh is everywhere a sacred feast with very special rules. In a letter written in 1634 by the Jesuit missionary Le Jeune, such an event among the Montagnais-Nascapi is reported in detail. The moment the bear had been brought into camp, one early evening, all the young girls and married women without children retired to a shelter of their own making, some distance away. The dogs were ejected from the wigwam in which the feast was to be held "lest they lick the blood," we read, "or eat the bones

or even the offal of this beast, so greatly is it prized." The meat was boiled simultaneously in two vessels, the contents of which were consumed separately, the first by the men and older women together, after finishing which the women left; the second was then emptied by the men alone. This latter feast was the more ceremonious, characterized by a special "eat all" feature; namely, a requirement that every morsel of the meat should be consumed, with every person required to eat the entire portion served him. "They will give to one man," wrote Father Le Jeune, "what I would not undertake to eat with three good dinners. They would rather burst, so to speak, than leave a thing. . . . Not a word is said; they only sing, and sometimes the shaman drums. . . . It is a banquet of devotion."[51]

This custom is followed not only by the Montagnais-Nascapi of Labrador, but also by the Tête-de-Boule and Eastern Cree south of Hudson Bay, as well as by the Asiatic Eskimo, the Lamut around the Sea of Okhotsk, and the Ainu of Japan.

No doubt the best-known example of the ceremonious killing of a bear is that recounted in Elias Lönnrot's reconstruction (1835) of the Finnish folk epic *The Kalevala*, "The Land of Heroes," which, by the way, provided the inspiration for Longfellow's invention of an Algonquian-Iroquois epic, *The Song of Hiawatha*, even to the detail of the archaic trochaic tetrameter verse. The hero of the Finnish episode is the old magician Väinämöinen, who, as he approaches the bear's den, sings out, using some of the flattering pet names, to let the animal know that he is coming:

'Otso, Apple of the Forest,
O thou lazy honey-pawed one:
If thou hearest me approaching,
Hearest me, the hero, coming,
In thy hair thy claws conceal thou,
In thy gums thy teeth conceal thou,
That thou never more shouldst move them,
That they motionless remain there.'

And when the bear has been slain, he again sings out, disclaiming responsibility:

'O my Otso, O my darling,
Fair one with the paws of honey,
Be not filled with causeless anger,
I myself have not o'erthrown thee,
Thou thyself hast left the forest,
Wandered from thy pine-tree covert,
Thou hast torn away thy clothing,
Ripped thy grey cloak in the thicket.'[52]

As he then approaches the village with his prize, he again sings out, to let the people know of the arrival of a great guest:

'What I bring is not an otter,
Not a lynx and not an otter,
One more famous is approaching,
Comes the pride of all the forest,
Comes an old man wandering hither,
With his overcoat he cometh.

'Where's my guest to be conducted,
Whither shall I lead my gold one?
To the barn shall I conduct him,
On a bed of straw to lay him?'

And the people gave him answer,
Shouted all the handsome people:
'Better lead our guest illustrious,
And conduct our golden beauty
Underneath these famous rafters;

260. A bear festival of the Gilyaks of the lower Amur River region (East Siberia); the bear is about to be sacrificed.

261. Conclusion of the Gilyak festival, when the sacrificed bear, as a revered guest, is served a ritual meal of its own flesh.

Underneath this roof so handsome.
There is food arranged for eating,
There is drink poured out for drinking,
All the floors have here been dusted,
And the floors been swept most cleanly,
All the women finely dressed them,
In their very finest garments,
Donned their headdresses the finest,
In their finest robes arrayed them.'⁵³

And when the inert guest has been carried into the fine house prepared for him, Väinämöinen reassuringly sings:

'Otso, Apple of the Forest,
Fair and bulky forest dweller,
Be not frightened at the maidens,
Fear not the unbraided maidens,
Be not fearful of the women,
They the wearers of the stockings.
All the women of the household
Quickly round the stove will gather
When they see the hero enter
And behold the youth advancing.'

And the people spoke in answer:
'Be not grieved of this, O Otso,
Neither let it make thee angry,
That we take thy hide an hour,
And thy hair to gaze on always.
For thy hide will not be injured,
And thy hair will not be draggled,
Like the rags of evil people,
Or the clothing of the beggars.'⁵⁴

Then the aged Väinämöinen stripped the bearskin from the body, laid it on the storehouse floor, and put the flesh into copper kettles, adding salt to the stew. The meat was placed in dishes on the long table, beer was poured, and Tapio, the God of the Forests, was invoked; also his

daughter Tellervo, son Nyyrikki, and all the rest of his people, to come to the feast where the Honey-Pawed One was to be eaten.

And when the people then asked for the legend of the bear's honorable birth, Väinämöinen sang to the accompaniment of his harp the Kantele of a maiden clad in "stockings blue," with gaily colored shoes and with a hair-filled basket on her arm. She walked, one night, through clouds near the moon, on the shoulders of the Great Bear, whence she cast from her bas-

ket the hair upon the sea. The wind tossed it, rocked it. The waves carried it to shore at the edge of a wooded headland. And there it was that Mielikki, Mistress of the Forest, took the soft fur from the water's edge, put it in her basket, and hung this beautiful cradle where the forest branches were thickest and the forest leaves most abundant. She rocked the charming object where it hung on the limb of a broadly spreading fir tree. And it was thus that the furry beast was nourished to life in a forest all dripping with honey.⁵⁵

The Bear Sacrifice

That the way to pay homage to a deity is by sacrificing and eating it is a notion justified, among the Ainu of Hokkaido, by their idea of the animal as a visitor from the spirit-world, to which they are returning it. *Iyomande*, "to send away," is the Ainu word for "sacrifice." For the deities like to visit this earth, and to do so they assume disguises; but they are then locked into their animal forms until relieved of them through the sacrifice. They consign their pelts and meat willingly, in gratitude, to those who have released them.[56]

and they are supposed to have a good happy time of communion together."[58]

The bear is a visiting mountain god, the owl a village god, the dolphin a god of the sea. The greatest visible power, however, is that which lives in the sun, the spirit by whose influence that body or "ball" (*num*) is made to shine and to move. And the chief power here below is fire, whose spirit is feminine and known as Ancestress or Grandmother (*Fuji*); also as Iresu-Kamui, "that divine spirit [*kamui*] who sustains and rears us [*iresu*]."[59] Plants are divinities, and of especial importance are the food plants. Even things made by man have spirits of their own—swords, for example, to wear one of which confers strength. Indeed, the whole environment is enspirited and recognized with gratitude as alive.

seated according to rank around the long, rectangular central hearth, play music and sing to entertain them. The bear is slaughtered the next day, cooked, and eaten. Offerings are made of his own meat to his pelt, which has been placed, with head attached, in the seat of honor. Words of thanks and praise are addressed to him, presents bestowed, and finally, with the most cordial expressions possible, the visitor is ceremonially dismissed to his spiritual mountain home.[61]

When a very young black bear cub has been brought alive into the village, he is adopted by one of the families and treated as one of the children, suckled by the mother, and affectionately pampered. When it becomes big enough to hurt the others when playing, however, it is put into a strong wooden cage, fed on fish

Further, as J. Batchelor points out in his fine piece on the Ainus in Hasting's *Encyclopedia of Religion and Ethnics:* "The very essence of Ainu religion consists in communion with the greater powers, and the people imagine that the most complete communion they can possibly hold with some of their gods—animals and birds, to wit—is by a visible and carnal partaking of their very flesh and substance in sacrifice. At the time of offering, the living victim is said to be sent to his ancestors in another place."[57] Therefore, as this observer recognized, "the bear festival is a kind of mutual feast—a feast of friendship and kinship—in which Bruin himself also participates. Indeed, the bear is offered to himself and his worshippers in common,

But, of all the visiting presences, the bear is the most important. When one has been killed in the mountains, the body is carried ceremoniously to the village and brought into the hunter's house, not by the door, but by a special opening known as the "god's window." To peer into a home through this opening is an insult and a sacrilege to be atoned for by a fine, which is interpreted as a gift and an apology to the god.[60] The bear's arrival by this portal is known as a "god's arrival"; and when he appears, he is welcomed by the fire-goddess, whose long, rectangular hearth occupies the center of the one room. The god and goddess will now converse together through the night, while the fire burns and while the people,

Three paintings from a Japanese scroll of 1840 depicting the bear sacrifice of the Ainu:

262. A black bear, captured as a cub, is raised in a cage.

263. Taken from its cage, the bear is held by two cords, led about before its worshippers, and shot at with blunt little bamboo arrows so as to bring it to a heat of temper, at which time it will be suddenly slain.

264. At the ritual meal that follows, the pelt of the bear, revered as a divine guest, is served a stew of its own meat.

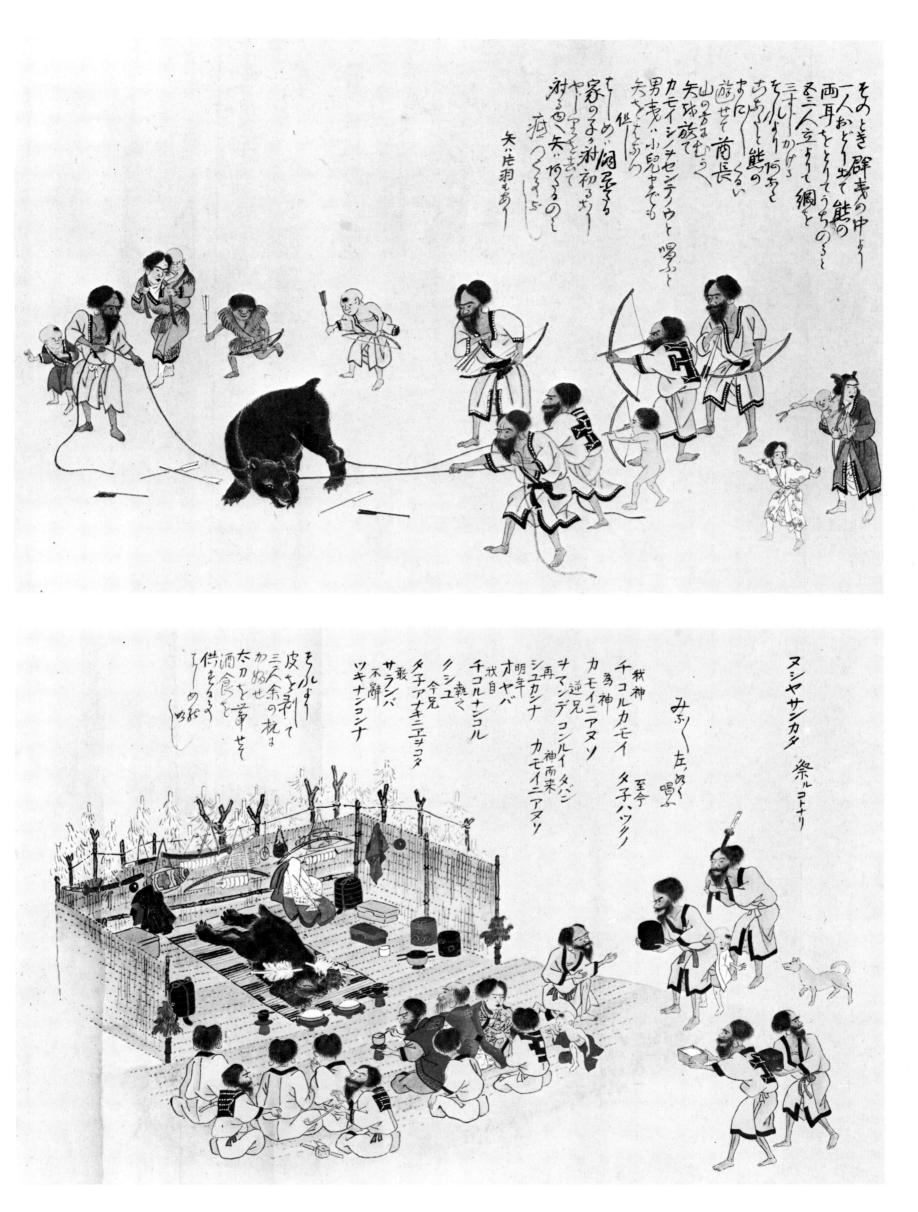

その時群衆の中より
一人おどり出て熊の
両耳をとりてうちのくと
ヌ三人立ちて網を
をとるゆくとくて
あるひとつ熊の
すゝに商長
遊せて山の方より
矢を放す
山の方より
カモイシリヤセテノウと唱ふと
男夷、小児やぞも
矢をとるより
ちゝめゝ閂をてら
家のよう初ます
ヤーンとまて
対る也矢やくるのく
疫つくるうと
矢ハ片羽もあり

ヌシヤサシカタ　祭ルコトナリ

みふ／＼左へぬく唱景　至今

秋神
チコルカモイ　　夕子ハツク
為神
カモイ二アヌソ
逆兄
ナマンデコンルイ　タシ　神雨来
シユカシナ　　　　カモイ二アヌソ
再
オヤバ
戎自
チコルナシコル
クシュ　今兄
タ子アナキ二ヲチコタ
歓
サラシバ
不離
ツキナシコシナ

そんまづ
皮を剥て
三人余の枕す
かむせ
太刀を章せて
酒食を
供もるゝ
ての

153

265. A photograph taken by Edward S. Curtis of a Kwakiutl canoe with an upright bear effigy arriving for a festival in 1910. The Kwakiutl are a prominent canooing and fishing people of the totem-pole culture of British Columbia, Northwest Pacific Coast.

and millet porridge, and kept for about two years, until the time is thought to have arrived for it to be released from its body and returned to its parents in their mountain.

The man who is to host the ceremony calls out to the people of his village, inviting them to the sacrifice of their dear little divine visitor from the hills. A number of prayer sticks are fashioned, whittled in such a way as to leave a head of shavings attached and clustered at one end. These sticks are stuck in the ground around the hearth of the house in which the bear has been raised, then brought out to the place where he is to be killed, and again stuck in the ground. Alongside them are laid two long, thick poles, known as *ok-numba-ni,* "the poles for strangling." The men approach the bear cage; the women and children follow, dancing and singing, and when the whole company has seated itself in a circle before the bear, one of its number comes very close to the cage and lets the little god know what is about to happen.

"O Divine One, you were sent into this world for us to hunt. Precious little divinity, we adore you; hear our prayer. We have nourished and brought you up with care and trouble, because we love you so. And now that you have grown up, we are about to send you back to your father and mother. When you come to them, please speak well of us and tell them how kind

we have been. Please come to us again and we shall again do you the honor of a sacrifice."

The bear, secured with ropes, then is taken from the cage and made to walk around in the circle of the people. Blunt little bamboo arrows, bearing a black and white geometrical design and a compact clump of shavings at the tip (called *hepere-ai,* "cub arrows"), are let fly at the animal and he is teased until he becomes furious. Then he is tied to a decorated stake; two strong fellows take hold of him and a third thrusts a kind of long wooden bit between his jaws; two more take hold of his back legs, two others of his front; one of the poles for strangling is held under his throat, the other above the nape of his neck, a perfect marksman sends an arrow into his heart in such a way that no blood spills to the earth; the poles are squeezed together, and the little guest is gone.

The bear's head is removed with the whole hide attached, carried into the house, and arranged among prayer sticks and valuable gifts by the east window, where the guest is to share the feast. A succulent morsel of its own flesh is placed beneath the snout, along with a hearty helping of dried fish, some millet dumplings, a cup of sake or beer, and a bowl of its own stew. Then the bear is honored with another speech.

"O Little Cub, we give you these prayer sticks, dumplings, and dried fish; take them to your parents. Go straight to your parents without hanging about on the way, or some devils will snatch away the souvenirs. And when you arrive, say to your parents, 'I have been nourished for a long time by an Ainu father and mother and have been kept from all trouble and

harm. Since I am now grown up, I have returned. And I have brought these prayer sticks, cakes, and dried fish. Please rejoice!' If you say this to them, Little Cub, they will be very happy."

The feast is celebrated, and there is dancing, while the woman who suckled the bear alternately weeps and laughs, along with some of the older women who have themselves suckled young bears and know something of the mixed feelings of saying good-bye. More prayer sticks are made and placed upon the cub's head; another bowl of his own stew is placed before him, and when time has been allowed for him to finish, the man presiding at the feast calls out, "The little god is finished; come, let us worship!" He takes the bowl, salutes it, and divides the contents among the guests, each receiving a small portion. The other parts of the beast are then eaten also, while some of the men drink the blood for strength and smear a portion upon their clothes. The head of the bear is then separated from the rest of the pelt and, being set upon a pole called *ke-omande-ni,* "the pole for sending away,"it is placed among a number of other skulls remaining from earlier feasts. And for the next few days the festival continues, until every bit of the little god has been consumed.[62]

Continuations and transformations of the cult of the bear in Europe are evident in many contexts. In classical times the goddess Artemis was identified with the bear. There was a Celtic bear-goddess, Artio, an image of whom (see Figure 267) was found at Bern (Bear City), which still preserves a trace of the ancient Celtic cult in its famous den of bears. And as the last secular echo of the bear sacrifice from pagan times, there were the popular bear-baiting arenas in the form of theaters, which in Elizabethan England competed with Shakespeare's stage for the patronage of a cultivated public. At a spectacle attended in 1575 by Queen Elizabeth, thirteen bears were provided; of which event Robert Laneham wrote:

"It was a sport very pleasant to see, to see the bear, with his pink eyes, tearing after his enemies' approach, the nimbleness and wait of the dog to take his advantage and the force and experience of the bear again to avoid his assaults; if he were bitten in one place how he would pinch in another to get free; that if he were taken once, then by what shift with biting, with clawing, with roaring, with tossing and tumbling he would work and wind himself from them; and when he was loose to shake his ears twice or thrice with the blood and the slaver hanging about his physiognomy."[63]

The sport survived until 1835, when prohibited by act of Parliament—the same Parliament which in that year forbade human sacrifice in India.

266

267. The Celtic bear-goddess, Artio, who was worshipped by the Helvetians in the neighborhood of Bern, feeds her attendant animal, a she-bear. (The City of Bern shows a bear in its coat of arms.) The inscription, in translation, states that "Licinia Sabinella [dedicated this] to the goddess Artio." There is a slit in the box pedestal through which coin offerings can be dropped. 7⅞ inches high and 11½ inches wide, this bronze artifact dates from c. A.D. 200.

Artio is the Celtic counterpart of the great Greek goddess Artemis, at whose temple at Brauron, a few miles southeast of Athens, dances were performed by little girls between the ages of five and ten who were called αρκτοι ("bears") and wore dresses that were saffron-dyed (**266**).[6] Iphigenia must have been one, for in Aulis, as she was being carried to be sacrificed at the goddess's shrine, her saffron-dyed dress slipped from her, and her bosom lay bare to the knife.[7] She was translated by Artemis to the Crimea (the "Tauric Peninsula") where, as the goddess's priestess among the barbarians, she supervised rites of *human* sacrifice. There is thus a long history of sacrifice of one kind or another associated with the bear. And something similar must surely be recognized in the bizarre Old Testament episode of II Kings 2:23–25: when some small boys jeered at the prophet Elisha (immediately after his companion-prophet Elijah had ascended in a fiery chariot into heaven) by shouting at him—"Go up, you bald-head!"—he cursed them in the name of the Lord, and two she-bears came out of the woods and tore forty-two of the small boys to pieces.

The name "Arthur" of King Arthur (from the Celtic verbal root *art,* "bear") was earlier the name of a Celtic god of about the sixth century B.C.: Ardehe, or Arthe (Latinizing as "Artio"), to whom there is inscribed an altar in the town of St. Pé-d'Ardet (Christianization of *Saint Père Ardehe,* "Our Holy Father Ardehe"), which is situated in the Pyrenees, in the *Vallée de l'Ourse* "Valley of the Bear"), not far from the miraculous waters of Lourdes.[8]

The name of the earliest legendary hero of England's Anglo-Saxon literature also means "Bear": Beowulf ("Bee-Wolf," so named because of the bear's passion for wild honey). And we have—have we not?—those two celestial bears, the Great Bear and the Little Bear, revolving forever as constellations around the Pole Star, *axis mundi* of the heavenly vault.

Moreover, the names, not only of the city of Bern, but also of Verona and Bayern (Bavaria) derive from the German noun *Bär.* Legends of the medieval hero Dietrich von Berne date from the reign in Italy of the Ostrogothic King Theodoric the Great of Verona (A.D. 493–526).[9] Dietrich = Theodoric = Theodore = Teddy = Teddy-Bear: the favorite doll of little girls between the ages of five and ten.

268. Bear-baiting scene on the lid of a bronze Etruscan vessel, c. sixth century B.C. Collection of the Villa Giulia, Rome. Whether the scene is of a religious rite or has already degenerated to such a pastime as remained popular in England until Shakespeare's time is unknown.

Shamanic Lore of Siberia and the Americas

The shaman is a particular type of medicine man, whose powers both to cause illness and to heal the sick, to communicate with the world beyond, to foresee the future, and to influence both the weather and the movements of game animals are believed to be derived from his intercourse with envisioned spirits; this intercourse having been established, usually in early adolescence, by way of a severe psychological breakdown of the greatest stress and even danger to life. The extraordinary uniformity in far-separated parts of the earth of the images and stages of this "shamanic crisis" suggests that they may represent the archetypes of a psychological exaltation, related on one hand to schizophrenia and on the other to the ecstasies of the yogis, saints, and dervishes of the high religions. Moreover, the typical way of functioning of the shaman everywhere is by passing into a state either of trance or of semitrance, and thus abstracted, performing his mysterious work.

In the Upper Paleolithic cave sanctuaries of Lascaux, Les Trois Frères, and Le Gabillou, at least six (and possibly nine) essential features of the shamanic art are illustrated:

1. The shaman's ritual dance (at Les Trois Frères and Le Gabillou)
2. His wearing of an animal costume (at Les Trois Frères, Le Gabillou, and Lascaux)
3. His identification thereby with a bird (Lascaux), a stag (Les Trois Frères), or a bull (Les Trois Frères and Le Gabillou)
4. His passage into an ecstatic trance (Lascaux)
5. His service as master of game animals (Les Trois Frères)
6. His role as master of initiations (Les Trois Frères)

Also possibly indicated are:

7. His possession of a wand or staff (the bird-on-a-staff at Lascaux and several actual *bâtons de commandement* that have been found at other Upper Paleolithic sites in France)
8. His control of a magical animal-familiar who supports him in his conjurations (possibly the rhinoceros at Lascaux)
9. The association of an animal sacrifice with his labors (the disemboweled bison at Lascaux) [64]

Like the cult of the master bear, that of the master shaman passed, at the close of the last glacial age, from northern Europe through Siberia to the Americas, along with the Aurignacoid industries that at that time were being carried across the inhabited Arctic to Alaska. (See maps, pages 34–35.) In Central Asia, subsequently, there were important developments that never crossed the Bering Strait; likewise, in the Americas, local developments occurred that were never carried back to Asia; so that there has been, through time and space, a history of shamanic forms. Yet, in all essentials, the complex remains constant from Norway to Alaska and south to Tierra del Fuego. Mircea Eliade has·described shamanism as "one of the archaic techniques of ecstasy."[65] And since in ecstasy it is the rapture, the inward psychological flight that is of the essence, and since, furthermore, the central nervous system of our species has hardly changed in the mere 12,000 to 15,000 years following the period of the shamans of the caves, there is an invariable, generally human strain that runs through all the historical modifications. The differing social systems within the bounds of which shamans have functioned have little affected the character of their experiences—as, indeed, the varieties of the historical religions have little affected the realizations of the mystics, the voices of whose raptures rise from the battlefields of world history in one polyphonic chorus of accord. "We have termed the ecstatic experience a 'primary phenomenon,'" states Eliade, "because we see no reason whatever for regarding it as the result of a particular historical moment, that is, as produced by a certain form of civilization."

In southern France, four prefigurements from the Magdalenian phase of the Paleolithic "creative explosion" (see page 129), showing shamans in costumes and roles that have remained classic through millennia:

269. The initiating *Sorcerer* of Les Trois Frères (see **132**, page 76).

270. The *Animal Charmer* of Les Trois Frères (see **131**, page 74–75).

271. The *Masked Shaman in Trance* of Lascaux (see **105**, page 65).

272. The *Dancer of Le Gabillou* (see **135**, page 78).

269.

272.

270.

271.

Rather, we would consider it fundamental in the human condition, and hence known to the whole of archaic humanity; what changed and was modified with the different forms of culture and religion was the interpretation and evaluation of the ecstatic experience."[66]

Through the centuries—indeed, the millennia—that have elapsed since the first passage of the bear and shaman complexes through Siberia to Beringland, most of the important later influences that have touched and transformed the original Paleolithic heritage in Siberia have entered the field from the southwest. Affecting first the peoples of the Uralo-Altaic ranges, they diffused northward along the valleys of the great rivers Ob, Yenisey, Lena, and Amur. The last peoples to be touched, of course, were those of the extreme northeast, beyond the Verkhoyanskiy mountains, namely the Paleo-Siberian (Americanoid) Chukchi, Koryak, Yukaghir, and Kamchadals. These stand, therefore, at the opposite historic pole to the Neo-Siberian Uralo-Altaics: the Ugrian Ostyaks, Finnic Voguls, Turkic Yakuts, Samoyedic tribes of the Arctic West, Tungusic peoples of the Siberian Far East, and Mongolic Buriats, Khalkas, and Kalmucs.

Among the historical forces that in the course of the long centuries shaped the cultures of these Neo-Siberians were the mythologies of the great Near Eastern Neolithic, Bronze, and Iron Ages, and the Indo-European of the horse and its rider, Zoroastrian dualism, Indian yoga, and the Tantric Buddhism of Tibet. Indeed, the word "shaman" itself, from the Tunguso-Manchurian *šaman,* is thought by many (but not all) authorities to have come ultimately, by way of China, from the Sanskrit *śramana* (Pali, *samana*), meaning "Buddhist monk." An apparent justification of this etymology is seen in the

Three transformations, west to east, of the antlered shamanic mask of Les Trois Frères:

273. Tungus shaman of sub-Arctic northeastern Siberia. Eighteenth-century engraving. Note the tipi-like dwellings.

274. Antlered mask from the Spiro Mound, Oklahoma (see **3**, page 11).

275. Deer and Buffalo Dancers (faces painted black) at San Ildefonson Pueblo, New Mexico, 1940.

evident interactions throughout eastern Asia between Buddhist and shamanic forms and practices. However, another, and more likely, etymology has been proposed: of *šaman* simply as a noun derived from the Tunguso-Manchurian verb *ša,* "to know," meaning "he who knows." In the strictest use of the term, "shaman" is applied by anthropologists only to those classic Neo-Siberian masters of the nineteenth and early twentieth centuries who, costumed in a certain type of gown, performed to their own beating of a sacred single-headed drum, and functioned finally by going into trances, either when their souls departed on visionary journeys or when spirits took possession of their bodies and spoke through them as oracles. A broader use of the term, however, recognizes the shamanic crisis and its aftermath as the essential component of an immemorial tradition, to which a number of characteristic and related features are attached, of which some may be accented in one region, others in another, but always in relation to the unmistakable crisis of vocation. It is in this larger, more inclusive sense that the term is understood in this chapter.

But to begin with a classic Neo-Siberian example (Figure 276): The horse shown tied to a sacrificial stake in this sketch of an Altaic shaman's visionary journey is evidence of an already-existing Indo-European influence. The great horse sacrifice (*aśva-medha*) of the Vedic Aryan war-

rior kings, through which they hoped to achieve world rule, has here become, in reduced form, the offering of a primitive shaman for access to the god Ülgen. His tent with a fire before it is seen at the start of the journey. Like the World Tree, the sacrificial post to which the horse is tethered is symbolic of the pivot of the storied universe. The branches of the tree are nine in number, as are the stages of the heavens, the importance of this number 9 and the notion of heavenly stages being of Mesopotamian origin. The slanting line across the head of the tree represents a pole on which the hide of the sacrificed horse has been hung, while the two little forms to the left and one to the right of the tree are offerings to the deities to be met: Bogdygan and Bobyrgan at the polestar gate, Kökysh along the way, and finally, the radiant Ülgen himself. Incongruously, the three regions beyond Kökysh are of water, sand, and cloud, representing perhaps some earlier, more primitive notion of the dangers of the visionary journey.

When an Altaic shaman has been summoned to a sickbed, his first task is to determine by divination the cause of the illness. If he finds that an object of some sort has been projected into the patient's body by the magic of another shaman, the healer will first perform a series of rites, to

276. An Altaic shaman's map of his visionary journey. Having sacrificed a horse, he proceeded from his tent and fire to the World Tree, hung the horse's pelt on a pole by the tree, and set down three offerings: to Bogdygan, Kökysh, and Ülgen. Then, mounting the nine branches (actually climbing, in the shamanic performance, the central pole of the yurt), he came to Bogdygan and his attendant, Bobyrgan, at the heavenly gate; next, he traversed nine fluctuating thresholds, to be welcomed by Kökysh; and finally, after three more trials—of water, sands, and cloud—he attained the radiant presence of Ülgen.[10]

the beating of his drum, to break the power of the magic, and then will apply his lips to the affected part and suck until—eureka!—he will spit from his mouth some pebble or even worm or roach that will represent the affliction. If it is found, however, that the reason for the indisposition is that the patient's soul has been abducted by the Messengers either of Ülgen above or of Ärlik below, the shaman will have to undertake a visionary voyage in trance to retrieve it. The voyage on high will be about as just described; that below, more dangerous and awesome.

''Passing through dark forests and crossing prodigious mountain ranges, where, time and again, he sees strewn the bones of shamans and their mounts who have met death in these terrible wastes, the shaman arrives at last at an opening in the earth. Here the most difficult stages of his journey are faced as he descends into abysmal underworld depths with their myriads of uncanny apparitions—all of which, in the course of his performance, the shaman illustrates in word and gesture, with especial emphasis on those awesome scenes of punishment where the souls of sinners are tortured and tormented. And when he has mollified the guardians of these regions and escaped their perils, he comes face to face

277. A Chukchi map of the heavenly ways. Two paths cross at the Pole Star's House: one, the sun's course from Dawn Man's House (lower left) to Evening Man's House (upper right); the other, the path of shamanic flight from the House of Darkness (below) to heaven. The Milky Way (double lines left of center) leads from the earth to the Pole Star's House. In the lower left portion of the map: Dawn Man, with rays around his head, holds high in his left hand a tray on which a sacrifice has been offered; in his right hand he holds a fox that he is giving in exchange; on one side of him sits the soul of the dog that was offered; a second fox comes on his other side; and two more sacrificial trays lie on the ground. In the upper right portion of the map: the family of Evening Man pays sacrifice to the gods of the sea. The members of his family are costumed in the guise of those gods: their faces are black; they wear ceremonial headbands; and they are clothed in loose white garments with walrus-gut tassles. The tall wand in their midst is symbolic of the axial pole.[11]

278. The soul of a Koryak shaman's sacrificed dog is intercepted in its flight to heaven by a demon. Above is the Heavenly Family; below, the shaman drums to heal a patient.[12]

279. A preliminary sacrifice (right, drummer facing west) is performed to appease the obstructing demon, who then allows the dogs of the main sacrifice (on left, drummer now facing east) to pass to their destination.

280. Shamans of the Huichol Indian tribe of Nayarit in western Mexico are today fashioning "yarn paintings" of their visionary flights: colorful pictures, about 2 feet square, made of vividly dyed wool yarns pressed onto beeswax-coated plywood. This "painting" by Ramón Medina is of a journey inspired by a supernatural summons to bring back to earth, in the form of a rock crystal, the soul of an ancestral shaman wishing to return. The star is the rock crystal to be found. The four wavy lines hanging to the left are the fiery curtain of solar rays through which the shaman had to pass. The path of his ascent is indicated by the footsteps; the beauty of the vision is betokened by the flowering plants; and the whole is framed by the mountains of the quarters: three in each direction, the ascent having begun from the central mountain (not depicted) of the West.[13] This visionary journey of a shaman from Mexico obviously resembles that of the shaman from Central Asia (276), even to the detail of the tree, which appears in the Altaic map at the start of the shaman's flight into space, and here in the Huichol painting at the center of the composition. Compare this tree with the Ladder and the World Tree up which the South American shaman climbs (281), thence to pass in trance to celestial heights.

with Ärlik himself, Prince of the Land of the Dead, who threatens terribly, violently bellowing, until the shaman (if clever enough) pacifies him with promises of rich offerings. The ceremony climaxes in this dialogue with Ärlik when the shaman collapses in ecstasy. In many regions it is believed that, returning from the Land of the Dead, the shaman rides a wild gander, as when returning from his voyages to heaven. With him is the patient's soul; and as he approaches in this flight, the prostrate shaman's agitation gradually subsides, until his eyes open at last, as though waking from sleep, and those present ask for an account of all that happened on his perilous journey."[67]

"Although the descriptions of the Land of the Dead associated with these ceremonies are undoubtedly of late and alien origin," comments the Finnish ethnologist Uno Harva, from whose work this passage has been quoted, "the belief that a shaman can transport himself to the other world to release souls is an authentic feature of Siberian shamanism."[68] It is a feature, also, of the medieval theme of Jesus's Harrowing of Hell—following his apparent death on the cross and before his resurrection—to release from Limbo the souls of the Old Testament patriarchs and prophets. "He descended into hell. . . . He ascended into Heaven"[69] Dante also descended and ascended, with especial attention (as in the shaman's journey) to the sufferings of the damned. There is an Iranian visit to the scenes of hell, followed by a flight to heaven, described in the seventh-century *Vision of Arda Viraf*, which is an account of the jour-

ney of a Zoroastrian seer. Moreover, the bull-like bellowing of Ärlik calls to mind the bull-headed figure of Yama, the Judge of the Dead, as represented in Tibetan tankas; while shamanic flight on a wild gander suggests, on one hand, the flying gander figurines of the Late Paleolithic Mal'ta site at Lake Baikal (see page 72), and on the other, the Vedic Indian meditation on the wild gander (*hamsa*), as symbolic of the spirit and of spiritual flight.

To escape these high-culture influences and uncover a shamanism more primitive, one must leave the Eurasian mainland, where such themes and images have been dispersed (even though with diminishing force) to the farthest reaches. In many parts of the other continents also, higher-culture influences are evident, as in the drum of the Mapuche shaman (Figure 281) and the ladder on which she stands, which has been clearly identified with the World Tree and, moreover, is topped by a sculptured head that is not of a primitive type. The Mapuche are an agricultural people, as are the Huichol of western Mexico, to whom we owe the colorful yarn painting of the shamanic visionary journey (Figure 280), here reproduced as a New World counterpart to that of the Central Asian Altaic shaman.

In Tierra del Fuego, the uttermost part of the earth, the Alacaloof and Yahgans, the Ona, and the Aush were as innocent of agriculture and the virtues of civilization as the penguins, dolphins, whales, and guanacos of their environment, when, on January 14, 1869, the Rev. Whait H. Sterling was left standing alone on the north shore of Beagle Channel, to inhabit

281. A female shaman of the Mapuche tribe of central Chile stands atop her carved ladder, symbolic of both the World Tree and her own power of spiritual ascent. Beating her drum, she will presently pass into trance; her spirit will rise with her people's prayers to the "Mother-Father" of all things, and her body, falling, will be caught in a blanket.[14]

159

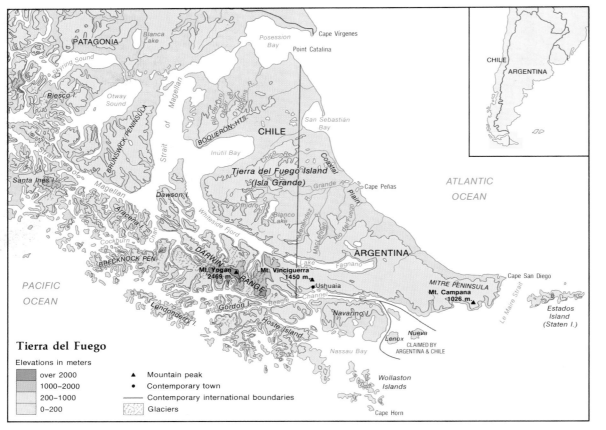

Map 35.

They were inspired and motivated, rather, by the practitioner's own familiars, acquired through visionary experiences of such profound, affective impact that the subject's personality and whole manner of life were radically—"to the root" —transformed.

*   *   *

Among the Yahgan (or Yamana), as Father Gusinde learned: "A man could be strolling alone along the seashore, lost in dreamland, without thought or purpose, when he would suddenly find himself in the midst of a visionary spectacle of what are known as *asikaku*, 'apparitions.' Around him crowds an immeasurable company of herrings, whales, swordfish, vultures, cormorants, gulls, and other creatures. All are addressing him in flattering terms, respectfully, in the most friendly way; and he is beside himself, has no idea what is happening. His whole body numb, he drops to the ground and lies there without moving. His soul (his *kešpix*), that is to say, is consorting with the spirits, and feeling, while among them, an inordinate joy. Then suddenly, they are gone.

"Waking from this heavy sleep, the man stumbles home. He hardly knows where he is. He falls onto his bed; is back in his dream; and again there appears the animal swarm. All the beasts are extremely friendly. They are inviting his soul to join them. And it does so, following them, presently, out onto the high seas. Moreover, there is one that is being especially amiable, in the most extravagantly attentive way, and this will become

282. Yahgan mother and child before a typical temporary hut. Although inhabiting a region hardly 1300 miles from the Antarctic Circle, these coastal, canoe and fishing people were practically naked, indifferent to the cold.

a little wooden house, 20 feet long and 10 wide, that had been set up there as his mission. Three previous attempts to bring the Gospel to the Yahgans had ended in disasters. The first had been of a young clergyman who arrived on the *Beagle* with Charles Darwin. He had been so threatened, mauled, and even stoned by those meant to have been his parishioners that he was immediately removed. The second, in the winter of 1850–1851, was a mission of seven, who had to flee for their lives into the wilderness, where they perished. A third attempt, in 1859, the year of Darwin's *Origin of Species,* got as far as to the building of a chapel; but on Sunday morning, November 6, in the middle of the first verse of the first hymn of their opening service, the little group of four was set upon, clubbed, speared, and stoned to extinction. The Reverend Sterling's mission, on the other hand, survived; and when, on the first day of October 1871, the Rev. Thomas Bridges disembarked there, with his wife and infant daughter, to inherit the mission and take charge, there were awaiting them on the shore a five-room bungalow and surrounding scatter of brush wigwams smelling of rotting whale blubber and smoke. Canoes were drawn up, and a naked congregation, squatting and standing, watched them as they landed.[70]

The Yahgan (or Yamana), whose huts and canoes these were, were a short and sturdy canoe people, inhabiting the coasts of the southern archipelago from Beagle Channel to the Horn, living largely on mussels, seals, fish, occasional whales harpooned or washed ashore, porpoises, gulls, and birds' eggs. North of the Channel and eastward to the Atlantic coast

were the Ona (known also as the Selk'nam), a tall, well-built and handsome, mountain-dwelling people living chiefly by the hunt. The Catholic Father Martin Gusinde has published two magnificent monographs based on his field studies of these two peoples from 1919 to 1923,[71] and of the greatest interest and importance to the student of primitive religions are his chapters on the myths, rites, and shamanism of these utterly primitive, marginal, hunting, fishing, and gathering tribes. Among both he found traditions of a High God of the kind that Andrew Lang and Father Schmidt had credited to the Kurnai of Australia.[72] (See pages 138–139.) In neither context, however, did the practices of the shamans have anything to do with this divinity.[73]

his familiar; though the others, too, will be at his call as friends and helpers."[74]

Or similarly, when strolling, musing, in the forest, one may suddenly find oneself in the midst of a large company of spirits, little people, very like men; and passing into a deep sleep, one then will see them sitting about a fire, keeping warm, talking quietly. In a friendly way they will invite one's soul to join them, and again, there will be one of the company especially cordial. Forest spirits of this kind are called *heštaka*-shamans. They like to live in the dead boughs of trees, and will sometimes cause such boughs to bend deeply down, turn on their axes, or quiver. Old rotten stumps are favorite resorts.[75]

In the Andaman Islands, it is recalled, the *oko-jumu* ("dreamers"), who functioned as medicine men, came into possession of their spiritual powers by consorting with spirits in the jungle, by dreaming, or by dying and returning to life. Similarly, in the early Celtic epics of the British Isles, those heroes who, when riding through a forest, allow themselves to be led into the pursuit of some visionary beast, presently find themselves inside the fairy hills, engaged in adventures of a timeless, dreamlike surreality. For the forest speaks to deeper centers than do city streets. And for those who have never been quite convinced of the high importance of the deeds and gossip of the marketplace or village compound, the excitement of the imagination that a forest fastness or wild seacoast can awaken may become an irresistible fascination, leading in the end to a transformed life. The annals of psychiatry provide examples, as for instance, the following report from the case of a sixty-eight-year-old widow:

"When she was between the ages of seven and nine, she was walking along a woodland path in the backwoods hill country near the mining town in Ken-

283/284. Two Ona shamans.

tucky where she lived. It was a warm summer day, and she was aware of buzzing insects in the foliage. But behind the drone she became aware of music, faint and distant at first, but gradually getting louder and closer. Finally she could distinguish a chorus of voices very light and high, but not children's voices. She stopped to listen, entranced, became aware that someplace on the path ahead there was an aura of light—not bright, but soft and luminous: it blotted out the landscape beyond. It seemed to pull her onward, and, as the singing grew louder, she began to move in its direction. Although she walked towards it, she could not get closer. It was always the same distance from her. It did not fade for some time. She was enchanted and then grieved by her experience.

"Many people have had such experiences," comments the physician of this report. "Their presence suggests another life hidden within us." And indeed, in the instance of the interesting case of this aging widow: "There was in her an underlying current of intense sadness, at times approaching a tragic grief. She felt . . . that she had not lived her life."[76]

Among the Yahgan, as Gusinde found, when an apparitional spirit has attached itself to a person, it never lets go. The person is forced to become a shaman. Should he refuse, the apparition takes revenge and the person dies. Gusinde cites the example of a Christian convert, Nelly Lawrence, who was walking one day with her little daughter in the forest when she heard break from the trunk of a tree a loud "Pah!" "I looked around," she told him, "and saw a cute little spirit in that rotten trunk who beckoned to me in a friendly way. I did not realize that it was an apparition (*asikaku*), but took it for an ordinary soul (*kešpix*). But an uncanny fear unstrung my limbs, and as though in a coma, I dragged myself on. Overcome then by a fatigue that was irresistible, I flung myself onto my bed, where I dreamed; and again there was that spirit before me, smiling in the friendliest way. It loaded me with presents: furs, baskets, necklaces and so on; even gave me a special song. And when, later, I woke with heavy senses, that song continued to sound for a long time within me."[77]

For many days the woman was faint and ill, feeling weak and helpless; but then she was visited by a female shaman who, when served a cup of tea, started back in horror. "Why," she asked, "do you hand me this disgusting beast?" Terrified, Nelly Lawrence replied, "But I gave you a cup of tea!" The shaman left, greatly troubled for her friend, but in a dream then realized what had happened to her. The apparition had thrown a leather noose around the woman's neck and a heavy cloak was upon her shoul-

285. A family of the Ona tribe, skillful hunters of the guanaco, are wrapped in the robes of guanaco fur, which, in spite of the sub-Arctic cold, were their only garments.

ders and was killing her because she had not begun to shamanize. "It was that cloak," the afflicted woman told Gusinde, "that had been so greatly oppressing and exhausting me that frequently I fell down." The shaman sent for her and, in a violent scene, tore from her throat and back those invisible things, the gifts, even the song, and so saved her life.[78]

Among the Ona it is understood that a child who frequently sings in its sleep, or in a half-abstracted state by day, will become a shaman; likewise, the young man or woman who, in a circle of companions, breaks unconsciously into song.[79] The Tierra del Fuegians do not have drums; their medicine songs are dull drones; and yet, in those strangely compelling songs there is heard a voice that is not of this practical life, but of a state of mind ordered to rapture. And it is through his personal song that the shaman invokes his familiar, as it was through that song, when it first came to him, that he was drawn from the normal world and way of life of the ungifted. The song sounds at the interface of the waking mind and dream. "Through it," in Gusinde's words, "a state of autosuggestion is induced, a kind of self-hypnosis, out of which the medicine man functions. . . . Most often," Gusinde continues, "it is after midnight or in the earliest morning hours that he can be heard intoning his song."[80] For the time for shamanizing is of darkness and the night mind of which the shaman is the incarnation.

Those to whom a song has come turn to a practicing shaman for induction into the mystery out of which their song arose, and the instruction then effects in them a total transformation, not of the mind alone, but of the body as well. As Gusinde learned among the Ona: "The whole external appearance of the medicine man is but an illusion. He is not made, as we are, of skin, bone, flesh, and blood, but of a thin, skinlike outer covering, beneath which his whole interior is filled with a soft, light substance that most closely resembles—according to an image of the Indians themselves—the most delicate feather-down . . . of which substance, when at work healing, he may on occasion bring forth a particle[81] . . . And it is thanks to this strange condition that medicine men possess the power of unhindered motion. Upon them there are no limitations, either of solid bodies or of great distances. Their power of sight can penetrate any object and traverse any reach of space."[82]

When the young aspirant, moved by the song that has come to him, goes to an elder for instruction, the accomplished master begins by singing his own song, kneading and squeezing his own body until, in a state of the highest half-conscious agitation, he brings forth a parcel of his own substance about the size of the head of a child—soft, white, and like the lightest down—which he then transfers to the other's body by pressing and rubbing it in. There it begins immediately to take effect, and in the course of the next four years or so it works a complete transformation. Commencing in the belly, it fills the breast, the head, the legs, and finally the arms. Meanwhile, the power of sight is increasing and exercises are undertaken to enhance it. And toward the end of the training time, the novice gives himself more and more to his dreams, until the experience comes upon him of being taken over by the *wáiyuwen*, the soul- or spirit-substance of some earlier medicine man; with that the initiate's own personality is wiped out; so that henceforth, it will not be he who acts, but the *wáiyuwen* of that earlier shaman acting through him.[83]

E. Lucas Bridges, the second son of the courageous couple who in 1871 stepped ashore with their infant daughter among the Yahgans of Beagle Channel, was invited by his Ona friends to study to become a shaman. But after an unpromising beginning, he thought better of the invitation, for, as he explains: "Medicine men ran great dangers. When persons in their prime died from no visible cause, the 'family doctor' would often cast suspicion, in an ambiguous way, on some rival necromancer. Frequently the chief object of a raiding party, in the perpetual clan warfare of the Ona, was to kill the medicine man of an opposing group. No, I would not become a *joön*, to be blamed, maybe, for a fatal heart attack a hundred miles away."[84]

"Some of these humbugs," he wrote, describing their shamanizing, "were excellent actors. Standing or kneeling beside the patient, gazing intently at the spot where the pain was situated, the doctor would allow a look of horror to come over his face. Evidently he could see something invisible to the rest of us. His approach might be slow or he might pounce, as though afraid that the evil thing that had caused the trouble would escape. With his hands he would try to gather the malign presence into one part of the patient's body—generally the chest—where he would then apply his mouth and suck violently. Sometimes this struggle went on for an hour, to be repeated later. At other times the *joön* would draw away from his patient with the pretence of holding something in his mouth with his hands. Then, always facing away from the encampment, he would take his hands from his mouth, gripping them tightly together, and, with a guttural shout difficult to describe and impossible to spell, fling this invisible object to the ground and stamp fiercely upon it. Occasionally a little mud, some flint, or even a tiny, very young mouse might be produced as the cause of the patient's indisposition. I myself have never seen a mouse figure in one of these performances, but they were quite common. Perhaps when I was there the doctor had failed to find a mouse's nest."[85]

An occasion to observe a considerably more mysterious exhibition of the shamanic arts occurred when a celebrated *joön* named Houshken, who had never seen a white man before, was induced to put on a performance. Here follows Bridge's account:

"Our conversation—as was always the case in such meetings—was slow, with long pauses between sentences, as though for deep thought. I told Houshken that I had heard of his great powers and would like to see some of his magic. He did not refuse my request, but answered modestly that he was disinclined, the Ona way of saying that he might try to do it by and by.

"After allowing a quarter of an hour to elapse, Houshken said he was thirsty and went down to the nearby stream for a drink. It was a bright moonlight night and the snow on the ground helped to make the scene of the exhibition we were about to witness as light as day. On his return, Houshken sat down and broke into a monotonous chant, which went on until suddenly he put his hands to his mouth.

286. The male initiation rites of the Ona were conducted in a special lodge of the men's society, the *klóketen*, from which women were excluded; and associated with the mystifications of this institution were a number of such Hallowe'en spooks as we see here. These apparitions would appear from time to time, ranging through the bush of areas about the men's house, and any woman or child seeing one or more of them was to suppose that they were the inhabitants of the *klóketen* with whom the men held converse in their meetings. An important moment in the initiations of a boy took place when he was compelled to get up and wrestle with one of these characters, who would let the youngster put him down, after which the masquerade was uncovered, and the boy turned into a man. There was a legend of the *klóketen* having been originally of the women, but taken and kept from them by the men.

When he brought them away, they were palms downward and some inches apart. We saw that a strip of guanaco hide, about the thickness of a leather bootlace, was now held loosely in his hands. It passed over his thumbs, under the palms of his half-closed hands, and was looped over his little fingers so that about three inches of end hung down from each hand. The strip appeared to be not more than eighteen inches long.

"Without pulling the strip tight, Houshken now began to shake his hands violently, gradually bringing them farther apart, until the strip, with the two ends still showing, was about four feet long. He then called his brother, Chashkil, who took the end from his right hand and stepped back with it. From four feet, the strip now grew out of Houshken's left hand to double that length. Then, as Chashkil stepped forward, it disappeared back into Houshken's hand, until he was able to take the other end from his

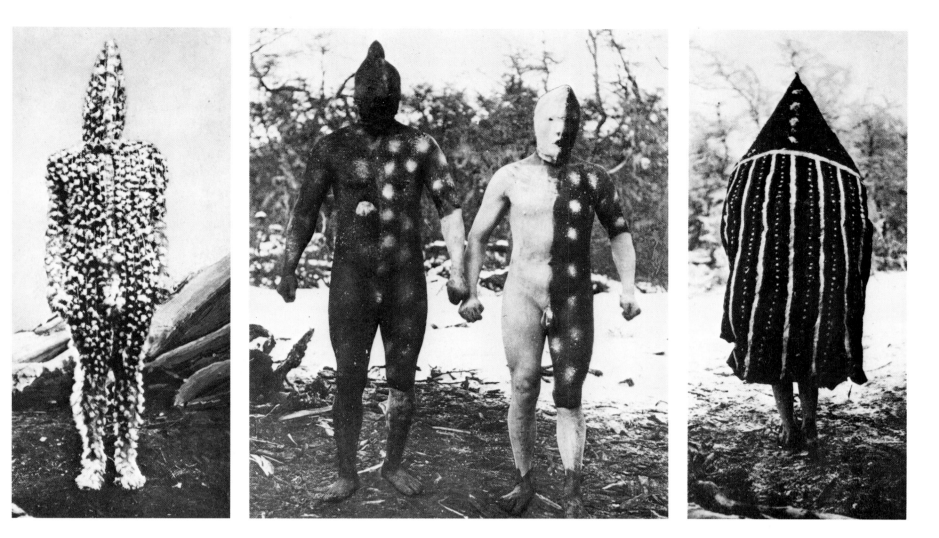

brother. With the continued agitation of his hands, the strip got shorter and shorter. Suddenly, when his hands were almost together, he clapped them to his mouth, uttered a prolonged shriek, then held out his hands to us, palms upward and empty.

"Even an ostrich could not have swallowed those eight feet of hide at one gulp without visible effort. Where else the coil could have gone to I do not profess to know. It could not have gone up Houshken's sleeve, for he had dropped his robe when the performance began [and, like all male Onas without their robes, was naked]. There were between twenty and thirty men present, but only eight or nine were Houshken's people. The rest were far from being friends of the performer and all had been watching intently. Had they detected some simple trick, the great medicine man would have lost his influence; they would no longer have believed in any of his magic.

"The demonstration was not yet over. Houshken stood up and resumed his robe. Once again he broke into a chant and seemed to go into a trance, possessed by some spirit not his own. Drawing himself up to his full height, he took a step towards me and let his robe, his only garment, fall to the ground. He put his hands to his mouth with a most impressive gesture and brought them away again with his fists clenched and thumbs close together. He held them up to the height of my eyes, and when they were less than two feet from my face slowly drew them apart. I saw that there was now a small,

almost opaque object between them. It was about an inch in diameter in the middle and tapered away into his hands. It might have been a piece of semi-transparent dough or elastic, but whatever it was it seemed to be alive, revolving at great speed, while Houshken, apparently from muscular tension, was trembling violently.

"The moonlight was bright enough to read by as I gazed at this strange object. Houshken brought his hands further apart and the object grew more and more transparent, until, when some three inches separated his hands, I realized that it was not there any more. It did not break or burst like a bubble; it simply disappeared, having been visible to me for less than five seconds. Houshken made no sudden movement, but slowly opened his hands and turned them over for my inspection. They looked clean and dry. He was stark naked and there was no confederate beside him. I glanced down at the snow, and, in spite of his stoicism, Houshken could not resist a chuckle, for nothing was to be seen there.

"The others had crowded round us and, as the object disappeared, there was a frightened gasp from among them. Houshken reassured them with the remark: 'Do not let it trouble you. I shall call it back to myself again.'

"The natives believed this to be an incredibly malignant spirit belonging to, or possibly part of, the joön from whom it emanated. It might take physical form, as we had just witnessed, or be totally invisible. It had the power to introduce insects,

tiny mice, mud, sharp flints or even a jelly-fish or baby octopus into the anatomy of those who had incurred its master's displeasure. I have seen a strong man shudder involuntarily at the thought of this horror and its evil potentialities. It was a curious fact that, although every magician must have known himself to be a fraud and a trickster, he always believed in and greatly feared the supernatural abilities of other medicine men."[86]

What Lucas Bridges had been shown, of course, was a living particle of that soft, light, interior substance "like delicate feather-down," the wáiyuwen, of which Father Gusinde later learned.

The Ona shamans undertook ascensions to the Moon when she appeared red in the sky, which was taken to be a certain sign of her displeasure with mankind and her intention to send some sort of plague. On such nights the various wáiyuwen of all the Ona shamans of Tierra del Fuego would be in flight to her, to appease her. For the Moon is a powerful shaman herself, and can send down death or life at will. The Sun-Man is even more powerful, and when he makes known his wrath by turning a burning red or by going into eclipse, even the shamans duck into their huts and wait in silence for his mood to pass; for, so powerful is the Sun-Man that, should they send up their wáiyuwen, he would burn them out of existence.[87] Lucas Bridges learned that not only the sun and moon, but also mountains, trees, and animals, could be shamans. There was a mountain near his father's mission at Ushuaia, on Beagle Channel, that was

287. Colored nineteenth-century engraving of a Siberian shaman clothed in a costume hung with animal skins, embroidered, and beribboned with a miscellany of magical features. Compare Catlin's drawing of a similarly festooned Blackfoot "Wolf Shaman" (**406** on page 239; also his painting from that drawing on page 127 at the opening of this section).

288. "The Sorcerer," an engraving published in 1590 by Theodore de Bry from a watercolor by John White, made in 1585, during his visit to Walter Raleigh's colony at Roanoke, Virginia (see pages 220–221). "They have sorcerers or jugglers," states the commentary, "who use strange gestures and whose enchantments often go against the laws of nature. . . . A small black bird is fastened above one of their ears as a badge of office."

thought to be a witch. To show her ill will, she could conjure up a storm.[88] He also tells of having once shot, high in the mountains, a solitary guanaco, which he and his Indian companions then discovered had been living alone in a small cave. "These guanaco recluses, braving the long winter in the mountains alone," he declares, "were very rare. . . . That night, discussing the matter round our campfire, I suggested that the hermit might have remained there alone in the cave to study guanaco magic. Instead of laughing, my companions agreed, with serious expressions on their faces, that this was quite likely."[89]

Thus, among the utterly primitive hunting, fishing, and gathering tribes of the southernmost inhabited pieces of land on this planet Earth, some eighteen or twenty of the typical features of shamanism have been identified by two qualified observers as follows:

1. The summons received in solitude from spirits of the wilderness
2. An association of song with this enchantment
3. Its compulsive character, illness and death ensuing if it be disregarded
4. The especial association of a spiritual familiar with this call
5. Its healing by way of a long season of intensive spiritual training
6. The sense thereby of an inward physical transubstantiation
7. The gaining thereby of supernatural powers

The powers thus gained are:

8. To see and to move through barriers and across distances
9. To mediate between man and the supernatural
10. To advise and guide in the search for game
11. To heal, whether by massage and suction, or by spiritual flights to the heavenly sources of the ill will; for example, the moon
12. To injure by occult means: projecting stones and other objects into enemies
13. To perform magic by sleight of hand or by actual necromancy
14. To assume the forms of animals or of mountains

In relation to this last faculty, there are:

15. The power of animals, mountains, trees, and such, to shamanize
16. The power of shamans (whether human, animal, vegetable, or geological) to influence the weather

Also to be noted as typical shamanistic conditions are:

17. The vicious atmosphere of rivalry and malice between practicing shamans

18. Schools of shamans dedicated to the search and fostering of likely talents

19. Perfected shamans who undertake the initiation of the young

Still another important feature noted by Gusinde is:

20. The shaman's reliance on dreams for information and warnings

Regarding this last point, the dreams to which the shaman pays attention are unexceptionally those foreboding evil. In such he believes that he is being shown the hostile intentions of his enemies, whether professional rivals or lay members of his tribe.[90] For, as Bridges also recognized, the shaman's life is beset on every hand by danger.

When this considerable list is compared with the above-numbered nine of the shamans of the caves (see page 156), only the following of that list are here missing: (2) the animal costume, (7) the (possible) wand or staff, and (9) the (possible) animal sacrifice. The function of the ritual dance (1) is served here by the enspelling song, while the passage into full trance (4) is reduced to the state of a semitrance. The animal transformation (3), mastery of the game animals (5), supervision of initiations (6), and the animal-familiar (8) remain. The additional fourteen or so features of the Tierra del Fuegian series are such as could not have been readily illustrated in the rock art; more than a few, nevertheless, must have been known. The arts of healing by massage and suction, and by spiritual flights to celestial realms, as we have already seen, were practiced by the Bushmen, who were also inheritors of the cavern legacy. The vocational call by way of a summons from spirits of the wilderness is recorded of the Andamanese. Reasonably, these may be assumed to have been features of a common Paleolithic inheritance, surviving among the most widely separated primitive peoples remaining alive to this day.

Between the Bushman and Tierra del Fuegian branches of this ancient heritage, an important distinction is evident in the contrast between the communal accent of the African rites (the women seated in a circle, singing, while the men dance around them and go into trance), and the solitary experiences and exercises of the South American masters. The relation between the Bushman experience of the heating and rising of the *ntum* to trance (see page 94) and the Tierra del Fuegian of the transubstantiation of the shaman's body has not, as far as I know, been studied. Nor do we know what to think of the possible relation of the haunting childhood experience of the Kentucky woman (page 161) and the mystic summonses reported generally of shamans.

289. Ona chieftain, wearing the usual cap and robe of guanaco fur. As hunters of the guanaco, the Ona dwelt chiefly inland, on the main island of Tierra del Fuego.

Only a little less remote than Tierra del Fuego from the painted caves of Europe are the coasts of glaciated Greenland; yet there again one meets shamans, called and trained in much the same way as those of the southernmost inhabited piece of the earth. Knud Rasmussen, in his trek from Greenland to Alaska across the whole of arctic North America in the early 1920s, collected from the shamans of those parts an extraordinary series of accounts of their visionary summonses and ordeals. "When my father died," he was told, for example, by the best-known and most feared of the Greenland shamans of that time, Autdaruta by name, "I often went out for long rambles among the hills, because I felt that I had been left alone. It was at the season when stonecrop springs up, and I gathered it, to preserve in blubber for the winter.

"One day, up among the rocks, I heard someone begin to sing; I looked, but could see no one. 'Now why should I have heard this song?' I thought to myself, and went home. The next morning, towards daybreak, I went up again to the hills, and then I heard the same thing again; it was someone beginning to sing. 'Now why is this happening to me?' I thought. Just then I saw two men coming toward me. They were inland-dwellers. 'We are sorry for you, because you are an orphan,' they said; and so they became my first helping spirits. Then I began to be a magician, but did not speak to anyone about it.

"The next year we moved south: that was in the season when the small birds come, and we settled down in company with an old and much venerated magician. He could not stand upright, and could walk only by propping up his thighs with his arms. He could not carry his kayak up and down himself, and so it came about that I used to help him. One day he came and said to me, 'Travel east with me, and I will teach you something. You may yet need help, my poor, fatherless boy.' So we traveled together, and he told me on the way that he was going to

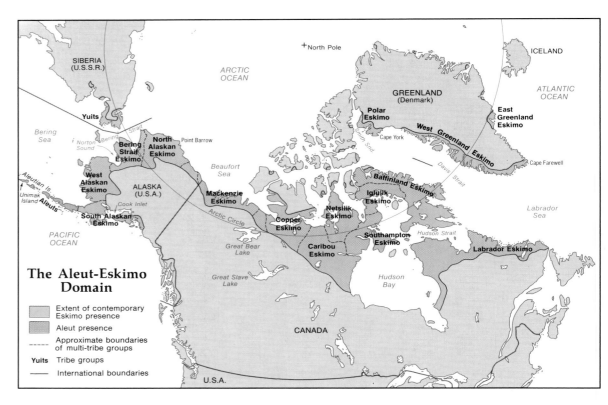

Map 36. The earliest confirmed evidence of a true Eskimo culture is from Unimak Island in the Aleutians, c. 1000 B.C. The occupation of the whole American Arctic seems to have been accomplished by the first centuries A.D., and a fairly constant population of 40,000 to 50,000 seems then to have been maintained in scattered enclaves throughout the region.

make a great magician of me. We went ashore up a fjord, close to a cave, and the old man took off his clothes and crept inside. And he told me to watch carefully what happened next. I lay hidden a little way off and waited. It was not long before I saw a great [polar] bear come swimming along, crawl ashore, and approach the magician. It flung itself upon him, crunched him up, limb for limb, and ate him. Then it vomited him out again and swam away.

"When I went up to the cave, the old man lay groaning. He was very much exhausted, but was able to row himself home. On the way, he told me that every time he allowed himself to be devoured alive by the bear he acquired greater power over his helping spirits.

"Some time afterward, he took me again on a journey and this time it was so that I myself might be eaten by the bear. This was necessary if I wished to attain to any good. We rowed off and came to the cave. The old man told me to take my clothes off, and I do not deny that I was somewhat uncomfortable at the thought of being devoured alive. I had not been lying there long before I heard the bear coming. It attacked me and crunched me

290. Polar bear of walrus-tusk ivory. Dorset culture, Melville Peninsula, Iglulik area, c. A.D. 1200. Both the posture and the skeleton in the x-ray style have shamanic associations. Compare the polar bear of the Eskimo Autdaruta's shamanic initiation (see text).

291. Ivory bow drill from Norton Sound showing shamans drumming inside a house and, outside, a magnificent catch of whales.

up, limb by limb, joint by joint, but strangely enough it did not hurt at all. It was only when it bit me in the heart that it did hurt frightfully. From that day forth I felt that I ruled my helping spirits. After that I acquired many fresh helping spirits and no danger could any longer threaten me, as I was always protected."[91]

The Animal Master of the circumpolar north has here become the initiator of a shaman. An externally venerated figure, that is to say, of the folk cultures of the region has been experienced inwardly by a hypersensitive individual in a symbolic role of the most profound personal import. We may term such a displacement from an outward to an inward space "the crisis of the object," using an expression coined by the surrealist artist Salvador Dali in the 1920s, when a bold generation of twentieth-century painters was recovering for Western man the understanding of art as a discipline of the interface between waking consciousness and night, as is shamanic song. Such an interiorization, furthermore, is an intrinsic element of the "mystical way," which opens when the generally venerated images and clichés of a popular cult—revered externally as agents and formulas for the production of health, wealth, progeny, victories, and good weather—become, through a crisis of introjection, operative as living symbols, initiating and enabling a spiritual transformation. The essential experience in all such crises is of a death and resurrection: death to the Old Adam (to use a technical Christian term) and rebirth in the image of the New, in Christ. In such primitive initiation rites as those, for instance, of the Aranda (see pages 143–146), the sense is of a death to infancy and return to life as men. Significantly, the psychological shamanic crisis typically occurs with approaching puberty. The affected child, in other words, undergoes spontaneously the transformation that in the general cult is ritually imposed; and since it is intimately inward and spontaneous, the shamanic-mystical experience is of a deeper, more authentic kind than anything the outward rituals can produce. Hence, in many tribal cultures, it is the medicine men, the "dreamers," who are the principal custodians and expositors of the myths on which the rites repose.

In the wastes of central Canada, just west of Hudson Bay, Rasmussen gained the confidence of Igjugarjuk, a Caribou Eskimo shaman, whose people, in Rasmussen's view, were the most primitive encountered on the expedition. When

young, this master shaman, who now served as an initiator as well as healer and seer, had been visited by dreams that he could not understand. As summarized by Rasmussen:

"Strange unknown beings came and spoke to him, and when he awoke, he saw all the visions of his dream so distinctly that he could tell his fellows all about them. Soon it became evident to all that he was destined to become an *angakoq*, and an old man named Perqanaoq was appointed his instructor. In the depth of winter, when the cold was most severe, Igjugarjuk was placed on a small sledge, just large enough for him to sit on, and carried far away from his home to the other side of Hikoligjuaq. On reaching the appointed spot, he remained seated on the sledge while his instructor built a tiny snow hut, with barely room for him to sit cross-legged. He was not allowed to set foot on the snow, but was lifted from the sledge and carried into the hut, where a piece of skin just large enough for him to sit on served as a carpet. No food or drink was given him; he was exhorted to think only of the Great Spirit and of the helping spirit that should appear—and so he was left to himself and his meditations.

"After five days had elapsed, the instructor brought him a drink of lukewarm water, and with similar exhortations, left

292. Eskimo shaman in flight, empowered by his animal familiars. Eskimo drawing by Jessie Oonark, 1971.

him as before. He fasted now for fifteen days, when he was given another drink of water and a very small piece of meat, which had to last him a further ten days. At the end of this period, his instructor came for him and fetched him home. Igjugarjuk declared that the strain of those thirty days of cold and fasting was so severe that he 'sometimes died a little.' During all that time he thought only of the Great Spirit, and endeavored to keep his mind free from all memory of human beings and everyday things. Toward the end of the thirty days there came to him a helping spirit in the shape of a woman. She came while he was asleep and seemed to hover in the air above him. After that he dreamed no more of her, but she became his helping spirit. For five months following this period of trial, he was kept on the strictest diet, and required to abstain from all intercourse with women. The fasting was then repeated; for such fasts at frequent intervals are the best means of attaining to knowledge of hidden things. As a matter of fact, there is no limit to the period of study; it depends on how much one is willing to suffer and anxious to learn."[92]

The accent upon suffering, solitude, and silence in this perhaps exaggerated account of an older man remembering his youth was matched, when Rasmussen reached Nome, Alaska, in the life story of another old shaman, Najagneq, who had

293. The Caribou Eskimo Igjugarjuk, who described to Knud Rasmussen the thirty-day ordeal of solitude, silence, and fasting of his shamanic initiation (see page 167).

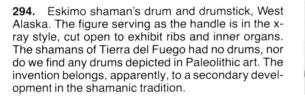

294. Eskimo shaman's drum and drumstick, West Alaska. The figure serving as the handle is in the x-ray style, cut open to exhibit ribs and inner organs. The shamans of Tierra del Fuego had no drums, nor do we find any drums depicted in Paleolithic art. The invention belongs, apparently, to a secondary development in the shamanic tradition.

just been released from a year in jail. For these fearless fellows were not exactly saints. When the primitive Caribou Eskimo Igjugarjuk, in his youth, had decided to take to wife a certain girl whose family objected to the union, he and his brother lay in hiding not far from the young woman's hut, and from there shot down her father, mother, brothers, and sisters—seven or eight in all—until only the girl whom he wanted remained. Autdaruta, in Greenland, had such a grim tally of murders to his credit that a Catholic missionary, zealous to instruct him, reported of their confrontations: "Sometimes I have a feeling that it is Satan incarnate that I have before me." Indeed, on one occasion, when about to meet his cluster of catechumens, the priest was seized with such a terror before facing this man that he wrote: "I was obliged to let them wait while I went down to the sea-

shore to fortify myself in solitude by prayer to Almighty God." [93] Each of his own solitude and familiar, one might say.

Najagneq, the old shaman just released from jail in Nome, had been apprehended for murdering seven or eight members of his village, where he had made a fortress of his house and from there waged war on the whole of his tribe. Taken by stratagem by the captain of a ship, he had been ferried to Nome and held in jail until ten witnesses of his killings could be fetched from his settlement to accuse him. Brought before them, Najagneq's small piercing eyes met theirs. His jaw hung in a slack bandage, his face having been injured by a man who had tried to kill him. And when the ten who had come expressly to get rid of him met his look in the witness box, they lowered their eyes in shame, the charges were dropped, and the case was dismissed.

Our usual association of the spiritual life with "virtue," in the modern sense of the word as referring to "moral excellence and practice," breaks down here. If applied at all to the spirituality of the shaman, "virtue" must be read in the earlier and now archaic sense of the word as referring to "the supernatural influence or power exerted by a divine being." The elementary mythology of shamanism, that is to say, is neither of truth and falsehood nor of good and evil, but of degrees of power: power achieved by breaking through the walls of space and barriers of time to sources unavailable to others. Shamanic combat is but one manifestation of this interest. The use of magical tricks and deceptions to impress and intimidate the uninitiated represents another. The crucial characteristic of this power quest is in its will and disciplines toward the mastery of spirits—which is to say, of the sha-

295. The Alaskan shaman Najagneq, who in Nome revealed to Rasmussen the message to be heard in the gentle voice of *silam inua,* the inhabiting soul of the universe. His jaw was broken by a man attempting to kill him (see page 168).

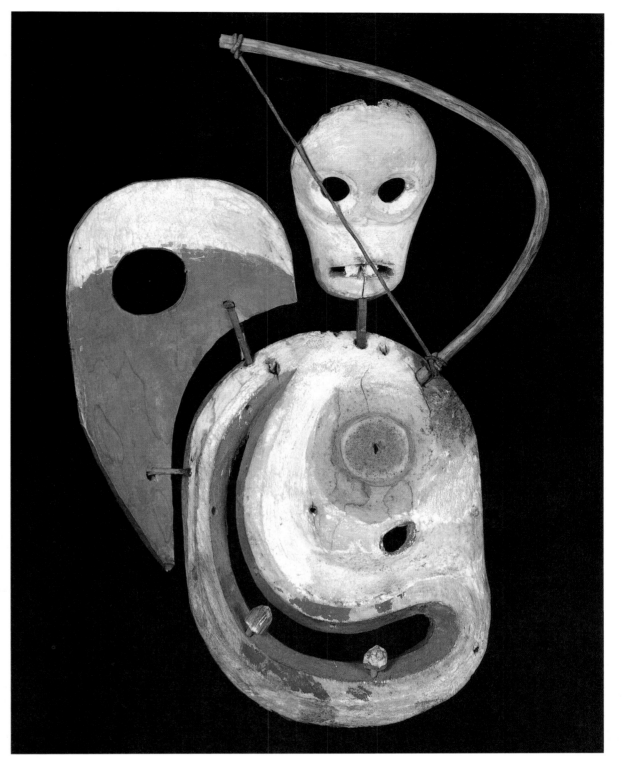

296. The Spirit of Water Bubbles, an Eskimo mask from West Alaska before 1900. The realm into which the shaman is transported by the sound of his drum is of such spirits: mythic apparitions from behind and within the appearances of things.

man's own projected and personified spiritual resources. And the fruits of these conquests, in the way not only of self-knowledge but also of what the Icelandic skalds knew as "the wisdom of the runes," were sometimes impressive indeed.

Najagneq, for example, had frequently employed deceptions to protect himself from his neighbors by playing on their superstitions, and he was not afraid to admit that he had made an art of pulling their legs. But when Rasmussen asked if he really believed in any of all the powers to which he pretended, he replied: "Yes, a power that we call Sila, one that cannot be explained in so many words. A strong spirit, the upholder of the universe, of the weather, in fact all life on earth—so mighty that his speech to man comes not through ordinary words, but through storms, snowfall, rain showers, the tem-

pests of the sea, through all the forces that man fears, or through sunshine, calm seas, or small, innocent, playing children who understand nothing. When times are good, Sila has nothing to say to mankind. He has disappeared into his infinite nothingness and remains away as long as people do not abuse life but have respect for their daily food. No one has ever seen Sila. His place of sojourn is so mysterious that he is with us and infinitely far away at the same time." To which Rasmussen comments: "Najagneq's words sound like an echo of the wisdom we admired in the old shamans we encountered everywhere on our travels—in harsh King William's Land or in Aua's festive snow hut at Hudson Bay, or in the primitive Eskimo Igjugarjuk, whose pithy maxim was: 'The only true wisdom lives far from mankind, out in the great loneliness, and it can be reached only through suffering. Privation

and suffering alone can open the mind of a man to all that is hidden to others.' " [94] When pressed concerning the mystery of Sila, or *silam inua,* "the inhabitant or soul *(inua)* of the universe," the old Alaskan shaman Najagneq replied: "All we know is that it has a gentle voice like a woman, a voice so fine and gentle that even children cannot become afraid. What it says is: *sila ersinarsinivdluge,* 'be not afraid of the universe.' " [95]

* * *

Spencer and Gillen have reported that in Australia, among the Aranda, those transformed into medicine men are supposed to have had magic crystals introduced into their bodies either by spirits of the Dream Time or by other medicine men. There is a cave near Alice Springs that is supposed to be occupied by such spirits, and when a man feels that he is capable of enduring their transformation, he goes alone to its entrance and lies down there to sleep. At break of day, one of the spirits, coming to the mouth of the cave and finding him there, hurls at him an invisible lance that strikes and penetrates his neck from behind, goes through his tongue, and leaves there an actual hole large enough to admit the little finger. A second lance goes through his head from ear to ear, and, falling dead, he is carried deep into the cave, which is supposed to run to a spot beneath the Edith Range some 10 miles distant. There the spirit removes his internal organs and implants an entirely new set, along with a supply of magical stones, after which the man returns to life, but in a condition of insanity. He is led back to his village by the spirit, who is invisible to all but the most gifted medicine men and to dogs, and after a certain number of days, the man paints himself in a certain way and the state of insanity ends. For a year, he does not practice, but consorts with other medicine men and acquires from them their secrets, "which consist," state Spencer and Gillen, "principally in the ability to hide about his person and to produce at will small quartz pebbles or bits of stick; and, of hardly less importance than this sleight of hand, the power of looking preternaturally solemn, as if he were the possessor of knowledge quite hidden from ordinary men." [96] If during this period the hole in the tongue closes, his virtues have departed and he will not practice. Otherwise, so long as the stones remain inside him, he is able to project them, either to heal or to injure. How the hole in the tongue is really made, Spencer and Gillen remark, it is impossible to say, but it is always present in the genuine medicine man. [97] (See Figure 298.)

A second sort of spirit, inspiring a second order of medicine man, takes aspirants underground instead of into a deep cave. Initiation by other medicine men, however, is a very different affair. The aspirant is taken to a secluded spot and told to stand with hands clasped behind his head and not to make a sound. Small quartz crystals, drawn (apparently) from the bodies of the initiators, are placed in the hollow of a spear-thrower. The aspirant is clasped from behind and, one by one, the crystals are taken from the spear-thrower and pressed slowly and strongly along the front of his legs and up his body to his breast bone. This scoring is repeated three times, it being supposed that by this means the crystals are forced into his body. The man is next told to lie down on his back and a pretext is made of projecting crystals into his head; after this, his legs, body, and arms are subjected to another scoring, and a crystal placed against his head is struck hard, as though to drive it into his skull. Next, a pointed

297. Shaman of the Aranda tribe of Central Australia. His body is not as of ordinary men but filled with quartz crystals and endowed with incorruptible internal organs.

298. Aranda shaman exhibiting the hole in his tongue that was made by an invisible lance hurled by spirits of the cave in which he received initiation.

stick is driven deeply under the nail of the middle finger of his right hand, making a hole into which a crystal is seemingly pressed. Two more scorings of his body are executed that day; he is given water to drink in which there are crystals to be swallowed as well as meat to eat in which he is to believe there are also crystals; and the next day there is more scoring, drinking, and eating. The third day, after yet another scoring, he is told to stand with his hands behind his back and his tongue out as far as it will go. The initiator then pretends to take a crystal from the back of his own neck and with this carves a hole in the other's tongue. The initiate is now painted in a certain way and told to remain in the men's camp until his wounds have healed, keeping his right thumb pressed, all the while, against the hole in his right middle finger, lest all the crystals now inside of him escape. [98] His shamanizing—even after all of this—will never be as effective as that of the men and women initiated by spirits. He will have gained a certain prestige, however, and will have the power to project lethal splinters of crystal into his enemies and to cure by suction.

The Western Aranda believe that, besides having a body full of crystals, the healer also has inside him a particular kind of lizard, supposedly endowed with great suctorial power. [99] Moreover, among tribes west of the MacDonnell Ranges, the medicine man can assume the form of an eagle-hawk, fly long distances at night, and bring suffering and death to the people of enemy tribes by digging into them his sharp claws. [100]

*   *   *

Not all the elements of what appears to have been a shared heritage of "techniques of ecstasy" from the period of the Upper Paleolithic caves have been equally well retained and cultivated in all the terminal provinces of the tradition: South Africa, in the trance dances of the Kalahari Bushmen; Tierra del Fuego, in the songs and visions of the Ona and Yahgan magicians; arctic America and Greenland, in the mystic realizations of the rugged challengers of the polar ice; and Australia, where the tradition seems to have devolved into a sort of sadomasochistic parody of itself. Father Gusinde's observation that in Tierra del Fuego the medicine men's protective spirits have nothing whatever to do with the High God of their traditions contrasts radically with Rasmussen's report of the role of Sila in Najagneq's thinking. It is possible that Gusinde simply failed to penetrate as deeply as Rasmussen into the secrets of shamanic thought and experience. It is also possible, on the other hand, that the shamans of Rasmussen's area may themselves have penetrated more deeply than did those of Gusinde's report, into the mysteries of their inward life. But in any case, from Rasmussen's Eskimo findings four distinct, yet related, levels of shamanic mythic thinking can be identified, the profoundest being of an unqualified "ultimate ground," experienced by the shaman as at once immanent and transcendent, not grasped but only suggested in images and speech: something very much more like the *ntum* of the African Bushman and the *megbe* of the Pygmies than like the High God of any monotheism, or the Sky God of academic anthropology. One has to wonder, indeed, whether either a missionary locked to the image of his own Almighty God, or an anthropologist professionally bound to the concepts of positivistic science would be able to recognize and follow a truly mystical and transtheological statement, even if he heard one. As remarked by Ananda K. Coomaraswamy: "To have lost the art of thinking in images is precisely to have lost the proper linguistic of metaphysics and to have descended to the verbal logic of 'philosophy.'" And as a consequence, in his view, our general inability to recognize the metaphysical content of primitive traditions "is primarily due to our own abysmal ignorance of metaphysics and of its technical terms." [101]

The second level of the shamanic mythic ambient, then, is that of those personal guardians, helpers, and familiars who capture and bind the imagination; and if the first level can be termed metaphysical, truly mystical, this second is more properly psychological, being conditioned both by cultural and by intimately personal circumstance. It may finally open to transpersonal, transcultural, metaphysical realizations by way of a pathological "crisis of the object" (as defined, page 167), which then becomes a destiny, setting the affected one spiritually and even physically apart from the commonality of his race. There are many mysterious features associated with the phenomenology of this level, occult features suggesting the actual acquisition of such powers as the Hindu yogis claim (and may, in fact, to some measure, acquire). But there is also a great deal of quackery involved; and it is with this that we come to the recognition of level three: that of the mythological image of the shaman, created in the popular mind by mystifications, theatrical scenes, and sleight-of-hand illusionism, the effects of which, however, turn back upon the mind of the shaman himself and become the aids and generators of his own translation to ecstasy.

The fourth level of the shamanic range is, finally, of those spooks and powers deliberately invented to intimidate and hold at bay the philistines. H. Ostermann, Rasmussen's posthumous editor, tells of the old shaman Najagneq, that when he was brought from his distant

village to Nome, although knowing only earth huts, kayaks, and sledges, he was not impressed at all by the large houses, steamers, and automobiles, but fascinated by the sight of a white horse hauling a big lorry; and when his villagers then arrived to accuse and undo him, he announced to them that the white man had killed him ten times that winter, but that he had had as helping spirits ten white horses which he had sacrificed one by one, thus saving his life. "He was no humbug," is Ostermann's comment, "but a solitary man accustomed to hold his own against many and therefore had to have his little tricks." [102]

We may call the first of these four levels the "metaphysical"; the second, the "psychological"; the third, the "social-historical"; and the fourth, the "exploitative." And not only in the matter of shamanism, but in every department of mythic and religious schooling, these four levels can be distinguished. That which is properly of moment for a historical atlas, of course, is the social-historical, treating of the variations in time and space of the forms through which psychological and metaphysical realizations are inspired and expressed. But the other three cannot be dismissed. And in some traditions—the biblical, Judeo-Christian-Muslim, for ex-

299. An East Siberian Yakut shaman invoking his familiar spirits, beating his single-headed drum, preparatory to passing into the trance of his shamanizing.

ample—the exploitative, racial or institutional, as well as masculine-sexual accent, has been to such a degree dominant that everything else has been structured to support it.

* * *

The historical development of shamanism that took place in Central Asia among the Neo-Siberian Tungus, Vogul, Yakut, Ostyak, and Buriat tribes brought into play a number of spectacular, post-Paleolithic ritual and mythic forms, which, however, did not alter the essential sense of the experience but, on the contrary, gave it accent. "When I shamanize," said the Tungus shaman Semyonov Semyon, when interviewed in his home on the Lower Tunguska River in the spring of 1925, "the spirit of my deceased brother Ilya comes and speaks through my mouth. My shaman forefathers, too, have forced me to walk the path of shamanism. Before I commenced to shamanize, I lay sick for a whole year: I became a shaman at the

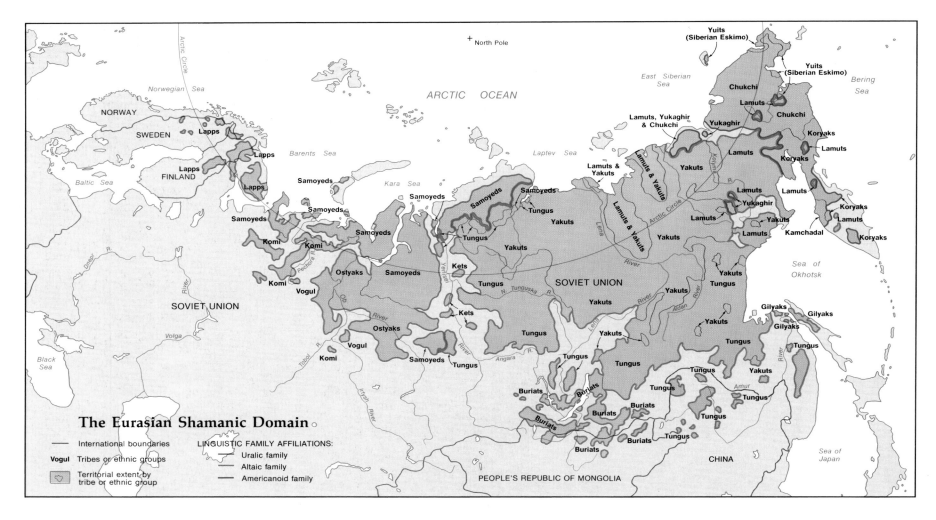

The Eurasian Shamanic Domain

International boundaries
Vogul Tribes or ethnic groups
Territorial extent by tribe or ethnic group

LINGUISTIC FAMILY AFFILIATIONS:
Uralic family
Altaic family
Americanoid family

Map 37. The peoples named above are classified according to linguistic affiliations. Of those named, the Finno-Ugric, Turkic, Tunguso-Manchurian, and Mongolian are of the Uralo-Altaic family, while the Paleo-Siberians and Aleut-Eskimo are Americanoid. Until Russian colonization in the mid-seventeenth century, there were three distinct domains of reindeer-herders (in the Arctic), as well as one of horse and cattle breeders (in the south): (1) *Northwest of the Ob:* Finno-Ugric Lapps and Komi, Voguls and Ostyaks; (2) *From the Ob to the Sea of Okhotsk:* Turkic Samoyeds and Yakuts, Tunguso-Manchurian Tungus and Lamuts, Mongolian Buriats and Mongols, Paleo-Siberian Kets and Gilyak; (3) *Northeast of the Lena:* Paleo-Siberian Yukaghir, Chukchi, Koryak, and Kamchadal, with a few Aleut and Eskimo.

age of fifteen. The sickness that forced me to this path showed itself in a swelling of my body and frequent spells of fainting. When I began to sing, however, the sickness usually disappeared.

"After that, my ancestors began to shamanize with me. They stood me up like a block of wood and shot at me with their bows until I lost consciousness. They cut up my flesh, separated my bones, counted them, and ate my flesh raw. When they counted the bones they found one too many; had there been too few, I could not have become a shaman. And while they were performing this rite, I ate and drank nothing for the whole summer. But at the end the shaman spirits drank the blood of a reindeer and gave me some to drink, too. After these events, the shaman has less blood and looks pale.

"The same thing happens to every Tungus shaman. Only after his shaman ancestors have cut up his body in this way and separated his bones can he begin to shamanize." [103]

"Up above there is a certain tree," this same shaman continued to his interviewer, G. V. Ksenofontov, a Russianized full-blooded Yakut, "a tree where the souls of the shamans are reared before they attain their powers. And on the boughs of this tree are nests in which the souls lie and are attended. The name of the tree is Tuuru. The higher the nest in this tree, the stronger will the shaman be who is raised in it, the more will he know, and the farther will he see.

"The rim of a shaman's drum is cut from a living larch. The larch is left alive and standing in recollection and honor of the tree Tuuru, where the soul of the shaman was raised. Furthermore, in memory of the great tree Tuuru, at each seance the shaman plants a tree with one or more cross-sticks in the tent where the ceremony takes place, and this tree too is called Tuuru. This is done both among us here on the Lower Tunguska and among the Angara Tungus. The Tungus who are connected with the Yakuts call this planted tree Särgä. It is made of a long pole of larch. White cloths are hung on the crosssticks. Among the Angara Tungus they hang the pelt of a sacrificed animal on the tree. The Tungus of the Middle Tunguska make a Tuuru that is just like ours.

"According to our belief, the shaman climbs up this tree to God when he shamanizes. For the tree grows during the rite and invisibly reaches the summit of heaven.

"God created the two trees when he created the earth and man: a male, the larch; and a female, the fir." [104]

The drum and the World Tree are post-

300. The axial World Tree on a Tungus (Gold tribe) shamanic garment.

301. Crown from a Scythian royal tomb, sixth to fourth century B.C., southern Russia, that illustrates the range of Scythian contacts. Head of goddess: Greek. World Tree with browsing reindeer: compare the Old Germanic World Tree, Yggdrasil, with four browsing deer consuming its leaves. Crowned king beneath the World Tree: Indo-Aryan idea of the World Ruler (*Cakravartin*) or World Savior (*Buddha*) enthroned at the *axis mundi*. The engraved boss on the animals' haunches also appears on ivory carvings at Ipiutak, Alaska (see pages 38–39).

Paleolithic innovations here; the feature of the *two* trees introduces a male-female polarity theme that is also new to the tradition and derived, as Hermann Baumann has shown, from the Near Eastern Neolithic and high-culture matrices.[105] A commonly recognized corollary of the male-female polarity theme is represented in the image of a single, androgynous, higher source or power out of which the opposites have sprung, as, for example, in Genesis 1:27, where we read, "God created man in his own image . . . male and female. . . ." (See, also, the image of Shiva the Great Lord, Figure 5, page 13.) Transvestite priests who castrated themselves in the service of Artemis at Ephesus, or of Attis and Cybele at Hierapolis on the Euphrates, were supposed to reflect, and so to approach, the condition of the Primal Bisexual Divinity. We have seen something of the kind in the subincision rites of the Aranda. Herodotus (I.105 and IV.67) in the fifth century B.C., wrote of what was known as the "female sickness" of the Scythian priests and soothsayers, the Enaries or Anandrieis ("non-men"), whose condition was supposed to have been inflicted upon them by the gods. W. Bogoras and Waldemar Jochelson discovered among the Paleo-Siberian tribes of the Chukchi Peninsula both male and female shamans who had ritually, psychologically, and to some extent even physically, "changed sex." We have already recognized a Scythian art motif in Alaskan ivories of the first centuries after Christ (see pages 38-39). It is not unlikely that some of the practices of the Scythian Anandrieis also crossed the Bering Strait at that time. "Transformation takes place," states Bogoras of the Chukchi, "by command of the ke'let [the spirit], usually at the age of early youth

302. Lappish shaman in trance, his drum on his back, with a female associate watching, brush in hand, to keep flies away; for it is believed that at this delicate time even the touch of a fly might break the power of the shaman's departed spirit to return to the vacated body. Seventeenth-century engraving.

The figure in a reindeer-drawn sleigh may have been added to remind us that the idea of the annual flight of Santa Claus in his reindeer-drawn sleigh (midnight of the winter solstice) was originally inspired by tales of the flights of the Lappish shamans. It was also once believed that the Old Germanic god Othin (Odin, Wodin, or Wotan) flew through the air with his Howling Host on that night of the birth of the new year, delivering gifts to those who were his worshipers and punishments to those who were not.

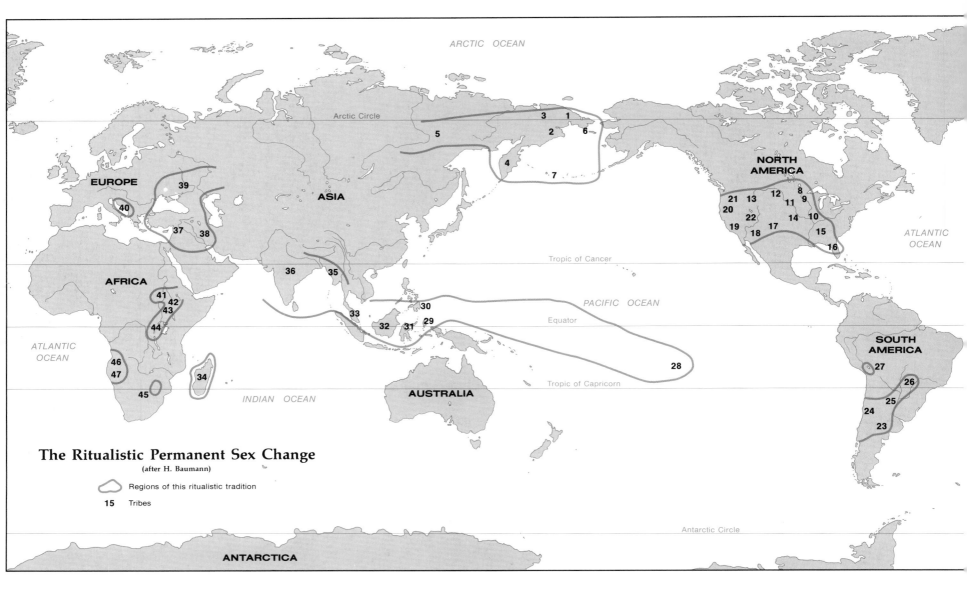

The Ritualistic Permanent Sex Change
(after H. Baumann)

⌒ Regions of this ritualistic tradition

15 Tribes

Labels on map: ARCTIC OCEAN; Arctic Circle; EUROPE; ASIA; AFRICA; ATLANTIC OCEAN; NORTH AMERICA; ATLANTIC OCEAN; Tropic of Cancer; PACIFIC OCEAN; Equator; INDIAN OCEAN; AUSTRALIA; Tropic of Capricorn; SOUTH AMERICA; Antarctic Circle; ANTARCTICA

Map 38. Generally hunters-and-gatherers maintain a scrupulous distinction between the sexes: such a bisexual power as the Mapuche "Mother-Father" of all things would find no place in their mythologies. North Australian hunting mythologies are grounded, however, in a bisexual creator, Ungud (pages 140–142), and Baumann has shown this concept to have been imported and proper rather to planters than to hunters (Map 33, page 142). Map 38 is of a related topic: for, where a bisexual creator is recognized, the contingent notion may follow of bisexuality as a condition spiritually superior to that of the untransformed male or female—hence, characteristic of shamans supremely endowed.

Mythologies based on the idea of a creative bisexual power that split into male and female and generated the universe first appear in documents from ancient Mesopotamia; and it was in areas proximal to that cultural matrix that ritualized transvestism, castration, and similar practices first became identified with the rites of a Universal Goddess. The extension of these practices southeastward to Indonesia, and thence eastward to Polynesia and westward to East Africa, accompanied the diffusion of an archaic megalithic temple complex. The northeastern thrust across Siberia to the Chukchi Peninsula, on the other hand, was an effect of Scythian influences in the eighth to second centuries B.C. The crown (**301** on page 173) is of these people. And we have already remarked the appearance in Alaska of Scythian art

when shamanistic inspiration first manifests itself. It is, however, much dreaded by the youthful adepts." Indeed, as he learned, the youths in some cases prefer suicide to answering this call.[106] And yet, as Jochelson avers: "The transformed shamans were believed to be the most powerful of all."[107]

Hermann Baumann has devoted an im-

motifs (pages 38–39). Since, in all high-culture areas, ritual transvestism and sex change have been abolished, their former prevalence in the Americas is known only from historical accounts of their extirpation by the Spaniards and from ethnological notices of their continuation into modern times in the zones indicated above.

Baumann's tribal catalog is as follows: *Northeast Asia:* (1) Chukchi; (2) Koryak; (3) Yukaghir; (4) Itelmen; (5) Yakut; (6) Asiatic Eskimo. *America:* (7) Aleut; (8) Ojibwa; (9) Sauk-Fox; (10) Illinois; (11) Dakota; (12) Mandan-Minitari; (13) Crow; (14) Ponca, Omaha, Kansas, Oto, Osage; (15) Choctaw and other Muskogee; (16) Seminole; (17) Pueblo [Zuni, Acoma, Laguna], Navaho; (18) Yuma, Mohave; (19) Juaneño; (20) Yakut, Yuki, Yurok; (21) Shahaptan-Flathead; (22) Ute-Shoshone; (23) Puelshe; (24) Araucanian; (25) earlier Guaycuru tribes of the Chaco; (26) Caduveo; (27) Titicaca villagers. *South Seas:* (28) Tahiti, Marquesas; (29) Palau. *Indonesia:* (30) Subanum [Mindanas]; (31) Celebes [Bugis, Makas, and such]; (32) Borneo. (33) Malaysia. (34) *Madagascar. Burma:* (35) Lushai, the Arakan Coast. *India:* (36) Vallabhacharyas and such. *Near East:* (37) Ancient Babylonia; (38) Nogai. *Eurasia:* (39) Scythians; (40) Serbo-Croatians; Albanians. *Africa:* (41) Nuba, Kunama; (42) Konso, Galla[?]; (43) Lango; (44) Rundi, Hunde; (45) Shona-Karanga, Lamba, Venda; (46) Humbe, Handa, Musho, Ovimbundu, Kimbundu; (47) Ambo-Kwanyama.[14]

portant work to the study and interpretation of this phenomenon: its beginnings in the archaic Near East in the cults of deities regarded, not merely as androgynous, but as beyond *all* "pairs-of-opposites"; its relevance to the post-Paleolithic mythological themes of bisexual gods, bisexual souls, the world parents, the world egg, world giant, and divine twins;

the truly astonishing reach of its distribution, not only throughout the Old World, but also into the New; and its relationship, on the one hand, to mythology, and on the other, to biology and psychology.[108] Among the Araucanians of Chile, of whom the Mapuche are an important tribe, the male shamans of earlier times were commonly transvestites;[109] and in a large part of North America, transvestite shamans have continued to be important up to the present. According to Bogoras, among the shamans of the Chukchi, various degrees of transformation are recognized. In the first, the shaman changes only the manner of braiding and arranging his hair; in the second, he adopts female dress; in the third, he leaves off all the pursuits and manners of his own sex and takes on those of a woman. "Even his pronunciation changes from the male to the female mode. At the same time his body alters, if not in its outward appearance, at least in its faculties and forces. . . . Generally speaking, he becomes a woman with the appearance of a man. . . . He seeks to win the good graces of men, and succeeds easily with the aid of 'spirits.' Thus he has all the young men he could wish for striving to obtain his favor. From these he chooses his lover, and after a time takes a husband.[110] . . . Moreover, each 'soft man' is supposed to have a special protector among the 'spirits,' who, for the most part, is said to play the part of a

303. A "soft man," transvestite, or transformed, shaman of the Chuckchi.

supernatural husband." [111] In the case of a woman transformed into a man, she cuts her hair, dons the dress of a male, adopts the vocabulary of men, and even learns in a very short time to handle a spear and to shoot with a rifle. She easily finds a quiet young girl who consents to becoming her "wife," and at last she marries. She obtains from the leg of a reindeer a gastrocnemius which serves her as a male organ; and should she wish to have children in this union she and her wife will enter into a bond of mutual marriage with some neighboring youth. [112]

An interesting feature of Baumann's map, charting the distribution of the evidence of these practices, is the large gap through Central Asia, between the time and place of Herodotus's report on the Enaries and Bogoras's and Jochelson's of the Paleo-Siberian "soft men." The period of development of the intervening Altaic complex must, therefore, have been later than that of the rise and spread of the Paleo-Siberian Scythian-Chukchi tradition. "The shamanism of the Chukchee has not reached a stage of development," states Bogoras, "high enough to have drums or clothing of peculiar form, or, indeed, any special belongings characteristic of itself. The Chukchee shaman uses the ordinary drum of his family, or perhaps he may make an extra drum for his own use; but this drum will have exactly the same form, and, moreover, it will

probably be employed in all the family ceremonials, where additional drums are used for making as much noise as possible. As to the shamanistic garb," he continues, "the Chukchee have nothing similar to the well-known type of coat covered with fringes and images, which is in general use among the Yakut and Tungus, and which probably was borrowed from the latter by the Yukaghir." [113]

Animal sacrifice in association with shamanic practice, on the other hand, is a feature known to both the Paleo- and the Neo-Siberians, and may be an original trait of the Paleolithic complex, as the rock painting at Lascaux of the shaman in trance before the bison pierced by a lance would seem to suggest. In our illustrations on page 158 we have already seen the account of an Altaic sacrifice of a horse, with the hide then hung on a pole (Figure 276); the sacrifice of a dog by a Koryak shaman, who is beating his drum while curing a patient (Figures 278/279); and a Chukchi map of the sky (Figure 277), where Dawn Man receives the sacrifice of a dog and offers a fox in exchange, while the family of Evening Man, costumed in the guise of the gods of the sea, pays sacrifice to those gods. [114]

These last two sketches, Koryak and Chukchi, are of the earlier, Paleo-Siberian tradition, among the characterizing features of which, the following seven may be named:

1. The dog sacrifice: which may represent a continuation from the Late Paleolithic; the offering then, however, was of game animals (the bear and possibly the bison), whereas here it is of a domestic beast

2. A reindeer sacrifice, which is again of a domestic species; the ancestors of these tribesmen having followed the great European herds northeastward as the glaciers melted, first as hunters, but then as owners and breeders of the herds

3. A family of anthropomorphic sky gods and another of sea gods, to whom the sacrifices are addressed: these necessarily of a post-Paleolithic, Neolithic vintage, very likely from the period of reindeer domestication

4. Intervening anthropomorphic enemy spirits, who may intercept and capture the offered sacrifices

5. The idea of a World Axis with the Pole Star at its head, along the line of which the sacrifices rise to their destination

6. The use of a drum in accompaniment to shamanistic rites, but a drum not yet especially sacred

7. Transvestite shamans: representing a sphere of spiritual power transcending the male-female polarity, this being a theme from the high Bronze Age of the Near East, carried into Central Asia by the Scythians about the fifth century B.C.

304. Northeastward of the Lena River and the Verkhoyanskig range are the Americanoid, Paleo-Siberian sea-mammal-hunting and reindeer-breeding Chukchi, Koryak, Yukaghir, and Itelman or Kamchadals. Among their most precious possessions are their dogs, and among their most important rites are reindeer and dog sacrifices, for which only the best are chosen. The animals are stabbed to the heart with a spear, an unsuccessful blow signifying the deity's displeasure. This early photograph is of a Koryak underground house with its best dogs' noses pointed to the sky, where their souls have flown. [16]

Of the later shamanic Uralo-Altaic system, these nine features may be noted:

1. The wearing of a special ritual costume, a trait already evident in the Paleolithic rock paintings

2. The sanctification and mythologization of the drum

3. The drum's association with the Neolithic image of the World Tree

4. The drum's association with the sacrificed reindeer, of whose hide the drumhead is made

5. An association of the World Tree with the central pole of the yurt, and of the shaman's ascent of this pole with his heaven journey

6. Anthropomorphic deities as guardians of the gates of the way

7. A horse sacrifice, which is an Indo-European feature

8. A radical dualism—a late Zoroastrian feature—of light and dark, sky and underworld, benign and terrible divinities and their worlds

9. An extreme development of the shamanic-crisis theme, with elaborate dismemberment and death-and-resurrection accents

Undoubtedly the most important, as well as most characteristic, of all these

Uralo-Altaic features is the drum. The shaman rides on his drum; and the Buriat of Irkutsk declare that by virtue of the power of his originally double-headed drum, their first shaman, Morgon-Kara, could bring back souls even from the dead.

Erlen Khan, the Lord of the Dead, complained to the great god Tengri, on high, that because of Morgon-Kara he was no longer able to hold the souls brought to him by his Messengers; and so Tengri himself determined to make trial of the shaman with a test. He took possession of the soul of a certain man, slipped it into a bottle, and then, sitting with the bottle in hand, his thumb covering its opening, he waited to see what the mighty Buriat would do.

The man whose soul had been taken fell ill, and his family sent for Morgon-Kara. The shaman immediately recognized that the soul of the man had been taken, and, riding on his wonderful drum, he searched the forests, the waters, the mountain gorges, indeed the earth, and then descended to the Underworld. The soul being nowhere in any of these, there remained but one domain to be searched: High Heaven. So, sitting on his drum, he flew aloft. And he cruised the heavens for some time before noticing that the radiant High God was sitting there with a bottle in his hand, over the top of which the ball of his thumb was pressed. Studying the circumstance, Morgon-Kara perceived that within the bottle was the very soul he had come to retrieve. So he transformed himself into a wasp, flew at the god, and gave him such a hot sting on the forehead that his thumb jerked from the opening and the soul escaped. The next thing Tengri knew was that the shaman, together with his prize, was on his drum again, sailing back to earth. He reached for a thunderbolt, let it fly, and the drum was split in half. And that is why shaman drums today have but one head.[115]

The Siberians

The Yakuts tell of a shaman of earlier times named Aadja, the younger of two brothers whose parents had died when they were very young.

Aadja's brother was thirty years of age, and he twenty when he married, and that year, there was born a red piebald stallion with all the signs and promise of an exceptionally beautiful steed. But that same fall, Aadja died. And although he lay there dead, he could hear everything that was being said around him, and felt as though he had simply fallen asleep. He could neither move nor speak, yet could distinctly hear them making his coffin and digging his grave. And so there he lay as though alive, unhappy that they should be coming together to bury him when he might very well have come back to life. They placed him in the coffin, put the coffin in the grave, and shoveled in the dirt.

As he lay in that grave, his heart and soul sobbed and cried. But then he heard someone

306. "The Three Worlds" on a Lapp drumhead, from northern Sweden, c. 1800. In the Upper World: the sun and the moon (or, perhaps, the sun setting and rising) are seen along with heavenly beings and their tent. In the Middle World (left to right): the Mistress of the Beasts sends animals to be hunted; a hunter shoots a reindeer; and a shaman, riding upward in a sleigh drawn by a reindeer, is followed by a dog. In the Lower World: three goddesses suggesting the Norns are pictured.

305. The Mongol (Bajongol) shaman Otsir Böö, in full regalia. On the vertical strut at the back of his drum is the image of his spirit helper.

up there begin to dig, and he was glad to think that his brother, believing that he might still be alive, had returned to disinter him. However, when the cover of his coffin was at last removed, he saw four black men whom he did not know. They took up his body and stood him upright on his coffin with his face turned toward his house. Through the window he could see a fire burning, and smoke was coming from the chimney.

Then, from somewhere far in the depths of the earth, he heard the bellowing of a bull. The bellowing came nearer, nearer; the earth began to tremble; he was terribly afraid; and from the bottom of the grave the bull emerged. It was completely black and its horns were close together. It took him sitting between its horns and went down again through the opening from which it had just emerged. And they reached a place where there was a house, from within which there came the voice of what seemed to be an old man, saying, "Boys, it is true. Our little son has brought a man. Go out and relieve him of his load!" A number of black, withered old men came hopping out, grabbed the arrival, carried him into the house, and set him on the flat of the hand of an old man, who held him to estimate the weight and said: "Take him back! He is predestined to be reborn up there!" With that, the bull again took him between its horns, carried him up along the old way, and set him down where he had been before.

When the living corpse came to its senses, night had descended and it was dark. Presently a black raven appeared. It shoved its head between the dead man's legs, lifted him, and flew directly upward. In the zenith was an opening through which they passed to a place where both the sun and the moon were shining and the houses and barns were of iron. All the people had the heads of ravens, yet their bodies were like those of men. And there could be heard inside the largest house something like the voice of an old man saying: "Boys! Look! Our little son has brought us a man. Go out and bring him in." A company of young men dashed out and, seizing the newcomer, bore him into the house, where they set him on the flat of the hand of a gray-haired old man, who first tested his weight and then said: "Boys, take him along and place him in the highest nest!"

For there was a great larch up there, whose size can hardly be compared with anything we know. Its top surely touched heaven. And there was on every branch a nest as large as a haystack covered with snow. The young men lay their charge in the highest of these, and as soon as they had set him down, there came flying a winged white reindeer that settled on the nest. Its teats entered his mouth, he began to suck, and there he lay for three years. And the more he sucked, the smaller became his body, until finally he was no bigger than a thimble.

Thus resting in his lofty nest, he one day heard the voice of the same old man, who now was saying to one of his seven raven-headed sons: "My boy, go down to the Middle World, seize a woman and bring her back." The son descended, and in time returned towing a brown-faced woman by the hair. They all danced in celebration. But the one lying in the nest then again heard the voice saying: "Shut this woman up in an iron barn, so that our son, who lives in the Middle World, may not come and carry her away."

They locked the woman in a barn; and in a little while, the nestling heard the sounds of a shaman's drum and song coming up from the Middle World. The sounds gradually grew, coming nearer—nearer—until, from below, a head appeared in the exit opening. From his nest, the watcher could then see a man of nimble body and moderate stature with hair already gray. Hardly had he fully appeared, when, pressing his drumstick to his brow, he was immediately transformed into a bull with a single horn projecting from the middle of its forehead. The bull shattered with a single blow the door of the barn in which the woman had been locked and galloped off with her, down and away.

Following him, there went up cries and shouts, laments and mourning, and the son of the old man again went down to the Middle World. He returned with a white-faced woman, who was first transformed into an insect and then hidden in the central structural pole of the heavenly yurt. Soon again the drum and song of a shaman could be heard. And this time, again, the one who arrived very soon discovered the patient, broke the pole in which she was hidden, and carried her off.

Whereupon the son of the old man went his way a third time, returning with the same white-faced woman, and this time the raven-headed spirit-people of the Upper World did

better than before for her protection. They set fire to a pile of wood at the exit hole, took glowing brands in their hands, and stood ready at the aperture, watching. When the shaman appeared, they smote him with the firebrands and forced him back to earth.

At last, the little watcher in the nest at the end of his three years, heard once again the voice of the old man. "His years are up," the voice said. "Throw our child down to the Middle World. He is to go into a woman to be born with the name Shaman Aadja, which we have given him. He shall be famous: no one shall take his name in vain in the holy month."

With songs and blessings, the seven hurled the nestling down into the Middle World, where he immediately lost consciousness, unable to recall by what means he had come to be where he was. It was not until he was five that this recollection returned—and then he knew that he had been born before, how he had lived on this earth, and how he had been born above and heard with his own ears and seen with his own eyes the arrival of a shaman.

Seven years after his new birth, he was seized by the spirits, compelled to sing, and

cut to pieces. At eight, he began to shamanize and to perform the ritual dance. At nine, he was already famous. And at twelve, he was a great shaman.

It turned out that he had this time come into the world some 15 versts [about 10 miles] from the place of his former residence. And when he paid a visit to his former brother, he found that his wife had again married and that the colorful stallion foal which had been born the

307. The Yakut (Karagasy) shaman Tulayev, of Irkutsk, wearing his reindeer-leather swan costume. On his cap of green cloth is sewn a wolf's muzzle with the moon above and stars on each side. A ribbon adorned with stars, representing his spine, hangs from the cap down his back. An x-ray-style representation, in a blue Chinese fabric, of his breast bone and ribs has been sewn to the chest of his garment; a similar x-ray of spine and ribs appears on the back; arm-bone applique, on both sleeves. And, whereas the shaman's left foot is bare, embroidered on the right boot are toe and leg bones in white reindeer hair. The head of the great drum is of reindeer hide, as is the cover of the head of the drumstick. Eagle-owl feathers on the shaman's shoulders are his wings. Photographed c. 1927.

year of his death was now, indeed, a famous steed. But his relatives failed to recognize him and he told them nothing.

One summer day, however, when a man of property was celebrating the Isyach Festival of the blessing of the sacred kumiss, which is accompanied by a ritual known as the Lifting Up of the Soul of the Horse, the young shaman met the one whom he had seen come into the Upper World while lying in his nest. The older shaman immediately recognized him and said in a voice loud enough for others to hear: "When I once was helping another shaman recover the soul of a sick woman, I saw you in the nest on the topmost ninth bough, sucking the teats of your animal mother. You were looking out of the nest." And the young Shaman Aadja, hearing these words, became furious. "Why do you bring out here, before everyone, the secret of my birth?" he asked. To which the other replied: "If you are planning evil against me, destroy me, eat me! I was formerly nurtured on the eighth bough of the same larch on which you were nurtured. I am to be born again and nurtured by the Black Raven, Chara-Suorun."

"And they say," concluded Ivan Popov, the Yakut narrator of this legend, on March 22, 1925, "that the young shaman that night killed the elder. The young shaman's spirits swallowed him and thus brought about his death, and no one saw. This ancient tale I was told by an old man."[116]

*   *   *

The Paleo-Siberian Yukaghir, now confined to the northern rim of the Chukchi Peninsula between the Lena and Kolyma Rivers, have adopted from their Tungus and Yakut neighbors the Altaic costume and drum. Their term for the drum, *ya'lgil*, means "lake," referring to the mythic lake through which the shaman descends to the underworld; and the infinitive, *yalgi'ne*, means both "to have a drum" and "to shamanize."[117] The shaman himself is called *a'lma*, from the verb *a*, "to do"; also *i'rkeye*, "the trembling one"; and he occupies, according to Jochelson, a very special place in the social system of the Yukaghir.

"He was the protector and priest of a definite group of relatives or of a clan," according to this author. "But he was not a professsional shaman in the sense of modern days. A'lma attended to the sick of his group, offered sacrifices, prayed to the gods for successful hunting and other benefactions, and had intercourse with the supernatural world and the kingdom of the Shadows. The ancient Yukaghir shaman represented his clan. Every Yukaghir clan traces its origin to some shaman. From the merging of the ancestor and the shaman in one person there developed the cult of the shaman-ancestor."[118]

Bogoras found that among the Chukchi, just eastward of the Yukaghir, shamanism is largely affiliated with the family ceremonials. "Each family," he reports, "has one or more drums of its own, on which its members are bound at specific periods to perform; that is, to accompany the beating of the drum with the singing of various melodies. Almost always, on these occasions, one member at least of the family tries to communicate with 'spirits' after the manner of shamans. Such a one will usually, with violent shouting and continuous exercise on the drum, work himself up to the highest pitch possible, and in this condition pretend that the 'spirits' have entered his body. In proof of this he acts in exactly the same way as do the shamans—jumping about, twisting his body in the most violent contortions, and uttering gibbering sounds and unintelligible words supposed to be the voice and the language of 'spirits.' Oftentimes he essays soothsaying and foretelling the future, though such attempts do not usually receive much attention. All this is done in the outer tent, where all the ceremonials are performed, and mostly in the daytime.

"The acts of real shamanism, on the contrary, are for the most part performed in the sleeping-room, at night-time and in perfect darkness."[119]

In October 1896, Jochelson recorded from the lips of a Yukaghir named Samsonov the following account of his people's way of disposing of the body of a deceased shaman:

"Our ancient people, when a shaman died, used to separate the flesh of the corpse from the bones. For that purpose they put on gloves and masks. Then they took iron hooks, and having caught the flesh of the corpse, drew it to them and cut it off. It was considered a sin to touch the corpse with bare hands, or to look at it with uncovered face. Thus they separated the flesh from the skeleton through its entire length. Then they made drying frames and hung up the flesh outside, to dry in the sun. After the flesh had been dried, the relatives of the dead shaman divided it among themselves. Then they made a tent of larch-tree rods, and each of them put his share in the middle of the larch tent separately. Then the relatives of the shaman killed dogs as offerings. They did not kill bad dogs; they killed only good ones. Then they added the killed dogs to their portions of dried flesh. After that they left the tent with the shaman's flesh and the offerings.

"Then they divided the bones of the corpse, and after having dried them, they clothed them. They worshiped the skull of the shaman. They made a trunk of wood and set on it the skull. Then they made for it a jacket and caps—two caps, a winter and a summer one. They embroi-

dered the coat all over. For its face they made a mask, with openings for eyes and mouth. Over the embroidered coat they put a coat of fawn-skins; and over that, a blanket of soft reindeer-skins.

"Then they placed the figure in the front corner of the house. Whenever they were going to eat something good, they first threw a piece of it in the fire and held the figure over the smoke. This they did at every meal; and thus they fed the figure, which they worshipped as a god."[120]

Pieces of the shaman's dried flesh were sewn into bags of waterproof smoked hide and worn under the clothes as amulets and, when traveling, the tribe carried in a wooden box the figure with the skull. It is called by the same name, *xiol*, that today is used when referring to the Christian god, to ikons, or to saints.[121]

The extraordinary reverence here shown before the remains and mystery of an extraordinary man is but an effect, intensely focused, of a general sense of wonder before the mystery of the universe and of all things, which inspires the secular, as well as religious, modes of experience, and action of the Paleo-Siberians. Bogoras found among the Chukchi the belief that every material object can act, speak, and walk by itself. Everything is spoken of as "having a voice." A stone endowed with a voice might roll down and crush a person against whom it had a grudge, or induce another person to pick it up and wear it as an amulet. The trees of the forest talk to one another. Both the rainbow and the sun's rays have "masters," who live above, on the highest part of the rainbow and at the place from which the sun's rays emanate, descending to earth along these paths of light. Even the shadows on the wall constitute definite tribes and have their own country, where they dwell in huts and subsist by hunting.

As Bogoras was told by a shaman of the Chukchi: "On the steep bank of a river there exists life. A voice is there and it speaks aloud. I saw the 'master' of the voice and spoke with him. He subjected himself to me and sacrificed to me. He came yesterday and answered my questions. The small gray bird with the blue breast sings shaman-songs in the hollow of the bough, calls her spirits, and practices shamanism. The woodpecker strikes his drum in the tree with his drumming nose. Under the ax the tree trembles and wails, like a drum under the baton. All these come at my call.

"All that exists lives. The lamp walks around. The walls of the house have voices of their own. Even the chamber-vessel has a separate land and house. The skins sleeping in the bags talk at night. The antlers lying on the tombs arise at night and walk in procession around the mounds, while the deceased get up and visit the living."[122]

It is because he hears the voices of the stones and trees that are speaking, unheard to us all, that the shaman does not live like other men in relation only to the appearances of things. Hearing their songs, he is led by them to the song within himself, through which he is sustained in a life inflated by the breath and winds of the unseen. The powers of which he thus becomes the vehicle may seem to be supernatural, but they are actually of nature itself. One thinks of the lines of the poet Wordsworth:

> For I have learned
> To look on nature, not as in the hour
> Of thoughtless youth; but hearing often times
> The still sad music of humanity,
> Nor harsh nor grating, though of ample power
> To chasten and subdue. And I have felt
> A presence that disturbs me with the joy
> Of elevated thoughts; a sense sublime
> Of something far more deeply interfused,
> Whose dwelling is the light of setting suns,
> And the round ocean and the living air,
> And the blue sky, and in the mind of man;
> A motion and a spirit, that impels
> All thinking things, all objects of all thought,
> And rolls through all things.[123]

The really great and final function of the shaman, then, is that of representing to his people the voices of things, their masters, opening behind their mere appearances intuitions of a power unseen; so that, as the rocks and trees once spoke to *him* of that something "far more deeply interfused," *he* now speaks to his tribe of that *mysterium tremendum et fascinans* which

has become so evidently the substance of his life that, even through the influence of his relics, it is able to sublimify theirs.

The living universe of the Chukchi is composed of planes both above and below the earth—variously, two, three, or four above, with equal numbers below. These planes are connected by a vertical succession of holes, culminating at the Pole Star. Through these the souls of the dead and spirits of shamans pass from one world to the next. Or one may ascend on a rainbow, on a ray of the sun, or in the smoke of one's funeral pyre; and there is also an alternate way, an exceedingly steep path toward the dawn. Some of these worlds have as many as eight suns. Game, when scarce on the earth, is abundant there, and when abundant here, is scarce there. The lowest plane is occupied by souls that have died twice; which is to say, are not only dead, but forgotten: these will never be reborn. There is a world in every direction of the compass (of which there are twenty-two); there is another under water; and on distant constellations there are those to which the clouds are the station stops.[124]

The power that pervades and sustains all this is imprecisely personified and variously named. Bogoras writes of it as similar to the *manitou* of the Algonquians and *wakanda* of the Sioux. It may be referred to as the Creator, the Zenith, Midday, and the Dawn; addressed in prayer as the Upper Being and the Outer One; known further as the Merciful Being, the Life-giving Being, and the Luck-bringing Being; it is also the Reindeer Being who looks after

the herds. This power is specifically connected with the amulets and the images by which specific herds are protected. Also, in its character of the Luck-bringing Being, it may be represented as a raven—and here we see connections, on the one hand westward, to the seven raven-headed sons of the Old Man on High in the Yakut legend, and on the other hand eastward, to the mythological Raven of the tribes of the American North Pacific Coast.[125]

Big Raven, among the Koryak, both is and is not the Creator; for when the Creator becomes Big Raven by putting on his raven coat, he is then subordinate to himself as the Supreme Being. Moreover, there is a folktale character, the bird raven, known as Raven Man, or Raven, who, as Jochelson describes him, is "a droll and contemptible personage, who feeds on dog carcasses and excrement, and has nothing to do with the cult."[126] We remember here the ambiguity of Mantis in Bushman folktales.

Jochelson has discussed in detail the similarities in myth and custom of the Koryak and American Indian tribes—not only the nearby peoples of the North Pacific Coast, but also those of the interior: Athapascans, Algonquians, and even Iroquois. As he remarks:

"Nothing points so plainly to a very ancient connection between the Koryak and Indian mythologies as the similarity of the elements of which they are composed; for while some of the religous customs and ceremonies may have been borrowed in recent times, the myths reflect, for a very long time and very tenaciously, the state of mind of the people of the remotest periods. . . . We find in the Koryak myths elements of the raven cycle of the Tlingit, Haida, and Tsimshian; those of the cycle of tales about Mink of the Kwakiutl and neighboring tribes; of myths about wandering culture-heroes, totem-ancestors; and of tales about animals current among tribes of British Columbia; also myths of the Athapascan of the interior, and the Algonquin and Iroquois east of the Rocky Mountains."[127]

308. A Koryak shaman with his congregation and the great single-headed drum to the sound of which his spirit flies. Dwelling in a region with a population of one person per ten square kilometers, this little company represents a considerable piece of the northern part of Kamchatka. The landscape is rugged, the climate severe, vegetation consists of tundra or thin birch forest, and the principal occupations today are fishing—mostly for crab—fur hunting and reindeer herding.

Myths and Tales of the North Pacific and Arctic

Folktales of the Maritime and Reindeer Koryak

Already by the end of the last century, the old myths of the Paleo-Siberians—the Yukaghir and the Chukchi, the Koryak and the Kamchadals—had disappeared, little more remaining than ill-told, fragmented folktales. Yet something of a long-forgotten mythological base can be discerned even through these. Moreover, analogous tales among the Eskimo and, more especially, the Indian tribes of the American North Pacific Coast, point back to a shared heritage—possibly from old Beringland—with elements also evident from the very much later East Asian, Neolithic, Bronze and Iron Ages. Recounted here for comparison are Koryak tales collected in 1900 and 1901, Eskimo stories from as far east as Greenland, and Raven episodes from the Indian tribes of the American North Pacific Coast.

Grass Woman's Abduction and Rescue

In this tale from the remotest northeast corner of Eurasia, it is difficult not to suspect a reflex of the distant Eleusinian legend of the wheat-goddess Persephone (here known as Grass Woman), who was abducted to the Underworld by the Lord of the Abyss, Hades (here appearing as Triton Man). But whatever the explanation may be, the Neolithic vegetation myth has in this story become incorporated in the context of an earlier, Paleolithic, shamanic tradition, centering on an ambiguous Creator and Trickster, known as Raven. As in Koryak folklore generally, so here, this figure is represented in two distinct, yet somehow related, characters: (1) Big Raven, who in Koryak tales represents primarily the "creator" aspect of the mythic being, and who, as "ancestor" of the Koryak, is known as Big Grandfather, Outer One, World, and Creator, and plays (or once played) an important part in religious observances; and (2) Raven Man, who represents primarily the Trickster aspect of the mythic being and is a more distinctly popular, inferior personification of the actual bird, the raven, represented as a greedy, droll, and contemptible, yet clever, magician. In the following folktale, he is shown to be a serviceable shaman, as well.

"Let us go to Big Raven," Gull Man said, "and serve for his two daughters." Raven Man agreed. And when they had served for some time, Big Raven said to Miti, his wife, "What shall we do? Shall we give them our daughters?" Miti consented, and so, Gull Man married Chanái-nyáut, and Raven Man, Yinyé-a-nyéut. Then Big Raven's son, Ememqut, said, "I, too, shall serve for a wife." And he went to the house of Root Man, whom he found at work making snowshoes.

Root Man looked up. "Oh, here's a visitor!" he said. "Come in!" They went into the house, and though refreshments were brought out, Ememqut, impatient to announce his suit, ate very little. "I have come to serve for your daughter," he said. "All right," said Root Man, "you may stay."

The daughter's name was Grass Woman. They married and she bore a daughter. Then Ememqut told his father-in-law he would like to take his wife home, and Root Man gave them four driving-reindeer for the journey.

One day, when Grass Woman had gone to pick berries, she failed to return, and Ememqut looked everywhere. Gull Man told him that Triton Man had carried her off, and his father warned, "Don't follow her. You will be killed." "Oh, I'm not afraid to die," said Ememqut, and he set forth.

Triton Man was out with his reindeer herd when Ememqut walked into his tent, took Grass Woman by the hand, and started for home. But Triton Man immediately felt something and jumped to his feet. "How my heart flutters," he muttered. "Something has happened at home." He rushed to the tent. "Where is my wife?" he asked. "Ememqut took her," his mother replied. And he started after, overtook the couple, slew Ememqut, and carried Grass Woman back to his dwelling.

Big Raven waited long for his son, then said to his two sons-in-law." "Go out and look for your brother-in-law." They found the body and returned with it. "You must do something to revive him," Big Raven said. And Raven Man replied, "I'll try. But first you must kill a white reindeer."

Big Raven waited long for his son, then said to his two sons-in-law, "Go out and look for Raven Man ordered the meat removed and only the blood left on the hide. Then he took up a drum, and, when he had beat it several times, he poured some of the blood over Ememqut's head. The body stirred. Raven Man pressed bone marrow to the mouth. "Do you taste the sweetness of the marrow?" he asked. "No," Ememqut responded. "It tastes like wood." Raven Man returned to the drum, poured more blood over Ememqut's head, and again gave him some marrow. "Do you taste the sweetness?" "Yes!" said Ememqut. "When I shot wild reindeer and ate the marrow of their bones, it was as sweet as what I taste now." "You have completely revived," said Raven Man. "You may rise."

However, the moment Ememqut got to his feet, he said, "I must set out again for my wife." "No!" his father urged. "Triton Man will again kill you." "I don't care if he does," said Ememqut; and he made away to Triton Man's place. "Come, Grass Woman, let's go!" he said. And again the couple made off. But Triton Man was again alarmed, ran home, heard the news, overtook the two, slew Ememqut, and cut him into small pieces.

"This time you will not revive," he said; and taking hold of Grass Woman, he carried her back to his tent.

Big Raven waited long, and when Ememqut failed to return, sent his sons-in-law to find him. They came back with the body in pieces. "Well, Raven Man," said the father, "revive him!" "I don't know whether I can, but I'll try," said Raven Man. "You will have to kill two reindeer." He beat the drum, and when he had drummed for some time the pieces reunited. He again poured reindeer blood on the head and pressed bone marrow to the mouth. "It tastes like wood," said Ememqut. More drumming, another pouring of blood, and again the marrow: "Do you taste the sweetness?" "It is as delicious," came the answer, "as the marrow I used to take from the wild reindeer I killed." "You may rise," said Raven Man. "You are completely revived." And Ememqut stood up.

A third time the adventure was attempted, and a third time, Big Raven's son slain. Triton Man, this time, burned the body and flung the bones into various lakes. And Big Raven, a third time, sent his sons-in-law to the search. They found the ashes. Then Gull Man flew out over the lakes, dove into them, and, one by one, came up with Ememqut's bones.

The two returned to Big Raven, who a third time ordered his son revived. "This time, I can't," said Raven Man. "Oh, try!" Big Raven pleaded. "Well then," said Raven Man, "let four white reindeer be killed." They were killed, and he beat his drum all day and night until at last the bones reunited and covered themselves with flesh. The blood was poured and the marrow put to the mouth. "Is it sweet?" "No," came the answer, "it is like wood." Raven Man again beat the drum, poured blood, and again asked about the marrow. "It is as sweet as the marrow from the leg bones of the wild reindeer I used to kill," Ememqut said; and up he stood, hale and well.

One whole day and Ememqut did not even mention his wife. Then he asked his father, "Should I not try again?" "No!" his father said. "Better go hunting!" So, next day, Ememqut went hunting, and when he had killed a wild reindeer, he lay down to rest beneath a stone-pine bush. And he had not been resting long when he heard a voice from underground, a child's voice. "Grandma, tell me a story." "What can I tell you?" an old woman's voice replied. "I don't know any stories, unless I tell you the one about Ememqut." "Well then, tell me that one," said the child.

"Triton Man," the old woman began, "carried Ememqut's wife away, and Ememqut took her back three times; but Triton Man overtook him each time and killed him." "And how is Ememqut going to get his wife back?" the child's voice asked, and the old woman replied: "He would be able to, if I told him how."

Ememqut searched beneath the stone-pine bush and found a hole leading to a house underground. Down he went and found old Spider Woman, who lived down there with her granddaughter. She greeted him and served him food, which, however, he did not touch. He only said to her, "You just told your granddaughter that you knew how Ememqut

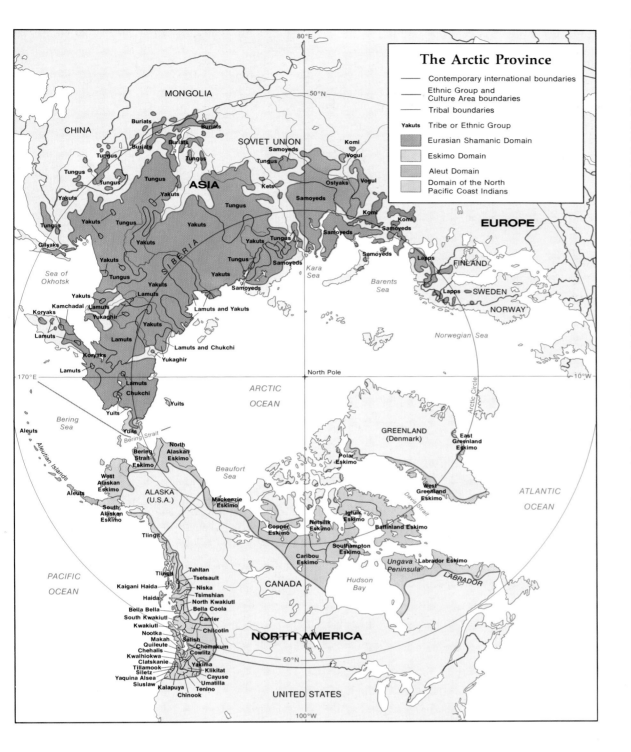

Map 39. A full circle of taiga, tundra, and ice! Culturally, the Eurasian half differs from the American in that reindeer herding is there practiced, and racially, it is more various. Animal sacrifices, like those of the Koryak to mythical beings (see **304** on page 175), are unknown in the American Arctic, since they are functions of a herding-culture stage, where the animals offered are valued possessions. Life in both halves depends on meat, however, and their fundamental festivals are petitions to the beasts. Furthermore, the shaman's drum resounds throughout, and there is everywhere an especial reverence for the bear.

The complexity of the Eurasian mixture follows from the number of its sources: first, Paleolithic Europe; next, the matrix (unidentified) from which the Paleo-Siberian races sprang; and finally, the Altai-Baikal region, whence migrants followed northward the Yenisei, Ob, and Lena valleys.

Whereas to the American Arctic there was but one gate, and as already noted (pages 34–36), after Beringland submerged there appeared in Alaska, c. 3000 B.C., a microlithic, small-tool industry, apparently of caribou hunters. By 1000 B.C. this Denbigh Flint complex had reached Greenland; and it was probably out of this base that the prehistoric Dorset Culture developed (c. 800 B.C. to A.D. 1200) in northeastern Canada and Greenland.

The Eskimo tradition emerged from a Bering Sea, seal-hunting culture, c. 500 B.C. By the first centuries A.D., Scythian influences were appearing in Ipiutak art (see pages 38–39). By A.D. 1200, this culture had reached Greenland, overlying the Dorset. In the next century the Norse arrived, and the circle was completed.

---

might get his wife back. I am Ememqut. Will you tell me?"

"Go to Triton Man's place," Spider Woman said, "but do not take your wife. First, you must open the box that stands in a corner of the tent. In that box is Triton Man's heart. Take his heart out of the box, and when you have done that, carry it away."

Ememqut gave the old woman the reindeer he had just killed, and hastened home. Big Raven was lying down, but on seeing his son, he sat up. "Why so cheerful?" he asked. "You must have heard good news." "Spider Woman," Ememqut answered, "has just told me how to get my wife back." "Then try once more," Big Raven said, and Ememqut hurried away.

When he arrived at the tent, he opened the box, took out the heart, and when he had reached home with it, built a great fire into which he threw it. The moment it began to burn, Triton Man—who again was out watching his herd—felt ill; and when the heart was completely burnt up, he died.

Then Ememqut went and brought his wife back home, after which they lived quietly with Big Raven.[128]

When Raven Man
Swallowed the Sun

In this amusing fragment of a larger tale, the negative aspect of the Trickster appears, but with a hint, also, of his cosmic role and power. In his service for a wife, he loses out to Little Bird Man, and in a pique creates a general disaster.

Raven Man and Little Bird Man went to Big Raven's place to serve for a wife. They both wanted to marry his elder daughter Yinyé-a-nyéut, but Little Bird Man won her hand. Some time later, when the couple had come to pay a visit to the bride's parents, it suddenly grew dark: someone had swallowed the sun. The second daughter, Chanái-nyáut, had a husband who claimed to be a shaman. Given a drum to beat, he tried his skill for a while and then cried, "I see! It's Raven Man! It's he who has swallowed the sun."

Yinyé-a-nyéut got up. "I'll go to him. I'll set it free," she said. She put on her reindeer-leather coat and went to Raven Man, whom she found in bed. He did not get up, but remained in silence so as not to open his mouth. Approaching, she said slyly, "I have left Little Bird Man. I have a longing for you." And, embracing him firmly, she tickled him under his arm. He laughed: his mouth opened, the sun escaped, and again there was light.[129]

Glutton, the Cannibal Giant

The character of the Glutton, the Voracious One, or Gourmandizer, takes the form in the following story of a young giant whose original identity with the Raven Trickster becomes evident in the end, when he marries Yinyé-a-nyéut, who is normally Raven Man's wife. Significant is the identification of Glutton's belly with the Underworld. Yinyé-a-nyéut's release of a multitude from this belly is a counterpart to the medieval legend of Christ's Harrowing of Hell releasing from the Devil's keep the souls of the

181

Old Testament patriarchs. It is analogous also to Yinyé-a-nyéut's release of the sun from Raven Man's mouth in the preceding tale. Or one may think of Little Red Riding Hood (the Sun-girl) released from the wolf's belly. For both in folktales and in major myths the great theme of the release of light, of life, or of innocent beings from the belly or keep of some evil power has been a universal favorite.[130]

Yinyé-a-nyéut was living alone, at that time, in the wilderness. Upstream was the young giant, Glutton, who had turned into a cannibal. He had devoured his mother, relatives, and neighbors, and was now going from village to village devouring the inhabitants. When he came to Big Raven's place, Yinyé-a-nyéut in her sleep saw him enter and eat Big Raven himself, Ememqut, and everyone else except Ememquet's wife, Grass Woman, whom he then married.

When Yinyé-a-nyéut woke, she hurried to her father's village, where there was no one; then to Glutton's place, where Grass Woman was alone. She had turned into a cannibal and threatened to kill her sister-in-law and feed her to her husband; but her intended victim contrived to extract her cannibal stomach and return her to her senses.

"What brought you here?" Grass Woman then asked. "When my husband returns, he will kill you." "Let him," said Yinyé-a-nyéut, "since he has already eaten my father, mother, and brothers!" Grass Woman hid her inside a bead, and presently Glutton was heard arriving outside, dragging a dead man on a sledge. He shouted, "Grass Woman, come out!" She went out and unloaded the sledge. "Why don't you exclaim over the catch?" he asked. "I am pleased," she replied, "but have just eaten." They hauled the body into the house and stowed it with many others. Then Glutton cut off a head to fry, and Yinyé-a-nyéut, watching from her place in the bead, saw that it was her father's.

Glutton sniffed the air. "It smells of human flesh here," he said. From within her bead Yinyé-a-nyéut whispered to Grass Woman, "Let him eat me. I'll revive all those he has killed." So Grass Woman drew her out and threw her to the cannibal, who devoured her at once.

Yinyé-a-nyéut found herself in the Underworld, with all her relatives and the others he had killed. "Hurry!" she cried. "Before the sides of the road come together!" She turned, they followed, and when Glutton, next morning, set out on his daily hunt, they all came up from underground into his house, filling it so full that the walls were pushed apart. And when Grass Woman saw among them her father and former husband, she said, "Why have you all come back? Glutton will eat you again." "Never mind!" Yinyé-a-nyéut answered. "Let him eat!"

Presently he arrived, and when he saw the multitude, he shouted, "What a lot of meat I shall have!" But Yinyé-a-nyéut walked up to him and with an iron hook pulled out his cannibal stomach, and he became sane. The people who had returned from underground departed for their homes. Glutton married Yinyé-a-nyéut, and at first would eat only once a month, but later he ate all kinds of food, as of old.[131]

How Universe the Supreme Being Makes Rain

Universe, the Koryak Supreme Being, and his wife, Rain Woman or Supervisor Woman, dwell in a heaven-village inhabited by people of the sky. Big Raven, dwelling on earth, is an aspect of this heavenly power. In the following tale, Universe and Big Raven are seen as separate; for, like the Father and Son of the Christian tradition, though theologically of "one substance," mythologically they are "two persons."

The following tale might be told to put a stop to rain or to a snowstorm. It was not to be told in fair weather.

309. Koryak shaman beating his drum. Walrus-ivory carving from the Chukchi Peninsula. Photographed reflected. Height, 2½ inches. Carried away on the sound of his drum, the shaman's spirit is said to ride on the animal whose hide has been stretched over the drum-frame. The drumstick is then his knout or whip. And lest his body, too, be carried away and possibly not return, the shaman is sometimes bound while in trance. The Northern Lights may be the flashing of shaman spirits somewhere in combat.

One time, when Big Raven was living on earth, it rained for so long that everything he owned got wet, his clothes and provisions began to rot, and his underground house filled with water. At last he said to his eldest son, Ememqut, "Universe must be doing something up there. Let us fly up and see." They went outside, put on their raven coats, and flew to Universe's place, where they heard the sound of a drum from within. It was Universe who was drumming. His wife, Rain Woman, was beside him. He had cut off her vulva and hung it on the drum; he had also cut off his own penis and was using it as a drumstick; and when he beat the drum, water poured from the vulva as rain.

When Universe saw Big Raven coming in, he hid the drum, and the rain stopped. Big Raven said to Ememqut, "The rain has stopped; we can leave." They went out, the drumming resumed, and the rain poured down as before. They returned, Universe put away his drum, and the rain stopped. Big Raven whispered to his son, "We'll pretend to go, but hide and see what they are doing." Then he said to Universe, "This time we're really going." Pretending to leave, the two turned into reindeer hairs and lay on the floor. They saw Universe ask his wife for the drum, she gave it to him, he beat it, and the rain poured as before.

Big Raven said to Ememqut, "I'm going to make them fall asleep. You watch where they put the drum and stick." Immediately, Universe and his wife fell asleep. Big Raven took the drum and stick and roasted them over the fire until they were dry and crisp, then returned them to their places and broke the sleeping spell. Universe picked up and beat the drum, but the more he beat it, the finer the weather became, until there was not a cloud in the sky. Universe and his wife then went to bed.

"Now," Big Raven said to his son, "let us really go home." The clear weather continued for days, but they had no luck in their hunting either of sea mammals or of reindeer. Everybody was starving because Universe was sleeping. "I'm going back to see what he's doing now," said Big Raven, as he again put on his raven coat and flew.

"We're now having very good weather," he told Universe when he arrived, "but everybody's starving. We can't find any game." "That's because I'm not looking after my children," Universe replied. "Go back home. From now on you'll have good hunting." Big Raven left, and when his sons thereafter went hunting, they got sea mammals and wild reindeer. Big Raven pulled from the ground the post to which his dogs were tied, and out came a whole herd of reindeer. He sacrificed many of these to Universe, and after that, he had only good luck in his hunting.[132]

Eskimo Tales

The uniformity of the Eskimo culture over its whole reach from Bering Strait to Greenland has been frequently remarked. However, a certain differentiation has also been remarked, east and west of the Mackenzie River. A linguistic distinction pertains to these areas, the Inupik dialect being spoken in the east, and the Yupik in the west. Moreover, influences from both Asia and the neighboring North American Indian tribes are significantly stronger in the west than in the east; and these find expression, as Franz Boas observed, "in a higher development of decorative art, in the occurrence of a few inventions unknown to the eastern Eskimo (such as pottery and the use of tobacco), and in religious observances, beliefs, and current tales not found in more eastern districts."[133] The tales of the following brief selection are chiefly from the eastern zone: Greenland, Baffin Land, Labrador, and Hudson Bay; the last two are from the northern slope of Alaska.

When the Earth Was Made

From a Polar Eskimo of Smith Sound, at the northernmost point of the western coast of Greenland, comes the following extraordinary recollection of an ancient cosmology. "Those who lived long before our day did not know how to store their words in little black marks, as you do," Rasmussen was told by the narrator. "They could only tell stories. And they told many things, and therefore we are not without knowledge of these things, which we have heard told many and many a time, since we were little children."[134]

A long, long time ago, when the earth was to be made, it dropped from the sky; earth, hills, and stones came down and thus the earth was made.

And when the earth had been made, came men. It is said that they came from the earth. From among the willow bushes, out of the ground came little children all covered with willow leaves, and there they lay among the bushes, lay and kicked, for they could not even crawl. And they got their food from the earth.

Then there is something told about a man and a woman: something not clearly known. When did they find each other? Where had they grown up? The woman sewed, made children's clothes, wandered forth and found the little ones, dressed them, and brought them home. And in this way men became many.

Being many, they desired dogs. So a man with a dog leash in hand stamped on the ground crying "Hok—hok—hok!" And the dogs came hurrying, each from its tiny mound, and violently shook themselves. For their coats were full of sand.

In those days, a long, long time ago, nothing was known of death. Children were born and grew to be old; and they were increasingly many on the earth, until at last they could neither walk nor lie down. They went blind. Nor did they know the sun: they lived in the dark. There was light only inside their houses, where they burned water in their lamps; for in those days water would burn.

Then there came from the sea a mighty flood. Many were drowned, and men became fewer. The marks of that flood can still be seen on the high hilltops, where mussel shells are found. And when men had thus become fewer, two old women debated: "Better to be without day," said one, "if thus we may be without death." "No," said the other, "let us have both light and death." And as she spoke, it was so: light came, and death.

It is said that when the first man died, others covered the body with stones, but the body, not rightly knowing how to die, tried to come back. It stuck out its head and tried to get up, but an old woman thrust it back, saying: "We have much to carry and our sleds are small." For the people were about to set out on a hunting journey. Having got light, they were able to go on journeys and to hunt. They had no longer to eat of the earth. And with death came also the sun, the moon, and stars; for when men die, they ascend to the sky and become brightly shining things up there.[135]

Sun Sister and Moon Brother

The action of these Eskimo tales is not assigned to the timeless Dream Time of a true Mythological Age, but, to quote again Franz Boas: "The general conditions of life supposed to prevail at the time of the story are the same as the conditions of life at the present time."[136] This fact results in such incongruities as those in the following tale, where, before there were sun and moon, there were already daylight and night. Likewise, in tales such as "The Old Woman, Sedna, of the Sea," where seals and whales are produced from Sedna's finger joints, they are not the first of their kind. As Boas states of these legends, "The animals created are rather individuals than the first of their species."[137] The version here reproduced of the Sun Sister and Moon Brother adventure is from the Central Eskimos of Baffin Land and Hudson Bay; it was published in 1888 by Franz Boas.

A brother and sister lived in a large village in which there was a big singing house where the sister and her friends went every night to enjoy themselves. One time, when the lights had been extinguished, a youth approached unseen and made love to her. This then happened several evenings, until finally she decided to find out who her unseen lover was. In the soot of the fire she blackened the palms of her hands and that night, when receiving his embrace, left the mark of her palms on his back. When the lamps were again lighted, she was appalled to see that he was her brother. She cut off her breasts and flung them at him with the words, "Since you relish me, eat these." She then fled from his pursuit about the room, and as they ran they were elevated to the sky. She became the sun, he the moon, with her black handprints still upon him. Occasionally he catches her, and then there is an eclipse.[138]

The Old Woman, Sedna, of the Sea

"Evidently," remarked Boas in 1888, "this tale is known to all the tribes from Greenland westward to Alaska, since fragments have been recorded in many places."[139] Robert F. Spencer, on the other hand, in northern Alaska some seventy years later (1959), found that "no ramifications of this myth, or the tale in any form of the goddess of the sea could be tracked down in the area."[140] W. Bogoras, among the Paleo-Siberian Chukchi in c. 1900, found a counterpart of the Eskimo Sedna in a sea-goddess known as Mother of the Walrus. She was supposed to have had two walrus tusks originally, but one had been recently broken, and this had so incensed her that she had thereafter reduced the game supply. When the second tusk is broken, all game will disappear from the surface of the earth. (There was also a Chukchi Reindeer Master with one eye closed, who had diminished the reindeer supply. When the other eye closes, the reindeer will disappear.) Bogoras discovered, among these people, the legend of a girl who was tossed overboard and whose fingers were chopped off; but she was not identified by the Chukchi with their Walrus Mother, as she is identified in the Eskimo legend with Sedna.[141] There was thus, at one time, a continuous province of the mythology of this sea-goddess extending from the Chukchi Peninsula to Greenland. She is known in Greenland as the Food Dish. And that she was once present in Alaska we know from a report published in 1886.[142] Her disappearance from the Barrow area, therefore, may be due to the success there of the Presbyterian mission, which has completely broken the power of her attendants, the local shamans, the last of whom died in 1939.[143] The folklore of the area now has the character, rather, of wonder-tales told for entertainment during the long winter night, than of myth.[144]

The best-known version of the legend of this old sea-goddess features a refusal-of-suitors motif. In folk traditions generally, and in those of North America especially, such a refusal of suitors is followed inevitably by a supernatural courtship.

Sedna, beautiful and proud, lived alone with her widowed father on a solitary Arctic shore and spurned every suitor who came to her. One springtime day, therefore, at the time of the breaking of the ice, a fulmar [an Arctic sort of seagull] came flying over the ice floes with a flattering song that seduced her. "Oh, come with me to the land of birds, where there is never hunger. My tent is made of the most beautiful skins. Your lamp will always be filled with oil, your pot with meat, you will rest on the softest bearskins, and my comrades will clothe you warmly with their feathers." She could not resist, and joined him in flight over the ice floes. His tent, however, was of broken fishskins, his bed of walrus hides; and there was no pot of meat, only miserable fish from the beaks of birds.

"Oh my father," Sedna sang, "if you knew my sorrow, you would take me away in your boat!"

Next spring, her father arrived in his boat, and when he saw the condition of his daughter, he killed the fulmar, took her aboard, and paddled for home. However, the fulmars very soon discovered their comrade slain and cried in mourning as they have been crying ever since. Then they flew, still crying, in pursuit of the fleeing couple, and conjured up such a terrible storm that the father and daughter in the tossing boat were in danger of their lives. And it was then that the ugly miracle occurred which transformed those two into underworld powers.

The father, in terror, to appease his pursuers, threw his daughter overboard, but she clung to the edge of the boat. He chopped off the first joints of her fingers, which fell into the sea and became whales. He chopped off the second joints, which fell into the sea and became seals. She continued to cling, so he chopped off her hands, which fell into the sea and became ground seals. The storm then subsided, for the fulmars thought she had drowned. And the father took his daughter back into the boat.

But she now bore him such resentment that when they had landed home and he had fallen asleep, she called her dogs, and they gnawed off his feet and hands. Waking in a fury, he so roundly cursed his daughter, and himself, that the earth opened and swallowed the hut, daughter, father, dogs, and all. And they have lived ever since in the place down there called Adlivun.[145]

Sedna sits in her dwelling, alone in front of a lamp beneath which is a vessel to receive the oil that continually flows from it. And it is either from this vessel or from the dark interior of her house that she sends forth the animals of the hunt. When angry, however, she withholds them and people starve. The Greenland Eskimos ascribe her anger to a plague of filthy parasites that fasten themselves to her head and are called by a name that means "abortions" or "dead-born children." As these accumulate, she becomes wrathful and withholds her herds, at which time it becomes the task of the *angakok*, the shaman, to go down to her and relieve her of her pain.

The Eskimos' earth plane of land and sea rests, like a vast table, upon four pillars. Above is the solid vault of the sky, revolving around a pivotal high mountain in the farthest north. Above the sky there is a land of mountains, valleys, and lakes, and below the earth another such land, which can be entered either by way of the sea or through certain mountain clefts. The shaman going to meet Sedna will first have his body tied with thongs. He then invokes his guardian spirits and his soul departs. The perils of the way are: first, a

passage through the region of the happy dead; next, the crossing of an abyss on the flat of an ever-turning wheel, as slippery as ice; next, a boiling kettle full of ferocious seals; and, at the entrance to the Old Woman's house itself, the seals and dogs by which it is guarded. Beyond these there is the crossing of a second gorge on a bridge as narrow as the edge of a knife. Other dangers are a large burning lamp, two rocks that strike together, and a pelvis bone. The task of the shaman, finally, on arrival, is to free the Old Woman's head of the unconfessed abortions that infest it and are the whole occasion of her anger.[146]

The Fox Wife

From the Eskimo of the Ungava district, Labrador, comes the following folktale, recorded in the 1890s, which is of a type known to scholarship as the Mysterious Housekeeper: Men find their house mysteriously put in order and discover that it is done by a girl, frequently an animal transformed into a girl.[147] The plot and action are certainly not of Eskimo invention, but originally from Asia—possibly Southeast Asia or Indonesia. Variants are distributed through Europe and Africa, as well as through both North and South America. There is a charming Japanese version, "The Crane's Wife," which the playwright Junji Kinoshita has turned into a popular children's theater piece, *The Twilight Crane*.[148]

A hunter, returning to his lodge, found it nicely put in order, as it would have been if he had had a wife. A hot meal was ready to be eaten. His leather clothing and boots had been cleaned and hung out to dry. Yet there were no tracks or signs to suggest who might have done these things. The next day, likewise, and so, too, the next; until the hunter determined to learn by ruse who this was that was being so attentive to his needs. He went out, as though as usual to go hunting, but circled back and hid in the brush within sight of the entrance to his lodge.

Presently there came a fox that trotted in through the entrance, in quest—he suspected—of food. When it did not reappear, he cautiously approached the lodge and, on en-

tering, saw a very beautiful young woman, dressed in skin clothing of wondrous make, and the skin of a fox hanging on a line. The man's entrance startled her, and he asked if it was she who had done these kind things, the past days. She replied that she was his wife and that to do these things was her duty; she only hoped that they had been done as he would have wished.

She then remained with him, and when they had lived together a number of days, the man detected a musty odor about the lodge and asked what it might be. She replied that the odor was hers and that if he was going to find fault with her because of it, she would leave. Throwing off her clothing, she resumed her fox-skin, slipped quietly away, and has never served any man since.[149]

The Wild Goose Wife

From the northwesternmost corner of Greenland, Smith Sound, some 900 miles from the North Pole, there comes this classic rendition (though with an ugly ending) of the folktale of the Swan Maidens: A man sees on a lake some geese who have taken off their feathers and become women. He steals the feathers of one, and the rest fly away as geese. She remains and marries him, but one day finds her feathers when she and her children fly away as geese.[150] Like the Fox Wife tale, this is not an invention of the Eskimo, but an importation from Asia—possibly first known in Central Asia. In the Arabian *Thousand Nights and One Night*, there are two fine examples: "The Story of Janshah" (Tale 131 b) and "Hassan of Bassora and the King's Daughter of the Jinn" (Tale 155). It is the fairytale of Tchaikovsky's popular ballet, *Swan Lake*, and in medieval India, it provided the inspiration for the episode of the trickster hero Krishna's stealing the Gopis' clothes.

A hunter once came to a lake upon which a

number of wild geese had descended. They removed their feather garments, and became young women bathing. Approaching stealthily, he gathered up the feather cloaks and hid, so that when the bathers came ashore they were dismayed. He then returned all the cloaks but one, whose owner, when the others had flown, became his wife.

They lived together some years, and she bore two children. But when her husband was away one day, she found some wings which she hid among the skin coverings of the walls, and when he was next away, she put these on herself and her two children and together, away they flew.

They were already far away, when the husband, returning, realized what had happened and decided to follow and recover them. He walked along the beach, and when he had walked for many days, saw before him a large man chopping with an axe and making of the great chips that flew walruses and seals. The man listened to his story and proposed to take him in his boat to the land of birds, but with the warning to keep his eyes shut all the way. There were times when he greatly wanted to look, but he was warned and reminded constantly, until finally they landed on a shore.

It was the children who first saw him coming. They ran and told their mother, who was incredulous, for they had flown, she thought, much too far for him ever to reach them. She refused to come out to see him, and when he walked into her tent, she feigned death. He took her out, buried her, covered the grave with stones, went back into the tent, and pulled down his hood in mourning. However, his wife, alive, broke out of the grave, strode into the tent, and began pacing about, when he took up his spear and killed her. A great many geese came down around him, and he killed them. But his two boys, meanwhile, had fled.[151]

The Raven Who Wanted a Wife

This piece and the two that follow are from the Old North Pacific Raven Cycle. In the first, from Upernavik in northern Greenland, the Trickster appears in his inferior character as the impudent, greedy bird, very like Raven Man of the Koryak; whereas, in the following two pieces, from Barrow, Alaska, he is in human form but with a raven's beak, like the Paleo-Siberian Big Raven in his higher role of the Creator—or more precisely, not the Creator, but the World Transformer, since the world was already in being when he arrived to reshape it. Noteworthy in these tales are: the virgin-birth motif; conception through the mouth; the origin of light (that is, of daylight-consciousness) through the accident of an infant's play; and the use of a spear to fix the earth upon the cosmic waters, this last being a motif prominent in the early Japanese cosmogony of the *Kojiki*.

A little sparrow was mourning for her lost husband, of whom she was very fond, for he caught worms for her. And as she sat there weeping, a raven came up to her and asked,

311. In western Alaska, an Eskimo grandfather teaches cat's cradle figures to his granddaughter. Compare the young Bushman girl exhibiting a cradle (**181** on page 101), as well as the Australian example (**244** on page 139).

"Why are you weeping?" "I am weeping for my lost husband. I was fond of him because he caught worms for me," said the sparrow. And the raven said, "One who can hop over high blades of grass should not be weeping. Take me for a husband. I have a fine high forehead, broad temples, a long beard, and a big beak. You will sleep under my wings and I shall give you lovely offal to eat." "I will not take you for my husband," she said, "for you have a high forehead, broad temples, a long beard, a big beak, and will give me offal to eat." So the raven flew away.

He went to seek a wife among the wild geese. He was so lovesick that he could not sleep. But when he came to the wild geese, they were about to fly off to other lands. The raven said to two of them, "Seeing that a miserable sparrow has refused me, I will have you." "We are just about to fly away," said the geese. "I'll go too," said the raven. "But consider," they warned. "No one can go with us who cannot swim on the surface of the sea; for along the way we go there are no icebergs." "That's nothing," said the raven. "I shall sail through the air." And the wild geese flew away, the raven with them.

Very soon the raven felt himself sinking from weariness and lack of sleep. "Something to rest on!" he cried, gasping; and to his two wives, "Sit on the water, side by side!" They did so, while their comrades flew on. The raven settled down on them and fell asleep. But they saw the other geese flying farther and farther away, and so dropped that raven into the water, and flew off. "Something to rest on!" the raven again gasped, as he met the water, sank to the bottom, and drowned. After a while his body broke into little pieces, and his soul turned into those little black mollusks that are known as "sea ravens."[152]

In the Beginning: Two Tales

In the beginning there was only darkness and a woman living with her father at the edge of the sea. She went out one time to get water, and, while scraping snow together, saw a feather floating toward her from the sea. She opened her mouth, it floated in, she swallowed it, and became pregnant. When the baby was born, it had a raven's beak, and the woman tried to find toys for it. There was a blown-up bladder hanging in her father's house, and the child, whose name was Raven, continually pointed at it and cried for it. At last she took it down and let him have it; but in playing, he broke it, and immediately there was light. When the father came home, he scolded. But Raven had disappeared.[153]

Men say that the world was made by Raven. He is a man with a raven's beak. When the ground came up from the water it was drawn up by Raven. He speared down into it, brought up the land, and fixed it into place.

The first land was a plot of ground hardly bigger than a house. There was a family in a house there: a man, his wife, and their little son. This boy was Raven. One day he saw a sort of bladder hanging over his parents' bed. He begged his father for it, again and again, but his father always said, "No!" until finally, he gave in. While playing, Raven broke the bladder, and light appeared. "We had better have night too," said the father, "not just daylight all the time." So he grabbed the bladder before the little boy could damage it further. And that is how day and night began.

Now the father had a kayak. "There is more land far away," he said, and Raven asked to be allowed to go there. At first his father said, "No!" but then agreed to let him go. The boy paddled a long time, and finally came to a place in the sea where there was land bobbing up and down on the water. It would rise and then sink. He was afraid and slowed up. As he watched, the land rose, then sank, then rose again. He had his spear in the kayak, and when the land again came up, he speared and held it fast with the lead rope. This secured it, and getting out of his kayak, he walked around upon its surface. The place where that was done is to this day called Umiat, "the landing place" [Colville River, 69° 30'N, 152° 16'W]. After the land had become fixed, the sea began to move away and there was dry ground all around. So it was because of Raven that people are now able to live in this world.[154]

185

The Great Kwakiutl Shaman Named Fool

I am a hunter of all kinds of animals, always paddling about for seals, which are what I want most; for I try out the oil from the blubber and sell it to my tribe for gravy. I have always killed lots of hair seals and so have never been poor. I used to be the principal doubter of shamans: what they said about curing the sick and about seeing people's souls. I would tell them out loud, they were lying. I would be sitting with those beating time for their curing ceremonies, and those shamans really hated me.

Well, I was out paddling for seals, one fine day, with the brave fellow named Leelameedenole who always served as my helmsman. Nothing ever frightened him, neither gales nor vicious animals, dangerous fish, or the sea monsters that we frequently see when hunting at night. That is why we have to have courageous fellows for our steersmen. I was paddling along at Axolis, when I saw a wolf sitting on a rock, scratching with both paws the two sides of his mouth. He whined as we approached and was not afraid of us; not even when I got out of my small traveling canoe and went to where he sat. He whined and I noticed that his mouth was bleeding. I looked in and saw a deer bone stuck crosswise between his teeth on both sides, very firmly. He was evidently expecting me to do something: either to kill him or to help him out of his trouble. So I said to him, "Friend, you are in trouble and I am going to cure you, like a great shaman—for which I expect you to reward me with the power to get easily everything I want, the way you do. Now you just sit still here while I fix up something to help me get rid of that bone." I went inland and picked up some twigs from a cedar tree which I twisted into a string, and when I returned the wolf was still sitting there on the rock with his mouth open. I took hold of the back of his head and put the string, thin end, into his mouth, tied it to the middle of the bone and pulled. Out came the bone. The wolf only sat staring at me. "Friend," I said, "your trouble is ended. Now don't forget to reward me for what I have just done for you."

When I had said that the wolf turned around to the right and trotted off—not fast. And he had gone only a little way when he stopped, turned his muzzle to me and howled—just once. He howled and went into the woods. I stepped into my small canoe and paddled away with my steersman. Neither of us spoke of the wolf. We paddled and anchored in a cove where no wind ever blows, called Foam-Receptacle; lay down in our small canoe, and our eyes immediately closed in sleep; for we had risen before daybreak and were very tired.

315. Wooden dance hat bearing the features of a wolf. Haida(?) The tower, composed of eight potlatch rings representing so many potlatches, contains sacred white eagle down, which is thrown out during the dance by quick head movements of the performer.

And I dreamed, that night, of a man who came and spoke to me, saying, "Why did you stop here? Friend, this island is full of seals. I am Harpooner-Body, on whom you took pity today, and I am now rewarding you for your kindness, friend. From now on there will be nothing you want that you will not obtain. But for the next four years you must not sleep with your wife." I woke and called to my steersman. He rose and pulled up the anchor. We went ashore, where I washed in the sea and stepped back into the canoe, eager to see whether, as Harpooner-Body had said in my dream, there were actually a lot of seals on the rocks of the island. For I did not believe in dreams, or in shamans, or in any of the beliefs of my people; but only in my own mind. We paddled out before dawn and approached the rocky, treeless shore, which I beheld covered with seals, all tight asleep. I took my yew-wood seal club, stepped ashore and clubbed four big ones, while the rest tumbled off into the water. I put the four aboard, and we traveled home.

So now there was at least one thing in which I believed, namely the truth of Harpooner-Body's words, delivered to me in dream. And from that time on it was easy for me, when out hunting, to get seals and every other kind of game.

Two years later, in the summer of 1871, I went to Victoria with my three nephews, my wife, and their wives and children. Returning home in our large traveling canoe, we came to Rock Bay, on the north side of Seymour Narrows, and went ashore there. Stepping out of the canoe, my eldest nephew saw four nice boxes on the beach, full of very nice clothing, two bags of flour, and all kinds of food. We could see no one around who might own those things and so, carried them aboard and moved on. When we came to Beaver Cove, a northeast wind sprang up and we stayed there for six days. It was then ten days after

we had found the box, and my whole company was now sick. In the morning we set off: it was calm. And when we arrived at Axolis we unloaded our cargo—all of us sick with the great smallpox, which had been contracted when we picked up the boxes. We all lay in bed in our tent. I saw that our bodies had swelled and were a dark red. I did not realize that the others were dead, but presently thought that I was dead. I was sleeping; but then woke because of all the wolves that were coming, whining and howling. Two were licking my body, vomiting up foam, trying hard to put it all over me; and they were rough when they turned me over. I could feel myself getting stronger, both in body and in mind. The two kept licking, and after they had licked off all that they had vomited, they vomited again; and when, again, they had licked this off, I saw that they had taken off all the scabs and sores. And it was only then that I realized that I was lying there among the dead.

Evening fell and the two wolves rested. I must have become afraid, being the only one alive there; for I crawled away, to the shelter of a thick spruce, where I lay all night. With no bedding and only the shirt I had on, I was cold. The two wolves approached and lay down on each side of me, and when morning came, got up and again licked me all over, vomiting up white foam and licking it off. I was getting stronger, and when strong enough to stand, I realized that one of those two wolves was the one from whose mouth I had taken the bone. All the others had remained in attendance too. And I now was, in fact, quite well. I lay down, and there came to me the figure that in my dream, in the place called Foam Receptacle, had told me that his name was Harpooner-Body. He sat down seaward of me and nudged me with his nose until I responded by lying on my back, whereupon he vomited foam and pressed his nose against the lower end of my sternum. He was vomiting magic power into me, and when he had finished he sat back. I became sleepy and dreamed of the wolf that was still at my side. In the dream he became a man, who laughed and said, "Now, friend, take care of this shaman power that has gone into you. From now on you will cure the sick, you will catch the souls of the sick, and you will be able to throw sickness into anyone in your tribe, who you wish should die. They will all now be afraid of you." That is what he said to me in my dream.

I woke and was trembling, and my mind, since then, has been different. All the wolves had left me, and I was now a shaman. I walked the way to Fern Point, where I remained alone for a long time in one of the seven abandoned houses there. On the way I met a man whom I told of the deaths of my whole crew, and he left me in fear and hurried home. I was not

depressed, but just kept singing my sacred songs, evening after evening, the four songs of the wolf. For I was just like someone drunk, completely happy, all the time. And I stayed there, at Fern Point, for more than the period of one moon.

A passing canoe-man heard my song, one evening, and spoke of it to the people at Teeguxtee; who immediately decided to invite the new shaman whose song had been heard to come and cure their sick chief, whose name was Causing-to-Be-Well. Meanwhile, the wolf had again appeared in my dream, warning me to make ready for the chief, who was indeed seriously ill. "You must suck out his sickness and fling it upward," he said to me in that dream. "When you are treating him do not apply your mouth more than four times." I woke and at once my body and stomach began to tremble. I sang my sacred song, and continued till late in the day, when I heard a number of men outside my house, talking. One whose name was Endeavoring-to-Invite said, "We have come to ask you, great treasured one, to have pity and to restore life with your water of life to our friend, our chief, Causing-to-Be-

Well." They all got into their big traveling canoe, while Endeavoring-to-Invite, coming into my house, begged me to join them: which I did, and we proceeded to Teeguxtee.

When we arrived at the beach before Causing-to-Be-Well's house, not I, but the others, stepped ashore and, entering the building, built a fire in the middle of it, and, when it had been lighted, four shamans came out and summoned everybody to come in—men, women, and children—to watch the new shaman. They then came and called me, still sitting in the big canoe. I rose and walked with the four of them into the house, where the song leaders were already beating time for me. And there I saw, in the rear of the house, Causing-to-Be-Well, sitting on a mat. The rhythm of the beating quickened as I entered, the beating of the batons on the boards. My body and my belly started to tremble, and, standing in the doorway together with the four shamans, I sang my sacred song. Then I went to where Causing-to-Be-Well was sitting, the four shamans following, and I treated him as instructed by the wolf. And I have now, as my shaman name, the name Fool.[160]

316. Regalia and mask of a Tsimshian shaman arriving to cure a patient. To warn of his approach, he taps the ground with his carved staff. Hanging from his beaded necklace is a carved ivory soul-catcher; his crown is of twenty-two grizzly-bear claws; and with the rattle in his left hand he will accompany the hum of his curing song, which, as the curing spirits begin to appear (visible only to himself) will gradually grow louder. A helper (often the shaman's wife) will be beating a large box drum to the rhythm of the shaken rattle. And the song sung will be something like the following:

O Supernatural Power, I beg you to take pity and to cure this our friend.
O Supernatural Power, I implore you, take pity and remove this sickness of our friend.
Take pity, O Supernatural Power, that I may make this friend of ours to live again.
O Great Real Supernatural Power, Great Life-Bringer, Supernatural Power,
Help me to remove easily this sickness of our friend.

The payments to shamans for this kind of work are serious. According to Franz Boas, they include canoes, chilkat blankets, sea otters, slaves, houses, and the daughters of chiefs. The goods accumulate during the course of the cure as inducing payments to the spirits; but in the end, of course, they are carried away by the shaman.[17]

NORTH AMERICAN TWILIGHT OF THE PALEOLITHIC GREAT HUNT

317. The calumet is held, stem to sky, so that the One Above may be the first to smoke. Then the Indian will himself send puffs in reverence to the four directions. His tobacco is an incense; his medicine pipe, an altar. The buffalo skull at his feet is a relic and sign of the necessary sacrifice of life to life and, in this regard, a token of the mysterious covenant of man and nature. Between its horns two decorated eagle feathers have been laid in symbolic offering: they are white and black, as in life and death all things are two. Consider Letakots-Lesa's feathers (**319**). That on his right is male; on his left, female. And each is two, half light, half dark; daylight and darkness, summer and winter. Man himself is two: two eyes, ears, nostrils, hands, and feet: one for man, one for woman. Or stand in the sun and—behold!—body and shadow, body and spirit.

The Idea and Ideas of God

On the banks of the Orinoco c. 1795, Alexander von Humboldt met a missionary who reported that a local jungle native had once said to him: "Your God keeps himself shut up in a house, as if he were old and infirm; ours is in the forest, in the fields, and on the mountains of Sipapu, whence the rains come."[161]

319. Letakots-Lesa. His otter-skin bonnet connotes wisdom; his necklace, the bear's virtue. His feathers are two: male and female, sun and moon.[19]

318. Rabbit-man, rock painting at Lake Mazinaw, Ontario. On vertical rock walls along the numerous waterways of this Canadian province, from Lake Mazinaw (north of Belleville) to the Manitoba border, more than 1000 petroglyphs have been recorded from approximately 100 sites. They were produced, apparently, by Algonquians of about the sixteenth century A.D. Most could have been painted only from the artist's bark canoe, at varying water levels. A paint of red earth (ferrous oxide) predominates, though white and black also occur, and the figures are of deer, caribou, rabbits, heron, trout, animal tracks, hand prints, canoes, and various mythic beings. The rabbit-man from Lake Mazinaw is undoubtedly an apparition of the Algonquian trickster hero, Nanabozho, the Great Hare.[18]

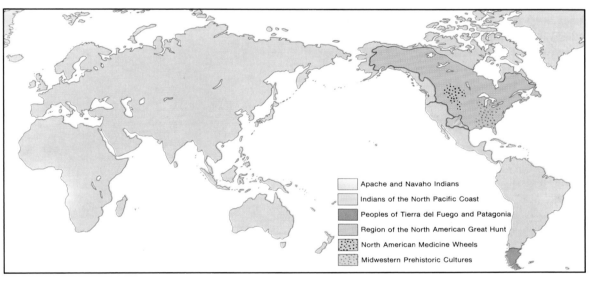

Apache and Navaho Indians
Indians of the North Pacific Coast
Peoples of Tierra del Fuego and Patagonia
Region of the North American Great Hunt
North American Medicine Wheels
Midwestern Prehistoric Cultures

Map 40.

Indians of the higher civilizations of America also recognized divinity as immanent in all things. The Aztecs of Tenochtitlan (old Mexico City), for example, as Richard Frazer Townsend has observed, "saw the relationship between their city and its natural environment as an integrated cosmological structure—an ordered universe within which the natural phenomena were regarded as intrinsically sacred, alive, and intimately related to the activities of man. This outlook contrasted with that of the Europeans, who saw cities as artifacts of civilization—places where religious and legal institutions sharply distinguished man's identity from that of untamed nature. The Spanish friars and soldiers automatically placed themselves as human beings on a higher level than other forms of life in a hierarchy of Creation. But the Indian approached the phenomena of nature with a sense of participation: the universe was seen as reflections of relationships between life forces, and every aspect of life was part of an interpenetrating cosmic system."[162]

The words of the Pawnee chieftain, Letakots-Lesa, already cited at the opening of this volume (page 8), are of the same mythic tone: "Tirawa spoke to man through his works." Not through any special, privileged revelation, but universally! Nor is only man made in the image of God: so, too, are the jaguar, buffalo, bear, eagle and serpent, butterflies, trees, rivers and mountains. For "All things speak of Tirawa."

This monistic philosophy is on the order of the Hindu and Chinese, in contrast to the biblical separation of nature and man.

Culture Areas of North America

— Culture Area boundaries

— Contemporary international boundaries

— Algonquian and Athabascan tribal areas

Hopi Indian tribes

Map 42.

1. *The Arctic:* Home uniquely of the Eskimo, homogeneous in its ecology, culture, mythologies, and art. The mythologies exhibit influences both from Asia (shamanic traits) and from America (animal tales), but differ from most American traditions in that they lack a Mythological Age: that is, conditions of life at the time of the beginnings were the same as they are now in the Eskimo's living present.

2. *The Northwest Coast:* A culturally isolated zone of salmon-fishing villages that is distinguished by an heraldic art based on monumental cedarwood sculpture and is motivated, like its rites and myths, by an obsession with caste and wealth.

3. *The Woodlands:* The formative zone of the whole North American development, this area comprises three distinct, yet culturally interlocked, regions:

(a) *The Northern Woodlands:* first region entered by Asian immigrants: the most recent were the Athabascans; earlier, the Algonquians; and much earlier, the ancestors of all other New World races.

(b) *The Mississippi Basin:* This region (with that of its tributaries, the Ohio, Arkansas, and Missouri) was the homeland of prehistoric builders of effigy mounds (the Adena culture, c. 500 B.C. to A.D. 100), of burial mounds (the Hopewell, c. 100 B.C. to A.D. 300), and of temple mounds (the Mississippian, c. A.D. 700 to 1600).

(c) *The Atlantic Seaboard:* once a region of advanced agricultural villages, from here tobacco and the potato were brought to England.

4. *The Plains:* An area with a history beginning in the Late Pleistocene, the period of Clovis, Sandia, and Folsom points. By c. 7500 B.C., when ice-age mammals had disappeared and climatic conditions approached those of today, a bison-hunting culture flourished here with Eastern Woodland affiliations. The equestrian "Wild West" developed only after Coronado entered the area (1540–42) and introduced the horse, sheep culture, and Catholicism.

5. *The Southwest:* From c. 5000 B.C., the terrain of a hunting-and-gathering Desert culture known as the Cochise: small family groups in search of acorns, nuts, and various seeds, roots, berries, and small game. Towards the close of the first millennium B.C., signs of settlements appeared: food-storage pits and pithouse dwellings. When pottery arrived, c. 100 B.C., the Desert culture gave way to four distinct regional developments:

(a) *The Mogollon Culture* (of southern New Mexico and Chihuahua): earliest maize, squash, and beans of the Southwest; subsequently arriving potteries were of a characteristic black-on-white ware and the graceful Mimbres designs.

(b) *The Hohokam Culture* (of southern Arizona

and Sonora): ceremonial ball courts of Maya-Aztec inspiration, carved stone bowls, and pallettes, a fine red-on-buff ware.

(c) *The Anasazi Culture* (of northern New Mexico and Arizona, southern Colorado and Utah): from c. 100 B.C., maize farming without pottery (the Basketmaker phase); from c. A.D. 700, the development of the Pueblo culture, of which the period of greatest expansion was A.D. 700 to 1300 (Mesa Verde, Canyon de Chelly, and so on). About the time of this greatest expansion, Athapascan tribes now known as the Navaho and Apache began arriving from the Canadian Northwest.

(d) *The Yuman, Patayan, or Hakatay Culture* (variously so named, along the Colorado River): poorly documented, but possibly ancestral to the Yuma tribe; maize and brown pottery from c. A.D. 600.

6. *The Far West, the Great Basin, and California:* early hearth of the Desert culture, where it persisted into historic times. Tribes of the area were the master basket weavers of the continent.

7. *Mesoamerica:* a major matrix of plant domestication and of Pre-columbian civilization.

8. *The Antilles:* formerly inhabited by Arawak and Carib tribes from South America that were exterminated in the early sixteenth century and supplanted by African slaves.

Mythologies of the North Pacific Coast

Landscape and Culture

The magnificent forests of the North Pacific Coast—the culture province defined landward by the Coast Range and extending from Yakutat Bay, Alaska, to Cape Mendocino, California—provided prodigious timber for the fashioning of totem poles, planks and beams for capacious buildings, and logs for the shaping of huge canoes, worthy of comparison with the greatest of Southeast Asia and Polynesia. Abundantly watered by its rivers from the mountains and by the warm rains carried from southern seas by the Kuroshio current, the region was rich in game, and its coastal waters, in fish. Indeed, salmon fishing was everywhere at the center of both the economic and the religious life, the fish being blessed and thanked in annual "First Salmon" cere-

327. The host of a Kwakiutl potlatch exhibiting to his guests an extremely precious "copper" that they are about to see destroyed. Hammered copper implements appeared early in North America, the richest known deposit of native copper in the world being on the Keweenaw Peninsula of northern Michigan. Tools and weapons of this material appeared in the upper Great Lakes area about 3000 B.C. in assemblages of what is known as the Old Copper Culture, which endured for about 2000 years. How or when knowledge of the metal reached the Northwest Coast, no one seems to know; but the prominence in potlatch ceremonials of such elegantly decorated, well-fashioned, hammered copper slabs as that exhibited by this chieftain testifies to a long history. One such copper—of no practical use whatsoever—would equal in value many hundred priceless Chilkat blankets.

328. Setting for a Kwakiutl potlatch at Alert Bay, Vancouver Island. The distinctive Northwest Coast institution of the potlatch was of a lavish, extremely formal, gift-giving ceremonial offered by a wealthy host to a large invited company, usually for the purpose of gaining or confirming social rank, prestige, or privileges for himself, or (alternatively) of passing on the like to his inheritors. With the increase in trade goods during the last half of the nineteenth century, a trend developed of extravagant display, with competitive challenge and face-saving aspects that led in extreme cases to the ostentatious burning of valuable objects. The fire in the foreground of the scene was for this purpose. Tales are told of incinerated grand pianos. But of traditional objects, the most valuable to be either given away or destroyed were coppers such as that of Figure 327.

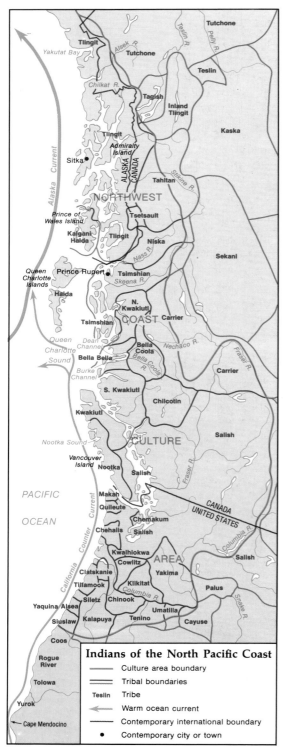

Map 43.

329. Possession by the Cannibal Spirit, which is by magic induced and by magic dispelled, is elegantly suggested in this double dance mask of the Haida, from the Queen Charlotte Islands, British Columbia.

monies dedicated to the return of their vital bones to their own villages under waves for renewal the following year. Up and down the coast, these ceremonies differed in detail, but typically included: welcoming speeches delivered to the salmon schools of the year; the cooking, blessing, and sacramental distribution of their flesh; and the performance, for their pleasure as well as for their renewal, of dances and other entertainments.

The people of this distinctive province were of a number of unrelated linguistic stocks. Brought and held together by the readily navigable waterways, however, they had come to share and elaborate a common culture, of which the typical settlement pattern was of villages, large and small, of wooden dwellings and ceremonial structures along protected beaches. The basic household consisted of a man, his wife or wives, and their children (or in the north, the man's sister's sons), and

each village was composed, typically, of a group of such nuclear families tracing descent from a common legendary ancestor, to whose legendary deeds were credited their rights to certain fishing, hunting, and berry-picking sites, as well as their claims to such intangible goods (of the greatest social and ritual importance) as family names, crests, songs, and dances.

Rank was a highly regarded value throughout this opulent region, and though reckoned according to the supposed genealogical proximity of each member of a village to the group's legendary ancestor, it was never automatically inherited, but had to be formally assumed in the lavish gift-giving ceremony known as the "potlatch." The word is from the Chinook *patshatl*, "gift" or "giving." Guests from villages far and wide were invited to a potlatch, the magnitude of the gathering being itself indicative of the host's rank. He and his kin exercised themselves to the limit in hospitality and generosity, the values of their gifts corresponding to the relative ranks of the recipients. Births, deaths, marriages, and initiations into any of the numerous secret societies of the region were standard occasions for such spectacles; but personages of great wealth, and with a taste for such affairs, might seize upon almost any incident (the first singeing of a baby's hair, for example) as an excuse.[166]

During the relatively mild winters, a number of related village groups would assemble in some well-sheltered cove for

the season of ceremonials, and it was during this festive time that the masked theatrical displays (unique on the North American continent) were presented. Judging from all accounts, they were both magnificent and terrifying; for, in not a few, the final aim was ecstasy (madness being a supernatural portent), when the chief dancer—wearing a prodigious Raven mask and dropping, perhaps, from a rafter into the middle of the performing area—might be expected finally to lose himself. Furthermore, associated with the secret-society initiations were ceremonies in which the madness could go very far indeed. Some time before such a ceremony, the candidate for initiation would be snatched away by the spirits and remained in the woods (in the keep, it was said, of the supernaturals, the powers that destroy man's reason), fasting and preparing for the demonstration of frenzy expected of him upon his return, when it would be the task of those in charge of the occasion to bring him back to secular consciousness.

Ruth Benedict in *Patterns of Culture* has devoted a major section to the review of a Kwakiutl Cannibal Society initiation. From the Paleo-Siberians we have already learned something of the nature of Cannibal Spirits (see page 184). A Kwakiutl so possessed had a passion for human flesh, bit pieces out of the spectators, and on great occasions, in the old days, even consumed portions of the bodies of slaves killed for his purpose. After such a defilement, however, he would be held tabu and kept alone in a small inner sleeping room for as long as perhaps four months, with a Bear Dancer keeping watch. On emerging, he would pretend to have forgotten how to be human, and would have to be taught to walk, to speak, and to eat. For some four more years, there would be further tabus put upon him until, at a Winter Ceremonial of a type intended for the taming of a Cannibal, he would be cured. An old man would be set out as bait to be bitten, and when the Cannibal approached to bite, he would discover himself surrounded. A woman co-initiate dancing naked before him with a corpse across her arms would be receding steadily backward, enticing him into the ceremonial building, where four priests with inherited supernatural powers for the exorcising of Cannibal Spirits took him in hand, and by means of fire, steaming water, and a smoke from cedar bark impregnated with the menstrual blood of four noble women, returned him to his senses.[167]

Cosmology

The mythic image of the universe that invisibly completes for these people the visible experience of their island-dotted waterways is best represented by an account received in the early years of this century from the Bella Coola tribe of British Columbia. These are a Salishan people from the south, now settled inland of Queen Charlotte Sound, along the lower Bella Coola River and the upper Dean and Burk channels. Their image is of a universe of five levels: two above, and two beneath the earth, those above being of the gods, those below of the dead, the earth-plane between being everywhere alive with the in-dwelling spirits of rocks and trees, watercourses, mountain peaks, and the ocean—also the Elders of the animal species. As Hartley Burr Alexander has remarked,[168] in every fire and along every trail are listening ears and watching eyes: the eyes that are so conspicuous in the Northwest Coast decorative arts. At the place of the sunrise, a great Heaven Bear stands watch. This is the warrior spirit that inspires battle frenzy. In the west, where the sun sets, a great pillar supports the sky; the Sun's way across the heaven dome is along a bridge as wide as the distance between the winter and summer solstices, at each of which turning places the Sun, as they say, "sits down." In summer he walks with his torch along the right side of this bridge; in winter, along the left. Three dancing Guardians surround him, and when he drops the torch, there is an eclipse.

The first of the two realms below the earth is of the remembered dead, who will be reborn. The second is of those forgotten, who have thus died a "second death" and passed into oblivion. The first of the heavens above is a mansion known as the House of Myths, where dwell the gods to whom prayers are addressed and of

whom the Sun is the master. But the second heaven is a windswept, treeless plain occupied by a single female presence named Qamaits. She is known also as Our Woman and as Afraid of Nothing; for, in the beginning, she waged war alone against the mountains, who had made the earth uninhabitable. She reduced them in height and now lives beyond them: not, however, quite alone; for a double-headed, horned serpent dwells behind her house in the saltwater pond in which she bathes.

The Sun, who is called the Sacred One, is also known as Our Father, since it was he, together with a goddess named Alkuntam, who generated mankind. This goddess's mother is a Cannibal who inserts her long, mosquito-like snout into people's ears and sucks away their brains. (When a Cannibal's body is burned, they say, its ashes turn into mosquitoes.) Other deities in the House of Myths include: ten who preside over the Winter Ceremonies; a flower-goddess and a cedar-bark goddess; the Sun and Alkun-

330. The idea of deceptive dual presences (animals in human guise and human beings as animals) which is so prominent in the folklore and myths, especially of peoples of the Arctic and north temperate zones is tellingly suggested in this Bella Coola grave post. For the Bella Coola, the remembered dead are not absolutely dead, but can return, reborn, so that behind the appearance of death there is life—which is again a deception. One notes that the uprights behind this mask were originally nine. Nine is the number of underworlds traversed by the dead in Maya-Aztec mythologies and may be here related to an equivalent Bella Coola mystery unknown to us.

tam's two sons, who inspire Cannibal frenzy; the Guardians who dance around the Sun as he moves across the sky; various sky-guardians and messengers; and four diligent brothers, forever carving and painting, who taught mankind the arts of hunting and fishing, canoe making, house building, box making, carving, and painting.[169]

Of greater interest than any of these, however, is the world-generating goddess Qamaits with her mysterious hidden consort. She is an altogether exceptional figure in North American mythology, and her associations appear to point to Asia, as do those—even more obviously—of the horned, double-headed demiurge in her pond. This serpent figure is known as Sisiutl to the arts and folklore of the Kwakiutl, where his representation so closely resembles the Chinese jade of Figure 320 that their kinship can hardly be doubted. Another evident association is with the Mayan "ceremonial bar."

Translated into the language of the Orient, the earth-plane of this Northwest Coast cosmology corresponds to what in India is known as the realm of the mind in its "waking state" (*jāgaritha-sthāna*), where it is outward turned, perceiving gross material objects in a field of extended space.

The first planes below and above the earth (where reside, on one hand, individuated souls and, on the other, a pantheon of anthropomorphic gods), are the matched aspects (subjective and objective) of the "dreaming or envisioning state" (*svapna-sthāna*), where the mind is inward turned, perceiving subtle luminous forms that are of the substance of the mind itself. And the second planes below and above (where, on one hand, individuated souls are dissolving into oblivion, and on the other, a primal couple is ever regenerating a universe out of an abyssal sea) are the matched aspects of a realm of "deep dreamless sleep" (*sushupta-sthāna*), into

331. Sisiutl, a Kwakiutl wood caving (see 321, page 194).

332. Photograph, taken in 1880, of the Haida village of Skidegate, Queen Charlotte Islands, British Columbia.

which all the worlds known to the mind dissolve and out of which they reappear. Covered with darkness, full of bliss, the mind there resides in itself, in wisdom, and is known as "the mask, mouth, or door, of consciousness" (*cetomukha*), since it opens both backward to the timeless ground of being and forward to the passing forms of dream and of waking.[170]

In India, the image at Elephanta of Shiva the Great Lord (see Figure 5, page 13) is symbolic of this "door." Out of its central face, which is the mouth or mask of Eternity, the pairs-of-opposites—left and right, female and male, mercy and justice—arise and proceed; back into and through it, they dissolve in death. In the Chinese ornamental jade pictured in Figure 320 (page 194), the central mask or face (known as *t'ao-t'ieh*, the "Glutton") is likewise flanked by a pair of symbolic (dragon) profiles. The pursed lips of the

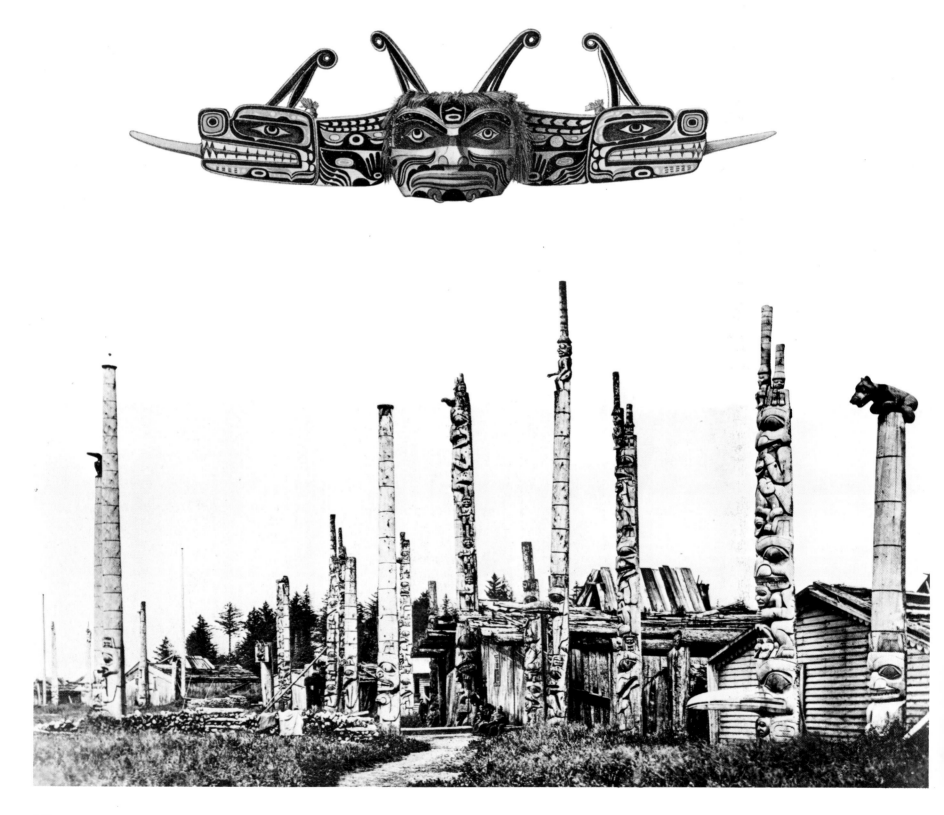

Kwakiutl cannibal ogress Tsonoqua (Figure 333) represent that door in its negative aspect, breathing out and inhaling death. And the central visage of the Sisiutl is symbolically of the same door, but dual in that it breathes both death and life. So that in the Bella Coola cosmological image of the horned and double-headed serpent (Sisiutl) in the lake at the top of the universe, we may now recognize the same demiurgic insight as that symbolized in India in Shiva the Great Lord.

The Mythological Trickster

The figure of the Trickster belongs, as Paul Radin has recognized, among the oldest expressions of mankind. "Few other myths," he declares, "have persisted with their fundamental content unchanged. The Trickster myth is found in clearly recognizable form among the simplest aboriginal tribes and among the complex. We encounter it among the ancient Greeks, the Chinese, the Japanese, and in the Semitic world. Many of the Trickster traits were perpetuated in the figure of the medieval jester, and have survived right up to the present day in the Punch-and-Judy plays and in the clown. . . .

"Manifestly," Radin continues, "we are here in the presence of a figure and a theme or themes which have had a special and permanent appeal and an unusual attraction for mankind from the very beginnings of civilization. In what must be regarded as its earliest and most archaic form, as found among the North American Indians, Trickster is at one and the same time creator and destroyer, giver and negator, he who dupes others and who is always duped himself. He wills nothing consciously. At all times he is constrained to behave as he does from impulses over which he has no control. He knows neither good nor evil, yet he is responsible for both. He possesses no values, moral or social, is at the mercy of his passions and appetites, yet through his actions all values come into being. But not only he, so our myth tells us, possesses these traits. So, likewise, do other figures of the plot connected with him: the animals, the various supernatural beings and monsters, and man. . . . The reaction of the audience in aboriginal societies to both him and his exploits is prevailingly one of laughter tempered by awe."[171]

Compare the case of the Bushman Creator and Trickster, Mantis (page 91)!

Along the Northwest Coast the most prominent Trickster figure is Raven, who is a glutton (like the *t'ao-t'ieh*). A second favorite, however, is Mink, who is a lover—ridiculous, of course, like Raven of the Greenland tale (page 187), yet, again like Raven, identified with the sun. There is, in fact, one Kwakiutl tale where his

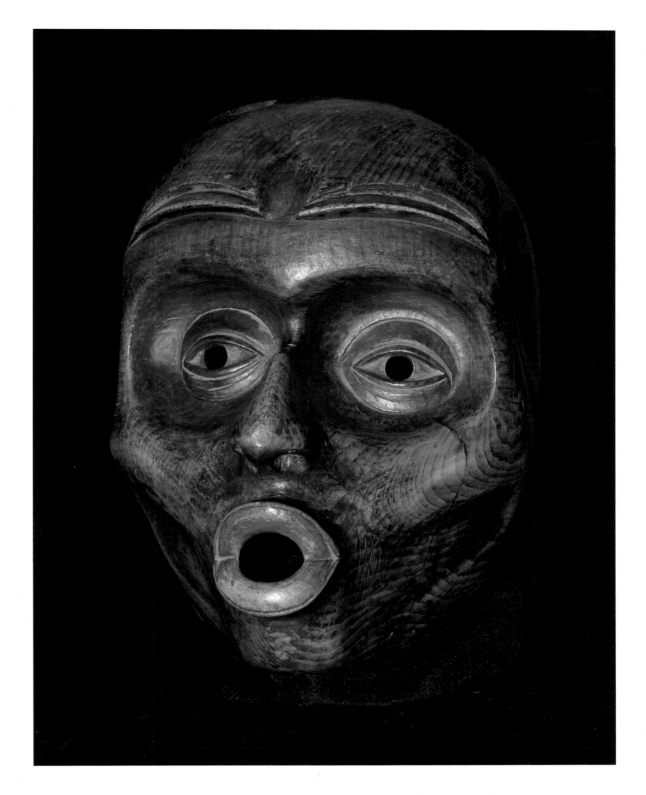

333. The giantess Tsonoqua, who roams the forest calling "ho, ho," searching for children to carry away in the basket on her back. Kwakiutl mask. Height, 12 inches. The pursed lips of her calling, as here pictured, are her identifying feature.

334. Tlingit forehead mask, representing a bear, from Sitka, Alaska. Height, 6¾ inches. Collected between 1882 and 1887. The form is of wood, covered with blanket cloth colored blue, red, and white; added features are of hair, haliotis, metal, and rawhide.

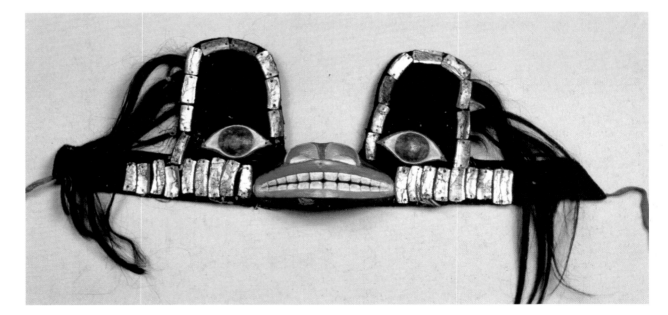

335. Niska (Tsimshian) sun mask, to be worn as a crest headdress. From the Nass River, Alaska. The projections carry sea-monster designs. As the dancer moved, the large flat area glowed, reflecting the firelight.

appearance in the solar role has attracted considerable scholarly attention because of its resemblance to the Greek Phaethon myth.[172]

The Kwakiutl version begins with the future mother of its hero weaving, facing the rear of her house, when the Sun's rays, shining through the cracks in the walls, struck her back, and she became pregnant. She gave birth to Mink, whose name, this time, was Born-to-be-the-Sun, since it was known how his mother had conceived him.

When still a child, Born-to-be-the Sun was quarreling with his little friend Bluejay, who taunted him, declaring that he had no father, and he went crying to his mother, who told him that his father was the Sun; whereupon he immediately announced that he was going to pay his father a visit.

The mother turned to the boy's uncle, her brother. "Make arrows for my child," she said, "that he may go to visit his father." The uncle fashioned four, and when Born-to-be-the-Sun shot one into the air, it hit the sky. He shot another, which went into the nock of the first. A third was shot with like result, and the fourth, as well, so that an arrow chain now reached the earth. His mother shook it and it became a rope, up which the boy ascended. When he reached the sky, he went on through, and was sitting on its upper side, not far from his father's house, when a boy who was there noticed him and asked, "Why are you sitting there like that?" "I have come to see my

father," Born-to-be-the-Sun replied; and the boy, going into the house, reported this to his chief. "Ah, ah, ah, indeed!" said his chief. "I got him by shining through. Show him in!" So the boy went out and called Born-to-be-the-Sun, who entered and sat down.

"Thank you, my child, for coming!" said his father. "I have grown tired of walking back and forth each day, so now you can go in my stead." But the Sun cautioned: "You mustn't walk too fast or look directly down! If you do, you will cause mischief." He dressed the boy with his own ear ornaments and gave him his sun mask, then pointed out the trail and again warned: "Don't expose yourself entirely! And don't brush aside the clouds, your aunts!"

Born-to-be-the Sun started, but when he had gone past noon, he brushed away his aunts, the clouds, and the sun shone blazing hot. The whole world began to burn. There was noise of cracking mountains, the sea began to boil, and the trees on the mountains caught fire. That is why the mountains have no trees and many of their rocks are cracked. That is also why the father of Born-to-be-the-Sun became furious. He rushed to his child and grabbed him—the sun being still very high in the sky—ripped away the ornaments and mask, and demanded, "Is this what I told you to do?" Then he took Born-to-be-the-Sun by the neck and flung him through the hole in the sky.

Down, down, down, he tumbled. A canoe was coming along, and it came to where Mink had dropped. "Is this not Born-to-be-the-Sun, our chief, here floating about?" they said. They touched him with the paddle, and he woke, raised his head, and puffed. "I've been here asleep on this water, a long long, long long time," he said. And he went ashore.

"Mother, I want to marry," said Born-to-be-the-Sun. "Whom do you want to marry?" she

asked. "Kelp," he replied. "I like her long wavy hair." "Then go ahead," she told him. So he married Kelp. He embraced her. "Let's go down to the bottom," he suggested; "down, down, down, to the bottom!" "We'll do that later, at half-tide," she replied. "No, now!" he insisted. "You're a funny fellow!" said Kelp. "You'll be out of breath." "No, I won't!" he declared. So down, down, down, they went. They were a long time under water. When he tried to pinch her to let her know that he needed air, however, he could not, because of the current. So he presently came floating up with foam on his mouth, and was drifting on the surface when a woman came paddling by.

"Is this not Born-to-be-the-Sun here floating about?" she asked. "Ts, ts, ts, so it is!" he said. "I've certainly had a long sleep." And he went home. His mother asked, "Where is your wife?" "Oh, she stayed under water too long," he replied, "so I left her."

"Mother," Born-to-be-the-Sun said, "I want to marry Frog." "Won't you get tired of hearing her croak?" she asked. "That's just what I like," he answered. "Well, go ahead, then," said his mother. So off went Born-to-be-the-Sun to marry Frog. "I want to marry you," he said to her. "All right, sit down," she said. "Come on," he urged, "let me hear you croak." She refused. "The others must start first," she said. He insisted. "Oh, come on! Come on! Wugé, wugé, wugé!" Where upon, she began to croak, and all the frogs round about followed, as did Born-to-be-the-Sun as well. But there was now so much croaking that Born-to-be-the-Sun got tired of it. "Stop it!" he yelled to his wife. "Oh, you funny fellow!" she croaked, and the noise went on. He became very tired of it; so he slapped her face and went home. "Well!" said his mother. "So where is your wife?" "Oh, they all made too much noise," he said. She wagged her head: "Didn't I tell you!"

"Mother," said Born-to-be-the-Sun, once again, "I want to marry Sawbill Duck." "Well then, go ahead," said his mother. He was wearing white feathers on his head when he went to Sawbill Duck, and one day when the two were paddling along a rocky shore, he looked down and saw sea-eggs below. He backed water and dived, and when he came up, "Go down again," she said, "stay longer, and get more." She was thinking of leaving him. He dove, and she paddled away, often looking back. It was only when she was some distance off that he came up with a great harvest, sat down on the rocks and ate sea-eggs, not caring that his wife had left him. She had returned home, and Born-to-be-the-Sun was now finished with having wives.[173]

336. Tlingit shaman's face mask, representing the spirit of a dead man with a protruding tongue. Wood, with traces of black and blue pigment. Measuring 8½ inches high, the mask was collected between 1884 and 1893 from a shaman's grave house on the Akwe River, where it had been the property of a shaman named Setan.

The Woodland Indians

"We know what the animals do, what are the needs of the beavers, the bear, the salmon, and other creatures, because long ago men married them and acquired this knowledge from their animal wives. Today the priests say we lie, but we know better. The white man has been only a short time in this country and knows very little about the animals. We have been here thousands of years and were taught long ago by the animals themselves."[174] This statement of a twentieth-century Athabascan hunter is supported by tales from every quarter of the continent, not only of animal wives, but also of animal husbands, and likewise, by unnumbered accounts of the Vision Quest commonly undertaken for the acquisition of knowledge, powers, and well-being. Indeed, among most of the North American tribes, such a vision was a fundamental requirement of every boy (and often, girl, as well) at the passage to adulthood.

As reported by George Catlin, in 1832, from the upper Missouri region (now the Dakotas): "A boy at the age of fourteen or fifteen years, is said to be 'making' or 'forming his medicine,' when he wanders away from his father's lodge, and absents himself for the space of two or three, and sometimes even four or five days; lying on the ground in some remote or secluded spot, crying to the Great Spirit, and fasting the whole time. During this period of peril and abstinence, when he falls asleep, the first animal, bird, or reptile, of which he dreams (or pretends to have dreamed, perhaps), he considers the Great Spirit has designated for his mysterious protec-

tor through life. He then returns home to his father's lodge, and relates his success; and after allaying his thirst, and satiating his appetite, he sallies forth with weapons or traps, until he can procure the animal or bird, the skin of which he preserves entire, and ornaments it according to his own fancy, and carries it with him through life, for 'good luck' (as he calls it); and his strength in battle—and in death his guardian *Spirit*, that is buried with him; and which is to conduct him safe to the beautiful hunting grounds, which he contemplates in the world to come."[175]

The instructive experience of a Winnebago youth who, in his Vision Quest, would be satisfied by nothing short of a sight of Ma-o-na, the Great Spirit himself, is recounted by Natalie Curtis:

"He blackened his face, as was the custom, and fasted four days or more, and dreamed of many things; then he ate a little, and fasted again. So he persevered until he had dreamed of everything on the earth, or under the earth, or in the air; he dreamed of the whole world, but he never saw Ma-o-na. The spirits said to him, 'You have dreamed of Ma-o-na because you have dreamed of all his works.' But the man was not satisfied. He blackened his face and lay down again, and again he dreamed of the whole world, yet still he wished to dream of Ma-o-na, but could not. But after four nights he dreamed again, and now at last he dreamed of Ma-o-na, who said: 'I am the Earth Maker. You will see me tomorrow at noon. But it is not well; you wish too much.'

"So the next morning the man rose up and made himself ready and took some tobacco for an offering, and before noon he set out for the place where Ma-o-na had said that he could meet him, a place

where mighty oak-trees grew to a vast height. There he stood still, and watched and listened, till just at noon he saw a large flag drop down to the earth and hang suspended before him. The man looked up and saw that Ma-o-na was there, among the tall oaks; he saw only the face of Ma-o-na, a long face with good eyes, for the flag covered all the rest. Then the face spoke to him and said: 'Nephew, you said that if you could not dream of me you would die. Nephew, you never can die. You never can die, because you are like me. You have dreamed of all my works, you know them all, and so you are like me. The spirits told you this, but you would not believe. You wanted to see me. Now you see me here today!'

"The man thought that he saw Ma-o-na, and he looked long at the face and never turned his eyes away, till at last the creature before him grew tired and drew back its wing; and then the man saw that it was only a chicken-hawk, one of the evil spirit's birds, that had flown down into a low oak close in front of him; and the chicken-hawk's wing had seemed to be the flag. The man cried for sorrow, and he lay four nights more, and then the spirits came and talked with him and took his soul away with them and said: 'Cease trying to dream of Ma-o-na. There are many more little birds and creatures of the evil spirit that may deceive you. You can dream no more, for you have seen all things.'

"So the man ceased in his fast and no longer tried to dream of Ma-o-na. He never saw Ma-o-na, nor he nor any one upon this earth. It is not possible to see Ma-o-na."

"Maona, to the Indian," Natalie Curtis adds, "is seen in all his works, and the whole world of nature tells of spiritual life. Maona is reflected in the mind of man himself, for man is like Maona when he has seen and understood Maona's works—the universe about him."[176] From the Algonquian-speaking, Northeast Woodland Abnaki (or Wabanaki) we hear the same: "The Great Spirit is in all things; he is in the air we breathe."[177]

The Athabascan-speaking Beaver tribe, Dunne-za, of the Peace River region of Alberta has it that, in the beginning, the roles of people and the animals were reversed. Gigantic progenitors of the present species roamed the woodlands, hunting and eating Indians; but they were overcome and reduced by a culture hero named Saya, who gained knowledge of their medicine songs and turned the power of these against them. As Robin

Ridington has noted in his studies of these people,[178] the Vision Quest on which every Beaver child is sent is interpreted as a repetition of the legendary culture deed of Saya; and the Medicine Song specific to the animal of the acquired vision confers on the initiate a wisdom that is in accord with all of nature. The song has a harmonizing, healing power that protects its owner, inspires prophetic dreams, and may be used for curing.

Such personal Medicine Songs are not for general use; but there are songs, also, called "Dreamers' Songs," on which the tribal ceremonies are founded. The shamanic Dreamers through whom these have become known are spoken of as Swan People; for, like swans, the sun, and the culture hero Saya, they can travel to, and return from, another land—a mythological land, where symbols are realities. The trails along which they fly are of songs sent down to earth by earlier Dreamers: songs only a Dreamer can grab hold of, following their turns as a trail.

Ridington points out that these songs combine two elements: one, the rhythm, which is carried by the drum and by the fall of the feet in the dance; the other, the melodic line, carried in the minds and voices of the singers. And as the power of the Medicine Songs is to heal, that of these Dreamers' Songs is to weld together a community in harmony with its environment. The hunters who sing and drum sit in the north and east of the lodge;

young women and their children, near the door to the south; the older men and women, among whom are the Dreamers, to the west; and all, from their places, come to join in the dance, circling sunwise round the fire on the trail of Saya: thus, for as long as three days and nights, while a Dreamer recites of the journey.

It was like going up on a sunbeam slanting down through a dark storm cloud, ascending to a place at the end of the trail of the mind, the place of the beginning. Sunset people dream of it, sunrise people sing it out, and all stamp their feet around the fire in the dust of many tracks, all on the one trail of Saya and the Swans.[179]

338. The classic snowshoe people of America are the northern Algonquian tribes. The Ojibwa (or Chippewa) snowshoe dance, recorded in 1833 by George Catlin, testifies to the importance of the snowshoe in their lives. Snowshoes of this shape, but with skin covering instead of web, were known to the Paleo-Siberian Yukaghir: the invention had opened the entire sub-Arctic to the Late Paleolithic hunters, giving them in winter a decisive advantage over the snow-bound beasts. According to Catlin, the Ojibwa performed this dance at the first snowfall, when they sang "a song of thanksgiving to the Great Spirit for sending them a return of snow, when they can run on their snowshoes in their valued hunts, and easily take the game for their food."[20]

The Iroquois and Algonquians

Separating the Algonquian tribes around the Great Lakes from those along the Atlantic Coast, there appeared, possibly in the twelfth or thirteenth century A.D., a people from the south known to history as the 'Iroquois' and to themselves as Ho-de-na-sau-nee (People of the Long House), with reference to the obvious contrast between their long, bark-covered dwellings (housing several matrilineally related families) and the circular, one-family huts of their enemy neighbors.

The carriage northward of strains from the formative culture centers of the south and their subsequent combination with influences from the north are illustrated in the histories, not only of the Iroquois in the East, but also of their linguistically related cousins of the Plains, including, among others: the Crow, Hidatsa, Winnebago, Omaha, Dakota (or Sioux proper), Caddo, Wichita, and Pawnee. The movement of the Iroquois northward along the Atlantic Coast brought them into New York state, Ontario, and Quebec, in which areas they became, from the beginning of the seventeenth century, the unrelenting enemies of the earlier Algonquians. And it was the talent of the Iroquois for coop-

erative organization, as well as their military prowess, that gave them everywhere the advantage.

According to their traditions, Hiawatha, one of their chieftains in the mid-fourteenth century, inspired by the peace message of Dekanawida (a prophet who had been born, it was told, of a virgin), founded the powerful league of five (later, six) Iroquois nations which the French and English colonists found dominant from the lakes Ontario and Erie to the Appalachians. Ironically, however, the legends recounted to this name in Longfellow's *Song of Hiawatha* (1855) were not Iroquois, but Algonquian, told of the

339. Traditional Iroquois longhouse, sheltering many families, built of poles lashed to construct a frame some 23 feet wide and from 40 to 300 or more feet long, then covered with bark. At one end was the men's door, at the other, the women's. Partitions jutting from the side walls left a long center aisle from end to end, each family (it is supposed) with a stall of its own.

340. The dwellings of an Algonquian people of the North, the Ojibwa (or Chippewa), at Sault Sainte Marie, Ontario. This painting by Paul Kane is now in the Royal Ontario Museum in Toronto.

Trickster Manabozho. They had been taken by the poet from the writings of Henry R. Schoolcraft (1793–1864), a government agent and ethnologist whose wife was an Ojibwa, and whose *Algic Researches* (1839) and *Historical and Statistical Information Respecting the History, Condition, and Prospects of the Indian Tribes of the United States* (six volumes published between 1851 and 1857), rank—along with the paintings and letters of his contemporary, George Catlin (1796–1872)—among our most important reports of American Indian life and lore at the vivid twilight hour of the Paleolithic Great Hunt. The following is the Ojibwa legend of the origin of maize which in Schoolcraft's redaction inspired Longfellow's Chapter 5, "Hiawatha's Fasting."

There was an unsuccessful hunter, who was poor therefore, but contented and always thankful to the Great Spirit for everything received. When the time came for the ceremonial fast of his eldest son, he built in a secluded spot a little lodge, to which the boy retired. His name was Wunzh. He spent the first two days rambling in the woods, wondering how the plants grew of themselves, why some were good to eat and others not, and whether in his vision he might learn of some easier way than hunting and fishing for his father to procure the family's food.

The third day, feeling weak and faint, he kept to his bed and saw, coming down from the sky and advancing toward him, a handsome youth wearing garments of yellow and green with a plume of waving feathers on his head. "I am sent," said the apparition, "by the Great Spirit, who knows your motive in fasting. You do not seek fame as a warrior, but only to benefit your people. I am sent to instruct you to that end." Then he challenged the boy to a wrestling match, and weak though Wunzh was, he responded. They wrestled long, and when Wunzh could no longer hold out, "My friend," said the beautiful stranger, "that will do for today."

Next day, he reappeared, and though Wunzh felt less strong than before, his courage was the greater, and again they wrestled. "Tomorrow," then said his challenger, "be again strong for the final test." And he rose to the sky. But when the wrestling of the third day had ended, the beautiful youth came into the little fasting lodge and sat down. "You have won your desire," he said. "Tomorrow, when you throw me, you are to strip me of my garments, clean the earth of roots and weeds, and bury me; then leave. But come back from time to time to see whether I have returned to life. Keep the grass and weeds from my grave and once a month lay on fresh earth."

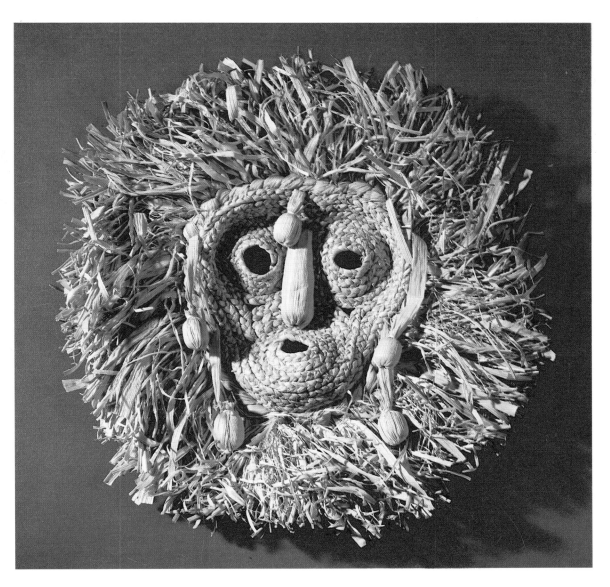

Wunzh's father came the next day with food, but the boy postponed eating until his friend again arrived, and all had developed as foretold. When the beautiful youth lay dead, Wunzh buried him as instructed, and returned to his father's lodge. He betrayed nothing of his experience, but for months tended the secluded grave, saw the green plumes coming up through the ground, watched them grow, and with delight one day brought his father to see a tall, graceful plant with brightly colored, silken hair and golden clusters on each side. "It is my friend," he said, "Mondawmin [maize]. We need no longer rely on hunting alone. For this I fasted, and the Great Spirit heard."[180]

There are Iroquois myths, also, of the origin of maize. According to a Seneca version collected in 1883:

Originally, people lived above, in the center of the Blue, and in the middle of their village

341. Cornhusk mask of the Seneca (Iroquois) "Bushyheads," or Husk Face Society. The masked members appear at the Midwinter Festival to dance among the people and, remaining mute, beg for food

grew a tree with blossoms giving light. A woman dreamed of a man who told her that that tree should be uprooted. "A circle must be dug around it," he said; "then a better light will come." So the people cut around their tree and, sinking, it disappeared. Darkness fell, and the chief, becoming furious, ordered the woman pushed into the hole.

Down, down she fell. Below there was only water, with waterfowl and aquatic animals at play. A duck looked up, saw something coming down, cried out, and a council was called to prepare a landing place. Loon said to Fishhawk, "Go catch and hold that creature until we are ready." The duck said, "I'll dive, and see if there is any bottom to this water." Long later it broke the surface, shot into the air, and fell back dead. Others tried with like result.

342. From pictures drawn on rocks to such on birch bark or on wood as those on this box lid is a major step, since rock pictures are normally representational of individuals or of scenes, whereas these are discursive, representing a sequence of connected thoughts, in the way of linear writing. The carved box itself is an Ojibwa tabernacle for the preservation of the sacred feathers used in meetings of the Midéwiwin, or Grand Medicine Society. Feathers were generally regarded in America, not simply as symbolic, but actually as carriers and communicators of spiritual power. The inscription on the lid is a record of Midéwiwin songs, to remind the singer as he chants.

Hell-diver, however, brought up mud, and Loon then sent all the members of that tribe down for more. "Put the mud on Turtle's back," he said. Beaver flattened it with his tail. Then Fishhawk brought the woman down and, work continuing, the earth increased; bushes presently appeared, and soon the woman gave birth to a girl.

Very quickly the child grew. And when a young woman, she was one day strolling, enjoying the animals and birds, when she met a nice young man. With their union, day and night came. At daybreak, she would go to meet him; at twilight, return home. One evening, she looked back and saw a big turtle walking where the man had just been. She thought: "A turtle has deceived me." At home, she told her mother and said, "I am going to die. You must bury me and cover me well. From my breasts will grow two stalks, on each of which an ear will appear. When ripe, give one to each of the boys I am to bear." She gave birth to twins, died, and was buried. And that was the origin of maize.[181]

Twin heroes are found everywhere in the mythologies of the Americas, North and South. But the boys are matched variously: as solar and lunar figures, warrior and medicine man, favored and unfavored sons, good creator and bad, and so on. In the present case, the first born is a competent creator, the second, incompetent and resentful.

The elder of the brothers molded mud into a shape, set it down, and asked, "Can you jump?" It didn't move. He blew on it, and it jumped. It was a grasshopper. Then he thought to make something to go higher, took red clay, and made the cherry bird, which flew and lighted on a bough. He shaped a deer, blew on it, pushed it, and it ran off. Then he thought, "Maybe I can make something like myself." Out of mud he fashioned such a thing and, wanting to give it a spirit like his own, bent down and blew into its mouth. It moved. He stood it on its feet and told it to whoop. The new man whooped. He had a fine voice.

Secretly watching, the younger brother thought, "I will make a man too." He went away and made something as like himself as he could, but it was deformed and strange. Another of his productions was a frog as large as a man. Others were man-eaters. One was known as *Shagodyowag*, or False Face. Its maker said, "Go and eat all the creatures my brother has made."

The elder brother, meanwhile, thought: "Let me make something like my grandmother." He made it of mud, breathed into it, brought it to the man he had made, and said: "This one I give to you. Be always together. You will have children like yourselves and will hunt the animals I have made for food. But you will not live forever. I now, go above the Blue. When you die, your spirit also will go above the Blue." Then he departed.

But when, from the Blue, he saw the creatures that his brother had made, he came down, put the man-eaters into the ground,

343. Great Doctor Mask of the Seneca (Iroquois) False Face Society. Such masks are worn by all the members when arriving as a group to cure a patient. The masks represent spirits of disease, which are without bodies, simply faces, and anyone dreaming of such a False Face is eligible for membership. All except the leader of the group were male. And here again we see a token of the Iroquois talent for organization; for these healers were not shamans, working individually: they always arrived as a company, masked, in single file, behind a female leader—this cooperation of male and female powers itself being an influence from the south. "On entering the house of the invalid," states Lewis H. Morgan, "they first stirred the ashes upon the hearth, and then sprinkled the patient over with hot ashes until his head and hair were covered; after which they performed some manipulations over him in turn, and finally led him around with them in the falseface dance, with which their ceremonies concluded. When these performances were over, the entertainment prepared for the occasion was distributed to the band, and by them carried away for their private feasting, as they never unmasked themselves before the people."[21] The Grand Medicine Society (Midéwiwin) of certain Central Woodland tribes was composed, likewise, not of shamans, but of members who either had dreamed of, or themselves been cured by, the group. Among the Pueblos there were such organizations as well.

and told them to remain there as long as the earth endured. Shagodyowag, however, spoke to him first: "Do not destroy me! I want to live on the earth and be your servant," he said. "I will inhabit the woods. The ashes of fire will be my medicine for men. I will scatter ashes over the sick and they will be well." Since he had spoken first, he could not be put into the ground; so the brother let him stay on earth. The true meaning of his name, Shagodyowag, is the Great One Who Protects Mankind.

The elder brother returned to the Blue, and the younger said to their grandmother: "I have tried to make a man, but have failed. Now I shall cause those that my brother has made to do evil."[182]

One recognizes in this final threat the influence of 200 years of Christian ethical dualism, the missions preaching God above and, on earth below, Satan and all those other evil spirits, *qui ad perditionem animarum pervagantur in mundo,* "who wander through the world for the ruin of souls."[183]

Even more evident influences from Europe—and from Africa as well—appear among the remaining fragments of the cruelly obliterated cultures of the Southeast of the United States. From the Creeks, for example, we learn that man was originally formed by the Great Spirit from fired clay; but the first batch was overbaked and came out black: these are the Negroes; the second was underbaked and came out pale: these are the Whites; the third came out just right in both color and form: and are, of course, the native Indian tribes.[184]

The Muskogean Creek

The Creeks, a Muskogean-speaking people, formerly of Alabama and Georgia, were demolished by General Andrew Jackson, 1813–14, and the remainder deported in the 1830s to what is now Oklahoma, where, together with the Muskogean Choctaw, Chickasaw, and Seminole, and the similarly exiled Iroquoian Cherokee (formerly of Tennessee and the Carolinas), they became known for a time as the Five Civilized Tribes.

The widely told tar-baby tale—originally from India by way of both Europe and Africa—reappeared among the Creeks as an adventure of the favorite Woodland Trickster, Rabbit.

A man who had been missing peas from his garden set a little image of pine tar before the plundered area, and when Rabbit came that night, he saw the figure. "Who are you?" he asked, and hopped closer. "If you don't answer, I'll hit you." He struck hard with his right forepaw, and the paw got stuck. "Let go of my paw," he said, "or I'll hit harder." He struck with his left paw, and that too got stuck. "I have another foot, stronger than these," he said, and he kicked. The foot got stuck. He kicked again, and again got stuck. "I'll kill you," he said, and he butted with his head and remained there, stuck in five places.

When the man arrived in the morning, Rabbit said to him, "Well, I've caught your thief! Here he is!" "Yes, indeed!" said the man. "I see my thief, all right, and I'm going to get rid of him." He tore Rabbit loose and tied him to a stake near his pigpen, then went off to get boiling water. When he had gone, Wolf came along and, seeing Rabbit tied, asked the meaning. "Oh, this fellow," said Rabbit, "asked me to eat up all his pigs and, since I couldn't, he tied me here." "Well, I can eat them for him," said Wolf. "Let me take your

place." He untied Rabbit, who in turn tied him to the stake, and when Rabbit hopped off and crawled into a hollow tree, the man returned.

"So!" he said, when he saw Wolf. "You are up to your old tricks and have made yourself look like a wolf!" He poured the boiling water on Wolf, who, howling in pain, tugged and broke the string, and ran off to the very tree into which Rabbit had crawled. As he sat there licking his scalded hide, Rabbit reached out and stuck him with a splinter. Wolf jumped up. "Not bad enough already!" he said. "So now I'm being bitten by ants!"[185]

We find also among the Creeks the following curious counterpart of the African Bushman tale of the Trickster Jackal who turned Lion into his horse. (See page 101.)

Rabbit wanted a wife, but Wolf, who was courting at the same house, was making a better impression because he was better-looking. So one day Rabbit said to the ladies: "Wolf is my riding horse." And when they refused to believe him, he declared that he would prove it by riding Wolf the next day.

Rabbit went to Wolf's house. "Let us go courting tomorrow," he suggested, and when Wolf agreed, Rabbit asked to be called for, so that the two could go together. When Wolf arrived next day, Rabbit pretended to be sick. "I can't walk," he said; "but if you would carry me on your back, I think I might go." Wolf consented; so Rabbit mounted him, and they started.

When they were ascending a hill, Rabbit fell off and declared that he could not stay on unless Wolf let him put on spurs. Wolf consented, and as they went on, Rabbit said, "Suppose you pretend you are my horse!" Wolf agreed, and they went on in a friendly way until they came within sight of the house where the ladies were watching for them. "We must make a good appearance," said Rabbit.

"As we approach, you must caper and dance." He struck his spurs into Wolf's sides, and they dashed up to the ladies in fine style. Then Rabbit tethered his horse to a post and, striding up to the ladies, said to them: "You see! I told you the truth. Here is my horse." They were impressed; and so he won his bride.[186]

The classic adventure of the Trickster, however, is the Fire Theft, and in the Creek's telling of Rabbit's miracles, the deed was accomplished as follows:

"How shall we obtain fire?" the people asked, and it was agreed that Rabbit should try. He crossed the Great Water to the east, and was received by the Fire People gladly. A dance was arranged, and when Rabbit joined the circle he was wearing a peculiar cap into which he had stuck four sticks of rosin. In the center of the circle was the Sacred Fire, and as the people danced, they circled nearer and nearer. Then they all began to bow to the Fire, bending lower and lower. Rabbit also bowed. He, too, bent lower and lower, and then suddenly very low. The sticks of rosin caught fire, and with his head ablaze, he ran. The people, amazed, all joined in pursuit of the impious stranger who had touched and stolen the Sacred Fire. Rabbit ran to the Great Water, sprang in, and the people pursuing stopped at the shore. Flames blazing from his cap, Rabbit swam. He swam across the Great Water and returned to his people; and so that was the way fire was obtained from the east.[187]

344. The Muskogean Creeks, who originally occupied Georgia and Alabama, dwelt in towns of rectangular houses arranged around plazas. The buildings were of poles plastered with mud, roofed with bark or thatch, and with smoke holes at the gables. The cabin here reproduced, described as a "Creek house in its best state of native improvement in 1790," shows the effects of 2½ centuries of association with European settlers. The Creeks were removed to Indian Territory (now Oklahoma) in the 1830s.

Prehistoric Societies in the American Midwest

Of especial interest in the Ojibwa legend of the origin of maize are two details: the appearance of the visionary messenger in human form, and the nature of the bestowed boon, not as a gift simply of personal power and protection, but as a transformation of the very body of the messenger himself. We are here at a juncture of two distinct, even contrary, mythologies: one, the northern, of those animal messengers who appear in vision as personal guardians; and the other, sprung from the plant world of the tropics, of a mythic being in whose death is the life of the world. For the great hunting tribes of the interior of North America were not simply hunters at the time of its discovery, but planters of maize, beans, and squash as well. And the myths associated with their horticulture had come to them, along with the art of plant domestication, from the south, where this art originated. The Iroquois legend of the first mother from whose buried body the food plants grew is another North American example of this widely known mythological motif. The global range of the idea is approximately the same as that indicated in Map 33, "The Diffusion of Bisexual Mythic Beings and Powers" (see page 142); for these two themes are akin. They are commonly associated, furthermore, with the moon that sheds its shadow and the serpent that sloughs its skin, even as they plant its seed, to be reborn.

The history of the entry of this plant-inspired mythology into the North American twilight zone of the Paleolithic Great Hunt is schematically illustrated on these pages in the chronological chart and in the drawings prepared by artist George Armstrong of Chicago's Field Museum. Based on the clearly stratified findings of an exemplary excavation begun in the 1970s under the leadership of Stuart Struever of Northwestern University on a farm (the Koster site) in southern Illinois, they reflect in continuous series the transformations of ceremonial forms through a range of 10,000 years.

THE KOSTER SITE: 8000 B.C. to A.D. 1200

At the lowest level of the dig (and of the chart) the artifacts are of the period known (for this area) as the Early Archaic, c. 8000 to 5000 B.C., at which time the early postglacial landscape of eastern North America, from southern Canada to the Gulf and from the Atlantic into the Plains, was transforming into woodland, and the big-game hunting of the terminal Pleistocene was giving way to small-game hunting, fishing, and wild-plant collecting. At the Koster site, c. 6400 B.C., among the remains of a hamlet of about twenty-five inhabitants, occupying three-quarters of

an acre, the first recorded signs of food grinding in North America appear in the form of metates and manos for the pounding of nuts and seeds. The earliest cemetery yet found in eastern North America lay at the western edge of this little settlement. Bodies with knees drawn up to the chest had been left exposed in prepared oval pits until decomposition set in, then covered. One eighteen-month-old infant had been dusted with red ocher. Some of the graves had been protected with limestone slabs or with logs. There were also the burials of three dogs, each in a very shallow pit, their legs curled up and heads turned inward toward the bodies. Finally, beads of a hematite not of this region tell of an already developing trade. Deer and various small mammals, fish, seeds, nuts, and fresh-water mussels were the people's food.

Following c. 6000 B.C., the site served for some two centuries as work camp for the fashioning of stone tools, after which a settlement twice as large as the first arose, covering an acre and a half, with a population dwelling in the earliest large and permanent houses yet found in North America, practicing more highly developed ceremonials than their predecessors, and equipped with more efficient tools. The village survived to c. 5000 B.C., after which the site remained uninhabited for a thousand years—except for a brief occupation at a date not determined.

The era from c. 5000 to 2000 B.C. is known (for this region) as the Middle Archaic, and at the Koster site, c. 3900 B.C., the dwellings of a settlement appear that survived to c. 2800 B.C. (five times as long as the history, to date, of the United States). A population of about 150 dwelt in a village of about 5 acres, still subsisting on wild foods, but at the beginning of an era of expanding trade (copper beads from Lake Superior, high-grade flints from Indiana) and of advanced ceremonial forms. The burials give evidence of improved life expectancy (to 60 or 70 years), care for the aged (some with severe arthritis), and, in a special cemetery apart, high-status burial rites. The village was abandoned apparently because of the exhaustion of available firewood.

The millennium from c. 2000 to c. 1000 B.C. is known here as the Late Archaic. At the Koster site, c. 1950 B.C., there arrived a people from the south (from the area of St. Louis), whose high-ranking burials in cemeteries remote from the village are furnished with beautiful flint daggers and engraved marine-shell pendants. The cultivated bottle gourd arrived (by trade) c. 1200 B.C., and maize (also by trade) c. 200 B.C., together with two pottery styles: "cord-marked" and "incised." No signs of local horticulture were to appear, however, until A.D. 800 to 950.

Apparently, during the Middle and Late Archaic periods the evolving Woodland cultures of eastern North America were so greatly gaining in their security and wealth that when agricultural products began arriving by trade, these were received and appreciated rather as supplements to, than as substitutes for, the bountiful natural resources. Hence, at the Koster site the villagers continued as hunters, fishers, and collectors for no less than 2000 years after learning of agricultural developments elsewhere. From c. 1200 B.C., the signs at the site increase of arrivals of domesticated products, yet it was not until c. A.D. 800 that these hunters began themselves to cultivate plants.

The great changes at the Koster site were introduced by: (1) the White-Hall People, c. A.D. 400 to 800, who brought the bow and arrow (formerly only spear and atlatl had been used); (2) the Jersey Buff People, who practiced horticulture (squash and pumpkins in small gardens), fashioned a thin-walled buff pottery, lived in a twenty-five-acre village of about one-hundred inhabitants, and during whose time the first evidences appear of armed warfare; and (3) a Mississippian people, c. A.D. 900 to 1200, who used ground and polished stone tools and cultivated fields of maize, beans, squash, and other crops; with them palisaded villages and large towns became numerous in the area, as did ceremonial plazas, temple mounds, and fortifications. Then, c. A.D. 1200, the Koster site was abandoned because of its vulnerability to attack.[22]

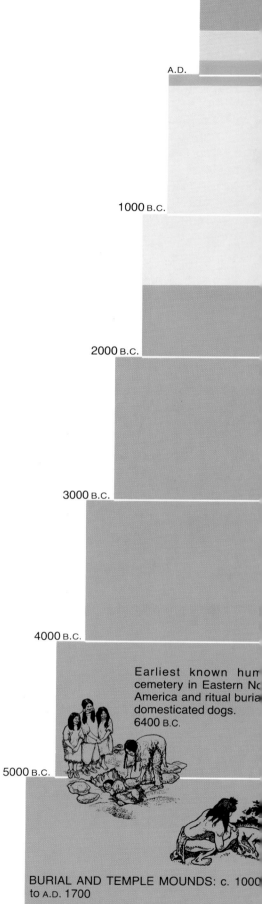

1000 A.D.

A.D.

1000 B.C.

2000 B.C.

3000 B.C.

4000 B.C.

Earliest known human cemetery in Eastern North America and ritual burial of domesticated dogs. 6400 B.C.

5000 B.C.

BURIAL AND TEMPLE MOUNDS: c. 1000 to A.D. 1700

6000 B.C. Parallel to, and finally reflected in, the later levels of the Koster site were three developments to the east and south that have been schematically represented in this chart, namely: (1) the Adena Culture of Ohio, c. 500 B.C. to A.D. 100 (Map 44 and lower figure grouping); (2) the Hopewell Culture, c. 100 B.C. to A.D. 300 (Map 45 and middle grouping); and (3) the Mississippian Culture, c. A.D. 900 to 1600 (Map and upper grouping).

7000 B.C. North American mounds are of two kinds, "burial" and "temple," classified chronologically as: Burial Mound I (c. 1000 to 300 B.C.) and II (c. 300 B.C. to A.D. 700), with the Adena and Hopewell Cultures as respective representatives, and Temple Mound I (c. A.D. 700 to 1200) and II (1200 to 1700), with the Mississippian Culture as model and source.

351. Interlaced pair of snake dancers emerging from a sloughed rattlesnake coil. Engraving on a large conch shell. Height, 12½ inches. Spiro Mound, Le-Flore County, Oklahoma.

352. Eye-in-palm motif (associated in Tibet with the Bodhisattva Chenrazi/ Avalokiteshvara), displayed in the oriental "fear-not" posture *(abhāya mudra)*, at midpoint of a cycle of two horned rattlesnakes. Engraved stone disk, diameter of 12½ inches, from Moundville, Alabama.

353. Figure in meditation, right hand in the oriental "boon-bestowing" posture *(varadana mudra)*. Stone. Height, 21½ inches. Raccoon Creek, Georgia.

Map 46. Sites of the Mississippian "Interaction Sphere": large towns with ceremonial plazas surrounded by earthen temple mounds. Formative area, Cahokia and environs (around St. Louis, Missouri). Classic period, c. A.D. 700 to 1200.

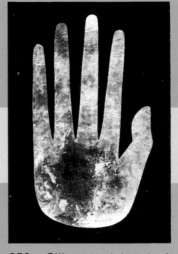

348. Snake cut from a sheet of mica about a foot wide. From the Turner site in southern Ohio. Mica imported from Virginia or North Carolina.

349. Swastika of native copper, beaten, cut, and annealed. From the Hopewell Mound Group in Ross County, Ohio. Animals, fish, crescents, and complex geometrical forms were also fashioned of native copper.

350. Silhouetted hand of sheet mica. Length, 10 inches. From the Hopewell Mound Group. Mica being too fragile for practical use, such delicate pieces were probably fashioned as burial gifts.

Map 45. Sites of the Hopewellian "Interaction Sphere": local cultures incorporating mortuary, iconographic, and other distinctive features of the sumptuous development in the Illinois and Ohio valleys known as the Hopewell Culture, c. 100 B.C. to A.D. 300.

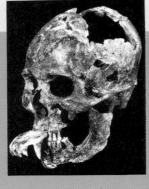

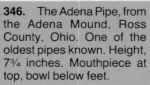

345. **(a)** Spatula-shaped artifact cut from a wolf's palate from Wright Mound, Montgomery County, Kentucky. **(b)** Skull with its upper incisors missing, from Ayers Mound, Owen County, Kentucky. **(c)** Ayers Mound skull with the Wright Mound artifact inserted through its incisor gap, suggesting a possible detail of shamanic semi-animal disguise.[23]

346. The Adena Pipe, from the Adena Mound, Ross County, Ohio. One of the oldest pipes known. Height, 7¾ inches. Mouthpiece at top, bowl below feet.

347. The Wilmington Tablet, showing a raptorial bird in mirrored negative reflex, head and wings above, feet and tail below. Sandstone slab, 5 by 6 inches, from Clinton County, Ohio.

Map 44. Distribution of Adena Culture sites: burial and effigy mounds, c. 500 B.C. to A.D. 100. Originating from the middle Ohio Valley, one of the earliest maize-cultivating cultures of North America.

354. The Serpent Mound, an effigy mound of the Adena Culture, about the first century B.C., near Locust Grove, Ohio: over 1300 feet long and 2½ to 3 feet high, it is in the form of an uncoiling serpent holding an egg-shaped object in its jaws. No one knows its function.

Most of what is known of the Adena has been derived from their burial and effigy mounds. That they were a numerous people is evident from the magnitude of their works; witness, for example, the great Serpent Mound (Figure 354) of the first century B.C., or the bird-effigy mound in Effigy Mounds National Monument (McGregor, Iowa) that measures, from wing tip to wing tip, 41 yards. Their numerous burial mounds greatly vary in both size and form, as well as in the number and kind of enclosed burials: flexed, extended, disarticulated, and cremated. There is one mound, in Mason County, Kentucky, that is 17 feet high and 120 feet in diameter, containing fifty-five burials and cremations;[188] another, in Doddridge County, West Virginia, only 3 feet high and 12 feet in diameter, with one burial.[189] The origins of the Adena and their customs are obscure, pointing as well to the north as to the south. A type of cremation anticipating theirs—using red ocher and with associated copper and galena fragments—has been radiocarbon-dated to as early as 2450 B.C. at the Red Lake site in

New York State;[190] and the astonishing shamanic wolf-palate masks (Figure 345), of which a number have been found,[191] likewise suggest an archaic, northern, Great Hunt culture background. However, the distinctive, artificially deformed skulls of the select individuals buried in the mounds indicate associations, rather, from the south.[192] Broad-headed (brachycephalic), in contrast to their long-headed (dolichocephalic) neighbors, they have been classified as a Gulf type;[193] and they so deformed their heads with circular bindings in infancy that their adult skulls exhibit foreheads that are among the highest known in the world.[194] Comparable deformations appear in skulls from early sites in the Valley of Mexico: Tlatilco, El Arbolillo, and Ticomán.[195] Furthermore, the large ear spools and the bent knees of the Adena Pipe figurine (Figure 346) come definitely from the south. It has been noted that this little fellow looks like an achondroplastic dwarf with a goiter and rachitic joints. Deformed subjects are not uncommon in Middle and South American art; indeed, some were deified. The skeleton of one such achondroplastic dwarf has been found in an Adena mound near Waverly, Ohio.[196]

The symbolic forms represented in the Adena remains and mounds mark the opening of an era of increasing icono-

graphic enrichment for the whole of the eastern Woodland region (see Map 44). Since we know nothing of the local social orders in relation to which these symbols functioned, we cannot interpret them ethnologically; however, their evident accordance with the forms of a widely known pictorial tradition makes it possible to suspect certain probabilities. The great Serpent Mound, for example, showing a snake bearing in its jaws an egglike form, suggests the mythic theme (once represented in the nineteenth-century flag of the Chinese Empire) of the cosmic dragon bearing the sun in its jaws; or in India, Ananta, the serpent of the cosmic sea, bearing the universe on his head; or in India again, the Tantric image and parable of the serpent of our mortal life incubating the egg, the golden germ, of the realization of our immortality. It has been suggested that the oval "in all probability marks the site of the ceremonies that must have been connected with this work."[197]

The split image of a raptorial bird on the Wilmington Tablet (Figure 347) suggests a shamanic theme from the Paleolithic northern context: for there is another such plaque, the Gaitskill Tablet (Figure 356), in which the bird's wings have become the hands of a masked personage whose feet are as a bird's talons. (Compare the masked bird-shaman of Lascaux,

355. The Lakin Tablet, an engraved stone tablet, 4½ by 3 inches, from an Adena mound in Lakin, West Virginia. Whereas in the Wilmington Tablet **(347)** the form is of a raptorial bird in mirrored negative reflex, that here is anthropomorphic, centered, yet bilaterally symmetrical, with arms and hands where the other shows wings, and with the feet modified to suggest talons. The head is masked: the subject, apparently, is of a shaman masked as a raptorial bird.

356. The Gaitskill Tablet, a clay tablet engraved in bas-relief, 4½ by 3½ inches, from the Gaitskill Mound, an Adena site in Mount Sterling, Kentucky. As in the Lakin Tablet **(355)**, so here (but more distinctly), the form is of a masked man with birdlike traits. The quadrated composition matches that of the Wilmington Tablet **(347)**: wings (or hands) above, taloned feet below. Dots mark the limb joints. The circle-in-palm anticipates the "hand-eye" design of the Moundville Disk **(352)**.

357. The Berlin Tablet, engraved sandstone tablet, from an Adena mound in Berlin, Jackson County, Ohio, is unique in that it is engraved on both sides, the two images being practically identical. As in the Wilmington Tablet **(347)**, the subject is a raptorial bird, but its eye has the form of a masked human face, suggesting the possibility of shamanic transformation. There are a total of thirteen of these engraved Adena tablets, all but three of which variously combine raptorial-bird and shamanic features.

358. Shell mask (miniature). Height, 3½ inches. From Anker site in Illinois. The "forked eye" is a Mississippian trait.

If the Adena tablets suggest a Paleolithic shamanic heritage from territories of the Great Hunt, the engraved Mississippian shells above testify to influences from the civilizations of Middle and South America. The "weeping eye" is of a native tradition that is represented in images from as far south as Argentina: see, for example, the Frontispiece **(1)**.

359. Shell gorget. Diameter, 4½ inches. From the Spiro Mound, LeFlore County, Oklahoma. Masks, apparently of deities of the world center and quarters, all with "forked-eye" markings.

360. Shell mask. Height, 6¾ inches. From Stafford County, Virginia. "Weeping-eye" motif.

Figure 105, page 65. The dots and circles at the joints of these figures suggest the eyes seen in the shamanic art of the Northwest Coast. Those in the palms anticipate the "hand-eye" of the Mississippian Moundville Disk (Figure 352). And one may think, as well, not only of the "eye of mercy" in the palms of Tibetan Taras and Bodhisattvas, but also of the pierced hands of the Risen Savior, Jesus Christ, who had descended into hell and was about to ascend beyond the blue.

The indentations along the lower margin of the Wilmington Tablet point downward along the left half, upward along the

right; and the matched heads, wings, and feet of the split image also contrast as positive and negative. The obvious suggestion would seem to be of a single transcendent power that has become manifest as a pair of opposites.

The human remains uncovered in the Hopewell mounds are of a long-headed race, differing in origin from the broad-headed Adena; yet the Hopewell, too, practiced cranial deformation.[198] They received and developed the Adena inspiration in their own way, constructing larger and more complex earthworks, some of which enclosed as much as 100 acres. And

361. Female statuette from a Hopewell burial mound. Clay. Height, 7¼ inches. Turner Mound, Ohio.

362. Stone pipe in the shape of a puma. Hopewell style. From Posey County, Indiana.

363. Hopewell statuette of a young woman. Marbled pottery, painted red, black, and white. height, 4⅜ inches. The Knight Mound, Illinois, c. 200 B.C.

364. Shell gorget (Mississippian) from the Spiro Mound, LeFlore County, Oklahoma. Swastika at center. Ring of twenty-seven spokes separating eye-in-hand circles.

365. Stone effigy pipe, 10 by 5 inches. From Spiro Mound. Warrior beheading a victim.

366. Shell gorget from Spiro Mound. Swastika at center on back of spider. Circles of seventeen spokes and of hands with shell-bead bracelets.

while many of the symbolic forms represented in their grave goods carry forward Adena themes (the cross, raptorial bird, hand-eye, and serpent, for example), others appear as new (sun-disks, swastikas, and various cut-out geometric designs in sheet mica and copper). Atlatl weights, flint and obsidian blades, masses of freshwater pearls, polished stone earspools, effigy pipes, and engraved human and animal bones also appear among the remains.[199] The high period was from 100 B.C. to A.D. 200; the extent of the influence was enormous (see Map 45). The decline and disappearance, for reasons unknown, occurred well before the rise of the second great Woodland phenomenon, the Mississippian, which developed and spread (as Map 46 shows) through the more southern part of the southeastern quarter of the continent.

367. Shell gorget, diameter of 7 inches, from Spiro Mound. Swastika in sun circle at center of cross that quarters the composition. Raccoon hangs from top, more raccoons from cross beam. Sun shields and rattles (with crosses) in the performers' hands.

The Mississippian tradition represents a reflex from the south of the Mesoamerican civilization, which in the latter half of the first millennium A.D. was at its classical apogee. The very great metropolis of Teotihuacán (the name meaning "City of Gods" or "Where Men Become Gods"), which around A.D. 650 was sacked and burned by the invading Toltec, has left upon its site, some 33 miles north of modern Mexico City, an imposing complex of remains covering an area of 8 square miles. In the northern part stands the Pyramid of the Moon, flanked by platforms and lesser pyramids; on the eastern edge, the Pyramid of the Sun, measuring at its base about 240 by 253 yards and rising by five terraces to a present height of 216 feet; while at the southern end of the vast complex, the symbolically decorated pyramid-temple of the "Feathered Serpent,"

ssippian symbolic designs
aved on large marine shells,
om Spiro Mound, LeFlore
nty, Oklahoma:

Fish pierced by arrows,
curved lines (wave forms?)
sun symbol on side.

Pumas with bird claws cir-
ambulating sun symbol coun-
ockwise.

370. Winged-rattlesnake
triad, axial serpent two-
headed (second head be-
low).

371. Winged-rattlesnake swastika, sun cross at center.

372. Two-faced personage
between serpent staves.

373. Dancer(?) in swastika
pose, eyes at elbow joints and
sun symbol on chest.

374. Crested birds on shaded
side of a three-rooted tree.

375. Crested-bird swastika with sun cross at
center. Engraved shell gorget, diameter of 3⅜
inches. From Castalian Springs, Sumner
County, Tennessee. Designs almost identical
appear on other gorgets from Tennessee, as
well as from Alabama and Mississippi.

376. Engraved shell gorget, diameter of 4 inches.
From Castalian Springs, Sumner County, Tennessee. The warrior (showing forked-eye motif) with
elaborate headdress holds in one hand a mace, in
the other a severed head.

377. Crested-bird swastika with sun swastika at center. Engraved shell gorget, diameter
of 3⅞ inches. From Spiro Mound, LeFlore
County, Oklahoma. The bird is apparently a
mythological species, combining heron,
woodpecker, and turkey.

Quetzalcoatl, confronts an expanse of 38
acres of ruined walls, known today as the
Citadel (*La Ciudadela*). The paved con-
course connecting the main groups of
these spectacular buildings is 1½ miles
long, 40 yards wide, and flanked along its
length by platforms that originally (it is
supposed) supported the public buildings
and palace residences of a governing élite.
The planning and early formation of this
city must have begun around the first or
second century A.D., and its influence extended as far south as to Guatemala and
north (at least) to Cahokia on the Mississippi.

The typical form of such a major Mississippian city as Cahokia was an arrangement of flat-topped, rectangular platform
mounds around rectangular open plazas,
the mounds having served as bases for
temples, chiefs' houses, and other impor-

378. Design from an immense engraved marine
shell, 13 inches long. From Spiro Mound, LeFlore
County, Oklahoma. Representation is of an eagle
dancer in full costume, with stepped (cloud?) design
overhead and a sun-circle at the throat.

tant buildings; and the period, known as
Temple Mound I, of the rise and expansion of this Mississippian culture-form
(c. A.D. 700 to 1200) matches the period of
Toltec ascendancy in Mesoamerica (c. A.D.
650 to 1160).

The fundamental legend of that somewhat obscure Mesoamerican period was
of the Feathered Serpent, Quetzalcoatl,
god-king of the fabled city of Tollan, who,
when old and hideous, sinned, commit-
ting incest with his sister after both had
partaken unwittingly of an intoxicating
potion. Ashamed, the god-king departed
from his city, set to sea on a serpent raft,
and after a period of fourteen days reappeared in the eastern sky as the Morning
Star.

We observe that the winged-rattlesnake
appears in the Mississippian designs reproduced in Figures 370 and 371. These

215

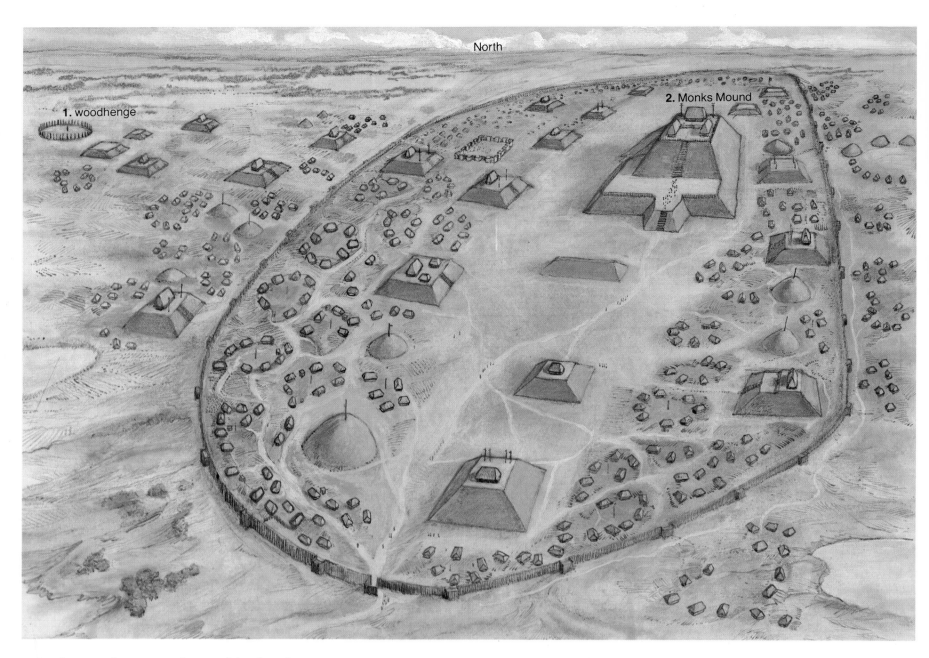

North

1. woodhenge

2. Monks Mound

examples are but two of a multitude of winged-rattlesnake arrangements in Mississippian works of art. In Mesoamerican art, the Feathered Serpent appears on monuments very much earlier than either Toltec Tollan or Teotihuacán, for example, on a carved stone of c. 800 B.C., from an Olmec ceremonial site at La Venta, Tabasco, on the Caribbean coast. The classic Mayans of c. A.D. 300 to 900 already knew the Feathered Serpent as Kukulcan. The winged rattlesnakes of the Mississippian designs, therefore, may represent a period of the god's symbolic history and associations antecedent to the relatively late Toltec-Aztec legend of the god-king of Tollan.

The geographical reach of the influence in North America of the Mississippian culture complex was enormous (see Map 46, page 211). How the Mesoamerican influences ever reached the Mississippi, however, is unknown. As reviewed by Gordon R. Willey: "The first appearances of the Mississippian tradition in the East remain clouded. Neither the place nor the exact time can be pinned down. Ultimate sources of origin are Mesoamerican, and the process of dissemination that crystallized in the Mississippian pattern appears to have been diffusion rather than mas-

sive migration of populations. The Mississippi Valley was the 'forcing ground' of the tradition, but whether its earliest emergence was in the lower Mississippi Valley, the Caddo region, or in the central Mississippi Valley cannot yet be answered. Certainly the most vigorous and viable branch of the new tradition was located in the central Mississippi Valley, probably between St. Louis and Memphis; and it was from here that emigrants set out to colonize places as distant as Aztalan, Wisconsin, and Macon, Georgia. Also at about the same time, influences spread and colonists perhaps moved from the lower Mississippi eastward into Florida and Georgia and probably northward up the Red River. These various events are estimated to have begun around A.D. 700, but it is likely the great Mississippian sites of the Temple Mound I Period did not reach their heyday until after A.D. 900.

"The Mississippian tradition," Willey continues, "attained its cultural climax during the earlier part of the Temple Mound II Period, presumably during those first two or three centuries following A.D. 1200, when population reached its maximum and the geographical extent of the tradition was greatest. All those regions formerly occupied by Mississippian peoples were included, as well as additional areas to the north, west, and

379. Plan of Cahokia. The shape and dimensions of this site, across the Mississippi from St. Louis, are of a huge lozenge, 2.8 miles long (east-west) and 2.1 miles wide (north-south). The area encloses over one hundred mounds, including Monks Mound (**2** above), the largest prehistoric earthen construction in the world. The axes of the lozenge intersect just west of this monument, the north-south axis passing through a large posthole on a burial mound (Mound 72) and the east-west cutting through a configuration of postholes known as Woodhenge (see **1** above, **380** on page 217, and text page 218).

east. . . . The Temple Mound II Period was also a time of regional culture differentiation and of modification of the Mississippian tradition by elements of antecedent Woodland cultures; yet in the majority of these blends the Mississippian patterns remained dominant."[200]

The nuclear site of Cahokia attained in this second period its final form, and as preserved today in the Cahokia Mounds State Park, the ruins suggest a population of some 5000 to 10,000, inhabiting a ceremonial complex with over 100 flat-topped and pyramidal earthen mounds arranged around ceremonial centers. Temples and the residences of priests and chieftains once stood upon these platforms, while beyond the city bounds were farmlands, intensively worked, of maize, beans, and squash. Outlying villages and towns with temple mounds of their own constituted, together with the metropolis, a theocratic empire; the inspiration from Mesoamer-

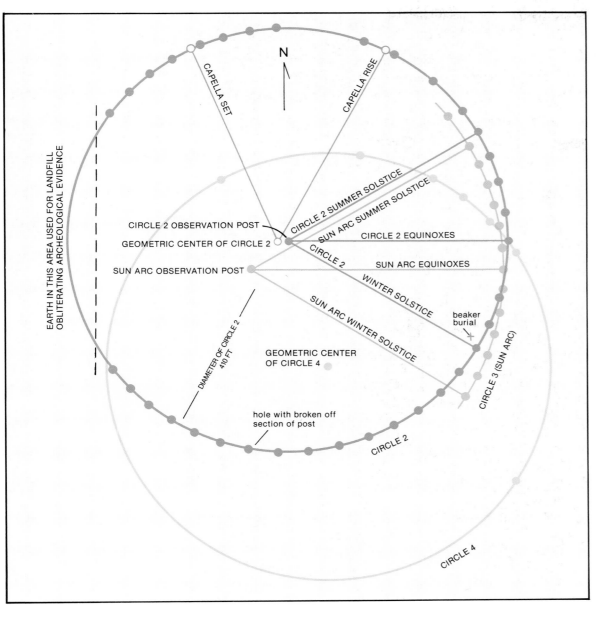

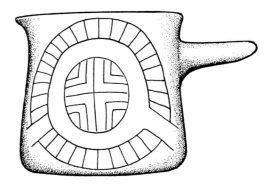

380. Circles 2, 3, and 4 of Cahokia's Woodhenge. *Circle 2:* diameter of 410 feet, composed of forty-seven posts set 27½ feet apart. *Circle 3:* an arc of fourteen posts intersecting Circle 2 at its eastern point (may represent a "sunrise arc," from winter to summer solstice). *Circle 4:* about the same diameter as 2, which it intersects at the point where Circle 3 cuts through. *Circle 1:* not yet reconstructed.

381. Fragment of a ceramic beaker found in a fire pit close to the winter-solstice posthole of Circle 2. Incised design appears to represent the relevant cosmological concept: the earth (crosses in center), the sun (radiating lines), and the sun's passage (circular pathway) opening to the winter-solstice sunrise (channel, lower right). Compare 380.

ica having been assimilated and adapted by local populations of Siouan, Muskogean, Iroquoian, and Caddoan language stocks.[201] So that from Spiro (Oklahoma) and Aztalan (Wisconsin) to Moundville (Alabama) and Etowah (Georgia), Mississippian communities were flourishing when, in 1540, De Soto began the work which, within three centuries, led to the extinction of even the memory of the native people and civilization.

Of the mounds at Cahokia, the greatest, so-called Monks Mound, covers fourteen acres and is approximately 1000 feet long, 700 feet wide, and 100 feet high in four stages. Since it is in the middle of the site, its symbolic function, as representing the axial height joining earth and sky, is evident. The idea of such a generative center is already represented in the Spiro

382. Victory celebration by the Timucuan chief Outina, here talking with the French Huguenot, René de Laudonnière, whose harquebusiers had contributed to the triumph. Scalps and limbs of the massacred foe hang from the poles. From a watercolor by Jacques Le Moyne de Morgues in c. 1564.

383. Seasonal festival at the Powhatan village of Secota (at the mouth of the Pamlico River in North Carolina). "They meet on a broad open plain enclosed by tall posts carved into faces resembling those of veiled nuns."[25] From a watercolor by John White, c. 1584.

Mound gorget of Figure 359 (page 213), which is an unmistakable representation of the mythological archetype of the quartered cosmos: an "elementary idea" (see page 9) of which the swastika and equal-armed cross are abstractions. The prominence of these symbols in the figures on pages 211–215 speaks for the importance of this concept in Mississippian thought. And that the idea was embodied in a system of ceremonials coordinating life in the earthly city with the celestial seasonal order has been confirmed in the recent discovery by Warren Wittry, of the University of Illinois, of the remains—about 880 yards due west of Monks Mound—of a solar observatory.

Wittry's name for this site is Woodhenge—by analogy with Stonehenge—for what he found was an arrangement of postholes in which cedar poles 18 inches in diameter had been set, forming intersecting circles and arcs (see Figure 380). Having persuaded a local electric company to donate four telegraph poles—one for the hole at the center of Circle 2; one for that directly east (where Circles 2, 3, and 4 intersect); one, four pits to the south; and one, four pits to the north—he demonstrated that, when observed from the central station, the equinoxial sun came up, September 23rd, directly behind the eastern pole; the winter-solstice sun, December 21st, behind that to the south; and the summer-solstice sun, June 21st, behind the pole to the north. Wittry has found that two other postholes might have served for sightings of the rise and set of the first-magnitude star Capella and has suggested that the whole layout of Cahokia might have been projected from the angles of these sightings.[202]

An idea of the way in which the circles might have served, not only for seasonal observations, but also for celebrations on the relevant festival days is given in the paintings of two sixteenth-century artists (Figures 382 and 383), reporting on the native tribes of Florida and Virginia. The earlier of the two, a Frenchman, Jacques Le Moyne de Morgues, had been sent to Florida in 1564 with a French expedition charged with the mapping of the seacoast, the indication of native towns, and the portrayal of the manners of the people. His watercolors—which have disappeared—were turned into engravings by the Flemish goldsmith, Theodore de Bry, and published in 1591. John White, the second of the two, sailed in 1584 with Sir Walter Raleigh's first expedition to Virginia. His watercolors—which have survived—were also turned into engravings by de Bry and published in 1590.[203]

The circles of poles pictured both by Le Moyne (in Florida) and by White (in Virginia) suggest the sun circles at Cahokia. The poles of Le Moyne's illustration display the limbs and scalps of a defeated enemy: at Cahokia, Wittry has unearthed

384. Annual offering to the sun at the spring equinox of the whole skin of a splendid stag, preserved and stuffed with produce of the fields; the prayer being that such good things as these may continue to appear through the coming year.[26]

385/386. From Key Marco, Florida, a carved and painted deer-head mask and a feline figurine that are among the oldest wooden artifacts recovered in the Americas. Mississippian, dating from six to eight centuries ago, they were probably used for unknown ceremonial purposes.

the bones of five different individuals, three leg bones and two arm bones, which may likewise have been hung as trophies. Le Moyne's description of the victory ceremonies that he witnessed states that when the Indians, returning from their wars, have assembled in the designated place, "they bring the legs, arms, and scalps of the fallen adversaries and with great solemnities attach them to tall poles. Then the men and the women sit down in a circle before the poles, where their sorcerer, holding a small image, begins to curse the enemy, uttering a thousand imprecations in a low voice. While the sorcerer is repeating his curses, three men kneel opposite him. One of them pounds on a flat stone with a club, marking time with the spells; two others rattle pumpkins filled with small stones or seeds and accompany the sorcerer's words with a chant. This is their way of celebrating whenever they win a victory over their enemies."[204]

A very different ceremonial witnessed by Le Moyne was of Outina's people's annual celebration of a solar stag festival, where the skin of the largest stag slain during that year was stuffed with the choicest roots, hung with garlands of the best fruits, and elevated on a pole to the sunrise—"just before spring"—to remain for the year as a constant prayer (Figure 384).[205] The festival was undoubtedly of the spring-equinox sunrise, and the pole upon which the symbolic stag was elevated can only have been the central, axial, solar pole of the symbolic circle. But as to whether any pole or poles of the circumference has been put to use in determination of the festival date, we are not told.

The Timucua tribes (who have long been extinct) were the dominant people of northern Florida at the time of the discovery. Their affinities are obscure. Once thought to have been of a Muskogean stock, their language (or what little is known of it) is today unclassified. Some scholars suggest Siouan affinities; others detect a possible link to Venezuela. In any case, the order of life illustrated in de Bry's engravings from the lost watercolors of Le Moyne is of a grace and elegance suggestive even of Polynesia. The fact that the bodies of the aristocrats, whether male or female, were from head to foot tattooed was, for North America, unusual. The bark trumpets blown before the young queen-elect were of a kind best known from the Amazonian rain-forests—where, however, they are tabu to women—and in use resemble the men's sacred forest-horn, the molimo, of the Congo Pygmies (see pages 103–104). The litter of the fully tattooed young queen, accompanied at either hand by attendants bearing tall fans, is, to say the least, surprising. And unless one can accept on faith the absolutely undemonstrable proposition that

387. The queen-elect is brought to the king. Four men carry her litter, each holding a forked stick on which to rest the poles when they halt. Two at the sides carry fans to shade her from the sun. The trumpeters blow horns of bark hung with oval balls of gold, silver, and brass that tinkle as they march. Behind are beautiful maidens—clad in skirts of Spanish moss, necks and arms decorated with pearls—each with a basket of choice fruits. At the end of the procession are the bodyguards.[27]

388. Transporting crops to the public granary. Twice a year they harvest, storing the produce in granaries built of stones and earth, thickly roofed with palm branches and "a kind of soft earth." They go there for supplies whenever in need, and no one fears being cheated. "Indeed," comments Le Moyne, "it would be good if among Christians there were as little greed to torment men's minds and hearts."[28]

219

389. Pocahontas in London as Lady Rebecca. Portrait by an unknown artist, 1616.

complexes of this composite kind can develop independently in various parts of the world through the influence solely of environmental conditions, the mind—as the eye takes in this attractive scene—cannot but fly to Southeast Asia.

*   *   *

The people of Virginia among whom John White found subjects for his elegant watercolors were of Algonquian stock, inhabiting some 200 coastal villages and towns from Chesapeake Bay to Cape Lookout (Figures 390 and 391). White had arrived in Virginia in 1585 with Sir Walter Raleigh's first colony, and although his stay in Roanoke was but a year, he produced some 75 paintings. In 1587 he returned as governor of the colony, accompanied by his daughter, Elinor, and her husband, Ananias Dare, whose child, Virginia, born in Roanoke, was the first child born of English parents in America. Nothing is known, however, of her life. Nine days after her birth, John White, her grandfather, sailed to England for supplies: there was a religious war going on at the time which rendered perilous, not

only the high seas, but life anywhere in the Christian world. Indeed, in 1565, the Huguenot settlement on the Florida coast where Jacques Le Moyne had been the artist had been wiped out by Pedro Menondez de Aviles, who had been sent with eleven ships to that task by Philip II of Spain. And when the slaughter of men, women, and children had been accomplished, the bodies were hung from trees by ropes passed through the pierced palms of their hands, to an accompanying inscription: "Not as Frenchmen, but as heretics." The Massacre of Saint Bartholomew's Day, when as many (some say) as 70,000 Huguenots were murdered throughout France, had occurred in 1572. And in 1588 (the year of White's proposed return to his colony), the entire battle fleet of Catholic Spain, sent against Elizabethan England, was wrecked by a storm off the coast of Ireland. The seas, therefore, were troubled, not only by natural, but also by supernatural, storms. White, thus

390. An elder of the Powhatan town of Pomeiock in his winter clothes: skins dressed without removing the fur and lined with other skins. A contemporary commentator wrote: "They wear their hair in a knot at the back and cut a crest in front. The country around Pomeiock is far more fruitful than England."[29]

delayed for three years in his return to Roanoke, arrived at last in the fall of 1590 and beheld on the shore only a plundered ruin overgrown with grass and weeds. What had happened no one knows to this day.

* * *

In the first decade of the next century, some twenty of the Algonquian tribes occupying tidewater Virginia were confederated under the leadership of a chief known to history as Powhatan—whose daughter, Pocahontas, was a child of about thirteen, when, in 1607, three British ships entered Chesapeake Bay with the settlers who founded Jamestown. Eight months later, when their adventurous leader, John Smith, thought to explore the Chickahominy River, he was ambushed and brought before Powhatan to be executed. And then it was that the pretty episode took place of which our schoolbooks tell: when Smith laid his head on the sacrificial stone to be clubbed to death, Powhatan's thirteen-year-old daughter threw herself between him and the lifted club. Smith then was adopted into the tribe; Pocahontas became his friend; and a period followed of peace and hospitality, when the native gifts of maize, beans, potatoes, and squash were what kept the invaders alive.

The tale, if it were not known as history, might be read as a variant of the legend, say, of Theseus saved by Ariadne, the daughter of King Minos; or that of Jason aided by the witch Medea in his theft from her father of the Golden Fleece. In both instances, the father was betrayed and the daughter eloped with her paramour—only to be herself betrayed, and in Ariadne's case, to die.

When Smith returned to England in 1609 and relations with Powhatan deteriorated, Pocahontas was kidnapped, held hostage, and used in negotiations with her father, by whom she then was ransomed. But she had meanwhile been converted to one of the recent English versions of the Christian faith and baptized as Lady Rebecca. She fell in love with a gentleman, John Rolfe; married him; and, in 1616, sailed with him to England—where she gave birth to a son, contracted smallpox, and in 1617 died.

Her father died the next year, and relations between Jamestown and the native towns again deteriorated. When the colonists began to realize what profits could be gained from cultivating and marketing the native tobacco to which they had been introduced, their fields expanded into native village lands; resistance resulted; two massacres occurred; and there followed the inevitable war (1622 to 1644), when the power of Powhatan's confederacy of some 200 native villages and towns was broken.

391. The town of Secota, at the mouth of the Pamlico River. "Those of their towns that are not palisaded are usually the more beautiful. The houses are farther apart and have gardens [marked E], in which they grow tobacco. They also have groves of trees where they hunt deer, and fields where they sow their corn.

"In the cornfields they set up a little hut on a scaffold, where a watchman is stationed [F]. He makes a continual noise to keep off birds and beasts. They sow their corn a certain distance apart [H] so that one stalk should not choke the next. For the leaves are large, like the leaves of great reeds.

"They also have a large plot [C] where they meet with neighbors to celebrate solemn feasts, and a place [D] where they make merry when the feast is ended. In the round plot [B] they assemble to pray. The large building [A] holds the tombs of their kings and princes. In the garden on the right [I] they sow pumpkins. There is also a place [K] where they build a fire at feast time, and just outside the town is the river [L] from which they get their water.

"These people live happily together without envy or greed. They hold their feasts at night, when they make large fires to light them and to show their joy."[30]

221

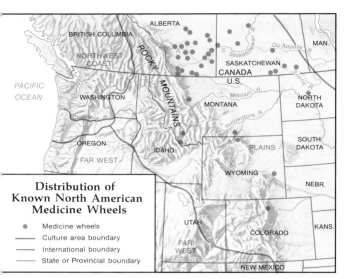

Distribution of Known North American Medicine Wheels

● Medicine wheels
— Culture area boundary
— International boundary
— State or Provincial boundary

Map 47.

The Rocky Mountain Medicine Wheels

Astronomical observations of the kind undertaken at Cahokia have been generally associated with settled agricultural peoples. There is now evidence, however, from the Western Plains of both Canada and the United States, of a number of observatories (known as medicine wheels) which can have been constructed only by hunters. Most, but not all, look like wagon wheels. There is one, how-ever, with the form of a turtle—head, tail, four legs, and all—at Minton, Saskatchewan. About fifty of these "wheels" are known, clustered along the bounding plains and foothills of the front range of the Rocky Mountains (see Map 47). In Alberta, Canada, at Majorville, there is one that has been extensively excavated (as well as vandalized) and gives evidence of "more-or-less continuous use from about 2500 B.C.," which, as noticed by John A. Eddy, one of the leading authorities in these matters, makes it "contemporaneous with the Egyptian pyramids and the early stages of Stonehenge. Other medicine wheels are probably a good deal more recent," he adds, "but no one is sure of this."[206]

Alberta, Saskatchewan, Montana, Wyoming, and North Dakota are remote, indeed, from the centers of agriculture in the Americas. Furthermore, as revealed in excavations at the Koster site (see pages 210–211), the cultivated pumpkin and bottle gourd first arrived in that neighborhood, by trade, c. 1200 B.C., and maize, also by trade, c. 200 B.C.; yet it was not until c. A.D. 800 that the hunting tribes of that area began cultivating gardens of their own. It is surely obvious, therefore, that medicine wheels in the Canadian Rockies can have had nothing whatsoever to do with practical economics: more likely, they reflect what I would call "mystical economics," which is to say, the delicate problem of keeping a human community in accord with the rhythmic order of the universe. The proper and primary function of such observatories as those here represented was based on an intuition which underlies all of the so-called "nature religions" (as distinguished from the monotheistic "historical religions"), namely, of accord—in depth—with the mystery of the order of nature as the first means and last end of well being.

At least two of the medicine wheels that have been studied coordinate lunar, solar, and stellar observations, the better known of the two being the Bighorn Medicine Wheel of Figure 392. Laid out on a lofty shoulder of Medicine Mountain (between Lovell and Sheridan in Wyoming) at an altitude of 9640 feet and with a sweeping view of the horizon, it is clear of snow no more than three months of the year, yet an admirable observatory, so

392. Aerial view of the Bighorn Medicine Wheel, high on Medicine Mountain in Wyoming. Estimated period of its use, c. A.D. 1250 to 1750. Besides summer-solstice sunrise and sunset, sightings from its various cairns mark the heliacle risings of the three first-magnitude stars: Aldebaran, morning of the summer solstice; Rigel, one lunar month later; and Sirius, after another lunar month.

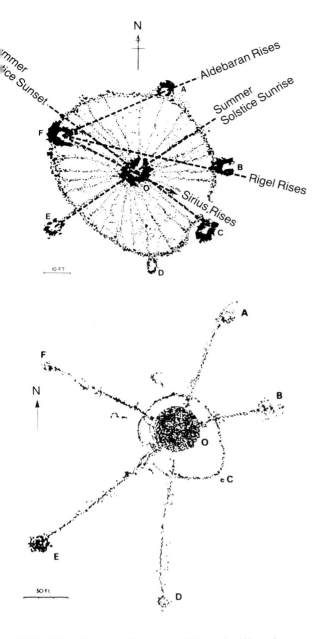

393. The Bighorn Medicine Wheel in Wyoming (above) and the Moose Mountain Medicine Wheel (below) in Saskatchewan, Canada, have similar arrangements of cairns. Both plans include alignments on the summer solstice sunrise and on three bright stars of the summer dawn. The Saskatchewan wheel is the larger and probably older. (*John A. Eddy*)

composed that on June 21, the morning of the summer solstice, sightings from two of its peripheral cairns, across the rock pile at the center, mark the points on the horizon of the solstitial sunrise and sunset. An earlier sighting that morning from another of the cairns will have marked the heliacle rising (the annual, very brief, first appearance in the dawn sky immediately before sunrise) of Aldebaran, brightest star in the constellation Taurus. Twenty-eight days (one "moon") later, another such sighting will greet Rigel, the brightest star in Orion. Again twenty-eight days (another "moon") and the sighting will be of Sirius, brightest star in the sky; after which the winter snows come down and the medicine wheel remains covered until the following June.

Now the number of lines radiating from the center of this medicine wheel is 28; and 28 is not only the number of days of one "moon," one lunar month, but also the usual number of poles set up to support the buffalo-hide covering of the med-

394/395. At the conclusion of the sacred ceremony, the Sun Dance Lodge (above) is left abandoned, but standing, as a sacred reminder exposed to the wind. The artist's plan and profile (right) show how each Lodge, like most medicine wheels, had a defined structure and celestial orientation.

icine lodges erected by the northern Plains tribes for the celebration of the Sun Dance. In the center of such a lodge there is a pivotal twenty-ninth pole (properly a freshly cut, still-living tree), which supports the twenty-eight roof beams and stands thus for the Sun, from whose life proceed the twenty-eight days of a lunar month. The time of year, furthermore, for the inauguration of the ceremony is precisely the day of the summer solstice. And so, although the Plains tribesmen of the late nineteenth century knew nothing of the functions of the medicine wheels remaining to them from an undetermined earlier time, in the canonical forms and informing ideas of their own most hallowed ceremonial, they continued to shape their lives to the correlative myth.

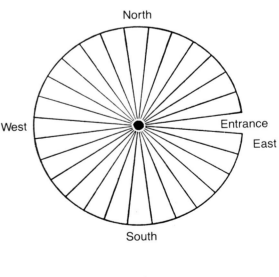

223

The Plains Indians

The Sun Dance

Something of the sense of the extreme tortures of the Plains Indian initiation rites can be learned from the explanation given of the Sun Dance of the Sioux by the old Oglala Holy Man and Keeper of the Sacred Pipe, Black Elk (Figure 397). Born in the early 1860s on the Little Powder River of Montana and Wyoming, he had experienced in early boyhood an extraordinary vision.[207] The painting executed in 1947 and 1948 by Standing Bear and called *Black Elk at the Center of the Earth* (Figure 396) is of one of the culminating moments of this revelation. And so it was not only through his lifelong participation in the ceremonials of his people as keeper of the symbol of their concord with the universe, but also through his long, long life of relevant visionary realizations, that he was rendered eligible to impart to his two best-qualified interviewers—John G. Neihardt in 1930–31 and Joseph Epes Brown in 1947–48—one of the most profoundly inspired native interpretations that we possess of a tribal people's ceremonial life.

The annual Sun Dance of the Sioux was held in June or July, when the moon was full; "for," as Black Elk noted, "the growing and dying of the moon reminds us of our ignorance which comes and goes; but when the moon is full it is as if the eternal light of the Great Spirit were upon the whole world."[208] The painting (c. 1930) by the Oglala Chieftain Short Bull (Figure 398) shows the interior of the sacred lodge, at the center of which is a cottonwood tree symbolic of Wakan-Tanka, the Great Spirit, who is the center of everything.[209] (There is such a tree at the center, also, of Figure 396.) Two thongs fixed to this central tree are really one thong passed around it; for all things which in appearance are two are in reality one.[210] They are tied to skewers through the chest of the warrior leaning backward. Blowing an eagle-bone whistle, whose sound is the voice of Wakan-Tanka as heard in the Spotted Eagle's cry,[211] the warrior will dance until the flesh breaks. Said Black Elk: "As we thus break loose, it is as if we were being freed from the bonds of the flesh."[212] The horned dancer near the entrance has four buffalo skulls skewered to his back, and at the central tree is a warrior offering pieces of his own flesh: two, four, eight, or twelve. The differing ordeals of this rite are voluntarily chosen and assumed.

Sitting at the back of the lodge is the Keeper of the Sacred Pipe, and to the south are the musicians. "The drum,"

396/397. *Black Elk at the Center of the Earth*, a watercolor on paper by Standing Bear. "Then in my vision a Voice said: 'Behold this day, for it is yours to make. Now you shall stand upon the center of the earth to see, for they are taking you.'

"I was still on my bay horse, and once more I felt the riders of the west, the north, the east, and the south, behind me in formation, and we were going east. Then I was standing on the highest mountain of them all, and round about beneath me was the whole hoop of the world. And while I stood there I saw more than I can tell and I understood more than I saw; for I was seeing in a sacred manner the shapes of all things in the spirit, and the shape of all shapes as they must live together like one being. And I saw the sacred hoop of my people was one of many hoops that made one circle, wide as daylight and as starlight, and in the center grew one mighty flowering tree to shelter all the children of one mother and one father. And I saw that it was holy."

Black Elk then told his interviewer, the poet John G. Neihardt, that the mountain upon which he stood in that vision had been Harney Peak in the Black Hills. "But anywhere," he added, "is the center of the world."[31]

said Black Elk, "is especially sacred to us. Its round form represents the universe and its steady strong beat is the pulse, the heart, throbbing at the center of the universe. As the voice of Wakan-Tanka, it stirs and helps us to understand the mystery and the power of things."[213] "O Wakan-Tanka," the musicians chant, "we are doing this that our people may live. Have mercy!"[214] And again: "O Wakan-Tanka when we are all at the center, may we have only you in our minds and hearts."[215] Blowing whistles, meanwhile, the entire company is dancing, first toward the west and back to the center, next to the north and back, next to the east, and finally to the south and back, thus beating a path in the shape of a cross.[216]

One woman is involved in this rite. She carries the pipe, attends the door, and at the time of the sacrifices offers one piece of her flesh.[217] She stands for the White Buffalo Cow Woman who brought to her people the Sacred Pipe and established the canon of their rites. Her coming is described in the following legend:

Early one morning, many winters ago, two Sioux warriors were standing on a hill, seeking game, when they beheld in the distance something approaching in a strange and wonderful manner. When it came closer, they saw that it was a very beautiful woman, clothed in white buckskin, bearing a bundle on her back, and one of the men had bad thoughts. The other rebuked him, declaring that this surely was a sacred woman; and when she drew near, she put down her bundle and bade the one with bad intentions come to her. As he approached, he and she were covered by a great cloud, and when it lifted, only she was there, with a heap of bones at her feet and great serpents gliding away. "Behold what you see!" she said to the other. "I am coming to your people and wish to talk with your chief. Return and tell him to prepare a great lodge in which to gather all his people. I have something of importance to tell."

When all had been prepared and young braves sent out to watch for her, something was seen approaching, and then, marvelously, she was in the lodge, walking around sunwise. She stopped before the chief, took the bundle from her back, and, holding it in both hands, said to him: "Behold and love this. It is holy [wakan]. No one impure should see it. For within it is a holy pipe by which to send your voices to your Grandfather and Father, Wakan-Tanka." She drew forth the pipe and with it a redstone rock which she placed on the ground. Then lifting the pipestem to the heavens, she said: "With this sacred pipe you will walk upon the Earth, your Grandmother and Mother. Every step taken upon her should be as a prayer. The redstone pipebowl is the Earth. The buffalo calf carved upon it represents all the four-leggeds that live upon your Mother; the wooden stem, all that grows upon her; and these twelve feathers hanging where the stem enters the bowl are from the spotted eagle, representing all the winged ones. For when you smoke this pipe all things of the universe are joined with you and lift their voices to Wakan-Tanka." She touched the foot of the pipe to the stone. "This round rock, made of the same redstone as the pipebowl, is the Earth: red, as the two-leggeds who live upon the earth are red." Then delivering to the chief instructions for the use of the pipe in seven ceremonials, she turned to depart and said to him: "I am now leaving, but remember, in me there are four ages. I shall look back upon your people in every age and, at the end, shall return."

She moved around the lodge sunwise and went out, but after going a short way, looked back and sat down. When she rose, she had become a red and brown buffalo calf, which walked a little way, lay down, looked back at the people, and rolled; then she got up and was a white buffalo cow, which walked on, and again rolling, became next a black buffalo, which walked away, stopped, and, after bowing to each of the quarters, disappeared over a hill.[218]

A variant has it that the maiden brought four differently colored grains of maize with the pipe, and that maize then sprang from the milk that dropped from the white cow's udder as she ambled away, so that maize and the buffalo were given together to be the food of all the red tribes.[219]

Both the Pawnee and the Sioux declare that a Cosmic Buffalo, Father and Grandfather of the universe, stands at the gate through which the animals come forth onto this earth, and back through which they return to be reborn; also, that in the course of a cycle of four world ages, this Buffalo drops one hair with the passage of each year, and with the passage of each age, one leg.[220]

"You should know," said Black Elk, "that the buffalo has twenty-eight ribs, and that in our war bonnets we have usually twenty-eight feathers."[221] The sundance lodge, he also pointed out, has twenty-eight enclosing posts, all resting on the central tree. Twenty-eight is the number of days of the moon's growing and dying, and as the twenty-eight poles rest on the one central tree, so the growing and dying of our ignorance reflects the one light of Wakan-Tanka, which is our center.[222] "The moon comes and goes, but the sun is forever."[223]

398. Sun Dance of the Sioux (the Dakota, or Lakota). Watercolor on paper by Short Bull, chief of the Oglala Sioux, c. 1930.

The Mandan Okipa Festival

By far the most vivid eye-witness account of an authentic, uncontaminated Plains Indian springtime ceremonial is that given by the artist George Catlin of the Mandan Okipa Festival, which, in 1832, immediately before the total dissolution of those people and their world in the following decade, he observed, depicted, and recorded as a privileged guest. According to Alfred W. Bowers' recent study of the remnants of Catlin's beloved tribe,[224] the Mandans, when first visited by white traders in the early part of the eighteenth century, were an agricultural people living in large, fortified villages of permanent lodges overlooking the wooded bottomlands of the Missouri River. Evidence of their southeastern origin is indicated, however, by the many ancient village sites downstream from the mouth of the Heart River, and their culture was consequently an amalgam of southeastern, agriculturally based, Mississippian traits and features recently acquired from the Plains and Central Woodland tribes. In Catlin's day, they inhabited two villages on the west bank of the Missouri about 800 miles above St. Louis. They were a people of Siouan linguistic stock, related to the Winnebago, and, according to their own account, the first people created in the world. As Catlin learned:

Originally the people lived inside the earth. They raised many vines, one of which grew up through a hole overhead, and when one of their young men climbed up this vine, he came out on the riverbank of the Missouri where the village stood in 1832. He saw many buffalo on the prairie, shot one with an arrow, and found that its meat was good. Then he returned, and when he had told what he had seen, a number decided to go up with him, including two very pretty young women. There was also a very fat woman, however whom the chief ordered not to attempt to climb. But she did, and when she was part way up, the vine broke. Thus the people above were separated from those below.[225]

According to another account:

The earth is a large tortoise covered with dirt, and there was a white-faced people, long ago, who used to dig into the dirt deeply to catch badgers. Once they struck through the shell and the tortoise sank. Water covered the earth, and all but one man drowned.[226]

Or, as some said:

There were four tortoises, one for each of the four directions. Each sent rain for ten days, and the waters covered the earth.[227]

Alfred Bowers has recorded another, much more complex and extensive version of this origin-and-flood myth, in which either one or four turtles are involved, and where the people are saved from the rising waters through the power of a sacred cedar and surrounding corral.[228] The Okipa ceremony was in part a commemoration of this salvation, the sacred cedar having been represented in the center of each Mandan village by a cedar post surrounded and hidden by an enclosure of standing planks, which in Catlin's account is likened to an ark.

This "Mandan religious ceremony," held annually, served four functions, according to Catlin: first, to appease the good and evil spirits and secure entrance into a pleasant paradise at death; second, to celebrate the subsidence of the mythological flood, called "the sinking down or settling of the waters"; third, to perform the Bull Dance, to which they attribute the coming of the buffaloes to supply them with food; and fourth, to conduct the young men of the tribe, as they annually reach manhood, through an ordeal to see which are the most hardy and best able to lead the war parties. Catlin described the Okipa Festival as follows:

In the center of the village is an open, circular area, 150 feet in diameter, kept clear for ceremonies and around which are their dwellings, as close together as possible and with doors facing the center. In the middle of the ground stands a large cylinder, 8 or 9 feet high, made of planks on end, bound with hoops, and called the Big Canoe, which is religiously preserved and protected, free from mark or scratch, as the rallying point of the whole nation.

The great religious ceremony began at the season of the full expansion of the willow leaves on the river bank; for "the twig that the bird brought home," to show that the waters had indeed subsided, "was a willow bough in full leaf." The bird that bore it was the turtle-dove, a medicine bird fully protected, never to be harmed even by their dogs. The opening morning of the ceremony, there was a deafening din and confusion: groups of women and children, all screaming, gathered on the tops of the earth-covered lodges; dogs howled; and all eyes were directed to the prairies in the west, where, at a mile distant, there was to be seen a solitary individual descending a prairie bluff and making his way directly toward the village. A great cry of alarm went up, as though the whole company were in danger of instant destruction. Bows were strung and thrummed to test their elasticity; horses were caught on the prairie and run into the village; warriors blackened their faces; dogs were muzzled; every preparation was made, as though for instant combat. Meanwhile, the figure on the prairie continued to approach with dignified step. All eyes were upon him, and at length, without opposition, he came

through the piquets and proceeded toward the center of the village. His body, chiefly naked, was painted with white clay; a robe of four white wolf skins fell back over his shoulders; he wore a splendid headdress made of two raven skins; and in his left hand he carried cautiously a large pipe, which he seemed to watch and guard as an object of great importance. All the chiefs and braves of the village stood ready to receive him, recognizing him as an old acquaintance and greeting him with his name: First or Only Man. After passing the chiefs and braves, he approached the medicine lodge, which had been religiously closed throughout the year and which he had the means of opening. He summoned four men to sweep it clean and strew green willow boughs over its floor. Wild sage and other aromatic herbs were gathered from the prairies and scattered over the floor. Willow boughs decorated the walls. Then, a number of buffalo and human skulls, along with some other articles to be used during the rites, were arranged over the floor. The whole day was devoted to this cleaning, while First or Only Man went about from door to door and, when greeted formally by the owner of the house, who would ask what the matter was, would answer with a full account of the catastrophe of the Flood, declaring that he had been the only person saved. He would tell how he had landed in his big canoe on a high mountain in the west, where he now resides, and whence he had now arrived to open the medicine lodge. He would require from every owner the gift of some edged tool, to be sacrificed to the water lest there should come another flood from which no one at all would be saved. Such tools had been used to make the Big Canoe. Collected, they were to be held in the medicine lodge until the afternoon of the fourth (the last) day, when, in a closing ceremony, they would be thrown into the river, in a deep place, from a bank thirty feet high, in the presence of the whole village—"undoubtedly," as Catlin wrote, "sacrificed to the spirit of the Water."

No one knew where First or Only Man spent the first night of this great ceremonial. Everybody was kept within doors: young and old, dogs, and all other living things. Dead silence reigned. Next morning, however, at sunrise, he again made his appearance, entering the medicine lodge and followed in single file by the young men, some fifty in all, who were the candidates of this year for the ordeal. Each one's body was chiefly naked and covered with clay of different colors—some red, others yellow, some white; and each carried in his right hand his medicine bag, on his left arm his shield of bull's hide, and in his left hand his bow and arrows, with his quiver slung on his back. When all had entered the lodge, they placed themselves in reclining positions around its sides, each having suspended above his place his weapons and medicine bag: "presenting together," in Catlin's words, "one of the most wild and picturesque scenes imaginable."

First or Only Man, now in the middle of the circle, lit and smoked his medicine pipe for their success, addressed them in a short speech of encouragement to trust in the Great Spirit during their severe ordeal, and then

called into the lodge an old medicine man, whose body was painted yellow and whom he appointed master of ceremonies for the occasion by passing to him the medicine pipe to which was attached all the power of holding these rites. The two shook hands, and First or Only Man returned to the mountains in the west, from where he would again appear in a year to open the medicine lodge.

The appointed Keeper of the Ceremonies, now lying beside the small fire in the center of the lodge, sent up prayers to the Great Spirit; his function was to see to it that none of the young men should escape from the lodge, eat, drink, or sleep during this period of preparation before the ordeal. On a small and delicate scaffold behind him, there rested a small object—too small to be identified—which none but the Keeper of the Ceremonies was permitted to approach. In Catlin's words: "This little mystery-thing, whatever it was, had the appearance from where I sat, of a small tortoise or frog lying on its back, with its

head and legs quite extended, and wound and tassled off with exceedingly delicate red and blue, and yellow ribbons or tassels, and other bright coloured ornaments; and seemed, from the devotions paid to it, to be the very nucleus of their mysteries—the *santissimus sanctorum*, from which seemed to emanate all the sanctity of their proceedings, and to which all seemed to be paying the highest devotional respect. The most urgent inquiries brought forth only the statement that it was *'great medicine,'* of which the nature 'could not be told.'"[229]

Beneath the frame on which this object lay were a knife and a bundle of splints or skewers. A number of cords of rawhide hung from the top of the lodge, and nearby were four sacks made of the skin of the buffalo's neck, each containing some three or four gallons of water and made to resemble a large tortoise lying on its back with a tail of eagle quills. On top of each lay a drumstick, with which it was to be beaten, and beside each, two gourd rattles. Catlin was very gravely told after the

399. Mandan Okipa Festival: Interior view of the medicine lodge with initiates assembled and the Keeper of the Ceremonies addressing a prayer to the Great Spirit. Painting by George Catlin.

ceremonies that "those four tortoises contained the waters from the four quarters of the world," and moreover, "that these waters had been contained therein ever since the settling down of the waters. I did not think it best," Catlin comments, "to advance any argument against so ridiculous a theory, and therefore could not even inquire or learn at what period they had been instituted, or how often, or on what occasions, the water in them had been changed or replenished."[230]

Outside the lodge during the period of this ceremonial, there were enacted in the open area in the middle of the village a number of mysteries and entertainments, of which the Bull Dance was the most prominent. Performed four times during the first day (once to each of the cardinal points), eight the second, twelve the third, and sixteen the fourth (four times to each of the points), and always around the Big Canoe, it was enacted principally by eight men. On their backs were the entire skins of buffaloes (horns, hoofs, tails, and all), their bodies were in a horizontal posture, and they looked out through the buffaloes' eyes as through masks. Their limbs, bodies, and faces were in every part covered with either black, red, or white paint; each had a lock of buffalo hair tied around his ankles, a rattle in his right hand, a slender white staff, six feet long, in his left, and a bunch of green willow boughs on his back. Divided into four pairs, these dancers took positions at the four sides of the Big Canoe, thus representing the cardinal points; and between each pair, as representing the points between, was another figure (four in all) with back turned to the Big Canoe, engaged in the same dance, and with a similar staff in one hand and a rattle in the other. Their bodies, chiefly naked, were clothed only in a kind of kilt of eagle feathers and ermine. They were painted: two of the four were black with numerous white spots, to represent the "firmament of night" and its "stars"; the other two were red with vertical white streaks, to represent the "ghosts [white] which the morning rays [red] were chasing away."[231]

The entertainment begins when the old man, the Keeper of the Ceremonies, comes dancing out of the medicine lodge, medicine pipe in hand, singing "a most pitiful lament" and approaching the Big Canoe, against which he leans, still crying. Four aged men, painted red, who have been guarding the four sides of the lodge, then enter it and come out with the four sacks of water. They set these down at the four sides of the Big Canoe, sit down by them, and start thumping with the drumsticks. Four other men shake the rattles, and all then lift their voices to the highest possible pitch, in the music of the Bull Dance, which then commences. After a quarter of an hour, all stop, and the whole nation shouts a deafening huzza of approbation. The Keeper of the Ceremonies dances back into the lodge; the sacks of water and all the rest are restored as before; and the four old men return to their places—until again called to action by the same method for another round.

A number of other characters, meanwhile, are also playing their parts. By the side of the Big Canoe are two with the skins of grizzly bears thrown over them, continually growling and threatening to devour everything before them and interfering with the forms of the ceremony. To appease them, the women are continually placing before them dishes of meat that are immediately snatched up and carried away to the prairie by two men called bald eagles—their bodies painted black and their heads white—who are chased by a hundred or more small boys—naked, with their bodies painted yellow and their heads white, representing antelopes—who at length get the food and devour it.

The chantings during the dances are of prayers to the Great Spirit for the continuation of his influence in sending buffaloes as food for the year. They are also chants of encouragement to the young men inside the lodge, announcing that "the Great Spirit has opened his ears in their behalf—the very atmosphere all about them is peace—their women and children can hold the mouth of the grizzly bear—and they are invoking from day to day the Evil Spirit, O-kee-hee-de, who has not yet dared to make his appearance!"[232] But then, alas! on the fourth day, in the last of the Bull Dances, about noon, and in the height of all these exultations, an instant scream bursts forth from the tops of the lodges. As described in Catlin's letter: "men, women, dogs and all, seemed actually to howl and shudder with alarm, as they fixed their glaring eye-balls upon the prairie bluff, about a mile in the west, down the side of which a man was seen descending at full speed towards the village! This strange character darted about in a zig-zag course in all directions on the prairie, like a boy in pursuit of a butterfly, until he approached the piquets of the village, when it was discovered that his body was entirely naked and painted as black as a negro, with pounded charcoal and bear's grease; his body was therefore everywhere of a shining black, except occasionally white rings of an inch or more in diameter, which were marked here and there all over him; and frightful indentures of white around his mouth, resembling canine teeth. . . . This unearthly-looking creature carried in two hands a wand or staff of eight or nine feet in length, with a red ball at the end of it, which he continually slid on the ground ahead of him as he ran."[233] "A small thong encircled his waist, from which a buffalo tail hung behind, and from under a bunch of buffalo hair covering the pelvis hung an artificial penis, carved in wood, of colossal dimensions, pendulous as he ran and extending below his knees; jet black, like his body, with exception of the glans, which was a glaring vermillion."[234] "Added to his hideous appearance, he gave the most frightful shrieks and screams as he dashed through the village and entered the terrified group, which was composed (in that quarter) chiefly of females, who had assembled to witness the amusements which were transpiring around the Big Canoe. . . . All eyes in the village, save those of the persons engaged in the dance, were centered upon him, and he made a desperate rush towards the women, who screamed for protection as they were endeavouring to retreat; and falling in groups upon each other as they were struggling to get out of his reach."[235] "For at his near approach to them he elevated his wand and as he raised it over their heads, there was a corresponding rising of the penis."[236]

"In this moment of general terror and alarm there was an instant check! and all for a few moments were as silent as death. The old master of ceremonies, who had run from his position at the big canoe, had met this monster of fiends, and having thrust the medicine-pipe before him, held him still and immovable under its charm! This check gave the females an opportunity to get out of his reach, and when they were free from their danger, though all hearts beat yet with the instant excitement, their alarm soon cooled down into the most exorbitant laughter and shouts of applause at his sudden defeat, and the awkward and ridiculous posture in which he was stopped and held. The old man was braced stiff by his side, with his eye-balls glaring him in the face, whilst the medicine-pipe held in its mystic chains his Satanic Majesty, annulling all the powers of his magical wand, and also depriving him of the powers of locomotion! Surely no two human beings ever presented a more striking group than these two individuals did for a few moments, with their eye-balls set in direct mutual hatred upon each other; both struggling for the supremacy, relying on the potency of their medicine or mystery. The one held in check, with his body painted black, representing (or rather assuming to be) his sable majesty, O-kee-hee-de (the Evil Spirit), frowning everlasting vengeance on the other, who sternly gazed him back with a look of exultation and contempt, as he held him in check and disarmed under the charm of his sacred mystery-pipe."[237]

"When the superior powers of the medicine-pipe (on which hang all these annual mysteries) had been thus fully tested and acknowledged, and the women had had requisite time to withdraw from the reach of the fiendish monster, the pipe was very gradually withdrawn from before him, and he seemed delighted to recover the use of his limbs again, and power of changing his position from the exceedingly unpleasant and really ridiculous one he appeared in, and was compelled to maintain a few moments before."[238]

"After repeated attempts thus made and thus defeated in several parts of the crowd, this blackened monster was retreating over the ground where the buffalo-dance was going on, and having (apparently by accident) swaggered against one of the men placed under the skin of a buffalo and engaged in the Bull Dance, he started back, and placing himself in the attitude of a buffalo bull in rutting season, he mounted onto him, repeating this act with four of the eight in succession, to the great excitement and amusement of the crowd, who were all praying to the Great Spirit to send them buffaloes to supply them with food during the season, and who attributed the coming of buffaloes entirely to the strict and critical observance of this ridiculous and disgusting part of the ceremonies.

"During the half-hour or so that he had been jostled about amongst men and beasts, to the great amusement and satisfaction of the lookers-on, he seemed to have become exceedingly exhausted, and anxiously looked out for some feasible mode of escape.

"In this awkward predicament he became

the laughing-stock and butt for the women, who being no longer afraid of him, were gathering in groups around, to tease and tantalise him; and in the midst of this dilemma, which soon became a very sad one—one of the women, who stole up behind him with both hands full of yellow dirt—dashed it into his face and eyes, and all over him, and his body being covered with grease, took instantly a different hue. He seemed heart-broken at this signal disgrace, and commenced crying most vehemently, when, *à l'instant*, another caught his *wand* from his hand and broke it across her knee. It was snatched for by others who broke it still into bits, and then threw them at him. His power was now gone—his bodily strength was exhausted, and he made a bolt for the prairie—he dashed through the crowd, and made his way through the piquets on the back part of the village, where were placed for the purpose, an hundred or more women and girls, who escorted him as he ran on the prai-

rie for half a mile or more, beating him with sticks, and stones, and dirt, and kicks, and cuffs, until he was at length seen escaping from their clutches, and making the best of his retreat over the prairie bluffs, from whence he first appeared."[239] The women returned with the colossal appendage, to the shouts of acclaim of the whole village. It was lifted and fixed above the door of the medicine lodge, the Bull Dance ended, and the time for the tortures had come.[240]

The master of ceremonies and the musicians with the four water bags reentered the medicine lodge, together with a number who were to administer the cruelties and the chief and doctors of the tribe, who were to look on and judge the youths. The old master, by the fire with his pipe, commenced smoking to the Great Spirit for the success of the aspirants;

400. Mandan Okipa Festival: The Bull Dance, with O-kee-hee-dee entering (left), the Keeper of the Ceremonies leaning on the "Big Canoe" (center), and O-kee-hee-dee fleeing (right). Painting by George Catlin.

401. Mandan Okipa Festival: The Ordeal. Keeper of the Ceremonies (center) smoking calumet for success of the initiates, and finger offerings at the buffalo skull (right). Painting by George Catlin.

the musicians took their places; and the excruciating, extreme ordeal began. The *sanctum sanctorum* scaffold was removed, as well as the buffalo and human skulls; two men—one with a scalping knife, the other with the bunch of splints—stood ready for their work; and the first of the young men came forward, placed himself on his hands and knees, or otherwise, as ordered, and submitted (without a change of face, or even smiling) to the operation. An inch or more of the flesh on each shoulder, or breast, was taken up by the thumb and finger of the man who held the knife, and the knife—ground sharp on both edges and notched to make it produce as much pain as possible—was forced through and, being withdrawn, was followed by a splint, or skewer, from the second man, who held a bunch of such in his left hand. Two cords were then lowered from the top of the lodge by men placed outside for the purpose; the cords were fastened to the skewers, and the youth raised until suspended just above the ground, where he rested until the man with the knife had skewered each arm below the shoulder and elbow and each leg on the thigh and below the knee. In other cases these operations were accomplished while the youths remained in a reclining position on the ground (as in Catlin's painting), to be then drawn up by the cords. The bystanders then would hang objects upon

the splints: each man's shield, his bow and quiver, and, in many instances, a buffalo skull or two. When all were adjusted, the youth was elevated until the weights swung clear of the ground. Someone would then advance with a pole and begin turning him—at first gently, but then vigorously—when the brave fellow, who could control his agony no longer, would burst out with cries of prayer to the Great Spirit to support and protect him in his trial. He was turned, then, faster and faster, until, fainting, his voice falters and he hangs, apparently a still and lifeless corpse. When, finally, his tongue is distended from his mouth, and his medicine bag, which he has been holding in his left hand, drops to the ground, the signal is given to the men at the top of the lodge, and they gradually and carefully lower him to the ground. One of the attendants pulls the two splints from the chest or shoulders, disengaging him from the cords but leaving all the other splints with their weights, and there he lies "in the keeping of the Great Spirit," until, after six or eight minutes, he has strength to move. He then crawls, with the weights still hanging to him, across the lodge to a buffalo skull, behind which there is a man sitting with a hatchet. The youth holds up the little finger of his left hand with a prayer of offering and lays it on the buffalo skull, where the man chops it off.

(Some were seen to offer, in the same way, the forefinger of the hand as well, leaving only the two middle fingers and thumb, which were essential for holding the bow.)

As soon as six or eight had passed the ordeal, they were led out of the lodge with the weights still hanging to their flesh; the old master of ceremonies, medicine pipe in hand, came running out of the lodge, and crying, leaned against the Big Canoe; two athletic young men, wearing headdresses of eagle feathers, took each of the exhausted initiates in hand and, after wrapping a broad leather strap around each of his wrists, stood with him, ready for what was known as "the last race." At a signal, with the weights still dragging, all then start to run, each striving to run longer than his comrades without, as they call it, "dying." When they faint, they are dragged by the straps with all possible speed. The start will have been at a moderate pace, but the speed is steadily increased, and the pain becomes so excruciating that they collapse and are dragged about unconscious until all of the weights are torn out—when the bodies are left lying as though dead, and the two that have dragged and left them run through the crowd and out onto the prairie, as though in flight. "In the keeping of the Great Spirit," each of the mangled bodies lies until, after a very few minutes, the youth can be seen moving, rising at last, reeling and staggering through the crowds, making for his lodge, where relatives and friends are waiting to restore him.[241]

402. Mandan Okipa Festival: The Last Race. Keeper of the Ceremonies encircled by young braves. Initiates running, dragged, and left "in the keeping of the Great Spirit." Painting by George Catlin.

*"When the sun died
[that is, was eclipsed, probably January 1, 1889],
I went up to heaven and saw God and all the
people who had died a long time ago.
God told me to come back and tell
my people they must be good and love one another, and not fight,
or steal, or lie.
He gave me this dance to give my people."*
—Wovoka[32]

403.

The Ghost Dance

At the time of Black Elk's vision, the Sioux were the dominant tribe from Minnesota to the Rockies and from the Yellowstone river to the Platte, with millions of buffalo to sustain them and thousands of horses. Formerly a Woodland people living around the source of the Mississippi, in the seventeenth century they were driven to the Plains when their neighbors, the Ojibwa, acquired firearms from the French. Linguistically, they are related (remotely) to the Iroquois, the earliest homes of both having been, apparently, along the South Atlantic slope.[242] Accordingly, their background was agricultural, and the wonder is that in their mythology they so perfectly adapted themes of a Southeast Woodland, Mississippian origin to their experiences as an equestrian, buffalo-hunting culture of the Great Plains.

The stunning three decades from 1860 to 1890 were, for every one of the Plains tribes, an irretrievable disaster. Helen Hunt Jackson's *A Century of Dishonor* (1881)[243] and James Mooney's *The Ghost Dance Religion and the Sioux Outbreak of 1890*[244] sufficiently review the sordid history. With their millions of buffalo van-

ished and themselves imprisoned on fraudulently managed, diminishing reservations, the shock was not only social, in the loss of an environment, but profoundly psychological, in the loss of their spiritual symbol. "The buffalo," said Black Elk, "represents the people and the universe. And is he not generous in that he gives us our homes and our food?"[245]

The spiritual reactions were chiefly of two orders: (1) a briefly flourishing eschatological movement (the Ghost Dance), anticipating an immediate regeneration of the earth, with the disappearance of the White Man and the resurrection of both the buffalo and all the Indian dead; and

(2) an enduring hallucinogenic movement (the Peyote Cult: a communal eating of peyote buttons), facilitating both a reactivation of the mythogenetic imagination and a regeneration of the symbolic life from within.

The Ghost Dance originated in the visions of Wovoka, a Paiute of Nevada, in 1889. Influential in his imagination were: Paiute myths of the aging and regeneration of the earth; the teachings c. 1870, of Tavibo, an earlier Paiute prophet; and certain echoes of the Christian eschatological expectation that stemmed chiefly from the Mormon community in Utah. Spontaneously, his message flew from reser-

The expectation of the Ghost Dance was of an imminent restitution of the Indians' destroyed world, with a resurrection of the buffalo herds, as well as of the Indians of all time, who then together with their grandchildren who are here dancing to hasten and welcome their return, would live in peace and joy forever on this earth. In trance and vision the returning Indian hosts could already be seen approaching, driving before them buffalo herds, ponies, and game of all kinds.

No drum was used in these dances. Men and women, hands joined, circled sunwise to songs brought back from the trances.

404. Ghost-Dancing Arapaho and Cheyenne. Drawing in colored ink on buckskin by Yellow Nose, a Ute captive of the Cheyenne, 1891.

All are in full costume, wearing medicine paint and consecrated feathers. The Cheyenne women's hair is braided, the Arapaho's hangs loose; two carry children on their backs; several wave the handkerchiefs that helped to induce the hypnotic effect; and one holds up the symbolic crow, sacred to the Ghost Dance. There is a man with a gaming wheel in hand, another with a shinny stick—reminiscent tokens of earlier visions. In the center, with arms upraised, are dancers in the rigid state; and toward the right, a medicine man is hypnotizing a woman. The spotted object on the ground behind him is a shawl from the shoulders of the woman above it.[33]

vation to reservation until the government agent on the Pine Ridge Reservation of the Sioux became alarmed, and on December 29, 1890, some 300 men, women, and their children were massacred by United States troops at Wounded Knee.[246] Elsewhere the dancing continued for another couple of years, until the undeniable failure of the Messiah's prophecies quenched the hope, and in the early 1890s the Peyote religion gained the field. Known today as the Native American Church, this movement claimed in the mid-1970s some 200,000 adherents among fifty or more of the surviving North American Indian tribes.

405. The Paiute prophet Wovoka of Mason Valley, Nevada (1856?–1932), whose visionary visit to the Other World inspired the Ghost Dance religion of hope, which rapidly spread among the western tribes immediately following the extermination of the buffalo. Photograph, c. 1920.

Myths and Tales of the Northern Plains

Three Blackfoot Medicine Legends

The Blackfeet are an Algonquian tribe that in the late seventeenth and early eighteenth centuries left the Woodlands for the northwestern Plains, where in the early nineteenth century their domain extended from the Saskatchewan River to the Missouri. The following three legends tell of the origins of their Bull Dance, their medicine lodge, and a certain sacred pipe. All conform to that universal pattern of the "Adventure of the Hero"—Departure/Initiation/Return—which, in *The Hero with a Thousand Faces*,[247] I have termed the Monomyth. The first takes place on the plane of earth; the second is of a journey to the Sun; and the third (an Orpheus and Eurydice type) concerns a visit to the Land of Shades.

The Buffalo's Wife

The people had prepared a buffalo fall, but the herds driven toward it always swerved to right or left, down the sloping hills, and across the valley to safety. So the people were in danger of starvation.

A young woman, early one morning fetching water, looked up and saw a herd on the cliff above the corral. "Oh!" she cried, "if you would jump I would marry one of you." To her amazement the buffalo began coming over, and she was then terrified when a big bull, with one bound, cleared the corral and was approaching. "Come!" he said, and he took her arm. "No, no!" she cried, resisting. "You said," said he, "you would marry one of us, and see! The corral is filled." Then he led her up over the bluff and away.

When the people had finished slaughtering, they missed the young woman, and when her father could not find her, he took his bow and quiver, climbed up the bluff, and went onto the prairie. When he had traveled far, he came to a wallow and saw a herd a little way off. Sitting down, tired and thinking what to do, he watched a magpie alight nearby. "Ha! You beautiful bird!" he said. "Help me! As you fly about, should you see my daughter, tell her, 'Your father waits by the wallow.'" The bird winged away toward the herd, and, seeing the young woman, alighted nearby. Picking around, turning his head this way and that, he came very close and said, "Your father is waiting by the wallow." "Sh-h-h!" she whispered; for the big bull was nearby, asleep. "Tell him to wait. I will come." The magpie flew and reported to the man, "Your daughter is with the herd and says to wait."

When the bull woke, he said to his wife, "Get me some water." She took from his head a horn and hurried to the wallow. "Oh father!" she said. "Why did you come? You

will be killed." "I came," said he, "to take my daughter home. Come! Let us hurry!" "No, no!" she said. "They would follow and kill us. Wait until he sleeps again. I'll be back." She filled the horn with water and returned to her husband. He took a sip. "Ha, ha!" said he. "There is a person here." Her heart rose. He drank some more, got up, and bellowed. What a fearful sound! Up rose the bulls, raised their short tails, shook them, tossed their great heads, and bellowed back. Then all pawed the dirt, rushed about, and coming to the wallow, found that poor man, trampled him, hooked and again trampled him, until not even a small piece of him could be seen. His daughter cried, "My father!" "Ah!" said the bull; "you mourn for your father. Now you see how it is with us. We have seen our mothers, fathers, and many of our relatives hurled over the rocky walls and killed for food for your people. But I will have pity and give you one chance. If you can bring your father to life, you and he may return to your people."

She turned to the magpie. "Pity and help me!" she said. "Go, search the mud. Try to find some little piece of my father." The bird flew to the wallow, searched every hole, tore up the mud with his nose, and at last found something white. Pulling hard, he brought out a bit of the backbone, with which he returned. The daughter placed this on the ground, covered it with her robe, and sang; then, removing the robe, she saw her father lying there, dead. Once more she spread the robe and sang, and when again she removed it, he was breathing. He stood up. The buffalo were amazed. The magpie was delighted and, flying round and round, set up a clatter.

Said the big bull to the others of his herd, "We have seen strange things today. The man we trampled is alive. The people's medicine is strong." Then he turned to his wife. "Before you go, we shall teach you our dance and song. Do not forget them." All the buffalo danced, and as befitted such great beasts, the song was slow and solemn, the step ponderous and deliberate. And when the dance was done the big bull said, "Now go home and do not forget what you have seen. Teach the dance and song to your people. Its medicine objects are the bull's head and robe. Those who dance the bulls are to wear these when they perform."

The joy of the camp was great when the man returned with his daughter. He called a council of chiefs, told them what had happened, and they selected braves to whom the dance and song were taught. And thus was formed the Blackfoot association called All Comrades, whose duty it is to regulate the tribal life and the rites through which the animals slain each year are returned to life.[248]

Scarface

In the earliest times, all the tribes were at peace. And in those days there was a man with a very beautiful daughter whom all the young men wished to marry, but she would only shake her head. Her father asked, "How is this?" Her mother said, "What shame for us should a child be born and our daughter still unmarried!" "Father! Mother!" the beautiful girl replied. "I have no secret lover, but now

hear the truth: the Person Above, the Sun, has told me, 'Do not marry, for you are mine. Take heed, and you shall be happy and live to a great age.'"

Now there was a very poor young man whose parents and relatives had all gone to the Sand Hills. He was handsome, except that on his cheek there was a scar, and his clothes were always poor and old. After the Bull Dances one year, some of the great braves whom the girl had refused taunted him. "Why don't *you* ask her?" And they laughed, but he did not. "Indeed," he said, "I shall do as you say." And he went to her. "I am poor," he said; "yet now, today, I ask you: will you be my wife?" She hid her face in her robe and brushed the ground with her moccasin, back and forth. "True," she said, after a time, "I have refused all the rich young men, yet now the poor one asks, and I am glad. I will be your wife, and my people will be happy. They will give us robes and furs, and you will be poor no longer. However, the Sun has spoken to me and has told me that I belong to him. So now, go to the Sun and say to him: 'She to whom you have spoken has heeded your words. But she now wants to marry and I want her for my wife.' Ask him to take that scar from your face, and that will be his sign. But if he refuses, or if you cannot find his lodge, do not return."

*   *   *

Scarface went to an old woman who had been kind to him and asked her to make him moccasins for a journey. She made seven pairs and gave him also a sack of food (pemmican), for she liked him. "Pity me, O Sun!" he prayed; and sad at heart, he set forth. Many days he traveled, over prairies, along rivers, among mountains, and the sack of food every day grew lighter. One night he stopped at the home of a wolf. "I seek the place where the Sun lives," he said. "I have traveled far," the wolf said, "and have never seen the Sun's place. But I know someone very wise. Ask the bear." The bear did not know, but suggested the badger, and the badger, then, the wolverine. Scarface, however, could not find the wolverine. Then he sat down, completely worn out, his moccasins broken, his food nearly gone. "O pity me, Wolverine!" he cried, and behind him heard a voice: "What is it, my brother?" Scarface told his story, and since it was already evening, the wolverine said he would show him the trail next morning to the big water beyond which the Sun lived. But when the youth then followed that trail and beheld the expanse of the big water, his heart failed him. "Here at this water," he said, "I shall die."

Two swans came swimming. They asked who he was and what had brought him to that shore. He responded, and they said, "Take heart. Across this water is the lodge of that Person Above whom you seek. Get on our backs, and we shall take you there." He waded in, lay on their backs, and they started. Very deep and black is that water. Strange beings inhabit it: monsters that seize people and drown them. Yet the two swans carried him safely to the other shore, where a broad trail led from the water. "*Hyi!*" said the swans. "Follow that trail."

Pretty soon there were some beautiful things to be seen lying along that trail: a war shirt, a shield, a bow, and some arrows. Scarface stepped carefully around them. Then he met an extraordinarily handsome young man with very long hair, wearing clothing of strange skins and moccasins sewn with colored feathers. "Did you see some weapons along the road?" the young man asked. "Yes," Scarface said. "But you did not touch them!" "No; I thought someone had left them there." "Then you are not a thief," the youth said. "What is your name?" "My name is Scarface." "Where are you going?" "To the Sun." "My name," the young man said, "is Early Riser [The Morning Star]. The Sun is my father. I will take you to our lodge. He is out now, but will be in tonight."

The lodge was large and beautiful: painted on it were strange medicine animals and behind, on a tripod, were weapons and beautiful clothes. The two entered, and within was Morning Star's mother, the Moon. She welcomed Scarface kindly, gave him food, and asked the purpose of his visit. When he had told her all, and when the Sun was soon to return, she hid him under a pile of robes. "I smell a person," the Sun said when he came in. "Yes, father," said Morning Star, "an honest young man has come to see you. I know that he is honest, for he did not touch my things when he passed them on the trail." They brought Scarface out from under the robes, and the Sun invited him to stay as long as he liked. "My son is sometimes lonesome," he said. "Be his friend."

So Scarface stayed a long time and hunted with Morning Star. Early in his stay the Moon told him neither to go, nor to let her son go, near the big water to hunt. "Great birds with long sharp bills are there," she said, "and they kill people. They have killed all of my sons but Morning Star." However, one day when the two were not far from the big water, Morning Star spied the birds. "Come," he said, "let us kill them!" And he started toward the water. Scarface, protesting, followed and then ran ahead; for he knew that to save his friend, he had to kill the birds himself, which he did; with his spear he killed them all. The two cut off the birds' heads, carried them home, and told the Moon what had been done. She was so elated that she kissed Scarface and called him "my son." She told the Sun when he came home, and he also called him "my son." "I shall not forget," he said, "what you have this day done for me. Tell me now what I can do for you." And when he had heard, he said, "I have watched and I know. She is good, she is wise, I give her to you, she is yours."

"And now," said the Sun, "let me instruct you. Be wise and listen! I am the only chief. I made the earth, the mountains, prairies, rivers and forests, the people and all the animals. I can never die. The winter makes me old and weak, but every summer I am young again. Now of animals the smartest is the raven: he always finds his food. And the most sacred is the buffalo. Of them all, I like him best. He is for the people, your food and shelter. And of his body, the most sacred part is the tongue. That is mine. And berries, too, are sacred; they too are mine. Come now with me and see the world." He conducted Scarface to the edge of the sky, and they looked down. They saw it round and flat and all around the edge were walls, straight down.

Then said the Sun: "When a man is sick or in danger, let his wife promise that if he recovers, she will build me a Medicine Lodge. If she is pure and true, I shall be pleased and help the man; but if she is bad and lies, I shall be angry. The lodge is to be built like the world: round and with walls. But first a sweat house is to be built of a hundred sticks, domed, like the sky. And half shall be painted red—for me; the other half, black,—that is the night. And now, which is the better, the heart or the brain? The brain; for the heart often lies, the brain, never."

The Sun then told Scarface how the Medicine Lodge was to be made and, when he finished, rubbed a medicine on the young man's face, and the scar disappeared. Then he gave him two raven feathers, saying, "These are the sign for the girl, that I give her to you. They must always be worn by the husband of the woman who builds a Medicine Lodge."

The young man was now ready to return home. The Sun and Morning Star gave him presents. The Moon cried, kissed him, and called him "my son." Then the Sun showed him the short trail, the Milky Way, and following that, he soon reached the earth.

* * *

It was a very hot day when he arrived. All the lodge skins were raised, and the people sat in the shade. One of the chiefs, early in the morning, had seen a person sitting on a nearby butte, closely wrapped in his robe, and when it was almost night and the person was still there, he sent some young men out to meet him. "He may be a stranger," the chief said; "go and ask him in."

When invited, the person arose, threw off his robe, and they were amazed. The clothes were beautiful; the bow, shield, and weapons of a strange make; but they knew his face, although the scar was gone. A shout of welcome went up, and all the people rushed to see him. And there in the crowd was that beautiful girl. He took the two raven feathers from his head, handed them to her, and said, "The trail was very long, I nearly died but, through his Helpers, found his lodge. He is glad. He sends you these two feathers. They are his sign."

Great then was her joy. When married, they constructed the first Medicine Lodge exactly as the Sun had described it. And the Sun, who was pleased, gave them both great age. They were never ill. And when they were both very old and, one morning, their children called, "Wake up!" they did not move. In the night, in sleep, without pain, their shadows had departed for the Sand Hills.[249]

The Sand Hills

There was once a young man so fond of his wife that when she died shortly after giving birth, he was disconsolate. He would take the child on his back and wander about the hills weeping, until one day he said to it, "My little boy, you will have to live with your grandmother, while I search for your mother, to bring her back."

When he set out for the Sand Hills, the fourth night away he had a dream in which he entered the little lodge of an old woman. "Why are you here, my son?" she asked. "I am mourning day and night," he answered. "For whom?" she asked. "For my wife," he replied. "Oh!" she said. "I saw her pass this way some time ago. I am not powerful medicine myself, but there is another old woman by that far butte. Go to her, and she will give you the power needed for your journey. Past the next butte beyond her lodge is the camp of the ghosts."

He woke and the next day went on. It took him long to reach the distant butte, and he found no lodge there. When he lay down, however, he dreamed, and there he saw a little lodge. An old woman came to the doorway, called, and he went in. "My son," she said, "you are very poor, and I know why you have come this way. You are searching for your wife in the ghost country. It will be hard for you to get there. You may not be able to bring your wife back. But I have great power and shall do for you all I can. If you do everything exactly as I say, you may succeed." Then she gave him a medicine bundle for the journey. "Wait here," she said, "while I go to their camp and try to bring back some of your relatives. You may return with them, but on the way must shut your eyes; for should you open them and look about, you would die and never come back. When you get to the camp, you will pass a big lodge. They will ask, 'Where are you going? And who said you might come here?' You must reply, 'My grandmother, who is out here standing by me, told me to come.' They will try to scare you, they will make fearful noises, and you will see strange, terrible sights. But do not be afraid." Then she left and, after a time, returned with one of his relatives, with whom he departed for the camp.

When they came to the big lodge, someone called out, and he answered as instructed, and when he then passed into the camp, the ghosts tried to frighten him, as predicted. But he kept on and came to another lodge, whose owner came out and asked where he was going. "I am searching for my wife," he said. "I so mourn for her that I cannot rest, and my little boy is crying for his dead mother. I have been offered other wives, but want only this one for whom I am searching." The ghost said, "That you have come here is a fearful thing. It is likely you will never leave. Never before has a living person been seen here." Then he invited him into the lodge. "You will remain here four nights and will then see your wife," he said. "But you must be extremely careful or you will die right there."

Then that chief ghost went out and called for a feast, inviting the man's father-in-law and other relatives. It was as though their son-in-law had died and arrived as a ghost. When they had gathered, they halted at the entrance. "There is a person in there," they called. It seems there was something about him, a smell that they could not bear. When the chief ghost burned sweet pine, they entered, and he told them the young man's mission. "Now pity your son-in-law. Neither the great distance nor the fearful sights have weakened his heart," he said. "He mourns, not only for his wife, but also because his little son is without a mother. He is tenderhearted. Do pity him, and give him back his wife." The ghosts consulted. Then one of them said to him: "Yes, you will remain here four nights, then we shall give you our medicine pipe, the Worm Pipe, and you will go home with your wife."

When the time came, the chief ghost again called and they arrived, bringing the man's wife. One came beating a drum. Following was another with the Worm Pipe, which they presented to him. "Now be careful," the chief ghost then said. "Tomorrow you and your wife will start on your homeward way. She will carry the Worm Pipe. Some of your relatives will be with you for four days, during which time you must not open your eyes, or you will return here and be forever a ghost. You can see that your wife is not now a person. But in the middle of the fourth day you will be told to look, and when you do, you will see that she has become a person and that your relatives will have disappeared."

The ghostly father-in-law then spoke to him. "When you reach your camp, you must not enter immediately, but let some of your relatives know you have arrived and ask them to build you a sweat house. Go into this and wash your body thoroughly. If you miss any part of it you will die. There is something about us ghosts that is difficult to remove. And do not whip your wife, or strike her with a knife or with fire. If you do, she will vanish from your sight and return to the Sand Hills."

Accompanied by their relatives, the reunited couple then left the ghost country for home, and on the fourth day the wife said, "Open your eyes!" Her husband looked about and saw that those who had been with them were gone and that they were standing before the old woman's lodge by the butte. She appeared and said, "Give back to me the medicines by which you accomplished your purpose." He returned them and became again fully a person.

When they drew near to the camp, the wife went ahead and sat down on a butte. Some curious people came out to see who that was, and she called to them: "Do not come nearer. Tell my mother and relatives to build a lodge for us, a little away from the camp, with a sweat lodge nearby." When this had been done, the man with his wife took a thorough sweat, then entered the lodge and burned sweet grass, purifying both their clothing and the Worm Pipe. Their relatives and friends then came to see them, and the man described his adventure, explaining that the pipe over the doorway was a medicine pipe, presented to him by his father-in-law in the Sand Hills. That is how the Worm Pipe was obtained, which now belongs to the Piegan band known as the Worm People.

However, not long after all this, the husband, one night, told his wife to do something, and when she hesitated, he picked up a firebrand—only to threaten, not to strike. But it was enough: she vanished and never again was seen.[250]

Two Creation Myths

George Bird Grinnell, who collected these legends directly from the lips of his friends of the 1870s and 1880s—Red Eagle, Almost a Dog, Four Bears, Wolf Calf, Big Nose, Heavy Runner, Young Bear Chief, Wolf Tail, Rabid Wolf, Running Rabbit, White Calf, All Are His Children, Double Runner, Lone Medicine Person, and many others: all members of the last generation of pre-reservation Plains Indians—states that he was unable to obtain anything like a complete account of the beginning of things.[251] In the legend of Scarface, the Sun appears as Creator; in the following tales, the Creator is Napi, Old Man, the Blackfoot Trickster. "There is some reason to suspect, however, that the Sun and Old Man are one," states Grinnell; "for I have been told by two or three old men that 'the Sun is the person whom we call Old Man.'"[252]

Originally there was a great womb in which were conceived the progenitors of all the animals now on earth, and among them was Old Man. One day the womb burst, and Old Man jumped first to the ground. That is why he calls the animals Young Brothers, and they call him Old Man.[253]

It is said that in the beginning, when all was under water, Old Man and the animals were floating on a large raft. One day Old Man told the beaver to dive and try to bring up some mud. The beaver was gone a long time, but could not reach bottom. The loon tried, and the otter, but the water was too deep. Then the muskrat dove and was gone so long they thought he had drowned; but he came up, nearly dead, and when they had pulled him onto the raft, they found a bit of mud in one of his paws. Of this, Old Man formed the earth and then the people.[254]

Among Algonquian tribes from the Atlantic to the Rocky Mountains, this "Earth Diver" motif is a standard feature of origin myths. That it was brought either with them or to them from Siberia becomes evident from such Asian examples as the following:

From the Yenisei Ostyaks: In the beginning all was water, and hovering over it was the Great Shaman Doh, accompanied by swans, loons, and other waterfowl. Since he could nowhere find a resting place, Doh asked the diver bird to bring up some earth from the bottom. The bird dove twice, and of the bit of mud then brought up, Doh made the earth as an island floating on the primal sea.[255]

A Buriat version: Water again, and Sombol-Burkhan sent down the white diver bird, who at half way was challenged by a crab of the depths that asked where he was going, and when told, the crab became angry. "I've been in this water forever," it said, "and have never

yet found its bottom. Now go back, right away, or I'll cut you in two with my scissors!" The bird returned, and when Sombol-Burkhan heard his excuse, he gave him a magic phrase by which, on his second dive, the power of the crab was annulled.[256]

From the Northern Yakuts: The Mother of God decided to create a world, but having no material, she created first the diver bird and the duck, commanding them to dive into the primal sea. First to return was the duck with some mud in her mouth; then came the diver with nothing. "There is nothing down there to be found," it said, and the Mother of God became angry. "Deceitful bird! Have I not given you more strength and a longer beak than the duck? You are lying, out of pity for the ocean. Well then, stay with it! Never shall you live on the sacred surface of the earth, but forever dip and dive in the waters, searching for refuse for your food!"[257]

Another Yakut example: The White Creator Lord moved in the beginning above the boundless ocean, and on seeing a bladder floating on the waters, inquired: "Who and whence?" The bladder replied that it was Satan and lived on the hidden earth underwater. God said: "If there is really earth down there, then bring me a piece of it." Satan dived and returned with a morsel of earth. God blessed it, placed it on the surface of the water, and seated himself upon it. Then Satan resolved to drown God by stretching out the land, but the more it stretched the stronger it grew, covering soon a great part of the ocean's surface.[258]

From eastern Finland: God sat in the beginning on a golden pillar in the middle of the sea. His shadow fell on the waters and, seeing it, he ordered it to arise. It was the Devil, and when God sent him diving for earth, he kept some of it hidden in a corner of his mouth. When God's word then caused the particle of earth placed on the sea to expand, that remaining in the Devil's mouth swelled too, and to keep from choking, he spat it out, thus adding rocks and mountains to the scene.[259]

In the Hindu Puranas: It is told that at the time of one of those universal floods which [in that mythology] recur every 311,040,000,000,000 years, the great god Vishnu himself, whose dream is the universe, assumed the form in his dream of a giant boar and, in this character, dove into the cosmic sea and brought the goddess Earth to the surface.[260] On another occasion, Vishnu took the form of a tortoise and, floating in the cosmic sea, supported on his back the cosmic mountain.[261]

In the Markandeya Purana the continent of India is described as resting on the back of the same tortoise.[262] The Puranas represent a relatively late development of Hindu mythology, c. A.D. 400 to 1000. However, already in the Vedas, c. 1200 to 800 B.C., the mythological tortoise is equated with Prajāpati, Lord of Creatures, the Creator, even receiving the epithet *svayambhū*, "self-created." In the Shatapatha Brahmana it is told that when Prajāpati was about to create the creatures of this earth, he changed himself into a tortoise; and it was this transformation of the ancient Vedic god that became in later myth the tortoise incarnation of Vishnu.[263] (Compare the turtle's role in the Iroquois creation myth on page 207; the rattle of the False Face, Figure 343 on page 208; and the mythic reference of the water-filled turtle drums of the Mandan Okipa Festival described on pages 226–231.)

A second Blackfoot account of Old-Man-in-the-Beginning tells of his coming from the south.

Traveling north, fashioning animals and birds along the way, he made the mountains, prairies, timber, and brush first, putting red paint here and there in the ground, covering the plains with grass for the animals to eat, putting trees in the ground and all kinds of animals upon it. When he made the bighorn with its big head and horns, he made it out in the prairie. It did not seem to travel easily there, so he took it by one of its horns and led it to the mountains, where it skipped about among the rocks with ease. So he said, "This is the place that suits you." And while he was there he made an antelope of dirt, turning it loose to see how it would go. But it ran so fast, it fell over the rocks and got hurt. So he took it down to the prairie, where it ran away fast and gracefully, and he said, "This is what you are suited to."

One day Old Man decided to make a woman and child, and he formed them both of clay. After he had molded them, he said to the clay, "You must become people." Then he covered it up and left. Next morning he returned and took the covering off and saw that the shapes had changed a little. The second morning there was more change, and the third still more. The fourth morning he told them to rise and walk, and they did so. They walked down to the river with their Maker, and he told them his name was Old Man.

As they were standing there, the woman asked, "How is it? Shall we always live? Will there be no end to it?" "I had not thought of that," said Old Man. "We shall have to decide. I'll take this buffalo chip and throw it in the river. If it floats, when people die, in four days they will be alive again. But if it sinks, there will be an end to them." He threw the chip into the river, and it floated. The woman turned and picked up a stone, saying: "No, I'll throw this stone into the river; if it floats, we shall always live; if it sinks, people must die, so that they may feel pity for each other and sorrow for each other." She threw the stone into the water and it sank. "There," said Old Man, "you have chosen."

Not many nights after that, however, the woman's child died, and she cried for it a great deal; and to Old Man she said, "Let us change this. The law that you first made, let that be it." "Not so!" he replied. "What has been made the law is the law. Your child is dead. That fact cannot be changed."

And so that is how we came to be people. And it was Old Man who made us.[264]

Trickster Tales

"In the serious tales, such as those of the creation," states Grinnell of the Blackfoot Trickster-Creator, Old Man, "he is spoken of respectfully, and there is no hint of the impish qualities which characterize him in other stories, in which he is powerful, but also at times impotent; full of all wisdom, yet at times so helpless that he had to ask aid from the animals. Sometimes he sympathizes with people, and at others, out of pure spitefulness, he plays them malicious tricks that are worthy of a demon. He is a combination of strength, weakness, wisdom, folly, childishness, and malice."[265]

The resemblance of this characterization to that already given of Mantis, the African Bushman Trickster, is manifest. (See pages 91–99.) For, indeed, as Karl Kerényi has pointed out in a commentary on the Coyote cycle of the Winnebago (a Siouan-speaking tribe now on reservations in Wyoming and Nebraska), the mythological Trickster is immediately recognizable in *whatever* cultural costume he assumes. Voracious, phallic, stupid, and yet sly, what he signifies is the spirit of disorder, the enemy of boundaries. "Disorder belongs," states Kerényi, "to the totality of life, and the function of his mythology is to add disorder to order and so make a whole."[266]

The Eye Juggler

One day, as Old Man was walking in the woods, he saw something very queer. A bird, making a strange noise, was sitting on a limb, and every time it made this noise, its eyes would go out of its head and fasten on the tree; then it would make another kind of noise, and its eyes would come back to their places.

"Little Brother," cried Old Man, "teach me how to do that." "If I do," replied the bird, "you must not let your eyes go out of your head more than three times a day. If you do, you will be sorry." "Just as you say, Little Brother," said Old Man. "The trick is yours."

When he had learned the trick, Old Man was very glad, and did it three times, right away. Then he stopped. "Why did he tell me to do it only three times?" he thought. "I will do it again, anyhow." So he made his eyes go out a fourth time, and could not call them back. "Oh Little Brother," he called to the bird, "come help me get back my eyes." But the bird did not reply; it had flown away. Old Man felt over the tree with his hands, but could not find his eyes; and he wandered about for a long time, crying and calling to the animals for help.

A wolf decided to have fun with him. He had found a dead buffalo and, taking a piece of the rotting meat, held it close to the nose of the Old Man, who, being hungry, tried to feel around for it, but the wolf kept jerking it away. Once, however, Old Man caught him,

and, plucking out one of his eyes, put it in his own head. Then he could see and was able to recover his eyes, but never again could he do the trick the little bird had taught him.[267]

The Sun's Leggings

Traveling around, Old Man happened to come to the lodge of the Sun, who invited him to stay a while, and he was glad to do so. One day they needed meat. Said the Sun: "Old Man, what do you say, shall we go and kill some deer?" "Very well," replied Old Man, "I like deer meat."

The Sun took down a bag and drew from it a beautiful pair of leggings, embroidered with bright feathers and colored porcupine quills. "These are my hunting leggings. They are great medicine," he said. "All I have to do is to walk around a patch of woods, and the leggings set it afire and drive the deer out to be shot." "Hai-yah!" How wonderful!" Old Man exclaimed. And he made up his mind to have those leggings, even if he had to steal them. The two set forth, and everything happened as the Sun had said. Each shot a white-tail deer.

That night, when going to bed, the Sun pulled off his leggings, and Old Man watched where he put them. Then, in the middle of the night, he stole them and went off. He had traveled a long way, when, becoming tired, he made a pillow of the leggings and lay down to sleep. In the morning he heard someone talking. "Old Man!" It was the Sun's voice. "Why are my leggings under your head?" Old Man looked around and saw that he was in the Sun's lodge. He thought he must have walked, unknowing, in a circle. The Sun asked again: "What are you doing with my leggings?" "Oh," replied Old Man, "I just couldn't find a pillow, so I used these."

Next night, again, Old Man took the leggings and, this time, did not walk, but ran. You see what a fool he was! He did not know that the whole world is the Sun's lodge. So when morning came, he was still inside that lodge, and the Sun said: "Old Man, since you like my leggings so much, I give them to you. Keep them." Old Man was happy and went his way.

One day, when his food was gone, he put on the medicine leggings, set fire to a patch of woods, and was just about to shoot a deer, when he saw that the fire was coming close to him. He turned and ran, but it followed. He ran as fast as he could, but the fire gained. It began to burn his legs, the leggings were afire. He jumped into a river and pulled off the leggings as fast as he could. They were burned to pieces.[268]

The Buffalo Hoarder

There came a time when the people were starving. There were no buffalo or antelope anywhere, the deer and elk trails were covered with grass, and not even a rabbit could be seen. Old Man decided to find out what had happened, and, taking with him the son of a chief, for many days he traveled, searching. Then one day, having climbed a ridge, they saw, far off by a stream, a single lodge. "What kind of person is that," the young man said, "camping alone, far from friends?" "That," Old Man replied, "is the one who has hidden all the animals. He has a wife and a little son."

They went down, and when close to the lodge, Old Man changed himself into a little dog and his companion into a digging stick. The lodge-dweller's child found the dog and brought it home. "Look, father!" he said. "What a pretty little dog I found!" "Throw it away," said the man. "That is not a dog." The little boy cried, but his father made him take it out, and it was then that he found the digging stick. He returned with both. "Look, mother!" he called. "See the pretty root digger I found!" "Throw those things away," the father said. "That is not a stick, and this is not a dog." But the woman argued. "I want that stick. And let our little boy keep his dog." "Very well!" said the man. "But remember, if trouble comes, you will have brought it on yourself." He sent them off to pick berries and, while they were gone, killed and slaughtered a buffalo. When his wife returned, he gave her the meat to roast, and when the boy began feeding some to the dog, the man snatched it away. "That is not a dog," he said again. "Don't feed it."

That night, Old Man and the chief's son returned to their proper shapes and quietly ate some of the meat. "You were right," the young man whispered, "this surely is the one who has hidden the buffalo." When they had finished their meal, they again became a little dog and a stick.

In the morning the man sent his wife and little boy to dig roots. The woman took the stick along, the dog followed the boy, and as they went along, searching and digging, they approached a cave. At its mouth stood a buffalo cow. The dog scampered into the cave, and the stick, falling from the woman's hand, followed, gliding like a snake. Inside were all the animals, and Old Man and the young man, in their proper shapes, commenced driving them out onto the prairie. Never before were so many buffalo, antelope, deer, and other game animals to be seen. The man came running. "Who is driving out my animals?" he cried. "The dog and stick are in there," his wife said. "Didn't I tell you!" he yelled. "See now the trouble you've brought upon us!" He put an arrow to his bow, waiting for the two inside to come out. But when the last animal, a big bull, was about to leave, the stick hid itself amidst the hair of its neck, and the little dog held on beneath, until they were far out on the prairie, where they changed again into their true shapes and drove the animals toward the people's camp.

When the people came out to turn the buffalo herd toward their buffalo fall, just as the leading buffalo were about to jump, a raven came croaking, flapping its wings before them, and they swung aside. When this happened again and again, Old Man knew that the raven was the buffalo hoarder. He changed himself into a beaver and lay on the riverbank as though dead. The raven dove to pick at it, and Old Man, catching its legs, ran to the camp, where he tied it over the smoke hole of the chief's lodge. There, as the days went by, it grew poor and weak, eyes blurred with the smoke, continually crying, until at last Old Man released it and told it to take its proper shape. Then: "Look at me!" said Old Man. "Why did you try to fool me? Of all the peoples and tribes I am the chief. I shall never die. I made the mountains, prairies, rocks, and they are standing still. You can see them. Now go home to your wife and child, and when hungry, hunt like anyone else, or you shall die."[269]

The Fire-Bed Game and Trickster Tricked

Another day, just wandering, Old Man heard some really queer singing. He had never heard anything like it. He searched and at last discovered a circle of rabbits making medicine. They had built a fire and produced a bed of coals on which all but one would lie down together and sing, while the remaining rabbit covered them. After a short while, the guardian would uncover them and they would all jump out, and this apparently was great fun.

"Little Brothers," said Old Man, "it is wonderful, how you lie there without getting burned. I wish you would teach me to do that." "Come on, Old Man!" they said. "We'll show you. You must sing our song and not stay too long; for those coals are really hot." Old Man began to sing, lay down, and they covered him with the coals, which did not burn him at all. "Why, this is very nice," he said. "You have powerful medicine. Now you lie down and let me cover you up." They lay down, and Old Man covered them. Then he piled the whole fire on top of them and only one old rabbit got out. When he moved to put her back, she begged: "Have pity, Old Man! My children are about to be born." So he let her go, that there might be more rabbits in the world. He piled more wood on the fire, and when his rabbits were cooked, cut some red willow brush and laid them on it to cool. The grease soaked into the branches, so that today, if you hold red willow over a fire, you will see grease on the bark. Also you can see that rabbits have a burnt place on their backs, where the one that got away was singed.

Old Man was sitting, waiting for his meal to cool, when a coyote came by, limping badly. "Pity me, Old Man," he said. "You seem to have a lot of cooked rabbits there, give me one." "If you're too lazy to catch your own food," said Old Man, "I'm not going to give you mine." "My leg is broken," the coyote pleaded. "I can't catch a thing. I'm starving." "I don't care if you die," said Old Man. "I've worked hard for these rabbits. I'm not giving them away. But I'll tell you what I *will* do. I'll run you a race to that butte out there, and if you win you can have one rabbit." "All right," said the coyote, and they started. Old Man ran very fast, and the coyote came limping behind, until they drew near the butte, when he turned and bounded back full speed, not lame at all. It took a while for Old Man to get back, and just before he arrived, the coyote had downed the last rabbit and was trotting off over the prairie.[270]

The Fire Theft

The classic Trickster adventure is the Fire Theft. We have already seen Rabbit, of the Southeast Woodland Creek Indians of Georgia and Alabama, cleverly contrive to carry it off (page 209). In southern British Columbia, some 2000 miles away, the Thompson River tribes tell a similar tale of Coyote.

Standing one evening on a mountain top, Coyote thought he saw a light in the distance. Not knowing what it was, he found by divination that it was fire, and determined to procure that wonder for mankind. He gathered a company of swift runners, the fox, wolf, antelope, and some others, and after traveling a long way, they came to the house of the Fire People. "We have come," they said, "to visit you: to dance, to play, and to gamble." And preparations were made for a dance that night in their honor.

Coyote prepared a headdress for himself, made of pitchy yellow-pine shavings with cedar-bark fringes to the ground. The Fire People danced first around the flame, and the fire was very low. Then Coyote and his people danced, but complained they could not see. The Fire People fed the flame, and Coyote complained four times, until at last the blaze rose to the ceiling. Then Coyote's companions pretended to be so hot that they had to go out to cool themselves, leaving only Coyote inside. They took up positions for running, while Coyote capered wildly until, when close to the door, he swung the long fringes across the flame and made for it, with the Fire People in pursuit. He gave the blazing headdress to Antelope, who ran and passed it on to the next, and so, in relay. The Fire People caught up with them one by one and killed them—all except Coyote, whom they nearly caught, but he ran behind a tree and gave the fire to that tree, so that, since then, people have been able to draw fire from the wood of trees with fire-sticks.[271]

Three Coyote Tales of the Winnebago

Coyote one day contrived to kill a buffalo, and while his right hand was skinning it, his left suddenly pulled the animal away. "Give that back to me," his right arm said. His left pulled again, and his right drove it off with the knife. Again his left pulled, and the quarrel became vicious. At last, with his left arm all slashed and bleeding, Coyote bawled, "Oh, why did I ever let *this* happen? How I suffer!"[272]

* * *

Another day, Coyote took an elk's liver and made a vagina of it, took the elk's kidneys and made breasts, donned a woman's dress that was too tight for him, and thus transformed himself into a very pretty woman. He let the fox have intercourse with him and make him pregnant, then the jaybird, and finally the nit. Then he walked to a village, married the chief's son, and gave birth to four handsome little boys.[273]

* * *

One day, when wandering about aimlessly, Coyote heard someone say, "Anyone who chews me will defecate." "Why should anyone say a thing like that?" thought Coyote, and he moved in the direction of the voice and heard it again. Looking around, he saw a bulb on a bush. "I know very well," he said to himself, "that if I chew this I will not defecate." So he took the bulb, put it into his mouth, chewed, swallowed it, and went on.

"Well," he said, "where now is the bulb that talked so big? How could such an object influence me? When I feel like defecating, I shall do so, and no sooner." But while he was speaking, he began to break a little wind. "Well," he thought, "I guess this is what it meant. It declared, though, that I would defecate, and I'm just breaking a little wind. In any case, I am a great man even if I do expel a little gas." Then it happened again, and this time it was really strong. "Well! Indeed! How foolish I was! Perhaps this is why I'm called the Fool!" It happened again, loudly, and this time his rectum began to smart. Next time he was propelled forward. "Well! Well!" he thought defiantly. "It may give me a little push but it will never make me defecate." Again it happened, and this time the hind part of his body was lifted into the air, and he landed on his knees and hands. "Well, just go ahead, do it again!" he cried. "Do it again!" It did, and he went far into the air, coming down flat on his stomach.

He began to take the matter seriously. He grabbed a log, and both he and the log were sent aloft. Coming down, the log was on top and, landing, he was nearly killed. He grabbed a cottonwood tree; it held, but his feet flew into the air, and he nearly broke his back. Next, the tree came up by the roots. He grabbed a large oak tree; it held, but again his feet flew into the air. He ran to a village and contrived to have all the lodges piled on top of him, together with the people, dogs, and everything else. His explosion scattered the camp in all directions, and the people, coming down, shouted angrily at each other, while the dogs howled. Coyote laughed until his sides were sore, but then he began to defecate. At first it was only a little, but then it was a good deal, and then so much that he had to begin climbing a tree to keep above what was happening. Up he went, higher, higher, and when he reached the top, he slipped, fell, and, from the bottom of the pile, came out covered and blinded by his own filth.[274]

Big Turtle's War Party

In an almost universally popular North American Indian tale, the great turtle, or tortoise, upon whose back the universe rests, comes to view as a Trickster. His story falls in two parts: (1) Turtle leads an incongruous fellowship to war; and (2) when caught, he chooses, for punishment, consignment to his own natural element, water. This second part, as Stith Thompson has shown, has worldwide affinities, specifically in the Philippines, Celebes, China, Burma, and Ceylon, also Angola, and among the North American Negroes in a tale told of Br'er Rabbit.[275]

A turtle went on the warpath, and as he traveled along, met Coyote, who asked, "And so where are you going, grandson?" "I am on the warpath," said the turtle. "May I join you?" "Let me see you run." Coyote ran. "Not fast enough," said the turtle, and moved on. He met a fox. "May I join you?" said the fox. "Let me see you run." The fox ran so fast the turtle could hardly see him. "Not fast enough," said the turtle, and he moved on. A hawk flew by, asked to join the adventure, flew as fast as he could, but was also refused. So it happened again, when a rabbit applied.

The turtle moved along, repeating as he went, "I am looking for people to join me." A flint knife asked, "Will I do?" "Let me see you run," said the turtle. The knife tried and failed. "You will do," said the turtle; "come with me." They met a hairbrush. "Let me see you run." The hairbrush tried and failed. "Come along," said the turtle. And so, also, they met and took with them an awl.

These four came to a big camp, and the turtle sent the knife in to attack. A man found it, took it home, and while trying to slice meat, cut his finger. He threw the knife away, and it returned with its report to the turtle. "Very good," said the turtle; "now, Brush, you go in." A young girl discovered it and picked it up; but when she began to brush her hair, it caught and pulled, so she threw it away. The brush returned to the turtle with its story, and, "Well done!" the turtle said. "So now, Awl, you go and be brave." A woman found the awl, but when she thought to repair her moccasins, it stuck one of her fingers, and she threw it out of her lodge. "Brothers," said the turtle, when all the reports were in, "you have done well. So now it's my turn."

Turtle entered the camp, and when the people saw him, "Look at Turtle!" they said. "He's on the warpath. Let us kill him." Somebody picked him up. "Let us throw him into the fire." "That's great," said Turtle. "I'll push out my legs, the coals will fly, and they'll burn you." "Well, then, let's put a pot of water on the fire," they said, "and when it boils throw him in." "Great! That's my element," said Turtle. "I'll splash and scald you." "All right," they said, "then throw him in the river." "Oh no! Oh no! Not that!" said Turtle. "He's afraid of water," they cried. So they threw him in.

Turtle came to the surface and laughed. "I'm a cheat," he called, and he poked out his tongue. And every time after that, when anyone went to get water, Turtle would come to the surface and say, "I fooled you! Water is my home." They would throw stones, and the turtle would dive.[276]

406. George Catlin's painting of a Blackfoot shaman illustrates the principle of man's acquisition of medicine power through identification with the energies that certain animals command. In addition to the pelt of a yellow bear (a great rarity), there are the skins of snakes, frogs, and bats; the beaks, toes, and tails of birds; the hoofs of deer, goats, and antelopes; "and in fact," quoting Catlin, "the odds and ends and fag ends and tails and tips of almost everything that swims, flies, or runs, in this part of the wide world."[34]

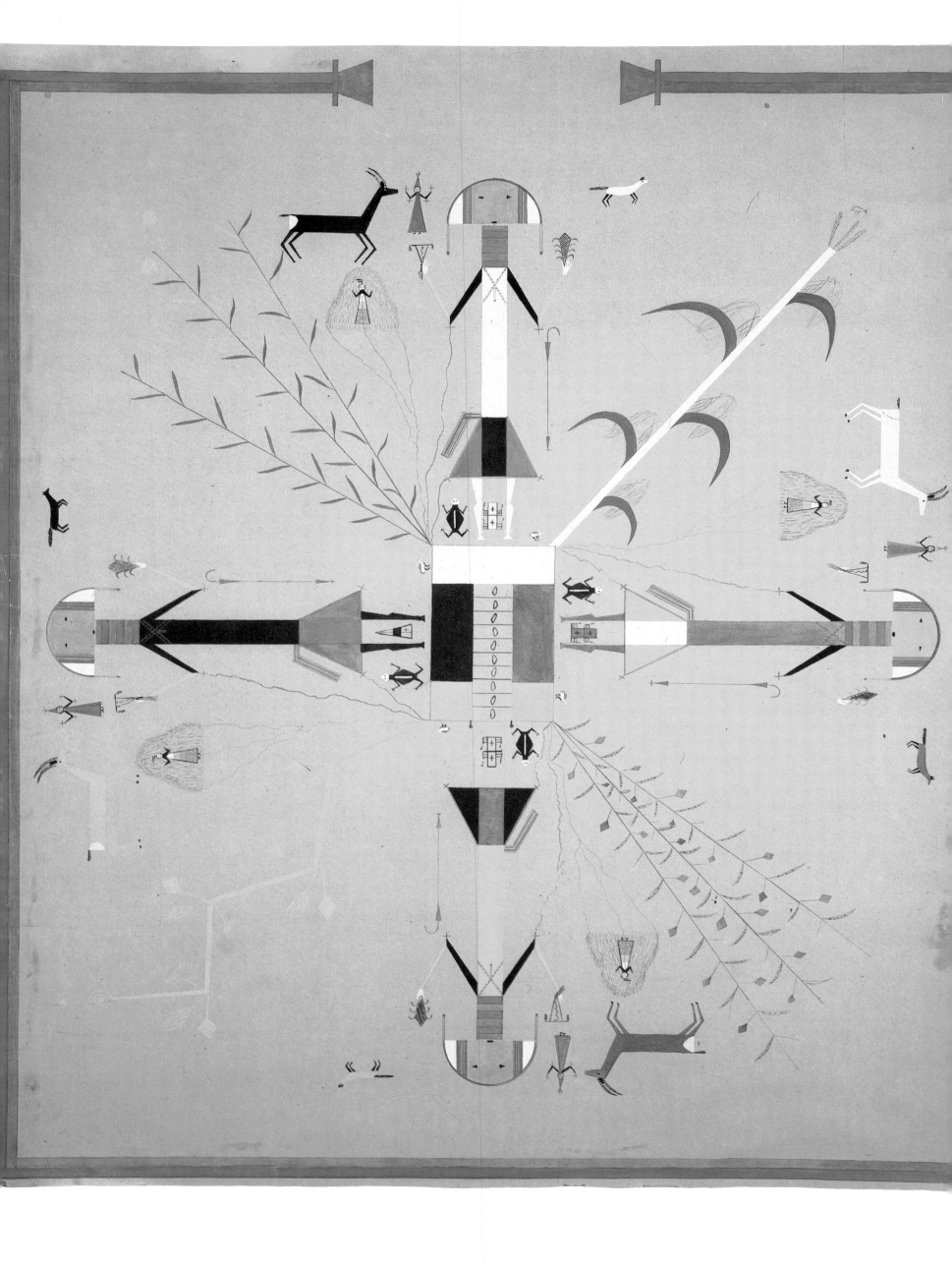

Mythologies of the North American Southwest

The mythologies of the North American Southwest are of the "way of the seeded earth": mythologies, that is to say, of agriculturalists and proper, therefore, rather to Volume 2 than to the present. Two major tribal groups, the Navaho and Apache, however, were recent arrivals from the Plains. They are of an Athabascan linguistic stock, the Apachean, whose nearest relatives are still hunters in the northwest Canadian woods. What caused the Apacheans to migrate south, across the buffalo plains into the desert country of the long-settled, maize-, beans-, squash-, and cotton-cultivating Pueblos (Spanish *pueblo*, "village" or "town") is unknown. As hunting-and-gathering nomads, they arrived some time between A.D. 900 and 1200, and while raiding and harassing their new town-dwelling neighbors, they nevertheless adopted and adapted to their own manner of life, not only a knowledge of plant cultivation, but also an associated mythology of the emergence of the First People from the womb of the earth.

In North America there is a distinct contrast to be noted between the Northeastern Woodland mythology of the woman who fell from the sky and gave birth on earth to twins (see pages 207–208 and the image here, in the Southwest, of twins born to a mysterious virgin-mother immediately after the First People's emergence from the womb of the earth. There is a contrast to be noted, also, between mythologies in which a solitary, masculine World Transformer goes about, in the Beginning, fashioning creatures of clay and mythologies such as that which follows, of the pouring of living creatures from the fertile body of a primal female power and presence—the natural laws of whose processes are known to, and administered by, a class of priestly deputies (here known as Hactcin), who, both in their character and in their entitlement to authority, substantially differ from the individually inspired, Paleolithic shaman. No comparative study has yet been made (as far as I know) of the distributions in North America of the myths and rites of these two orders of mythology. Immediately evident, however, is a preponderance of Emergence myths in the Southwest and a significant distribution, also, up the Mississippi, Ohio, and Missouri valleys.

An expertly recorded version of the Emergence, collected in 1934 from the Jicarilla Apache of New Mexico, is of especial interest for its vivid account of the conflict (which at some time must have been experienced by the Jicarilla themselves) between the spiritual claims of their shamans of the earlier, nomadic, hunting-and-gathering days—each with his own powers and familiars—and the priestly ordinances of the socially authorized ceremonials of an agriculturally grounded commonality. It will be observed, also, that in this telling (possibly as a reflex of the biblical mythology introduced to this whole region by the Spanish friars) there has been retained an account (possibly from their own nomadic legend) of the special creation of man by an anthropomorphic divinity—though he is here in no way alone. And so, as the legend is now told:.

The Emergence

In the beginning there was nothing where the world now stands: no ground, no earth; only Darkness, Water, and Cyclone; no people, fishes, or living things; only the Hactcin [the gods]. These had the material out of which everything was to be made. The earth they made in the form of a living woman; sky in the form of a living man. He faces downward; she, upward. They are our mother and our father.

In the underworld, at that time, there were all kinds of Hactcin. The mountains had a Hactcin; each kind of fruit had a Hactcin; everything had its Hactcin. And it was then that the Jicarilla Apache dwelt under the earth. There was no light there, only darkness. Everything was spiritual and holy, just like the Hactcin. The people were not real, no

407. *The Emergence*, a Navaho sandpainting associated with the Upward-Reaching rite. In the center is the Place of Emergence, showing the Emergence Ladder with the ascending people's footprints starting from the white east and emerging at the yellow west. Cultivated plants on which the people live are rooted in the Ladder: yellow squash, a green medicine plant, white and green maize, and many-colored beans. Four People of the Myth (not otherwise identified) wear the colors of the Four Directions. Red lines of strength proceed from them to the roots of the growing plants, and at their feet are water creatures (frogs) that can also live on land. Between their feet are offerings. Rivers flow to the roots of the plants from the Mountains of the Four Directions (each mountain with its guardian). Antelopes of the Four Directions lend power to the painting, as do what have been said to be Coyote in the Four Directions. The blue and red framing stripes are where Sky and Earth meet; they are left open at the east to permit an inflow and reception of the spirit.

408. The magically sculpted landscape of Monument Valley.

flesh and blood. They were like the shadows of things. Everything was as though in a dream.

And it was there, before anything else was made, that Black Hactcin made the animals. He made an animal of clay with four legs and put a tail on it. "Let me see," he said, "how you are going to walk with those four feet." (That is why little children like to play with clay images.) It began to walk. "That's pretty good," he said. "I think I can use you." And then he said: "But you are alone. I think I will make it so that you will have others from your body." Then all sorts of animals came from that one body; for Black Hactcin had power. He could do anything.

He held out his hand and a drop of rain fell into the palm, which he mixed with earth: it became mud. Then he fashioned a bird from that mud. "Let me see," he said, "how you are going to use those wings." The mud

You can do it, though," the Hactcin said. They all chased the grasshoppers and other insects. And that is what they are doing to this day.

The birds and animals came to Black Hactcin and told him they wanted a companion. "We need man," they said. "You are not going to be with us all the time." And he replied, "I guess that's true." So he told them to gather objects from all directions, and they brought pollen from all kinds of plants, red ochre, specular iron ore, water scum, white clay, white stone, jet, turquoise, red stone, Mexican opal, abalone, and assorted valuable stones. And when they had placed these before Black Hactcin, he said, "You must go a little away. I don't want you to see what I'm doing." He stood to the east, then to the south, then to the west, then to the north. He took pollen and traced with it the outline of a figure on the ground, like that of his own body. Then he placed the precious stones and

on his arms. The birds were now very much excited. (And it is because those birds and animals were so eager to see, that people are so curious today, just as you are eager to hear the rest of this story.) "Sit up," said Black Hactcin to the man. Facing him, he helped him up. Then he taught him to speak, to laugh, to shout, to walk, and to run. And when the birds saw what had been done they burst into song, as they do in the early morning.

But the animals thought this man should have a companion; so Black Hactcin put him to sleep, and when the man's eyes became heavy, he began to dream. He was dreaming that someone, a girl, was sitting beside him. And when he woke there was a woman sitting there. He spoke to her, and she answered. He laughed, she laughed. "Let us get up," he said, and they rose. "Let us walk." And he led her the first four steps: right, left, right, left.

turned into a bird and flew around. It flew to the east, south, west, and north, then returned and said, "I can find no one to help me." So Black Hactcin took up that bird and whirled it around rapidly in the sunwise direction. It grew dizzy and, as one does when dizzy, saw many images round about: all kinds of birds—eagles, hawks, and small birds too. And when it was itself again, there were all those birds there, too.

The birds asked Black Hactcin, "What are we to eat?" He raised his hand to each of the four quarters, and because he had so much power all kinds of seeds fell into his palm and he scattered them. "All right, now pick those up," he said. The birds went to do so, but the seeds all turned into insects, worms, and grasshoppers, which moved and hopped around. "Oh, it's hard work to catch them.

other objects around inside, and they became bones and flesh. The veins were of turquoise, the blood of red ochre, the skin of coral, the bones of white rock; the fingernails were of Mexican opal, the pupils of the eyes of jet, the white of abalone; the marrow of the bones were of white clay, and the teeth, too, were of Mexican opal. He took a dark cloud and turned it into hair: it becomes a white cloud when you are old.

Black Hactcin sent Wind into the form that he had composed. The whorls at the ends of our fingers indicate the path of the wind at the time of that creation. The whorls at the bottom of the feet represent its exit at the time of death. The man was lying face downward, arms outstretched. The birds tried to look, but Black Hactcin warned them back. For the man was coming to life. He braced himself, leaning

409. Four Mountain Spirit Dancers of the Mescalero Apache of south-central New Mexico, who have been joined by a boy prepared for participation in a Corn Dance. With the terminal points of their headgear aflame, these beneficent spirits arrived at night from the cardinal points of the universe, dancing into the circle of light of a ceremonial bonfire, there to fight away in allegorical encounters representations of the powers of illness and evil.

"Let us run." They ran. And then once again the birds burst into song, so that the two should have pleasant music and not be lonesome.

Now all of this took place, not on the level of the earth on which we are now living, but below, in the womb of the earth; and it was dark; there was neither sun nor moon at that time. So White Hactcin and Black Hactcin together took a little sun and moon out of their bags, caused them to grow, and sent them up into the air, where they moved from north to south, shedding light all around. This caused a great deal of excitement among everyone: the animals, the birds, and the people. But there were among them at that time a lot of shamans, men and women who claimed to have power from all sorts of things. These saw the sun going from north to south and began to talk.

One said, "I made the sun"; another: "No, I did." They began quarreling, and the Hactcin ordered them not to talk like that. But they kept making claims and fighting. One said, "I think I'll make the sun stop overhead, so that there will be no night. But no, I guess I'll let it go. We need some time to rest and sleep." Another said, "Perhaps I'll get rid of the moon. We really don't require any light at night." But the sun rose the second day and the birds and animals were happy. The next day it was the same. When noon of the fourth day came, however, and the shamans, in spite of what the Hactcin had told them, continued to talk, there was an eclipse. The sun went right up through a hole overhead, and the moon followed, and that is why we have eclipses today.

One of the Hactcin said to the boastful shamans, "All right, you people say you have power. Now bring back the sun."

So they all lined up. In one line were the shamans; in another all the birds and animals. The shamans began to perform, singing songs and making ceremonies. They showed everything they knew. Some would sit singing and then disappear into the earth, leaving only their eyes sticking out, then return. But this did not bring back the sun. It was only to show that they had power. Some swallowed arrows, which would come out of their flesh at their stomachs. Some swallowed feathers; some swallowed whole spruce trees and spat them up again. But they were still without the sun and moon.

Then White Hactcin said, "All you people are doing pretty well, but I don't think you are bringing the sun back. Your time is up." He turned to the birds and animals. "All right," he said, "now it's your turn."

They all began to speak to one another politely, as though they were brothers-in-law; but the Hactcin said: "You must do something more than speak to one another in that polite way. Get up and do something with your power and make the sun come back."

The grasshopper was the first to try. He stretched forth his hand to the four directions, and when he brought it back he was holding bread. The deer stretched out his hand to the four directions, and when he brought it back he was holding yucca fruit. The bear produced choke-cherries in the same way, and the groundhog, berries; the chipmunk, strawberries; the turkey, maize; and so it went with all. But though the Hactcin were pleased with these gifts, the people were still without the sun and moon.

Thereupon, the Hactcin themselves began to do something. They sent for thunder of four colors from the four directions, and these thunders brought clouds of the four colors, from which rain fell. Then, sending for Rainbow to make it beautiful while the seeds that

the people had produced were planted, the Hactcin made a sand-painting with four little colored mounds in a row, into which they put the seeds. The birds and animals sang, and presently the little mounds began to grow, the seeds began to sprout, and the four mounds of colored earth merged and became one mountain, which continued to rise.

The Hactcin then selected twelve shamans who had been particularly spectacular in their magical performances, and, painting six of them blue all over to represent the summer season, and six white to represent the winter, called them Tsanati; and that was the origin of the Tsanati dance society of the Jicarilla Apache. After that the Hactcin made six clowns, painting them white with four black horizontal bands: one across the face, one across the chest, one across the upper leg, and one across the lower. The Tsanati and clowns then joined the people in their dance, to make the mountain grow. When its top nearly reached the hole through which the sun and moon had disappeared, it stopped and would grow no more. Two disorderly girls, when no one was watching, had climbed to the top, chasing each other, tumbling and trampling on the holy plants up there, even using the place as a toilet. "Something must have happened up there," said the Holy Ones, the Hactcin. They went up, cleaned and fixed everything, and the mountain grew a little higher, but stopped again.

This time Fly and Spider were sent to see what they could do. They went up to where the sun was, took four rays of the sun, each of a different color, and pulled them down to the mountaintop, like ropes, one to each corner of the opening. Of these the Holy Ones then made a ladder, up which the people could ascend to the surface of our present earth. But there was a great deal of water up there, so great that no ground could be seen. The Holy

410. Geronimo and three of his warriors, photographed in 1886, after their defeat. The Apache were among the toughest resisters to confinement in reservations, and from 1870 to 1886, under a number of leaders, of whom Geronimo was the last, they repeatedly outwitted and outfought detachments of both the United States and Mexican armies.

Ones made four hoops of the four colors: black, blue, yellow, and glittering, which they tossed to the east, south, west, and north. The waters rolled back, and when four Big Winds of the different colors had blown the wet mud dry and were holding the waters back, the people ascended the four ladders. The six clowns went ahead with magical whips, laughing in a certain way to chase disease away, and they were followed by the Hactcin, who made a different noise for the same reason. Then the twelve Tsanati went up, and after them, the people and the animals. And when they came up onto the earth, it was just like a child being born from its mother. The place of emergence is the earth's womb.

But there were two old people down there, an old man and a very old woman, who had not been able to come up. Their sight was dim. They had been far behind the animals, and when their turn came, the ladders were worn out. They stood there and called, "Come, get us. Take us up too." But there was no way to help. Finally they became angry. "All right," they called, "we'll stay here. But you will all come back some day." And that is why people return to the underworld when they die.[277]

Where the Two Came to Their Father

When the young men of the Navaho reservation were being inducted into the U.S. Army for service in the Second World War, an old medicine man, Jeff King (born between 1852 and 1860; served the Army as an Indian scout from 1870 to 1911; awarded the Army's Indian Campaign Medal for service against the Apache, 1885–1886; died January 22, 1964; buried with honor in Arlington National Cemetary), brought from his memory an old Navaho ceremonial for the initiation of warriors, which he then celebrated, whenever invited to do so, for the spiritual preparation of any young man of the reservation about to be inducted.[278] Its mythological base was a Navaho version of the general southwestern cycle of the First People: their emergence from the earth, and the deeds, then, in the first years of the world, of the two sons of the virgin, Changing Woman.

Changing Woman had herself been born miraculously near the summit of Gobernador Knob (New Mexico), where for four days a dark cloud had been seen resting. Talking God, the benevolent grandfather of the pantheon, ascended to investigate, circling as he climbed, and when he reached the place where the cloud rested, found a rainbow and soft rain falling. Hearing an infant's cry, he looked, and there on a bed of flowers lay a baby girl. She had been born of Darkness. Dawn was her father. The god carried her down to First Man and First Woman, who were dwelling at the foot of Mountain Around Which Moving Was Done, and there they nourished her on sun-ray pollen, cloud pollen, plant pollen, and the dew of flowers.

When she had grown and come of age, one day she felt lonely and, wandering from the hogan, sat playing with her hair in the sun. She lay back and fell asleep, and when she woke, felt tired and sweaty. There were tracks from the east, approaching and leaving her. She hoped they were not of Big Giant, for she had seen giants carry girls away.

In two days she knew she was going to have a baby, and in two more gave birth to a boy. She cried a little, not knowing what to do with it, then wrapped it in a piece of cradle-bush bark, brought it to the hogan, and dug a hole in the center of the floor, next to the fire. A second hole she dug, sideways, at the bottom of the first, lined it with soft grasses, and tucked the baby in, so that no one should see. Then she went to wash at a pool where there was water dripping. It fell on her legs and body, and again in two days she knew she would have a baby, and dug another hole at the bottom of the first, for she was afraid of owls and buzzards, monsters and the giants.

In four days the boys walked. She warned them not to go far and made for them little bows and arrows, with which they played

411. Jeff King (c. 1852/60–1964), Navaho singer of the legend *Where the Two Came to Their Father.*

412. Gobernador Knob, New Mexico, on the summit of which the virgin mother was born of Monster Slayer and Child Born of Water, the Two Who Came to Their Father.

around the hogan. When they were twelve, however, they disappeared around a cliff toward the east, stepped onto a cloud, and from there onto a rainbow. They were going to the Sun, their father, for weapons with which to kill the monsters of which their mother was so greatly afraid.

In Figure 413 we see Changing Woman's hogan and around it the four cardinal mountains, full of the seeds of all things. The white cross in the center is the fire. The blue crosses are the boys' spirits, by which they rose to the clouds. The right footstep is of the elder brother, Monster Slayer, the left of Child Born of Water, the younger. The triangles are clouds of the four directions, upon which the boys mounted, and the rainbow is Rainbow Man, who carried them on their way. "This painting is used for a warrior going to war," said Jeff King; "also for people who are out of their minds or do not think straight. It is very holy, because on this mountain Changing Woman gave birth to her sons and from it the Navaho tribe increased."[279]

The rainbow carried the twins south, where they came to white sands and the world guardian of that quarter, Sand Dune Boy. With his long arms, he would grab people and push their heads into the sand. "You can't

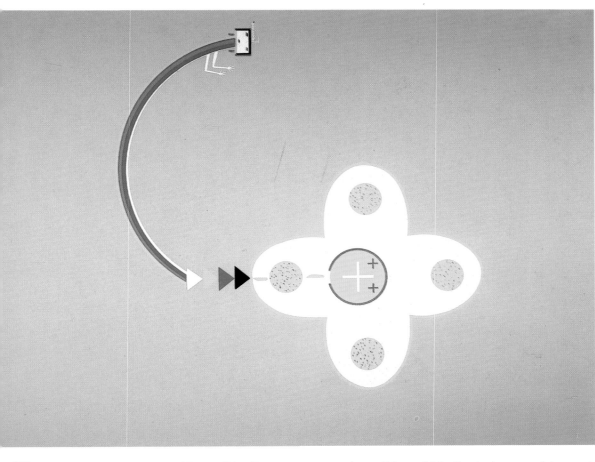

413. *Mountain Around Which Moving Was Done,* the home of Changing Woman, mother of the warrior twins, Monster Slayer and Child Born of Water. Pollen painting on buckskin by Jeff King, recorded by Maud Oakes, to whom he gave the legend, together with a blessing, in 1942.

pass here," he said to the twins, reaching out at them. But standing on two waterspouts, they sang songs of praise to him, and having never been treated that way before, he was pleased and let them pass. At the other quarters they praised the guardians the same way, and Rainbow carried them on.

They were now beyond the hoop of the known world, in the realm where death leads to rebirth, and there they saw an old woman heading west with a bundle on her shoulder. Her name was Old Age. "What are you people doing here?" she asked. "We are on our way to our father, the Sun," they replied. "You will die before you get there," she warned. "But go on, my son and grandson. Only, don't walk on my path. Keep to the left of it." They went on, but forgot to and, walking in her path, felt heavy, then stooped; their steps became shorter; they got sticks and still could not walk. They sat down, and the old woman returned. She had been watching. They asked to be helped. She rebuked them, but began to sing, naming the four directions, saying after each, "old age!" Then she explained: "I sang this song so that in the future everything should reach old age: people, animals, birds, insects, everything that grows. I mentioned the four directions, so that no matter how far the earth goes, there should always be old age." She spat on her hands, rubbed it into her armpits and body, then rubbed her hands together and pressed them on the boys, first the elder, then the younger, and again sang, mentioning old age. So they again were young, and she bade them go their way.

Ahead they saw coming out of the ground a little thread of smoke. The younger was afraid, but the elder had no fear, and as they approached, there appeared a little old woman in black. She was Spider Woman. That was her house. "My grandsons," she said to them, "this is no place for earth people." "We are going for help," they explained, "to the Sun, our father. We and our people are being troubled by monsters." "My grandsons, that is a

long long way, and you are going to face many dangers. Better come down and let me help."

The door of her house was small, but she blew her breath four times and it grew to receive them. Then, with her web she made the Sun descend, so that they should spend the night. "I have not much to eat," she told them, as she set out four sorts of cornmeal in baskets made of white shell, turquoise, abalone, and jet. Into the elder's she dropped a bit of turquoise; into the younger's a bit of white shell; and as they ate, the bowls kept filling, until they rubbed their bodies and legs and declared, "From here on, we shall have strength to continue." Then she gave a live eagle feather to each, and warned, "Whatever you do, don't show this to the Sun, your father. I stole it from him. Keep it hidden, close to your heart."

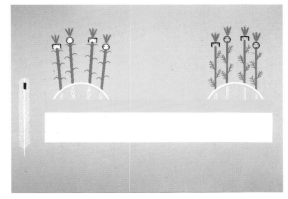

414. *Rock That Claps Together*

Figure 414 shows the dangers of the way now before them. The feather is their eagle feather charm. The yellow is a passageway, and the white stands for rocks. On the left are the Reeds That Cut; on the right the Cattails That Stab; between, though visibly there is nothing, is the Rock That Claps Together: it would open, as though to let people through, then crush them.

Beyond these dangers the boys came to a river with lots of people on the water having a wonderful time playing with hoops. They were Water Bug People, who, when they saw the twins, stopped playing, asked where they were going, parted to let them pass, but then closed in. The boys' feathers began to sing. Little Wind and Big Fly, who now arrived to become their guardians, whispered, "Blow them away." So they blew four times and passed through, to the other side.

They arrived at a great water, so wide it went into the sky and became one with it. Not knowing where to go, they stood on their feathers and thought, "We shall know where we are going when we get there." Then they saw in the distance the Sun's house, on the water yet in the sky. Little Wind and Big Fly flew ahead to reconnoiter and came back. "The house is guarded by four big bears," they reported, "four big snakes, four big winds, and four thunders. But don't be afraid. You have within you the power to enter."

Figure 415 is the Sun's house. Along the top of the water is a rainbow. The four crosses are holy places. The square is the house, each section a room. The horse is

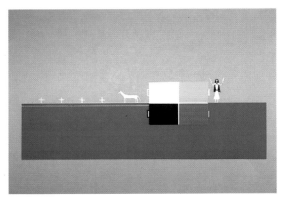

415. *Sun's House*

416. *Lightning Armor House*

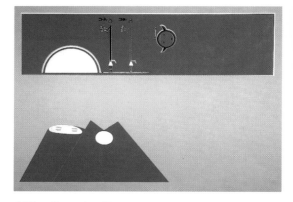

417. *Guessing Tests*

the Sun's mount; the girl, his daughter. In her hands are male and female corn. Every morning she shakes a rattle, to call the horse for her father to ride. The whole house is made of white clouds.

The bears growled and their hair stood on end. But Little Wind and Big Fly sang songs over the twins and told them to throw their breaths at the bears. They did so and passed by; so too with the big snakes, winds, and thunders. "My father is away," the girl said when they arrived. "When he comes home, he will kill you." She wrapped them in clouds to hide them—the elder in black, the younger in blue—and stowed them over the doorways to their rooms, the black room and the blue, then told her mother about them. The Sun arrived. He looked around and asked, "Where are those two people I saw brought into my house?" "You have always told me," his wife replied, "that you are faithful to me as you pass from east to west. These two people say they are your sons."

The Sun said nothing, but began searching, taking down every cloud in the house. (Whenever he wanted to use one, he would unroll it and put it in the sky.) One boy he found, then the other, wondering how they had got into his clouds. "Perhaps they are Holy People," he thought. He would test them, to find out.

The Sun had a servant named Water Carrier, whom he sent to heat up the sweat lodge, but his daughter, already anticipating, had dug two holes inside and covered them with flat stones and dirt, of which refuges she advised the twins. When their father then made them undress, they had to leave their protective feathers with their clothes, and the lodge was hot, fiercely hot, so hot they could hardly enter. But by the girl's device they were saved.

Recovering their clothes, they recovered also the feathers, and while following their father to the next test, they heard a little voice call from a shrub, "Wait!" It called four times. They looked, and there, with a hunched back, was an inchworm. "He will try you," it said, "with a basket of poisoned cornmeal. Turn it halfway around, only half is poisoned. Here is something to put in your mouth against harm." And it gave them some of its spoor.

When they had survived that relatively easy trial, the next and last was of being thrown against poles of the cardinal colors, jagged with sharp flint knives. Here the eagle feathers alone saved them, and their father at last recognized them as his sons.

He showed them all the contents of his house of clouds: the east room (white) full of

black clouds, lightning bolts, and wild flowers; the south room (yellow), full of game animals; the west room (blue), with grain and domestic beasts; and the north (black), full of armor, flint knives, a bow, white-tailed eagle arrows, and, over the doorway, a medicine bundle. Then he asked what they had come for, and Little Wind said, "Ask for the bundle," for by this their father would always know when they were in danger.

Figure 416 shows the brothers in their father's Lightning Armor House (the house of initiation), where they learned their names and acquired distinct powers.

In a room full of sparklings of all colors, so strong that when you looked it could be for only a second, the Sun made them stand on two buffalo rugs to receive strength, courage, and wisdom for what lay ahead. Little Wind and Big Fly whispered, "When the Thunder People arrive, don't be afraid." And just then, Black Thunder and Blue Thunder came in.

Each brother in the picture stands on a rainbow and buffalo hide, each within his own frame, which is a rainbow of protection and strength. "Monster Slayer," Jeff King explained, "is black. He has a male flint knife and a war club. On his feet are flint shoes; on his head is a flint cap. Child Born of Water is blue. He, too, is dressed in flint. He has a female flint knife and a war club. And each is tall, of his own color and full of power, because they have received their names. This painting is made at dawn, over a warrior going to battle, or starting on a raiding party. It is used, also, for people who have had bad dreams."[280]

Black Thunder stood at the left of Monster Slayer, and Blue Thunder at the left of Child Born of Water, and the Sun gave to each of the twins a little image of a man to swallow. That of the elder brother was of jet; that of the younger, of turquoise. The Sun pressed his hand to each chest to make the image within stand upright. Then calling Monster Slayer his son and Child Born of Water his grandson, he bestowed on them their names. That done, he again asked why they had come, and they replied that what they wanted was to kill the Big Lonesome Giant on Mount Taylor, for it would be only after his death that the lesser monsters could be slain.

The Sun said nothing for a moment, for that giant, too, was his son. But then he promised

weapons when they reached the earth and sent them on their way. They stood on a lightning flash, and it carried them off and away to the hole in the sky.

Figure 417 illustrates the sequence of the twins' descent to the earth and arrival on Mount Taylor, where the Big Lonesome Giant lived beside Hot Spring Lake. The white circle is the lake. The footsteps show where the brothers came down. The feather on which they are standing, above, is not the one from Spider Woman, but was given them by the Sun, their father, who is here testing them with questions.

"You must name the Holy Mountains in order," he said. "If you fail, you can't go down." Little Wind and Big Fly whispered the answers. The answers were correct, and the Sun was satisfied. "I shall give you now my wisdom," he said. "Use it and hand it on, so that it may be known forever on earth." Then he let them go.

Down they went, but did not know it until they landed, for there were clouds and fog all about them. Big Lonesome Giant immediately noticed their reflections in the lake and, since it is the nature of monsters to mistake shadow for substance, mistook the reflections for themselves, drank up the lake at one gulp, and then, looking at the mud and not seeing them there, thought he had swallowed them. So he threw up the water and saw them again. This happened four times, after which, not feeling so well, he lay on his back and spied the two alive against the sky, across the lake.

He got up to shoot his arrows. The Sun, who was watching, joined in the fight, and when the Big Lonesome Giant was slain, his blood ran. Little Wind and Big Fly quickly warned the twins: "If that blood runs up Mount Taylor, he will come back to life, put a flint in front of it. Do the same for all four mountains. And if it starts toward the lake, do the same again." So having no place to go, the blood stayed on the flat and became hard.

Figure 418 shows the youths heading homeward, returning to their mother's place. When they had descended from Mount Taylor and were passing along its southern slope, they tripped, fell, and dropped their male and female lightning arrows, which flashed away and cut the mountain in two, for they had passed from the sphere of sheer mythic power to

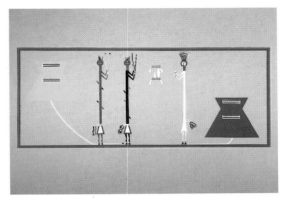

418. *Talking God Painting*

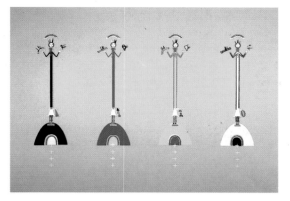

419. *Holy Ones on Holy Mountain*

Mountain Around Which Moving Was Done, where Changing Woman gave birth to the Two Who Came to Their Father.

According to Jeff King, "When they put the extra mountains around, they took Mountain Around Which Moving Was Done out of First Woman's belt."[282] There is a blessing prayer addressed to it, which Jeff King gave to the artist Maud Oakes when she received from him these paintings.

"He gave me," she tells, "two prayersticks, male and female, to hold and told me to keep all bad thoughts out of my mind. Then he prayed: 'I am Changing Woman's Son! I am Changing Woman's Son! Eastern Mountain, Chief of all Mountains, I walk with your feet, I walk with your legs, I walk with your body, and with your mind, and with your sound. The feathers on your head I walk with; they are in front of me, beautiful; under me, beautiful; on top of me, beautiful. Oh, Mountain of the East, I am the one that lives on forever. Everything is beautiful. Everything is beautiful. Out of my mouth, beauty, and around me, beauty. I AM EVERLASTING MAN! Around me everything is beautiful. Around me everything is beautiful. Around me everything is beautiful. Around me everything is beautiful.' "[283]

that of life on earth. The Sun, their father, was displeased but returned the male and female arrows, which, in the painting, they are holding in their hands. And they are being greeted by the same Talking God, who, in the beginning, attended their mother's birth. He is giving them a talking prayer stick such as advises gods where to go and where not to go. It is of male and female corn. The yellow mountain is Mount Taylor. The blue is Mountain Around Which Moving Was Done, to which the First People went immediately after their emergence from the earth and where Changing Woman was raised and the twins were born.

When Talking God received the youths, he embraced them and sang for them twelve songs. [On approaching their father's realm, they had been helped by Spider Woman; returning now to their mother's, they are greeted by Talking God.] The songs accompanied them to Changing Woman's hogan, but when they arrived they saw no footsteps about, for no one was there. They heard, however, a *hish* sound inside and went in. It was the fire-poker. "Your mother and the people," it said, "are hiding from the monsters." Then it told them where to go to find her.

The end of the adventure was their killing, in five spectacular battles, of five monsters: a great Horned Monster; a Monster Eagle, living near Ship Rock; a monster called Slayer With Eyes, who with his big, staring eyes made people unable to move and then ate them; a giant bear, known as Bear That Tracks; and a huge rock, known as Traveling Stone, that would roll after people and crush them. The battles were exhausting, and, when done, the twins were losing weight, getting thinner each day, and nearing death. So the gods, the Holy People, deciding that the twins had killed too much and had gone where earth people were not to go, came down and performed over them, four times, this ceremony of the story of their lives, after which the two were so full of power, they became four.

Figure 419 is greatly powerful. "It is used," said Jeff King, "for young warriors about to go into battle for the first time. It is given at dawn. Also, it is used for protection against all evil and harm. It is very holy and protects the entire Navaho tribe today."[281] Monster Slayer is shown standing on the mountain of the east, Child

Born of Water on the mountain of the south, Reared Underground (Monster Slayer's double) on the mountain of the west, and Changing Grandchild (Child Born of Water's double) on the mountain of the north. A rainbow frames the doorway of each mountain, and leading into each are pollen crosses to mark the four holy steps that each of the four brothers took to enter his mountain.

Figure 420, called *Earth and Sky*, is a summary map of the defining holy sites and powers of the mythic Navaho universe. The blue area is sky, framed by three lines of sun-rays. Along its top is Milky Way Man, and below, from east to west (left to right), are: Boss Sparkling Star of the East, the White Sun (of the east), yellow Coyote Star, the seven Eastern Stars, seven stars of the Pleiades, twelve stars [sic] of the Big Dipper, the Moon, and the Big White Star of the West. The earth is yellow, framed by four lines of sun-rays (three for the sky, four for the earth). Its cardinal mountains are white (of the east), blue (of the south), yellow (of the west), and black (of the north). The brown mountain is Fir

420. *Earth and Sky*, mythological power centers in the Navaho universe. Pollen painting by Jeff King for a blessing ceremony. Recorded by Maud Oakes.

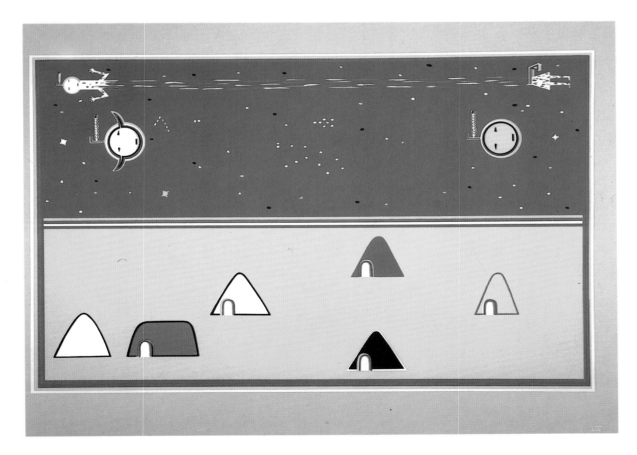

The ceremony of Where the Two Came to Their Father could be celebrated either for two nights and one day or for five nights and four days, depending on circumstances and the desire of the family. The paintings were not made of colored sands, as in most Navaho ceremonials of this kind, but of ground charcoal and flower petals, cornmeal, and the pollens of various plants and trees; and they were laid down, furthermore, on buckskin, not on a cleared piece of ground. For each there were special prayers and songs recited from memory by the celebrant, while the initiate or patient (when the ceremony was used for curing) either sat or stood and walked on the design.

For the point was that he or she should become identified in spirit with the mythic subject of the legend, the painting itself being understood as spiritually equivalent to the mythic landscape it represented—not simply as an illustration, but as intelligibly identical, its form being that of the informing sense of the represented mythic scene. "Art," Cezanne has somewhere said, "is a harmony parallel to nature," correcting thus what Plato called the "corrupted courses of the head" by renewing in each his "original nature . . . which is akin to the harmonies and revolutions of the universe."[284] The sand or pollen paintings—with their associated chants and prayers, ceremonial lustrations, visionary jouneys, and pictured revelations, continuing their spell through nights and days within the sacred space of a Navaho hogan (which itself is in its form symbolic of the cosmos)—remove the mind from the usual considerations of mortality by confirming it (to quote Plato again) in "thoughts immortal and divine."[285]

In fact, the whole of Navaho life, in its traditional sense, is grounded this way in myth. The eight sides of the hogan represent the four world quarters and four points between, so that anyone lost in Navaho country need only to see a hogan, its doorway always facing east, to know again his bearings. The fireplace in the center of the lodge floor, where Changing Woman cradled her twins, sends its column of smoke through the centered smoke hole, in the way of an axial aspiration to that hole in the dome of the sky through which, in return, the Sun sends down his boon of life. Every Navaho home is thus, for its inhabiting family, the universe in a likeness.

And so, also, in a larger way, the entire Navaho country. The mythic model of the universe, which is of no local when or where, but of the mind—as represented, for example, in Jeff King's pollen painting called *Earth and Sky* (Figure 420)—has been identified, as by reflection, in certain actual landmarks of the extensive Navaho reservation (which includes the point of juncture of four states: Utah and Colorado, Arizona and New Mexico). As stated by Jeff King, in his own telling of the emergence myth:

"When the people were ready and had everything to dress the mountains in, they stood on a rainbow and traveled to the east, to plant the Holy Mountain of the East. They put down a blanket of white shell and on it some white shell, and on top of it they sprinkled some sand of the mountains of the world below. They wrapped this up in its blanket and planted it to the east. And since they all agreed and all wanted it, it became and was called *Blanca Peak*. With the Mountain of the South they did likewise, only it was planted on a turquoise blanket and was made of sand and turquoise, and it was called *Mount Taylor*. The Mountain of the West was made on an abalone blanket and out of sand and abalone, and it was called *San Francisco Peak*. The Mountain of the North was made on a jet blanket and was made of jet and sand, and it was called *La Plata Range*. . . . After those mountains had been made, the people decided to place a Holy Person in each, to guard it and to listen to the prayers, songs, and offerings made to it. . . . In the Mountain of the East they put Talking God of the East; in the Mountain of the South, Call God of the South; in the Mountain of the West, Talking God of the West; in the Mountain of the North, Call God of the North."[286]

By such a method of land claiming for the myth—which has been common in the histories of cultures—an indifferent landscape is transubstantiated, turned into an icon, and the elementary idea is established in a local habitation. Moreover, not alone the landscape: for in this particular mythology of the Pollen Path of Beauty, every water bug and local beast and fowl has been mythologized, so that in the whole known world there is nothing apart from the beauty, since (to make use of another symbolic vocabulary) all are in God, and God is in all.

421. Detail of a Navaho curing rite: one moment of a ceremony that may continue for three or more nights and days. The patient is to identify with the spiritual forces symbolized through a sequence of pollen or sand paintings with their associated chants, prayers, and ceremonial lustrations, visionary journeys, and pictured revelations. The mind, in this way removed for a time from its usual daily anxieties, becomes centered and brought to order in what Plato called "thoughts immortal and divine" (see text).

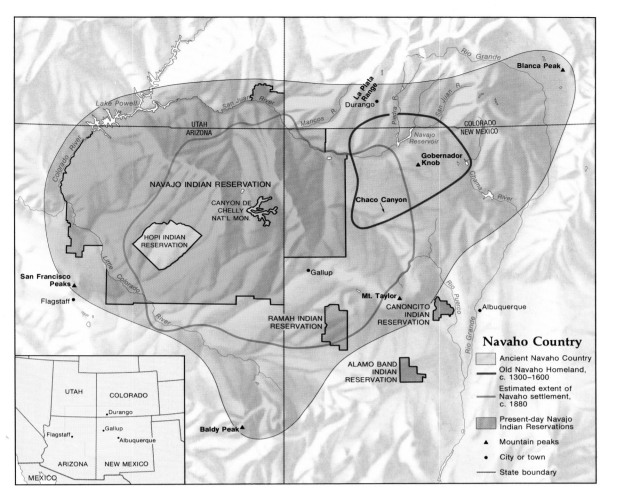

Map 48. Sacred mountains demarcate the mythologized landscape of Ancient Navaho Country. In evidence is the shifting settlement pattern of the Navaho over the centuries. Note that, although "Navaho" is the traditional spelling of the people, the United States Government officially insists on "Navajo."

Navaho Country

- Ancient Navaho Country
- Old Navaho Homeland, c. 1300–1600
- Estimated extent of Navaho settlement, c. 1880
- Present-day Navaho Indian Reservations
- ▲ Mountain peaks
- • City or town
- State boundary

422. Navaho hogan, a dwelling constructed of logs and adobe, always with eight sides and with its one door opening east to the sunrise. The smoke-opening in the domed roof corresponds to the mythological opening in the heaven dome. The fireplace in the center of the floor is symbolically the center of the world.

Not Man Apart

During the 1880s, when in the United States the buffalo herds of the Great Plains had been wiped out, and the brief moment of expectation of the Ghost Dance had failed, a new way to the realization of identity with the life and being of all that passes in the course of time was opened to the disinherited tribes then being gathered onto reservations. From northern Mexico—specifically, the desert between the Rio Grande and San Luis Potosi, where the desert-cactus peyote grows and is harvested most reverently by the native Huichol tribesmen, who know it as *hikuri*, the plant of eternal life—there came to the people of the Plains a realization of the power of this plant to break open the walls of space and release to the mind visionary realities such as in primeval times had been known to the shamans. Accepted first about 1885 by the Kiowa and Commanche of Oklahoma (which at that time was known as Indian Territory), the peyote cult during the next decade spread as far north as to Canada. It is recognized today among some fifty tribes and incorporated as a distinct religion, the Native American Church, with a membership said to be of some 200,000. The doctrines vary from area to area, and in some may include modified Christian elements—such as, for example, an identification of the Peyote Spirit with Jesus, who was killed by the Whites and has turned now to the Indians. But, whatever the doctrines, the sense and function of the movement has been to recover knowledge from within of the spiritual ground of native life. For the spiritual predicament following the extinction of the buffalo herds was of a people deprived suddenly, not only of their way of life, but also of the mythological forms by which that life-way had been sustained. And the contrast of the values of that mythology with those of the life-way and way of thought that had been imposed by force in its stead could hardly have been more extreme.

Some sense of the violence of the contrast may be gained from the reported

423. *Peyote Drummer*, a photograph taken in 1927 by Edward S. Curtis.

424. *A Blackfoot Travois*, a photograph taken in 1926 by Edward S. Curtis.

words of the Suquamish Chief Seattle, one of the last spokesmen of the Paleolithic moral order, when required about the year 1855 to transfer his tribal lands to the arriving people of the United States:

"The President in Washington sends word that he wishes to buy our land. But how can you buy or sell the sky? The land? The idea is strange to us. If we do not own the freshness of the air and the sparkle of the water, how can you buy them?

"Every part of this earth is sacred to my people. Every shining pine needle, every sandy shore, every mist in the dark woods, every meadow, every humming insect. All are holy in the memory and experience of my people.

"We know the sap which courses through the trees as we know the blood that courses through our veins. We are part of the earth and it is part of us. The perfumed flowers are our sisters. The bear, the deer, the great eagle, these are our brothers. The rocky crests, the juices in the meadow, the body heat of the pony, and man, all belong to the same family.

"The shining water that moves in the streams and rivers is not just water, but the blood of our ancestors. If we sell you our land, you must remember that it is sacred. Each ghostly reflection in the clear water of the lakes tells of events and memories in the life of my people. The water's murmur is the voice of my father's father.

"The rivers are our brothers. They quench our thirst. They carry our canoes and feed our children. So you must give to the rivers the kindness you would give any brother.

"If we sell you our land, remember that the air is precious to us, that the air shares its spirit with all the life it supports. The wind that gave our grandfather his first breath also receives his last sigh. The wind also gives our children the spirit of life. So if we sell you our land, you must keep it apart and sacred, as a place where man can go to taste the wind that is sweetened by the meadow flowers.

"Will you teach your children what we have taught our children? That the earth is our mother? What befalls the earth, befalls all the sons of the earth.

"This we know: The earth does not belong to man, man belongs to the earth. All things are connected like the blood which unites us all. Man did not weave the web of life, he is merely a strand in it. Whatever he does to the web, he does to himself.

"One thing we know: Our god is also your god. The earth is precious to him and to harm the earth is to heap contempt on its creator.

"Your destiny is a mystery to us. What will happen when the buffalo are all slaughtered? The wild horses tamed?

425. *The Medicine Man, Slow Bull*: photograph taken by Edward Curtis in 1907, seventeen years after Wounded Knee. His garment: United States Government issue. The broken buffalo skull: a species thirty years extinct. The noble calumet: His unbroken pride.

What will happen when the secret corners of the forest are heavy with the scent of many men and the view of the ripe hills is blotted by talking wires? Where will the thicket be? Gone! Where will the eagle be? Gone! And what is it to say goodbye to the swift pony and the hunt? The end of living and the beginning of survival.

"When the last Red Man has vanished with his wilderness and his memory is only the shadow of a cloud moving across the prairie, will these shores and forests still be here? Will there be any of the spirit of my people left?

"We love this earth as a newborn loves its mother's heartbeat. So, if we sell you our land, love it as we have loved it. Care for it as we have cared for it. Hold in your mind the memory of the land as it is when you receive it. Preserve the land for all children and love it, as God loves us all.

"As we are part of the land, you too are part of the land. This earth is precious to us. It is also precious to you. One thing we know: There is only one God. No man, be he Red Man or White Man can be apart. We *are* brothers after all."[287]

251

Cultural Geography

In the Americas, the nuclear sourceland—both of the arts of food production and of mythologies and associated ceremonials appropriate to the structuring of village-, town-, and city-based societies—was the large Central and South American zone represented on Map 49 by the areas colored tan. Within the red zone, a civilization unfolded that was distinguished from all others in the New World by its possession, not only of writing, but also of a mathematically structured and astronomically accurate calendar (correlating cycles of the sun, the moon, the planet Venus, and an artificial round of 13 x 20 = 260 days), which could be projected to an extreme cycle of time (known in Mayan as an *alautun*) of 23,040,000,000 differently named and numbered days. Distinguished by an architecture in stone, with pyramids rising from astronomically oriented ceremonial compounds; by consecrated priesthoods; wars of conquest; dynastic empires; taxes, tribute, and all the rest that goes with what is known as high civilization: this monumental flowering—which by the second or third centuries A.D. had extended its influence north as far at least as to Teotihuacán—corresponds in grade to the stage of civilization attained in Mesopotamia c. 3500 B.C., in Egypt c. 2850 B.C., India and Crete c. 2500 B.C., and in China, with the founding of the Shang Dynasty, c. 1523 B.C. It is of the grade, that is to say, which will be dealt with in Volume 3 of the present writing, *The Way of the Celestial Lights*.

The first signs in the Americas of any such high-cultural mutation appeared along the Caribbean coasts of southern Vera Cruz and Tabasco, c. 1300 to 1150 B.C., in a little constellation of ceremonial establishments, of which La Venta, San Lorenzo, and Tres Zapotes seem to have been the most important. A stone sculptural art of the highest distinction, whether of small jade carvings or of colossal portrait heads, is the hallmark of this culture. Associated with ceremonial compounds, of which at least one (La Venta) contained a pyramid, the productions are of a school of art that was already, on first appearance, fully matured; its dominant motif was of an anthropomorphized jaguar face that bears comparison with the Shang Chinese *t'ao-t'ieh* (see Figure 320, page 194). The antecedents of this culture—which today is recognized as representing the initial phase of the whole Mesoamerican development—are unknown.

To Volume 2 of the present study, *The Way of the Seeded Earth*, belong the mythologies of the world's village cultures, grounded in agriculture and, secondarily, animal domestication. Three major centers of origin of these economies have been identified: Southwest Asia, Southeast Asia, Central and South America (on Map 49, the areas colored gold), with a fourth center, of less extensive influence, in Africa in the Western Sudan.[288] The number of plant domesticates cultivated in the native Americas was enormous: maize, squash, pumpkins, manioc, tobacco, many varieties of beans, the potato, sweet potato, peanut, pineapple, tomato, guava, avocado, papaya, vanilla, three species of cotton, rubber, quinine, cacao, and coca—besides the bottle gourd, coconut, and banana, all three of which by one means or another (the issue is hotly debated) arrived on these shores from elsewhere. In contrast, the only animals domesticated were the turkey and dog, and in South America, the Muscovy duck, llama, alpaca, guinea pig, a breed of low-slung dog that was fattened for food, and chickens that reportedly laid blue and olive-green eggs and the meat and bones of which were black. There were no draft animals, hence, no drawn vehicles; the wheel was used only for children's toys. Of the wool of the llama and alpaca, yarns were spun for some of the finest hand-loom-woven textiles of all time.

The general dating now proposed for what is known in the Americas as the Period of Incipient Agriculture is c. 6500 to 1500 B.C., when gradually the transition was made in various parts of the areas colored gold from Paleolithic hunting

Map 49.

Cultural Geography of the Pre-Columbian Americas

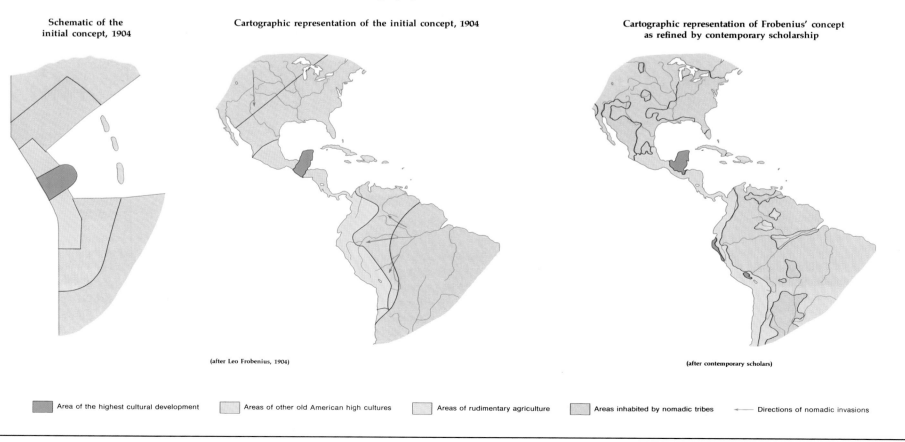

Schematic of the initial concept, 1904

Cartographic representation of the initial concept, 1904

Cartographic representation of Frobenius' concept as refined by contemporary scholarship

(after Leo Frobenius, 1904)

(after contemporary scholars)

Area of the highest cultural development Areas of other old American high cultures Areas of rudimentary agriculture Areas inhabited by nomadic tribes Directions of nomadic invasions

and foraging to a settled, Neolithic style of village life and farming. The same regions, centuries later, received from the red-colored domain contributions and influences that not only directly enriched the native inheritance, but also worked as motivation stimuli to local creativity. It is not often easy and, indeed, sometimes impossible to estimate the ratio in a given culture context between what has been received and what locally initiated: a formidable example of this ambiguity appears in the history of Peru, where an undoubted contribution from the Olmec has been recognized in the initial monumental ruin known as Chavín de Huantar, although the subsequent development to the culminating moment of the Inca Empire (which in its engineering, military, and political achievements surpassed the exactly contemporary Aztec) was of a distinctive and self-consistent order—incongruously, and for no discoverable reason, without a literature of any kind or even a knowledge of writing.

The green areas of Map 49 are (schematically) of regions beyond the Formative zone, which were nevertheless significantly illuminated and transformed by influences from the sourceland. In our chronicle of the Koster site, the Hopewell culture, and Mississippian Cahokia (see pages 241–251), we have already recognized the evidences of such influences, culminating in ceremonial compounds containing temple mounds, although not of stone, but of heaped up tons of earth.

A contemporary and equivalent development in the Southwest was of the Anasazi culture, ancestral to the graded stages of the Pueblo.

In South America, the matching culture zone (also colored green on Map 49) is of the manioc-cultivating, rain-forest tribes of the Orinoco and Upper Amazonian riverlands; also, of the Caribs and Arawak of the Antilles; and, at the southern bound in northern Chile, of the sturdy Araucanians, who successfully resisted, not only inclusion in the Inca Empire, but also subjugation by the Spaniards, holding their own even into the nineteenth century, until they were subdued by the Chilean Army in the War of the Pacific (1879–1884) and settled on reservations, these dates being precisely those of the United States Army campaigns against the Apache.

The beige-colored areas of Map 49, finally, are of the hunting and foraging nomads, both of South and of North America; in these regions, the culture tides flowed for centuries in two directions: one was of peoples and influences moving from the more developed zones out into the wilderness—as, for instance, the relatively recent movements up the Atlantic coast and Mississippi valley of the Iroquois and Mandan; the contrary movement was of nomads—like the Athabascan Apacheans—driving into and ravaging the settled lands of the agriculturalists. The arrows shown striking from the beige into the green areas of the map are

426. Taos Pueblo.

intended to suggest the force of this inevitably destructive impulse that often threatened even the roots and generative life-forces of the nuclear sourcelands of civilization. The Mesoamerican chronicles of the Aztecs themselves tell of devastating invasions from the barbaric north by one tribe after another: the destruction of Teotihuacán; then, of Tollán; and finally, of Tenochtitlán by Cortés, which did, indeed, accomplish the demolition of a civilization. The process is one that has been documented for every quarter of the earth: beneath the ruins of Homer's Troy, the ruins of earlier Troys. And not always are the later strata of a higher grade than the earlier; more often, the warmth and life of creative inspiration, growth, and grace are of the earlier phases of an historic course, while in the later phases, practical applications and disciplines take over. This we recognize when we turn, for example, from Greece to Rome, or from Mayan to Aztec ruins and remains.

In any broad review of the entire range of transformations of the life-structuring mythologies of the native Americas, one outstanding feature becomes immediately apparent: the force, throughout, of shamanic influences, undoubtedly as a consequence of the repeated incursions into the settled village provinces of one horde after another of nomadic tribesmen. In fact, as Frobenius once remarked:

"The great problem of the cultural geography of America lies in the question of how, between the two prodigious negative fields of the northern hunting nomads and the southern forest and water nomads, the American high civilizations could have originated and developed at all."[289] They originated, one observes by Map 49, in the hemisphere's one defended area, equidistant, north and south, from the two nomadic zones. In their development, however, they were carried and brought to fulfillment by the same nomads who, initially, had broken upon them as destroyers. There is a quality of ferocity in the myths and ceremonies of these civilizations that will, depending upon one's temper, either chill or boil the blood; for they are grounded in the hunter's recognition of the ferocity that is of life itself, which lives on life.

427. A posed trophy photograph (above), made about 1918, of Julio Popper and his squad on an Indian hunt. The body in the foreground is of a Selk'nam. The Indian's bow is in his left hand, an arrow in his right. In a still-earlier photograph (below), taken in Paris in 1889, M. Maître exhibits a group of Tierra del Fuegans that he has captured, transported to France, and presented to society.

At the Uttermost Part of the Earth

Of the myths and folktales of the South American nomadic tribes, those from Tierra del Fuego merit special regard, because they both are free of planting culture influence and are of aborigines whose progenitors must have been among the earliest to enter the New World. Moreover, we have two full collections of all that could be learned of their tales in the early 1920s, compiled by the same Martin Gusinde from whose intimate reports of their shamanic practices and experiences we have already had occasion to quote (see pages 160–163). Furthermore, Johannes Wilbert has published translations of these tales and an index of their folklore motifs, classified according to the categories of Stith Thompsons's *Motif Index of Folk Literature*.[290]

I have selected ten tales of the Selk'nam (or Ona), the land-nomads of the large, northern, main island of the archipelago, and twelve tales of the Yamana (or Yahgan), the canoeing people of the numerous small islands south of Beagle Channel. I have taken the liberty of compressing and telescoping the tales of my selection with a mind rather to the interest of the narratives than to ethnology.

Myths of the Selk'nam of Tierra del Fuego

How the Ancestors Came to Be

Kenós was alone on the earth. "Someone Up There," Temaúkel, had appointed him to set everything down here in order. He was the son of the South and the Heavens. He wandered over the world, came back here and looked around, then went to a swampy place, dug out a lump of mud mixed with matted roots and grass tufts, shaped a male organ, and placed this on the ground. He dug another lump, squeezed the water out, shaped a female organ which he placed beside the first, then went his way. During the night, the two lumps of earth joined. From this arose something like a person: the first Ancestor. The two objects separated and, during the following night, joined again. Again someone arose who quickly grew. Night after night this occurred, with every night a new Ancestor. Thus their number steadily increased.[291]

How the Old Were Given New Life

When Kenós and three Ancestors who had joined him reached old age, they lay down and tried to fall into a long sleep, but failed. They tried a number of times and finally succeeded, lying like dead. But they did not die. They got up and were still old. So they went north, to try up there, wearily dragging themselves along, speaking feebly, in the way of the old, mortally tired. When they reached the north, they let the Ancestors up there wrap them in their mantles and put them in the ground, where they lay as though dead. After a few days they stirred, then began to move their lips, whispering, then talking. Then they rose, looked at each other, and saw that they were young again. Those who had been weeping for them were now joyous. In their transformation sleep they had finally succeeded. And so it was thereafter for all the Ancestors. After rising from the long sleep, each would go to Kenós, saying, "Wash me!" and he would wash them clean of the odor of death.

The people would age again and again, lie down to sleep and rise again, until, no longer wishing to come back, one would be transformed into a mountain, a bird, or a wind, a sea animal, rock or land animal. Others, following Kenós to the sky, became stars or clouds.[292]

How the Sky Was Raised

In the beginning the celestial vault lay close to the earth. But Kenós, before ascending, lifted it to its present place, where he himself stands, now, as a star.[293]

Kwányip, the First Herdsman

Kwányip was from the north. His father, Háis, was a *xon* (shaman) who had wished to marry the daughter, Hósne, of a rival *xon* named Nánenk. The lovers would meet secretly, and when Nánenk, unknown to them, discovered them embracing, he planned a devastating revenge. He contrived that Háis's own daughter, Alekwóin, should be lying, one day, where Hósne should have been, so that when Háis arrived, blind with desire, he threw himself on his own daughter. She conceived. And the child was Kwányip.

In his youth, this brother of his own mother was notoriously selfish. He had a herd of domesticated guanacos, but would share none of their meat with his tribesmen, who were hunters of wild guanaco in the mountains, often with little to show. He came from the north to our country, driving his herd, helped by his dogs. You can still see on the stones the footprints of that first herd. But he never shared their meat, and for this he was greatly disliked.[294]

Kwányip and Chénuke: a Shaman Contest

At that time, here in the south, there was a mighty and dangerous *xon*, named Hásapa when he lived on earth, but Chénuke when he became a star. A woman was strolling along a beach looking for mussels, when he called to her, "Give me some!" She approached, and he burst into laughter, peered at her with his peculiar glance, and she fell dead.

This monster greatly resented Kwányip and wanted to undo him. Discovering where he

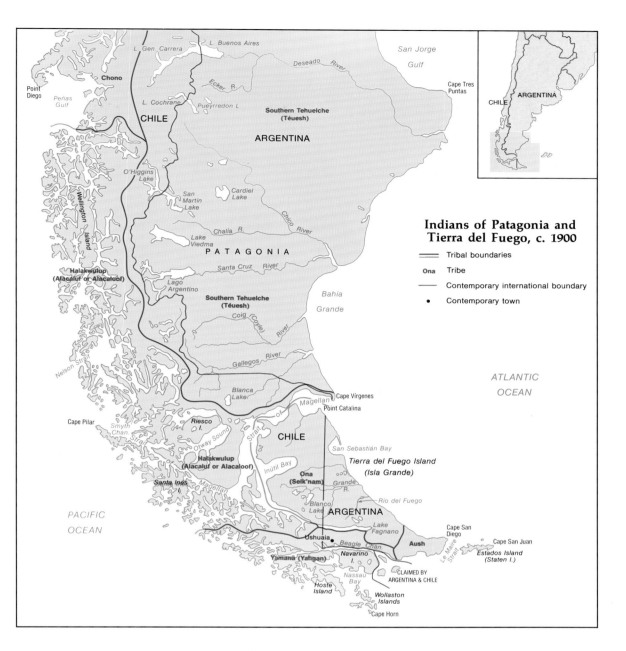

Indians of Patagonia and Tierra del Fuego, c. 1900

- ⎓ Tribal boundaries
- Ona   Tribe
- ── Contemporary international boundary
- • Contemporary town

Map 50. Formerly the coasts of the whole Chilean archipelago were inhabited by canoeing tribes—the Chono, Halakwulup (or Alacaluf), and Yamana (or Yahgan)—living on shellfish, seals, birds, and occasional stranded whales, while on the forested, large main island were the guanaco-hunting Selk'nam (or Ona). The coastal landscape, as described in 1741 by George Anson, the Commander of a British squadron rounding the Horn on an expedition to the South Seas, "had an aspect extremely barren and desolate. . . . It seems to be entirely composed of inaccessible rocks without the least mixture of earth or mould between them. These rocks terminate in a vast number of ragged points which spire up to a prodigious height and are all of them covered with everlasting snow. The points themselves are on every side surrounded with frightful precipices, and often overhang in a most astonishing manner. The hills which bear them are generally separated from each other by narrow clefts which appear as if the country had been frequently rent by earthquakes; for these chasms are nearly perpendicular, and extend through the substance of the main rocks, almost to the bottom; so that nothing can be imagined more savage and gloomy than the whole aspect of this coast.[35]

The Chono, the northernmost of the aborigines of this coastline, "became extinct" (as they say) in the nineteenth century. The Halakwulup, when visited by Martin Gusinde in 1923–24, had been reduced in number to eighty, dwelling along Smyth Channel; they could recall of their traditions no more than

fragments. And the Yamana, the southernmost of the canoeing tribes, with whose surviving numbers Gusinde worked from 1919 to 1922, numbered in his time no more than seventy, among whom, however, there was one—Julia, the fifty-five-year-old wife of an occasional worker on a sheep ranch at Punta Remolino—who could recall from long memory a coherent series of the folktales of her people.

On the large main island—where E. Lucas Bridges (the early English missionary's son, see page 160) had, from 1874, played, hunted, and grown up with various companies of the Selk'nam (or Ona, as he and his father always called them)—Gusinde in 1918 could find no more than 250 of the tribe: an encampment of five families near Lago Fagnano, and another cluster of twenty-seven families in a village by a mission station near the Rio del Fuego. Bridges, returning in 1932, found, as he tells, "pitifully few Ona faces" to welcome him. For there had meanwhile been two epidemics of measles, one in 1924 and another in 1929, which had completed the work of extermination begun earlier by such squads of Indian hunters, armed with repeating rifles equipped with telescopic sights, as that of Figure 427. Bridges, reporting the situation in 1947, stated that: "Of the seven to nine thousand natives—Yahgan, Ona, Aush, and Alacaloof—who inhabited the country when the story began, there are now less than a hundred and fifty pure-blooded Indians and possibly a slightly larger number of half-breeds. The white population at the last census was 9560."[36]

428/429. The only garment of the Selk'nam male was the "man's robe" (*chohn k-oli*), which was usually of guanaco hides, not fastened in any way, but held in position with the left hand, in which the hunter also carried his bow and quiver. On his forehead when fully dressed, he wore a triangular piece of blue-gray skin from the head of a guanaco that was held in place by a band of plaited sinew: the *göochilh* (Bridges' spelling) or *kóchel* (Gusinde's). An identification of the hunter with the animal of his hunting would seem to be implied by this symbolic detail (compare the Bushman's identification with the wounded eland, pages 92–93). In the Selk'nam story of Kwányip and the Cannibal, the *kóchel* is explicitly identified with the pubic area of a woman. Thus, the bleeding wound and menstruating vagina would seem to have been identified: the animal as willing victim, even yearning for the dart, and the hunter's bow and released arrow as the male organ, generating life. Viewed in this light, each of the hunters here pictured symbolically attired is a living counterpoint to the symbolic image of the shaman and wounded bison in the holy of holies of Lascaux (Figure 105 on page 65). When going into action, the hunter lets his robe fall and is naked save for the *kóchel* on his brow.

The five Selk'nam here photographed were the friends of E. Lucas Bridges around 1900; left to right: Aknikin, Shishkolh, Halimink, Chalshoat, and Puppup. "Under the eye of the camera," Bridges comments, "Halimink finds it impossible to retain his beaming smile."[37]

liked to catch nesting cormorants along the rocky coast, he hid above one of the nesting cliffs and waited; so that when the other was perilously climbing to one of the nests, he was able to send down a rain of pebbles, stones, then rocks, and finally boulders. Kwányip slid to the bottom and still they came. He shook his fist. He knew who had done this, and would reply.

Chénuke liked to catch birds at a swamp, far to the south, where there were geese and ducks. Kwányip, when he got there, felt astray and anxious, and when night fell was glad to see Chénuke's torch in the dark. Immediately, he caused a blizzard of hail and snow to come down and a high wall of ice to press Chénuke and his family out to sea. They all began waving their arms, as if to fly. "Kwányip has done this," Chénuke thought, as he and his family kept waving their arms, like birds. And then they rose out of the water and were flying east.[295]

How Kwányip Separated Night from Day

In the beginning, the Older Sun Man was up there in the sky. As father of the Younger Sun Man, he was so much the more powerful that there was hardly any night. When the Younger Sun Man took his place, the old father went away forever.

The people had never liked it to be light so long, it left too little time for love-making without being seen and laughed at. Kwányip also wanted more darkness. So he made the nights longer and longer, until there was no less night than day. Then everybody was pleased; for now men and women could lie a

long while together, and no one could watch and laugh.[296]

Kwányip and Cháskels, the Cannibal

Cháskels was a giant who hunted and ate people. His immense hut [a long ravine] can be seen to this day on the shore of the Rio MacLelan. His slingshot carried far, so that people everywhere were in danger. No one could hunt; everybody was starving. He had powerful dogs that would pursue and run people down, either consuming them on the spot or dragging them to their master. In his lust, he particularly relished women. A pregnant victim he would roast with the child intact within the womb. Sucklings he carried stacked on his head behind his triangular forehead ornament, his kóchel [see Figures 428 and 429]. Larger children he hung from his belt. His mantle was of human skins, and his kóchel of hairy patches cut from the pubic area of captured women.

One day, this cannibal-giant came across the two young nephews of Kwányip, seized and hung them from his belt. "I'll set these to work in my hut," he thought. The hut, with bones, intestines, flesh, and excrement strewn all about, was a horrifying sight. The boys were given the filthiest task, cleaning out the intestines of the bodies to be consumed, besides fetching wood for a huge fire, kept always burning.

When Kwányip became aware of what had happened to his nephews, he made his way to Cháskels' hut, where the giant sat musing by the fire, and there he beheld the two boys, covered with blood and filth. Unseen by the giant, he made a sign to them, pointed to where he would await them, then turned, and hastened away. First chance, they fled, and when their captor realized they were gone, he followed their tracks. When the boys had reached a broad river, Kwányip brought the two banks together, and they stepped across. When the giant arrived, the two banks were again apart, and he waded across. But when he started to ascend the opposite bank, Kwányip caused it to become so soaked with water that great chunks broke loose as he climbed. Stumbling about, sinking deeper into the saturated mud, he was about to give up, when Kwányip caused a freeze to occur. The ground became hard. Cháskels pulled himself to the top and collapsed, face down, exhausted.

"My back!" he groaned, when he saw Kwányip approaching. "It feels terrible." "I'll put my foot there, very softly," Kwányip said. "That will draw the pain away. Don't move!" And with his right foot he came down with all his might, the back broke, and the monster screamed and died.

The boys came out of hiding when they heard that scream and flung two stones from their slings that burst the dead giant's eyes. The entire inside of each eye, spurting out, fell into the water, and one sees to this day the greenish-gray spots on lagoons. Also from each eye came an insect, loudly buzzing. Horseflies: they like to sit on rotting meat and excrement. And so, Kwányip and his young nephews left that loathsome giant lying there, where the body turned into stone and can still be seen on the bank of that broad river, the Rio Grande of Tierra del Fuego.[297]

How Kwányip Caused the Dead to Rise No More

Aukmenk, Kwányip's elder brother, began to act as though he wished to die; so Kwányip wrapped him in his mantle and put him in the ground. Displeased to think of his elder brother reviving, however, he sat down by the place where he lay, and when the body stirred, brought his *xon* power to bear, so that Aukmenk should *not* come alive. Since then, no one has come alive again. All now remain forever dead.

When the people realized what Kwányip had done, they turned against him, and the most indignant against him was his rival, Chénuke, who took revenge by throwing his *xon* power at Kwányip's older sister-and-mother, Alekwóin, who soon lost strength and died, to rise from her sleep no more. Kwányip, greatly saddened by this loss, painted himself red and ascended with his whole family to the sky, where he now can be seen with his relatives all around him.[298]

When the Women Ruled

In those days, the sun, moon, stars, winds, rivers, and mountains walked the earth as human beings, and everywhere the women were in control. They told the men what to do, as today men tell women what to do. But since the men were numerous and strong, the smartest of the women were afraid that some day they might rebel; so they got together to consider what might be done to keep them in submission.

Their leader was Kra, the Moon, a powerful *xon*. She was the wife of Kran, the Sun. When the women were assembled, they arrived at an idea, and at some distance from the village erected a big hut, large enough for them all, where most of them thereafter remained most of the time. No man was allowed to approach. And to deceive their men into thinking that they had been joined by powerful spirits, they painted their bodies with various designs, covered their heads with masks of bark, and would appear from their big house, either singly, in pairs, or in long lines, hopping, skipping, or stiffly striding. They let it be known that these were extremely powerful spirits, who wished to be kept informed of the men's behavior. There were many of these spirits, each with a name, all desiring that the men should behave as required. And when the

430. The "women's robe" (*nah k-oli*), like the men's, was of guanaco hide, but smaller; unlike the men's, however, it was fastened around the shoulders by means of two strips of hide. A baby traveling on its mother's back was carried inside the robe for warmth, with a little net of thongs outside to hold it in place. "If the mother had some burden," Bridges states, "the child would be seated on top of that, but still inside the *oli*. Women never carried children any distance in their arms."[38]

In addition to an outer robe, each woman wore a kind of petticoat called "hip-tied" (*kopiyaten*), which was of soft guanaco skin wrapped one-and-a-half times around the body and tied with a long guanaco thong. It reached from just below the breasts to the knees, and although, like a man, a woman would discard her *oli* without hesitation, she would not further uncover herself in public, or even in her own home.

women would return to their own dwellings, it would be only to assign to their husbands tasks invented for them by Kra, the Moon, their mistress. "Xálpen, the Chief Spirit in the Big Hut, needs plenty of meat and needs it often," they would say. And so, their men were kept busy, hunting, with their entire catch then going to their wives in the Big House.

Now Kran, the Sun, was a great hunter. One day, having killed a large guanaco, he was returning with the animal on his shoulders, when, fatigued, he threw it to the ground and sat down beside it to rest. He was within sight of a lagoon, not far from the women's Big House, and on the beach saw two of the younger women, who had been bathing, laughing, and practicing the stiff, short steps of one of the supposed spirits. "We've nearly got it," they were shouting. "So *that's* it!" thought Kran, incensed. He got up and ran at them, yelling, "You wretches!

Deceivers!" Terrified, the two jumped into the water and ducked under. "Stay there!" Kran shouted, "for your own good!" And with that, they were transformed into water birds of a kind that dive and stay under when people approach.

Returning with his guanaco to the village, Kran tried to behave as though nothing had happened, and, one by one, secretly told his story to the men in their huts. They gathered for a meeting and, to check on the situation, sent one of their number, a swiftly running little bird, to investigate. He approached the Big Hut unseen, darted in and ran along the inside wall and out the other side. "There are no spirits," he reported; "only women, seated along the wall, and behind each, her mask." To make sure, a second bird was sent; then a third. And just then, Kran's own daughter arrived with two other women to collect meat for the spirits. Kran grabbed the guanaco he had just brought in, threw it furiously at his daughter's feet, and shouted, "Take it! Take it

tempted, the most extreme: that of sending the mask known as *Xálpen ke xat*, "The Chief Spirit, the Devourer." In two lines the women filed out of the Big Hut, while Kra, the Moon Woman, stood shouting at the men to come near and see for themselves how furious Xálpen had become because of their recent behavior. "All your wives are about to be devoured, one by one, by Xálpen," she screamed, thinking to frighten them back into submission.

And indeed, the men came forward, but when Kran, the Sun Man, gave a scream and yelled, "Strike them down!" the slaughter began. Swinging cudgels even at their own daughters and wives, the furious men moved in, grabbing and throttling every female they laid hands on. Sun Man, with a flaming torch, went after his powerful wife, and, at his first blow, the entire sky trembled; at the second, it threatened to fall. So he hesitated, and she escaped, rising to the sky as the moon with the sun in pursuit. You can still see the burned

431. Angela, a young Selk'nam matron. The horizontal stripes are of red paint.

432. Selk'nam males disguised as the supposed inhabitants of the *klóketen*, the special lodge of the men's society (see **286**, pages 162–163).

to your mother and her women. It's not much, but enough for *them*."

Shocked and terrified, realizing that the secret was out, the three went back with the frightening news, and immediately Kra, the Moon Woman, realized the need for action. She had herself painted particularly beautifully and with four others proceeded to the village, demanding meat. The five were given all there was, but overheard much murmuring. Another mask was sent, attended by a large company, and on seeing her, every man ran to his hut and hid his face in his mantle. Her attendants scattered, each to her own husband, and what they overheard were such comments as: "Who knows if these be really spirits?" and "Maybe we have been tricked!" Everywhere, the men were so threateningly restive that the women, afraid, returned to the Big House.

As a last resort, one more ruse was at-

and bruised spots on her face. The other women, who had all been slain, were transformed into animals whose markings tell what designs they were wearing when killed. And the only females left were little children, knowing nothing of their mother's fraudulent secret.[299]

Foundation of the Men's Secret House

When the women had been killed and their *Klóketen* (Big House) destroyed, the men assembled to organize a *Klóketen* of their own. Each brought from his own region a great log of stone. The seven greatest logs were the first set up, the others filled the spaces between. The form of the hut was conical, the whole thing tremendous. One can still see among the mountains of Máustas the form of that mighty ceremonial structure, the tremendous posts and beams. Whoever even thinks of it and calls out, "Máustas, Máustas!" will find many sea lions, or else a whale stranded on a beach. And anyone falling asleep near there will in dream see everything that happened at that place in those earliest times.[300]

Myths of the Yamana of Tierra del Fuego

The Older and the Younger Sun Man

The women, at one time, were in authority, and it was they who then decided to get rid of the Older Sun Man, who, in a rage, had caused a universal conflagration: the forests had burned, the ocean had boiled, and to this day the mountaintops are bare. All the women attacked and almost strangled him. But he was strong, broke free, and fled to the sky, to

become a star, which has since faded and disappeared.

The Younger Sun Man, his son, was altogether different. He was kind and loving, helpful, an excellent hunter, and marvelously handsome.[301]

The Flood

Once, when spring was approaching, someone saw a spectacled ibis fly over his hut and shouted to his neighbors, "Look! There is an ibis flying over my hut." They all joined him, shouting with joy, "The ibises are flying. Spring is here."

However, the ibis herself, who is a very delicate woman, wishing to be treated with deference, not noise, took offense at all that shouting and, in revenge, let it snow so hard and long that the whole earth was blanketed.

The sun came out, the snow melted, and the earth then was flooded. People hurried to their canoes, but only the very lucky reached one or another of the five mountain peaks that remained above the waters. When the flood subsided, these came down, rebuilt their huts along the shores, and ever since that time, women have been ruled by men.[302]

According to another version:

It was the Moon Woman, who, in anger, caused the flood, after the men had seized power.

The Culture Bringers

A mother, three sisters, and two brothers, the Yoálox family, wandered over the world until they came to where we now live, and it was they who taught us to arrange our lives: to make tools and weapons, to hunt on water and on land, how to make use of the animal skins, and how to prepare the meat. Of the brothers, the younger was the smarter and more talented, but the cleverest of all was the eldest sister.[303]

The Invention of Fire

Once the elder brother was amusing himself, striking small stones together. Among them was a firestone that gave sparks. Surprised, he struck it in such a way that a spark ignited some very dry down. Then he fetched kindling and had a fire.

"Fire," he said to his younger brother, "is both pleasant and useful. Let us keep it burning all the time, so that people may have it without trouble."

"I disagree," said the younger. "It will be very much better for people to have to make some effort and to work." He took a stick,

433/434/435. Although the Selk'nam hunted with bow and arrow, the Yamana held to the earlier spear and harpoon. Nor did they have the atlatl, the Late Paleolithic spear-thrower. Their shamans, likewise, had no drum. Their huts were the crudest shelters. And to appreciate their deliberate nakedness, it is necessary to realize that they were living, not in the tropics, but within five degrees of the South Polar ice pack. They were the ultimate representatives of what Jamake Highwater has termed the "primal mind."[39]

436. *Selk'nam Bowmen*

And so, to this day, hunters break or lose harpoons if they have not learned to hurl them with good aim; or if they are not thrown with enough force, they remain stuck in the sea lion's back as he swims away.[306]

The Invention of the Harpoon Point

A short time later, the two began fashioning harpoon points out of whalebone, but when they hunted with them, the sea lions were unharmed by the light wounds, and the harpoons were lost, one after another. Disheartened, they went to the eldest of their three sisters for advice. She looked at one of their points. Both sides were smooth, and it was firmly fixed to the shaft. She carved a large barb on one side of it, then loosened her loincloth, from which she cut a long leather thong. She tied one end of this to the lower peg of the bone point, then laid the next part of the thong along the shaft, securing it there [and thereby the point to the shaft] by wrapping it once around the lower part, after which she rolled up the long free end and taught her brothers how to use the new weapon.

The right hand grasps the middle of the shaft, the left loosely holds the rolled up thong. The weapon is hurled, and when the sea lion is struck, the shaft becomes detached from the head; but since it is loosely fastened to the long thong, one end of which is in the hunter's hand, the other fixed to the barb in the animal's body, the shaft floats on the surface, following the movements of the sea lion, which has plunged but will finally cease tugging at the line, since every time it does so, the sharp side-barb digs deeper into the flesh. Brought in at last, it is clubbed with a heavy cudgel, and for the hunter's family there is blubber and meat. The two Yoálox were nearly beside themselves with delight at the successes that they enjoyed with this clever device.[307]

The First Menstruation

In the beginning, the two Yoálox lived with their eldest sister, since neither had a wife. But then the time came when they no longer enjoyed sleeping alone, and she agreed to help them find one.

Now the Wren had so many wives that he was unable to supply them with sufficient meat, whereas the Yoálox were good hunters, and so, had plenty. Wren's wives suggested

scattered the embers, and since that time people have had to work to make fires.[304]

Bird Hunting

Those two Yoálox, when they needed meat, would kill birds with their slings. "I would like it better," said the elder, "if we killed them just by a glance. That way, people would have food without effort." He turned his sharp eyes on some birds that were flying overhead, wishing them to fall dead. They did, and he was overjoyed. "From now on," he said, "It will always be like this."

"Not at all," said the younger. "It is better that people should have to make their weapons and use cunning to sneak up on their prey. *That* is how it shall be. Everybody must work."

Next day, when a flock of birds flew overhead, the elder stared at them with the thought that they should fall, but they kept flying. Since then, every hunter must use effort and cunning. And frequently, from clumsy hunters the quarry escapes.[305]

The Sea-Lion Hunt

The elder Yoálox was given by his eldest sister a harpoon that never missed the mark and always returned to his hand. One day, on a big sea lion, he broke and lost it. "How convenient it would be," said he to his younger brother, "if I had a harpoon that would always hit the mark, return to my hand, and never get lost or break! That way, we should all be saved much toil and trouble."

The younger became angry. "It must never be like that," he said. "All the benefits of work and effort would be lost if we handed people any such weapon as you propose. It is good that unskilled hunters should break and lose their harpoons. Each should work to learn through his own effort."

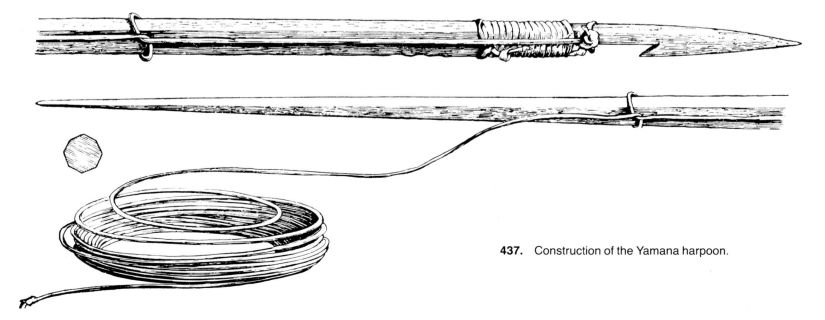

437. Construction of the Yamana harpoon.

438. Tenenésk, headman and shaman of a remnant Selk'nam group of five families (thirty-two persons) that in Gusinde's time (1918) were encamped near Lago Fagnano. When Lucas Bridges knew him (1895–1910), the hunting grounds of the party of six or seven families of which he was, not the headman, but the shaman, reached to the Atlantic coast, extending from Cape Santa Inés to Policarpo Cave. In summer, the company hunted southward as far as to the hills overlooking Sloggett and Moat bays. Tenenésk was Gusinde's principal source for his Selk'nam legends. In 1895 he had offered to initiate Bridges into shamanism. His wife, Leluwachin, was the only Selk'nam woman Bridges ever met who was credited with magic powers. "Many Yahgan [Yamana] women," he states, "were considered to be witches, but Leluwachin was unique as a sorceress among the Ona."[40]

439. Julia, the fifty-five-year-old wife of an old ranch-hand on a sheep ranch at Punta Remolino. "Most of the narratives current among the Yamana," states Gusinde, "I owe to the intelligent Julia. She is considered by all who know her to be the person best informed of them all."[41]

that they might ask for help from the Yoálox, and so he dressed them up very beautifully, ordering each to paint and decorate herself [that was the origin of ceremonial body painting], and one by one they went to beg for meat.

The brothers looked over each of the women carefully, and to all that were not to their liking they bade their sister give plenty of meat. When the last and most beautiful arrived, however, they were enchanted and asked their sister not to give her meat, but to persuade her to remain.

"Just sit down quietly here beside my brothers," said the sister. "They both like you very much."

Without embarrassment, the woman sat down on the bed, and the two began caressing her. They told her how deeply they desired her and this pleased her very much. "All right," she said; "I'll stay." And so the Wren lost the most beautiful of his wives.

The two took turns sleeping with her, and one day, when the elder rose early to hunt, he returned only when it was getting dark, and overhearing, as he approached, certain sounds within the hut, he realized that his brother had been making love, in bed, all day. He drew closer quietly and overheard the woman whispering: "I really like your penis a lot. It is large and fills my vagina. Your brother's is too small. It doesn't excite me." The hunter presently entered and sat for a time warming himself by the fire, then turned and let the woman know what he had heard. He got up and approached her, and his brother moved away. He lay on top or her, and his penis, entering her vagina, swelled until she was torn and started to bleed. "Are you satisfied?" he asked. "Do you want it to grow larger?" He got up. "You have now had your first menstruation," he said, and he thereupon established the rules to be observed (which are still observed) at the time of the first menstruation. The brothers' sister was helping her and giving advice as well. And then: "Now that this woman is menstruating," she said, "let us have a big celebration." The brothers agreed. They prepared a lot of meat. And that was the first menarchia celebration.[308]

The First Childbirth

After that, the younger Yoálox lived alone with that woman, who gave birth eventually to a son. He informed her of the rites for childbirth, and women still follow those instructions. The child, however, cried incessantly, most loudly during the night, and Yoálox couldn't stand it. He built a hut apart, from which to go hunting and in which to fashion his weapons. Whenever he entered the other hut, the child would scream more loudly than ever, until once, in desperation, he grabbed it under the armpits, lifted it, stared fiercely into its face and yelled, "Will you stop screaming?" Whereupon, the little boy split right down the middle, so that Yoálox now had two sons. They were the first children brought into the world through an actual birth.[309]

Death Is Introduced

When the mother of the five Yoálox died, her body was placed on the grass where the warm sun would shine upon her, and the elder brother, sitting down beside her, fixed his eyes on her in silence, until the body moved a little and its eyes slowly opened. He got up and ran to the hut to tell his brother, who became angry. "No, no!" the brother cried. "It must not come to that. She is decrepit and old and must sleep now forever." The elder returned to where the body lay, to stare as before. But it was now rigid and remained that way. Since then, all people die.[310]

The Sea-Lion Husband

The two youngest sisters enjoyed bathing and playing in the waves. One day a big sea lion approached, offering to join in the play and, unafraid, they accepted him. Daily thereafter he joined them, and a special attachment developed with the elder. He would come swimming to her under water, and the younger sister would ask, "What is that big black thing I just saw passing between your legs?" To which the other would respond, "What do you mean? You must have seen my shadow." The younger was not satisfied, but the daily play continued, until the elder was clearly

pregnant. Then the sea lion took her on his back and swam away to his cave.

He was tremendously happy when a son was born, but anxious to know what the brothers would do when they understood what had happened. "They will kill me," he said. "But perhaps, if you return and tell them how fond of each other we are and how lively our little son is, they will let me live with them." She prepared herself to leave, he took her on his back, and when they came close to her brothers' hut, the sea lion set her ashore.

The brothers had had for some time an idea of what was going on, and when their sister returned with her story, "You say the sea lion is your husband," they said. "Very well, he may come in." So with his wife and child on his back, the sea lion confidently arrived. They had to enlarge the hut door to admit him, but his place in the family seemed assured. Every day, he would swim away to hunt and return with mussels, fish, and crabs enough for the whole family.

One day, however, the brothers sent the women off on an errand of some kind, and while they were away, treacherously slew their guest. It was a beautiful day, and when the sea lion had returned from the hunt, he had stretched out on a large rock to sleep in the sun. The brothers had been sitting before their hut, preparing harpoons and, when they heard the sea lion snoring, sneaked up on him, raised the two harpoons, and thrust the cruel barbs home. He woke with a roar of pain, which the women in the distance heard, and the wife came running. But by the time she arrived, the brothers had already finished butchering, and had even given a piece of the meat, roasted, to the little boy. Unknowing, he had liked it, begged for more, and was eating a second piece of his father when his mother arrived, horrified. In a flash, she flung at the child's head a spiney sea urchin that turned him into a thornfish [which the Yaghan do not eat, because it used to be a boy]. Then she gazed, speechless, at her husband's butchered body, fell down and wept, while her brothers flung some of the parts at her with insults. "Here you have the mouth that spoke to you with love; here the flippers that embraced you; the back on which you rode; the part that satisfied your desire.'' A long time passed, after which, at first timidly, she tasted a bit of sea lion's flesh and liked it very much. In the end, reconciled to her loss, she was eating sea lion blubber and meat with as much relish as her two brothers.[311]

The Ascension

The Yoálox family remained a long time on earth. They gave names to all things and places. When they grew old, they rose to the sky and are seen today as stars.[312]

Noteworthy in the Yamana tale of *The Flood* is the actual number of escape mountains, namely five, which is the number of sacred mountains of the Navaho (see Map 48). The Navaho mountains are of the world center and four directions. It is possible that the Yamana five were also of this sense. Such mountains are of eternity, whereas the floods and tides of fortune are of time. And in terms of the *philosophia perennis* (of which the archetypes of myth are the everlasting symbols), man's true being, as well as the being of all things, is not in the vicissitudes of time, but aloft on the mountaintop of the still point of this turning world.

A second theme to be remarked is of the overthrow of female dominance by the masculine community; it appears in both traditions: in the Selk'nam tale of *When the Women Ruled* and in the Yamana of *The Older and the Younger Sun Man*. Compare the Pygmy version of the same mythological event as rendered in the ceremonial dance observed by Colin Turnbull in the Congo (see page 111).

The Blackfoot tale of *The Buffalo's Wife* (see page 234) and the Yamana of *The Sea-Lion Husband* are variants of a theme that has been popular throughout the world, apparently from the beginning of mankind's time on earth. The Blackfoot is in the form of a myth; the Yamana is a folktale. The myth had to do with the origins of the rites by which the Blackfoot tribe rendered veneration to the animals upon whose willing giving of their lives the survival of the tribe depended. The Yamana tale, on the other hand, has become disengaged from any properly mythological context with which it may once have been associated and has been turned to entertainment. We do not know whether, for the Yamana, the sea lion may once have stood in the role of Master Animal, as did the buffalo, not only in North America, but on back to the period of Lascaux. In fact, we know next to nothing of what must once have been the *mythology* of the tribes of Tierra del Fuego. The people who gave Gusinde what they remembered of their traditions were the last representatives of already extinguished races. As Jochelson found among the Yukaghir of northernmost Siberia, the master guardians of the mythology were no more; all that could be collected in the first decades of the twentieth century were the recollections of individuals already acculturated. Of Gusinde's Selk'nam collection, the principal source was the headman and shaman, Tenenésk, of a small group near Lago Fagnano; and of the Yamana tales, fifty-five-year-old Julia—of Punta Remolino—and her friends. The differences of interests and concerns of these two distinct personalities are evident in the selections of their contributions, through which the last reflections come to us of a long long day, the sun of which, with its light, has set.

440. Selk'nam departure.

APPENDIX

ENDNOTES

FOREWORD

[1] John E. Pfeiffer, *The Creative Explosion* (New York: Harper & Row, 1982).

[2] André Leroi-Gourhan *Treasurers of Prehistoric Art* (New York: Harry N. Abrams, n.d.), p.112.

[3] Ibid., p. 118.

[4] Ibid., p. 144.

[5] Ananda K. Coomaraswamy, "The Philosophy of Mediaeval and Oriental Art," in Roger Lipsey (ed.) *Coomaraswamy*, 2 vols. Bollingen Series LXXXIX (Princeton University Press, 1977), vol. 1, p. 43.

[6] *Māṇḍūkya Upanishad*, complete. In verses 3 and 4, "by way of the body, its senses. . ." etc., I have followed an interpretation by Vedantic commentators of the two technical terms, "seven limbed" (*saptāṅga*) and "nineteen mouthed" (*ekonaviṁśatimukha*). See *Vedāntasāra* 62–89.

[7] Sigmund Freud, *The Interpretation of Dreams*, translation by A.A. Brill, *The Basic Writings of Sigmund Freud* (New York: The Modern Library, published by Random House, Inc., 1938), pp. 499–502.

[8] Sankara's Commentary to *Māṇḍūkya Upanishad* Verse 4, citing *Bṛihadāraṇyaka Upanishad* 4.3.9-14. Sankara translation, from Swami Nikhilananda, *The Māṇḍūkyopanishad with Gauḍapāda's Kārikā and Sankara's Commentary*. Sri Ramakrishna Centenary Publication (Mysore: Sri Ramakrishna Ashrama, 1936), p.20. Brihadāraṇyaka translation, following (with slight stylistic modifications) Robert Ernest Hume, *The Thirteen Principal Upanishads* (London, New York, etc., Oxford University Press, 1921), pp. 134–135.

[9] Marguerite Anne Biesele, *Folklore and Ritual of !Kung Hunter-Gatherers*, thesis presented to Harvard University, Department of Anthropology, Cambridge, Mass., 1975, p. 1.

[10] Lorna Marshall, "The Medicine Dance of the !Kung Bushmen," *Africa*, vol. 39, no.4 (October 1969), pp. 350–352. Richard B. Lee, "The Sociology of the !Kung Bushman Trance Performances," in Raymond Prince (ed.), *Trance and Possession States*, Proceedings of the Second Conference of the R.M. Bucke Memorial Society, Montreal, 1966, p. 42.

[11] Ibid., p. 352.

[12] *The Gospel of Sri Ramakrishna*, translation, with a preface, by Swami Nikhilananda (New York: Ramakrishna-Vivekananda Center, 1942), pp. 829–830.

[13] A.A. Brill, op. cit., p. 12.

[14] Sigmund Freud, "Das Ich und das Es," *Gesammelte Schriften*, vol. 6 (Leipzig, Wien, Zurich: Internationaler Psychoanalytischer Verlag, 1925), p. 401.

[15] Ibid., p. 400.

[16] *Vivekacūḍāmani* 308.

[17] Freud, *The Interpretation of Dreams*, in Brill, op. cit., pp. 307–309.

[18] C.G. Jung, *Two Essays on Analytical Psychology*, translated by R.F.C. Hull, *Collected Works*, Bollingen Series XX (Princeton University Press, 1953–1979), vol. 7, p. 64.

[19] C.G. Jung. *The Archetypes of the Collective Unconscious*, translation by R.F.C. Hull, *Collected Works*, vol. 9.1 pp. 42–43.

[20] C.G. Jung, *Psychological Types*, translation by R.F.C. Hull, *Collected Works*, vol. 6, pp. 442–443. In a letter to Freud, Nov. 11, 1912, reporting on a recent visit to the United States, Jung wrote, "I analysed fifteen Negroes in Washington, with demonstrations." He did this at St. Elizabeth Hospital (a government facility) through the cooperation of its director, Dr. William Allison White. See ibid., p. 443, Note 62.

[21] Gaudapāda, Kārikā 3 to Māṇḍūkya 6. Text and translation in Nikhilananda, op. cit., p. 31.

[22] Biesele, op. cit., p. 1.

[23] *Phaedo* 66 c–d. Translation by Hugh Tredenick, in Edith Hamilton and Huntington Cairns (eds.), *The Collected Dialogues of Plato*. Bollingen Series LXXI (New York: Pantheon Books, 1961), p. 49.

[24] James Joyce, *A Portrait of the Artist as a Young Man* (London: Jonathan Cape, Ltd., 1916) p. 233; Penguin Books edition, p. 205.

[25] *The Gospel According to Thomas*, Coptic text established and translated by A. Guillaumont, H. -Ch. Puech, G. Quispel, W. Till and Yassah 'abd al Masih (New York: Harper and Brothers, 1959), Logion 113, p. 57.

[26] Brill (ed.), op. cit., Book V, "Totem and Tabu," end of Section 5, p. 919.

[27] Ibid., p. 903; citing a certain Dr. Savage, in the *Boston Journal of Natural History*, vol. V, 1845–7.

[28] Ibid., pp. 915–916.

[29] Leroi-Gourhan, op. cit., p. 58.

[30] Joyce, op. cit., p. 241; Penguin Books edition, pp. 211–212.

[31] Robert Snyder, *Buckminster Fuller* (New York: St. Martin's Press, 1980), p. 100.

[32] Daisetz Teitaro Suzuki, *Essays in Zen Buddhism (First Series)*, Published for the Buddhist Society, London. (London, New York, Melbourne, Sydney, Cape Town: Rider and Company, n.d.), p. 58.

[33] Joyce, op. cit., pp. 241–242; Penguin Books edition p. 212.

[34] Lorna Marshall, "!Kung Bushman Religious Beliefs," *Africa*, vol. 32, no. 3 (1962), p. 251.

[35] Ananda K. Coomaraswamy, "A Figure of Speech or a Figure of Thought?" in Roger Lipsey (ed.), op. cit., vol. 1, p. 20.

[36] John G. Neihardt, *Black Elk Speaks* (Lincoln: University of Nebraska Press, 1961), pp. 198–200.

[37] Johann Peter Eckermann, *Gespräche mit Goethe in den letzten Jahren seines Lebens, 1823–1832*, 2 vols. in one (Berlin, Leipzig, Wien, Stuttgart: Deutsches Verlagshaus Bong & Co., 1916), vol. 1, p. 251.

[38] Quoted from motto page of Oswald Spengler, *Der Untergang des Abendlandes* (Munchen: C.H. Beck'sche Verlagsbuchhandlung, 1931), vol. 1.

[39] Joyce, op. cit., pp. 242–243; Penguin Books edition, p. 213.

[40] *The Gospel According to Thomas*, Coptic text established and translated by A. Guillaumont, H.-Ch. Puech, G. Quispel, W. Till and Yassah 'abd Al Masih (New York: Harper and Brothers, 1959), pp. 43, 55, 3, and 55–57.

[41] Marshall, "!Kung Bushman Religious Beliefs," op. cit., p. 251.

[42] Abbé Henri Breuil, *Four Hundred Centuries of Cave Art* (Montignac, France: Centre d'Etudes et Documentation Préhistoriques, 1952), pp. 170–171.

[43] Ananda K. Coomaraswamy, "Svayamātṛṇṇā: Janua Coeli," in Lipsey (ed.), op. cit., vol. 1, pp. 483 and 481.

[44] Eugen Herrigel, *Zen in the Art of Archery*, translated by R.F.C. Hull (New York: Pantheon, 1953), p. 20.

[45] *Muṇḍaka Upanishad* 4.

[46] Abbé H. Breuil, translated by Mary E. Boyle, *Four Hundred Centuries of Cave Art* (Montignac, Dordogne: Centre d'Etudes et de Documentation Préhistoriques, 1952), pp. 91–101.

[47] *Ibid.*, p. 95.

[48] Leo Frobenius, *Das Unbekannte Afrika* (Munich: Oskar Beck, 1923), p. 164.

[49] Marija Gimbutas, *Goddesses and Gods of Old Europe: 7000–3500 B.C.* (Berkeley and Los Angeles: University of California Press, 1974).

[50] Frobenius, op. cit., pp. 162–163 and Fig. p. 163.

[51] Ibid., p. 128.

MYTHOLOGIES OF THE GREAT HUNT

Text

[1] John E. Pfeiffer, *The Creative Explosion* (New York: Harper & Row, 1982).

[2] Frobenius, *Kulturgeschichte Afrikas*.

[3] Coon, op. cit.

[4] Ibid., pp. 651–652.

[5] Nance, *The Discovery of the Tasaday*.

[6] Jamake Highwater, *The Primal Mind* (New York: Harper & Row, 1981).

[7] Chard, op. cit., p. 15.

[8] Lewis Henry Morgan, *The League of the Ho-dé-no-sau-nee, or Iroquois*, 2 vols. (New York: Dodd, Mead, 1901; 1904; 1-vol. ed., 1922).

[9] James George Frazer, *Totemism and Exogamy, a Treatise on Certain Forms of Superstition and Society*, 4 vols. (London: Macmillan, 1910).

[10] Emile Durkheim, *Les Formes élémentaires de la vie religieuse, le système totémique en Australie* (Paris: F. Alcan, 1912).

[11] Sigmund Freud, *Totem und Tabu: Einige Übereinstimmungen in Seelenleben der Wilden und der Neurotiker von Prof. Dr. Sigmund Freud* (Leipzig: H. Heller, 1913).

[12] T. G. H. Strehlow, *Aranda Traditions* (Carlton, Australia: Melbourne University Press, 1947), p. xviii.

[13] Ibid., pp. 1–5.

[14] Fritz Graebner, "Wanderung und Entwicklung Sozialer Systeme in Australien," *Globus*, vol. 90, no. 12 (1906), pp. 181–186.

[15] Adapted from A. W. Howitt, *The Native Tribes of South-East Australia* (London: Macmillan, 1904), p. 493.

[16] Ibid., pp. 488–489.

[17] Ibid., pp. 489–491.

[18] Ibid.

[19] Ibid., p. 492.

[20] Ibid., p. 500.

[21] Wilhelm Schmidt, *Der Ursprung der Gottesidee*, 12 vols. (Munster in Westfalia, W. Germany: Aschendorff, 1912–1955).

[22] See Lang's important article, "God (Primitive and Savage)," in James Hastings (ed.), *Encyclopaedia of Religion and Ethics*, 13 vols. (New York: Charles Scribner's Sons, 1928), vol. 6, pp. 243–247. See also, the discussion of the controversy in Mircea Eliade, *Australian Religions: An Introduction* (Ithaca, N.Y.: Cornell University Press, 1973), pp. 8–41.

[23] Ronald M. Berndt and Catherine H. Berndt, *Man, Land and Myth in North Australia: The Gunwinngu People* (East Lansing: Michigan State University Press, 1970), pp. 117–118.

[24] Ibid., p. 118, abridged.

[25] Andreas Lommel, *Die Unumbal: Ein Stamm in Nordwest-Australien* (Hamburg, W. Germany: Museum für Völkerkunde, 1962), pp. 10–12; following commentary in Eliade, *Australian Religions*, pp. 67–69.

[26] Ibid., pp. 12–13; Eliade, *Australian Religions*, pp. 69–70.

[27] A. P. Elkin, "Rock-Paintings of North-West Australia," *Oceania*, vol. 1, no. 3 (1930), p. 263.

[28] Hermann Baumann, *Das Doppelte Geschlecht: Ethnologische Studien zur Bisexualität in Ritus und Mythos* (Berlin: Dietrich Reimer, 1955), p. 9.

[29] Ronald M. Berndt, "Badu, Islands of the Spirits," *Oceania*, vol. 19, no. 2 (December 1948), p. 98.

[30] Spencer and Gillen, op. cit., pp. 215–216.

[31] Ibid., pp. 246–249.

[32] Ibid., p. 257.

[33] Baumann, op. cit., pp. 213–223.

[34] Spencer and Gillen, op. cit., p. 364.

[35] Ibid., pp. 363–367, with insert from p. 350; abridged.

[36] A. Irving Hallowell, "Bear Ceremonialism in the Northern Hemisphere," *American Anthropologist*, new series, vol. 28, no. 1 (January-March 1926), p. 30; citing Knud Leems, *Account of the Laplanders of Finmark, Their Manners, Language, and Religion* (Copenhagen, Denmark, 1767), in John Pinkerton, *A General Collection of the Best and Most Interesting Voyages and Travels in All Parts of the World* (London, 1808-1814), vol. 1, p. 415.

[37] Ibid., p. 28; citing Baron de La Houton, *New Voyages to North America* (1703), reprinted with addenda by R. G. Thwaites, 2 vols. (Chicago: A. C. McClurg, 1905), vol. 2, p. 484.

[38] Ibid., p. 27; citing P. F. X. Charlevoix, *Journal d'un voyage fait par ordre du roi dans l'Amerique Septentrionale* (Paris, 1744), letter 6 (March 1721) at Three Rivers, Quebec, p. 117.

[39] Bächler, op. cit., pp. 162–164.

[40] Hallowell, op. cit., pp. 43–51.

[41] Karl Meuli "Griechische Opferbräuche," in *Phyllobolia für Peter von der Muhll* (Basel, Switzerland: Benno Schwabe, 1940), p. 225.

[42] Bächler, op. cit., p. 167.

[43] J. Batchelor, *The Ainu and Their Folklore* (London: Religious Tract Society, 1901), p. 476.

[44] Ernest George Ravenstein, *The Russians of the Amur* (London: Trubner, 1861), p. 379.

[45] Hallowell, op. cit., pp. 53–54.

[46] Ibid., pp. 54–61.

[47] Adapted from Carl Etter, *Ainu Folklore* (Chicago: Wilcox & Follett, 1949), pp. 56–57.

[48] Hallowell, op. cit., p. 60, paragraphing and wording modified; citing James Teit, *The Lillooet Indians*, in Franz Boas (ed.), *Jesup North Pacific Expedition Publications* (Leiden, 1900–1908), vol. 2, p. 274.

[49] Ibid., pp. 60–61, n. 236, paragraphing and wording modified; citing James Teit, *The Shuswap*, in Boas (ed.), *Jesup North Pacific Expedition Publications*, vol. 2, p. 602.

[50] Ibid., p. 60, n. 233.

[51] R. G. Thwaites (ed.), *The Jesuit Relations and Allied Documents*, 73 vols. (Cleveland, Ohio: Burrows Brothers, 1898), vol. 6, *Quebec, 1633–1634*, pp. 283–293; see also, vol. 5, *Quebec: 1632–1633*, p. 131.

[52] W. F. Kirby (trans.), "Väinämöinen and the Bear," runo 46 in *Kalevala, the Land of the Heroes*, Everyman's Library, no. 260, 2 vols. (New York: E. P. Dutton, 1966; reprint of 1907 ed.), vol. 2, pp. 213–215, ll. 63–70, 107–114.

[53] Ibid., pp. 216–218, ll. 177–182, 225–242.

[54] Ibid., pp. 218–219, ll. 267–276, 283, 291–298.

[55] Ibid., pp. 219–222, ll. 298–299.

[56] Kyosuke Kindaiti, *Ainu Life and Legends*, Tourist Library, no. 36 (Tokyo: Maruzen, 1941), p. 50.

[57] J. Batchelor, "Ainus," in Hastings (ed.), *Encyclopaedia of Religion and Ethics*, vol. 1, p. 249.

[58] Ibid.; see also, Batchelor, *The Ainu and Their Folklore*.

[59] Ibid., pp. 241–242.

[60] Takakura Schinichiro, "The Ainu of Northern Japan: A Study in Conquest and Acculturation," *Transactions of the American Philosophical Society*, new series, vol. 50, part 4 (1960), p. 21 and n. 68.

[61] Kindaiti, op. cit., pp. 51–52.

[62] Batchelor, "Ainus," pp. 249–250; Kindaiti, op. cit., pp. 52–54.

[63] Robert Laneham, *Laneham's Letter Describing the Magnificent Pageants Presented Before Queen Elizabeth, at Kenilworth Castle in 1575* (Philadelphia: Hickman & Hazard, 1822).

[64] On this point, see Karl J. Nard, "Bärenzeremoniell und Schamanismus der Älteren Steinzeit Europas," *Saeculum*, vol. 10 (1959), pp. 233–272. Nard dates the beginning of the bear cult to a time earlier than 50,000 to 30,000 B.C., and of shamanism, to c. 25,000 B.C.

[65] Mircea Eliade, *Shamanism: Archaic Techniques of Ecstasy*, Bollingen 76 (New York: Pantheon, 1964), p. xix.

[66] Ibid., p. 504.

[67] Uno Harva, *Die religiösen Vorstellungen der altaischen Völker*, F F Communications, vol. 52, no. 125 (Helsinki, Finland: Porvos, 1938), pp. 558–559.

[68] Ibid., p. 559.

[69] From the Roman Catholic "Apostles' Creed."

[70] E. Lucas Bridges, *Uttermost Ends of the Earth* (New York: E. P. Dutton, 1948), pp. 27–59.

[71] Martin Gusinde, *Die Feuerland Indianer*, vol. 1, *Die Selk'nam: Von Leben und Denken eines Jägervolkes auf der grossen Feuerlandinsel*, vol. 2, *Die Yamana: Vom Leben und Denken der Wassernomaden am Kap Horn* (Mödling bei Wien, Austria: Verlag der Internationalen zeitschrift "Anthropos"—vol. 1, 1931; vol. 2, 1932).

[72] Ibid., vol. 1, pp. 496 ff.; vol. 2, pp. 1045 ff.

[73] Ibid., vol. 1, pp. 802–803; vol. 2, p. 1139.

[74] Ibid., vol. 2, pp. 1397–1398.

[75] Ibid., vol. 2, p. 1397.

[76] Mary Jo Spencer, "A Hidden Life," in Gareth Hill et al. (eds.), *The Shaman from Elko: Papers in Honor of Joseph L. Henderson on His Seventy-Fifth Birthday* (San Francisco: C. G. Jung Institute of San Francisco, 1978), pp. 177, 179.

[77] Gusinde, op. cit., vol. 2, pp. 1398–1399.

[78] Ibid., p. 1399.

[79] Ibid., vol. 1, pp. 734, 779–780.

[80] Ibid., p. 753.

[81] Ibid., p. 741.

[82] Ibid., p. 742.

[83] Ibid., p. 743.

[84] Bridges, op. cit., p. 264.

[85] Ibid., p. 262.

[86] Ibid., pp. 284–286.

[87] Gusinde, op. cit., vol. 1, pp. 772–775.

[88] Bridges, op. cit., pp. 232, 302–304.

[89] Ibid., p. 290.

[90] Gusinde, op. cit., vol. 1, pp. 752–753.

[91] Joan Halifax, *Shamanic Voices: A Survey of Visionary Narratives* (New York: E. P. Dutton, 1978), pp. 104–106; citing Knud Rasmussen, *The People of the Polar North: A Record*, compiled and edited by G. Herring (Philadelphia: J. B. Lippincott, 1908), pp. 305–309.

[92] Knud Rasmussen, *Across Arctic America* (New York: G. P. Putnam's Sons, 1927), pp. 82–84. A verbatim translation of Igjugarjuk's account of his trials to Rasmussen appears in Knud Rasmussen, *Intellectual Culture of the Hudson Bay Eskimos*, Report of the Fifth Thule Expedition, 1921–1924, vol. 7 (Copenhagen: Glydenalske, 1930), pp. 52–55.

[93] Halifax, op. cit., p. 104; citing Rasmussen, *The People of the Polar North*, pp. 305–309.

[94] H. Ostermann (ed.), *The Alaskan Eskimos, as Described in the Posthumous Notes of Dr. Knud Rasmussen*, Report of the Fifth Thule Expedition, 1921–1924, vol. 10, no. 3 (Copenhagen: Nordisk Forlag, 1952), pp. 97–99.

[95] Ibid., p. 128.

[96] Spencer and Gillen, op. cit., p. 525.

[97] Ibid., p. 523.

[98] Ibid., pp. 526–530.

[99] Ibid., pp. 531.

[100] Ibid., p. 533.

[101] Ananda K. Coomaraswamy, "Primitive Mentality," in Lipsey (ed.), *Coomaraswamy, Selected Papers*, vol. 1, pp. 287, 296–297.

[102] Ostermann (ed.), op. cit., pp. 97–98.

[103] G. V. Ksenofontov, *Legendy i rasskazy o shamanach u. yakutov, buryat i tungusov* (Moscow: Izdatel stvo Bezbozhnik, 1930); translated into German by A. Friedrich and G. Budruss, *Schamanengeschichten aus Sibirien* (Bern and Munich: Otto Wilhelm Barth Verlag, 1955), pp. 211–212.

[104] Ibid., pp. 213–214.

[105] Baumann, op. cit., pp. 14–81.

[106] W. Bogoras, *The Chukchee*, Reports of the Jesup North Pacific Expedition (New York: Memoirs of the American Museum of Natural History, 1907), vol. 11, part 2, p. 450.

[107] Waldemar Jochelson, *The Koryak*, Reports of the Jesup North Pacific Expedition (New York: Memoirs of the American Museum of Natural History, 1905), vol. 10, part 1, p. 52.

[108] Baumann, op. cit., pp. 343–382.

[109] John M. Cooper, "The Araucanians," in Julian H. Steward (ed.), *Handbook of South American Indians*, 7 vols., Smithsonian Institution, Bureau of American Ethnology, bulletin 143 (Washington, D.C.: Government Printing Office, 1946–1959), vol. 2, p. 750.

[110] Bogoras, op. cit., pp. 450–451.

[111] Ibid., p. 452.

[112] Ibid., p. 455.

[113] Ibid., p. 457.

[114] Ibid., p. 310.

[115] Harva, op. cit., pp. 543–544; citing "Pervyi buryatskii Šaman Morgon-Kara," *Isvestiya Vostočno-Sibirskago Otdela Russkago Geograficescago Obščestva*, vol. 11, no. 1–2. (Irkutsk, Russia, 1880), pp. 87 ff.

[116] Ksenofontov, op. cit., pp. 179–183.

[117] Waldemar Jochelson, *The Yukaghir and Yakaghirized Tungus* (New York: Memoirs of the American Museum of Natural History, 1910–1926), vol. 13, part 2, p. 162.

[118] Ibid., p. 163.

[119] Bogoras, op. cit., p. 413.

[120] Jochelson, *The Yukaghir and Yakaghirized Tungus*, p. 163.

[121] Ibid., pp. 163–164.

[122] Bogoras, op. cit., pp. 280–281.

[123] William Wordsworth, "Lines Composed a Few Miles Above Tintern Abbey, July 13, 1798," in Thomas Hutchinson (ed.), *The Poetical Works of William Wordsworth* (New York: Oxford University Press, 1923), p. 207, ll. 88–102.

[124] Bogoras, op. cit., pp. 330–332.

[125] Ibid., p. 315.

[126] Jochelson, *The Koryak*, pp. 18–19.

[127] Ibid., p. 355.

[128] Jochelson, *The Koryak*, pp. 227–230. Told by a Maritime Koryak man in Mikano, January 10, 1901.

[129] Ibid., pp. 251–252. Told by a Maritime Koryak woman in Talovka, December 29, 1900.

[130] See Antti Aarne, *Verzcichnis der Märchentypen*, F F Communications, no. 3; translated and enlarged by Stith Thompson, *The Types of the Folktale, a Classification and Bibliography* (Helsinki, Finland: Suomalainen Tiedeakatemia, Academia Scientiarum Fennica, 1928; rev. 2d ed., 1964), type 333, "The Glutton."

[131] Jochelson, *The Koryak*, pp. 302–303. Told by a Maritime Koryak woman in Talovka, December 30, 1900.

[132] Ibid., pp. 142–143. Told by a woman of a Reindeer Koryak village on the Chaibuga River.

[133] Franz Boas, "The Folk-Lore of the Eskimo," *Journal of American Folk-Lore*, vol. 17 (1904), p. 1; reprinted by Franz Boas, *Race, Language and Culture* (New York: Macmillan, 1940), p. 503.

[134] Knud Rasmussen, *Eskimo Folk-Tales*, edited and translated by W. Worster (London: Gyldendal, 1921), p. 16.

[135] Ibid., pp. 16–17.

[136] Boas, "The Folk-Lore of the Eskimo," p. 5; reprinted in Boas, *Race, Language and Religion*, p. 507.

[137] Ibid.

[138] Franz Boas, "The Central Eskimo," *6th Annual Report of the Bureau of American Ethnology* (1888), p. 597; also, "The Eskimo of Baffin Island and Hudson Bay," *American Museum of Natural History Bulletin*, vol. 15 (1901), p. 395.

[139] Ibid., p. 583.

[140] Robert F. Spencer, *The North Alaskan Eskimo*, Smithsonian Institution, Bureau of American Ethnology, bulletin 171 (Washington, D.C.: Government Printing Office, 1959), p. 310.

[141] Bogoras, op. cit., pp. 215–216.

[142] J. Murdock, "A Few Legendary Fragments from the Point Barrow Eskimo," *American Naturalist*, vol. 20, no. 7 (July 1886), p. 594.

[143] Spencer, op. cit., pp. 378–382.

[144] Ibid., pp. 383–439.

[145] Boas, "The Central Eskimo," p. 583.

[146] Henry (Heinrich Johannes) Rink, *Tales and Traditions of the Eskimo* (Edinburgh: William Blackwood & Sons, 1875), pp. 37–40; also, Boas, "The Folk-Lore of the Eskimo."

[147] Stith Thompson, *Motif-Index of Folk Literature*, 6 vols. (Bloomington: University of Indiana Press, 1932–1936); also issued as F F Communications, nos. 106–109, 116–117 (Helsinki, Finland, 1932–1936), topic N 831.1; see also, Stith Thompson, *Tales of the North American Indians* (Cambridge, Mass.: Harvard University Press, 1929), pp. 161, 342, n. 233.

[148] Junji Kinoshita, *Twilight of a Crane*, translated by Takeshi Kurahashi (Tokyo: Miraisha, 1952).

[149] Lucien M. Turner, "Ethnology of the Ungava District, Hudson Bay Territory," *11th Annual Report of the Bureau of American Ethnology, 1889–1890* (Washington, D.C.: Government Printing Office, 1894), p. 264.

[150] Thompson, *Tales of the North American Indians*, p. 356, n. 284; *Motif-Index of Folk Literature*, topic D 361.1; also, Antti Aarne and Stith Thompson, *The Types of the Folktale*, F F Communications, no. 184 (Helsinki, Finland, 1964), type 400*.

[151] Alfred L. Kroeber, "Tales of the Smith Sound Eskimo," *Journal of American Folk-Lore*, vol. 12, no. 7 (1899), p. 171.

[152] Rasmussen, *Eskimo Folk-Tales*, pp. 77–78.

[153] Spencer, op. cit., p. 285.

[154] Ibid., pp. 384–385.

[155] Hartley Burr Alexander, *North American Mythology*, vol. 10 in Louis Herbert Gray (ed.), *The Mythology of All Races* (Boston: Marshall Jones, 1916), p. 259; citing John R. Swanton, *Tlingit Myths and Texts*, Smithsonian Institution, Bureau of American Ethnology, bulletin 39 (Washington, D.C.: Government Printing Office, 1909), pp. 80–88.

[156] Swanton, *Tlingit Myths and Texts*.

[157] Thompson, *Tales of the North American Indians*, pp. 19–21, 280–281, nn. 38, 39; citing Franz Boas, "Tsimshian Mythology," *31st Annual Report of the Bureau of American Ethnology, 1909–1910* (Washington, D.C.: Government Printing Office, 1916), p. 58.

[158] Ibid., pp. 22–24, 281–282, nn. 42, 43, 44; Boas, "Tsimshian Mythology," p. 60.

[159] Curtis, op. cit., pp. 299–302, abridged and recast.

[160] Adapted from Franz Boas, "Talk About the Great Shaman of the Na'k!wax'da^{e}x^{u}, Called Fool," in *The Religion of the Kwakiutl Indians*, part 2, Columbia Contributions to Anthropology, vol. 10 (New York: Columbia University Press, 1930), pp. 41–45.

[161] Hartley Burr Alexander, *Latin American Mythology*, vol. 11 in Gray (ed.), *The Mythology of All Races*, p. 275; citing Alexander von Humboldt, *Voyage de Humboldt et Bonpland, aux régions équinoxiales du Nouveau Continent, fait en 1790–1804*, 24 vols. (Paris, 1807–1833); translated in part by T. Ross, *Personal Narrative of Travels to the Equinoctial Regions of America*, 3 vols. (London, 1852–1853), vol. 3, pp. 362–363.

[162] Richard Fraser Townsend, "State and Cosmos in the Art of Tenochtitlan," *Studies in Pre-Columbian Art and Archaeology*, no. 20 (Washington, D.C.: Dumbarton Oaks Trustees for Harvard University, 1979), p. 463.

[163] *The Gospel of Sri Ramakrishna*, translated by Swami Nikhilananda (New York: Ramakrishna-Vivekananda Center, 1942), pp. 365–366, 858–859.

[164] *Tao Teh King* 1.

[165] *Svetasvetara Upanishad* 4.4, translated by Robert Ernest Hume, *The Thirteen Principal Upanishads* (New York: Oxford University Press, 1921), p. 463.

[166] Phillip Drucker, "Northwest Coast Indians," in *The New Encyclopaedia Britannica*, Macropaedia, vol. 13 (Chicago: Encyclopaedia Brittannica, 1978), pp. 251–255. See also, Drucker, *Indians of the Northwest Coast*, American Museum of Natural History Anthropological Handbook, no. 10 (New York: McGraw-Hill, 1955; reprinted, Garden City, N.Y.: Natural History Press, 1963), and Drucker, *Cultures of the North Pacific Coast* (San Francisco: Chandler, 1965).

[167] Ruth Benedict, *Patterns of Culture* (Boston: Houghton Mifflin, 1934), chap. 6.

[168] Alexander, *North American Mythology*.

[169] Franz Boas, *The Mythology of the Bella Coola Indians* (New York: Memoirs of the American Museum of Natural History, 1900), vol. 2; also, Alexander, *North American Mythology*, pp. 249–250, 253–255.

[170] *Mandukyopanishad* 3–5, translated with Gaudapada's "Karika" and Sankara's "Commentary," by Swami Nikhilananda (Mysore, India: Sri Ramakrishna Ashram, 1936), pp. 14–18.

[171] Paul Radin, *The Trickster*, with commentaries by Karl Kerenyi and C. G. Jung (New York: Philosophical Library, 1956), pp. ix–x.

[172] Ovid, *Metamorphoses*, I:747–II:328.

[173] Franz Boas, *Kwakiutl Tales* (New York: Columbia University Press, 1910), vol. 2, pp. 123–135, adapted and abridged.

[174] Olivia Vlabos, *Body, The Ultimate Symbol* (New York: J. B. Lippincott, 1979), p. 62; citing Diamond Jenness, *The Indians of Canada*, National Museum of Canada Anthropological Series 15, bulletin 65 (1955).

[175] George Catlin, *The North American Indians, Being Letters and Notes on Their Manners, Customs and Conditions, Written During Eight Years Travel Amongst the Wildest Tribes of Indians in North America, 1832–1839*, 2 vols. (Philadelphia: Leary, Stuart, 1913), vol. 1, p. 42.

[176] Curtis, op. cit., pp. 262–263.

[177] Ibid., p. 11.

[178] Robin Ridington, "Metaphor and Meaning: Healing in Dunna-za Music and Dance," *The Western Canadian Journal of Anthropology*, vol. 8, nos. 2–4 (1978).

[179] Ibid.

[180] Mentor L. Williams (ed.), *Schoolcraft's Indian Legends* (East Lansing: Michigan State University Press, 1956), pp. 59–60, abridged and recast.

[181] Jeremiah Curtin, *Seneca Indian Myths* (New York: E. P. Dutton, 1923), pp. 192–194.

[182] Ibid., pp. 195–197.

[183] "Ordinary" of the Roman Catholic Mass, part 6, prayers at the foot of the altar, concluding phrase.

[184] John R. Swanton, *Myths and Tales of the Southeastern Indians*, Smithsonian Institution, Bureau of American Ethnology, bulletin 88 (Washington, D.C.: Government Printing Office, 1929), p. 75; citing "Narrative of a Voyage to the Spanish Main in the Ship 'Two Friends'," author unknown (London, 1819).

[185] Ibid., p. 68.

[186] Ibid., p. 67.

[187] Ibid., p. 46.

[188] William S. Webb and Raymond S. Baby, *The Adena People—No. 2* (Columbus, Ohio: Ohio State University Press for the Ohio Historical Society, 1957), p. 1, mound 176.

[189] Ibid., p. 8, mound 218.

[190] Ibid., p. 103; citing William A. Ritchie, *Recent Discoveries Suggesting an Early Woodland Burial Cult in the Northeast*, New York State Museum and Science Service, circular 40 (1955).

[191] Ibid., pp. 61–71.

[192] Charles E. Snow, "Adena Portraiture," in Webb and Baby, op. cit., pp. 47–60.

[193] Ibid., pp. 48–49.

[194] Ibid., p. 55.

[195] Ibid., pp. 56–59.

[196] Ibid., p. 55.

[197] "Serpent Mound," in Frederick Webb Hodge (ed.), *Handbook of American Indians North of Mexico*, Bureau of American Ethnology, bulletin 30 (Washington, D.C.: Government Printing Office, 1910), vol. 2, pp. 511–512.

[198] Snow, op. cit., p. 51; also, Willey, op. cit., vol. 1, p. 273.

[199] Willey, op. cit., vol. 1, pp. 274–275.

[200] Ibid., pp. 297–298.

[201] Ibid., pp. 293–294.

[202] D. Norrish, "Woodhenge—Work of a Genius," *Cahokian* (Collinsville, Ill.: Cahokia Mounds Museum Society, February 1978), pp. 1–16.

[203] Stefan Lorant, *The New World: The First Pictures of America* (New York: Duell, Sloan & Pierce, 1946).

[204] Ibid., p. 67, translated from Le Moyne's Latin narrative.

[205] Ibid., p. 105.

[206] John A. Eddy, "Medicine Wheels and Plains Indian Astronomy," in Anthony F. Aveni (ed.), *Native American Astronomy* (Austin: University of Texas Press, 1977), p. 149.

[207] John G. Neihardt, *Black Elk Speaks: Being the Life Story of a Holy Man of the Oglala Sioux* (New York: William Morrow, 1932; Lincoln: University of Nebraska Press, Bison Book, 1961), pp. 20–47.

[208] Joseph Epes Brown, *The Sacred Pipe: Black Elk's Account of the Seven Rites of the Oglala Sioux* (Norman: University of Oklahoma Press, 1953), p. 67.

[209] Ibid., p. 80.

[210] Ibid., pp. 94–95.

[211] Ibid., p. 71.

[212] Ibid., p. 85.

[213] Ibid., p. 69.

[214] Ibid., p. 93.

[215] Ibid., p. 83.

[216] Ibid., pp. 80–81.

[217] Ibid., pp. 81, 83, 85.

[218] Ibid., pp. 3–9; Neihardt, op. cit., Bison ed., pp. 3–5. See also, James Mooney, "The Ghost Dance Religion and the Sioux Outbreak of 1890," *14th Annual Report of the Bureau of American Ethnology, 1892–1893* (Washington, D.C.: Government Printing Office, 1896), part 2; edited and abridged by Anthony F. C. Wallace, *The Ghost Dance Religion and the Sioux Outbreak of 1890* (Chicago: University of Chicago Press, 1965; Phoenix ed., 1976), pp. 297–299.

[219] Wallace (ed.), *The Ghost Dance Religion and the Sioux Outbreak of 1890*, Phoenix ed., p. 298.

[220] Brown, op. cit., p. 6, n. 8; also, George A. Dorsey, *The Pawnee: Mythology*, part 1 (Washington, D.C.: Carnegie Institution of Washington, 1906), p. 134.

[221] Ibid., p. 80.

[222] Ibid., pp. 80–81.

[223] Ibid., p. 71.

[224] Alfred W. Bowers, *Mandan Social and Ceremonial Organization* (Chicago: University of Chicago Press, 1950).

[225] Catlin, op. cit., vol. 2, p. 202.

[226] Ibid., p. 204.

[227] Ibid., p. 205.

[228] Bowers, op. cit., pp. 156–163; see also, two additional accounts of the Okipa Ceremony that Bowers collected from informants, pp. 111–115.

[229] Catlin, op. cit., vol. 1, pp. 183–184.

[230] Ibid., pp. 184–185.

[231] Ibid., p. 186.

[232] Ibid., p. 188.

[233] Ibid., pp. 188–189.

[234] Harold McCracken, *George Catlin and the Old Frontier* (New York: Dial, 1959).

[235] Catlin, op. cit., vol. 1, pp. 188–189.

[236] McCracken, op. cit.

[237] Catlin, op. cit., vol. 1, pp. 188–189.

[238] Ibid., p. 189.

[239] Ibid., pp. 189–191.

[240] McCracken, op. cit.

[241] Catlin, op. cit., vol. 1, pp. 176–200.

[242] Wallace (ed.), *The Ghost Dance Religion and the Sioux Outbreak of 1890*, Phoenix ed., pp. 69, 293–296.

[243] Helen Hunt Jackson, *A Century of Dishonor* (London: Chatto & Windus, 1881).

[244] Ibid.

[245] Brown, op. cit., p. 72.

[246] Wallace (ed.), *The Ghost Dance Religion and the Sioux Outbreak of 1890*, Phoenix ed., p. 120.

[247] Joseph Campbell, *The Hero with a Thousand Faces*, Bollingen 17 (New York: Pantheon, 1949; Princeton, N.J.: Princeton University Press, 1953), pp. 3 ff.

[248] George Bird Grinnell, *Blackfoot Lodge Tales* (New York: Charles Scribner's Sons, 1916), pp. 104–107, abridged.

[249] Ibid., pp. 93–103, abridged.

[250] Ibid., pp. 127–131, abridged.

[251] Ibid., p. 271.

[252] Ibid., p. 258.

[253] Ibid., p. 271, abridged.

[254]Ibid., p. 272, abridged.

[255]Uno Holmberg, *Siberian Mythology,* vol. 4 in Gray (ed.), *The Mythology of All Races,* p. 323; citing V. I. Anučin, *Sbornik Muzeya po Antropologii i Etnografic pri Akademi Nauk,* vol. 2, no. 2 (Petrograd, Russia, 1914), p. 14.

[256]Ibid., p. 325; citing *Zapiski Vostočno-Sibirskago Otdela Russkago Geografičeskago Obščestva,* vol. 1, no. 2 (Irkutsk, Russia, 1890), p. 30.

[257]Ibid., pp. 324–325; citing P. I. Tretyakov, *Turuchanskiy Kray, ego priroda i zitali* (Petrograd, Russia, 1871), p. 207.

[258]Ibid., p. 313; citing V. L. Priklonskiy, ''Tri goda v Yakutskoy oblasti,'' *Zivaya Starina,* vol. 4, no. 66 (Petrograd, Russia, 1891).

[259]Ibid., p. 321; citing *Antero Vipunen* (Helsinki, Finland, 1908), pp. 25–26.

[260]*Visnu Purāna* 1.4.

[261]Ibid., 1.9.

[262]*Mārkandeya Pūrāna* 58.47.

[263]*Satapatha Brāhmana* 7.5.1.5, 14.1.2.11; *Taittirīya Sarihita* 6.2.42; *Taittirīya Aranyaka* 1.13. For the Tortoise incarnation, see *Mahābhārata* 1.18.45–53; *Rāmàyana* 1.45; *Agni Purāna,* chap. 3; *Kūrma Purāna,* chap. 259; *Visnu Purāna* 1.9; *Padma Purāna* 6.259; *Bhagavata Purāna* 8.7, 8.8.

[264]Grinnell, op. cit., pp. 137–139, abridged.

[265]Ibid., p. 257.

[266]Karl Kerényi, ''The Trickster in Relation to Greek Mythology,'' in Radin, op. cit., p. 185.

[267]Grinnell, op. cit., pp. 153–154, abridged.

[268]Ibid., pp. 167–168, abridged.

[269]Ibid., pp. 145–148, abridged. In reading this story, compare the Koryak tale of the expedition of Big Raven and Ememqut to the dwelling of Universe to bring rain (p. 184), the Sioux and Pawnee buffalo guardian at the gate through which the animals come and go (pp. 238–239), the great bull in the Crypt of Lascaux (Figure 105, p. 65), and Odysseus' exit from the Cyclops' cave (*Odyssey* 9.415–470).

[270]Ibid., pp. 155–156, abridged.

[271]James A. Tait, ''Thompson Tales,'' in Franz Boas (ed.), *Folk-Tales of Salishan and Sahaptin Tribes,* Memoirs of the American Folk-Lore Society, vol. 11 (New York: G. E. Stechert, 1917), p. 2, abridged.

[272]Radin, op. cit., p. 8, abridged.

[273]Ibid., pp. 22–23, abridged.

[274]Ibid., pp. 25–27, abridged.

[275]Thompson, *Tales of the North American Indians,* pp. 75–77, 302–303.

[276]George A. Dorsey, *Traditions of the Skidi Pawnee* (Boston: Houghton Mifflin, 1904), pp. 274–276, abridged.

[277]Morris Edward Opler, *Myths and Tales of the Jicarilla Apache Indians,* Memoirs of the American Folk-Lore Society, vol. 31 (New York: G. E. Stechert, 1938), pp. 1–26, abridged.

[278]*Where the Two Came to Their Father: A Navaho War Ceremonial,* given by Jeff King, text and paintings recorded by Maud Oakes, edited and with commentary by Joseph Campbell, Bollingen 1 (New York: Pantheon, 1943; 2d ed., Princeton, N.J.: Princeton University Press, 1969). The material published here is a radical abridgement of this now-inaccessible publication.

[279]Ibid., Pantheon ed., p. 38.

[280]Ibid., p. 39.

[281]Ibid., p. 41.

[282]Ibid., p. 19.

[283]Ibid., p. 48.

[284]Plato, ''Timaeus,'' in *The Works of Plato,* 4 vols. in 1, translated and with analysis and introductions by Benjamin Jowett (New York: Dial, 1871), p. 377.

[285]Ibid.

[286]*Where the Two Came to Their Father,* Pantheon ed., pp. 12–13.

[287]From an anonymously edited and popularly circulated speech delivered by Chief Seattle (Seathl) in 1855; other versions have been published by Virginia Armstrong, *I Have Spoken: American History Through the Voices of the Indians* (Chicago: Sage Books, 1971); by Thomas Sanders and Walter Peck, *Literature of the American Indian* (New York: Macmillan, 1973); and in German, as Chief Seattle, *Wir sind ein Teil der Erde* (Olten und Freiburg i Brsg.: Walter-Verlag A. G. Olten, 1982).

[288]For the African center, see George Peter Murdock, *Africa: Its Peoples and Their Culture History* (New York: McGraw-Hill, 1959), pp. 21–22, 64–71.

[289]Leo Frobenius, *Geographische Kulturkunde* (Leipzig: Friedrich Brandstetter, 1904), p. 605.

[290]Thompson, *Motif-Index of Folk Literature.* Martin Gusinde, *Die Feuerland Indianer,* vol. 1, *Die Selk'nam,* translated with commentary and analyses by Johannes Wilbert, *Folk Literature of the Selknam Indians,* U.C.L.A. Latin American Studies Series, vol. 32 (Los Angeles: University of California Press, 1975); vol. 2, *Die Yamana,* translated with commentary and analysis by Wilbert, *Folk Literature of the Yamana Indians,* U.C.L.A. Latin American Studies Series, vol. 40 (Los Angeles: University of California Press, 1977).

[291]Wilbert, *Folk Literature of the Selknam Indians,* pp. 21–22; Gusinde, op. cit., vol. 1, pp. 574–575.

[292]Ibid., pp. 23–25; Gusinde, op. cit., vol. 1, pp. 576–578.

[293]Ibid., pp. 26–27; Gusinde, op. cit., vol. 1, p. 579.

[294]Ibid., pp. 30–34; Gusinde, op. cit., vol. 1, pp. 584–586.

[295]Ibid., pp. 27–28, 34–36; Gusinde, op. cit., vol. 1, pp. 580–581, 586–588.

[296]Ibid., pp. 33–34; Gusinde, op. cit., vol. 1, p. 586.

[297]Ibid., pp. 39–43; Gusinde, op. cit., vol. 1, pp. 593–595, 597–599.

[298]Ibid., pp. 37–39; Gusinde, op. cit., vol. 1, pp. 588–589.

[299]Ibid., pp. 147–158; Gusinde, op. cit., vol. 1, pp. 859–869.

[300]Ibid., pp. 161–164; Gusinde, op. cit., vol. 1, pp. 871–873.

[301]Wilbert, *Folk Literature of the Yamana Indians,* pp. 17–18; Gusinde, op. cit., vol. 2, pp. 1145–1146.

[302]Ibid., pp. 25–30; Gusinde, op. cit., vol. 2, pp. 1232–1233, 1155–1156.

[303]Ibid., pp. 30–31; Gusinde, op. cit., vol. 2, p. 1160.

[304]Ibid., pp. 31–32; Gusinde, op. cit., vol. 2, pp. 1160–1161.

[305]Ibid., pp. 32–33; Gusinde, op. cit., vol. 2, pp. 1161–1162.

[306]Ibid., pp. 34–35; Gusinde, op. cit., vol. 2, pp. 1162–1163.

[307]Ibid., pp. 38–40; Gusinde, op. cit., vol. 2, pp. 1165–1167.

[308]Ibid., pp. 42–47; Gusinde, op. cit., vol. 2, pp. 1168–1172.

[309]Ibid., pp. 47–50; Gusinde, op. cit., vol. 2, pp. 1174–1176.

[310]Ibid., pp. 58–59; Gusinde, op. cit., vol. 2, pp. 1182–1183.

[311]Ibid., pp. 51–57; Gusinde, op. cit., vol. 2, pp. 1176–1182.

[312]Ibid., pp. 60–61; Gusinde, op. cit., vol. 2, p. 1183.

[17]Norman Bancroft-Hunt and Werner Forman, *People of the Totem* (Toronto: Doubleday Canada, 1979), pp. 78–81; Franz Boas, *Kwakiutl Culture as Reflected in Mythology,* Memoirs of the American Folk-Lore Society, vol. 27 (New York: G. E. Stechert, 1935), pp. 97–98. The prayer is from Franz Boas, *Ethnology of the Kwakiutl,* Smithsonian Institution, *35th Annual Report of the Bureau of American Ethnology, 1913–1914* (Washington, D.C.: Government Printing Office, 1921), p. 1295, modified.

[18]Selwyn Dewdney and Kenneth E. Kidd, *Indian Rock Paintings of the Great Lakes* (Toronto: University of Toronto Press, 1962), pp. v–vi, 76.

[19]Curtis, op. cit., pp. 97–98.

[20]Catlin, op. cit., vol. 2, p. 159 and fig. 243.

[21]Morgan, op. cit., vol. 1, pp. 158–160.

[22]Stuart Struever and Felicia Antonelli Holton, *Koster* (Garden City, N.Y.: Doubleday, Anchor, 1979); also, *Early Man,* an archaeological publication of Northwestern University, Evanston, Ill., no. 2 (June 1977).

[23]Webb and Baby, op. cit., pp. 61–67.

[24]Ibid., pp. 83–101; a recently discovered, thirteenth site was noted by Martha Otto, Ohio Historical Society, in a personal communication.

[25]Lorant, op. cit., p. 260; quoting from Thomas Hariot, *A Brief and True Report of the New Found Land of Virginia,* a text to engravings by Theodore de Bry from a watercolor by John White, c. 1584 (London, 1588).

[26]Ibid., p. 105.

[27]Ibid., p. 109.

[28]Ibid., p. 79.

[29]Ibid., p. 243.

[30]Ibid., pp. 264–265.

[31]Neihardt, op. cit., Bison ed., pp. 42–43.

[32]Wallace (ed.), *The Ghost Dance Religion and the Sioux Outbreak of 1890,* Phoenix ed., pp. 2, 16.

[33]Ibid., pp. 176–177.

[34]Catlin, op. cit., vol. 1, p. 46.

[35]Bridges, op. cit., p. 59.

[36]Ibid., p. 521.

[37]Ibid., p. 368 and plate 23.

[38]Ibid., p. 370.

[39]Highwater, op. cit.

[40]Bridges, op. cit., pp. 212–213.

[41]Wilbert, *Folk Literature of the Yamana Indians,* p. 6; citing Gusinde, op. cit., vol. 2, p. 1142.

Captions

[1]Andreas Lommel, *Prehistoric and Primitive Man* (New York: McGraw-Hill, 1966), p. 41 and map p. 42.

[2]Strehlow, op. cit., pp. 7–9 and fig. 4.

[3]Following Dacre Stubbs, *Prehistoric Art of Australia* (New York: Charles Scribner's Sons, 1974), pp. 41–42 and map p. 109, modified.

[4]Berndt and Berndt, op. cit., pp. 117–118 and illustration ff. p. 158.

[5]Baumann, op. cit., p. 250.

[6]Martin P. Nilsson, *Geschichte der Griechischen Religion,* 2 vols. (Munich: C. H. Beck'sche, 1955), vol. 1, p. 485.

[7]Karl Kerényi, *The Heroes of the Greeks* (New York: Grove Press, 1960), p. 333; citing Aeschylus, *Agamemnon* 239, and Euripides, *Iphigenia in Aulis* 1579.

[8]See the remarkable article by Charles Musès, ''Celtic Origins of the Arthurian Cycle: Geographic-Linguistic Evidence,'' *Journal of Indo-European Studies,* vol. 7, no. 1–2 (1979).

[9]Ibid., p. 36.

[10]Harva, op. cit., pp. 557–558.

[11]Bogoras, op. cit., pp. 310–311.

[12]Jochelson, *The Koryak,* p. 93.

[13]Peter T. Furst, ''The Roots and Continuities of Shamanism,'' in Anne Trueblood, Rose Danesewich, and Nick Johnson (eds.), *Stones, Bones and Skin: Ritual and Shamanic Art* (Toronto: Society for Art Publications, 1977), p. 25.

[14]Baumann, op. cit., pp. 14–44, 343–355 map 1.

[15]Cooper, op. cit., vol. 2, pp. 743, 750.

[16]Jochelson, *The Koryak,* pp. 90–98.

A NOTE ON THE INDEXES

References to pages, captions, maps, and map captions

In the Place Name Index and the Subject Index, references to pages are page numbers, e.g.,

Barrow (Alaska), 187

which means that a reference to Barrow is to be found on page 187. In both indexes, commas, rather than dashes, are used to indicate separate mentions of a topic in adjacent pages, e.g.,

125, 126

References to captions consist of a boldface caption number (or range of caption numbers), followed by a hyphen and a page number. For example,

254-147

126–130-72

References to maps consist of a boldface capital "M" and map number (or range of map numbers) followed by a hyphen and a page number, e.g.,

M50-255

M44–46-211

Map captions are referred to similarly, but with an additional letter "C," e.g.,

MC29-122

271

CREDITS AND ACKNOWLEDGEMENTS

MYTHOLOGIES OF THE GREAT HUNT

223 JV; **224** PF; **225** AIS; **226** Linden Museum, Stuttgart; **227** Kühn, *Rock Art of Eruope;* **228** JV; **229–231** AL; **232** Robert R. R. Brooks, *Stone Age Painting in India* (New Haven, Conn.: Yale University Press, 1976); **233** AL; **234** Edward L. Ruhe, Lawrence, Kansas; **235** MV; **236** AL; **237** Charles Kerry/National Library of Australia, Canberra; **238-239** AIS; **240** Mountford Sheard Collection of Ethnology, State Library of South Australia; **241** AMNH; **242** BM; **243** NYPL; **244** AIS; **245** Robert Edwards, Internationall Cultural Corporation of Australia, Sydney; **246** MV; **247–248** J. E. Stanton/Anthropology Research Museum, University of Western Australia; **249** Kerry/National Library of Australia; **250** NYPL; **251–253** AMNH; **254** National Museum, Copenhagen; **255** George Kopak Tayarak, Sugluk La Fédération des Cooperatives du Nouveau, Quebec/Ernest Mayer, Winnipeg Art Gallery; **256** LB; **257** Vince Ambromitis/Carnegie Museum of Natural History, Pittsburgh; **258** FM; **259** NYPL; **260–261** AMNH; **262–264** BNM; **265** EC/PMA; **267** MSGL; **268** Soprintendenza alle antichità dell'Etruria Meridionale, Rome; **269–272** GA; **273** NYPL; **274** MAI; **275** Alice Marriott Collection, University of Oklahoma, Norman; **276–279** AMNH; **280** PF; **281** Louis Faran, Stony Brook, New York; **282–284** ABM; **285–286** MG; **287** N. Bouvier, Cologny-Genève; **288** NYPL; **289** ABM; **290** National Museum of Canada, Ottawa; **291** SI; **292** Jessie Oonark, Winnipeg Art Gallery/Ernest Mayer; **293** KR; **294** Sam Kimura/Sheldon Jackson Museum, Sitka; **295** KR; **296** Lowie Museum of Anthropology, Berkeley; **297–298** Spencer and Gillen, *The Native Tribes of Central Australia;* **299–300** AMNH; **301** HL; **302** Radio Times Hulton Picture Library, London; **303** KR; **304** AMNH; **305** Sakan Pals/National Museum of Finland, Helsinki; **306–307** MV; **308** AMNH; **309** LB; **310** GA/KR; **311** Burt Glinn/Magnum; **312** MAI; **313** University of Washington Extension Series, adapted from Viola E. Garfield, 1940; **314** EC; **315–316** Werner Forman Photo Archives, London; **317** EC; **319** J. A. Shuck Collection of Western History, University of Oklahoma Library; **320** Freer Gallery, Washington, D.C.; **321** AMNH; **322** Musée Cernuschi, Paris; **323** University Museum of Archaeology and Ethnology, Cambridge, England; **324** AMNH; **325** Collection Tropen Museum, Amsterdam; **326** Museo Nacional de Rio de Janeiro; **327–328** Eberhard Otto, Toronto; **329–332** AMNH; **333** Bill McLenan/Museum of Anthropology, University of British Columbia; **334** AMNH; **335** MAI; **336** AMNH; **337** EC; **338** GC/NCFA; **339** NYPL; **340** Paul Kane/Royal Ontario Museum, Toronto; **341** MV; **342** MAI; **343** National Museum of Man, National Museums of Canada, Ottawa; **344** NYPL; **345** BNM; **346–347** OHS; **348** MAI; **349–350** FM; **351** MAI; **352** University of Alabama Museum of Natural History; **353** Bob Campagna/Cote Library Powers Collection, Cornell Library, Mt. Vernon, Iowa; **354** George Gerster/Photo Researchers; **355–357** OHS; **358** FM; **359** MAI; **360** John W. Melton, Jr., Glen Allen, Va.; **361** Peabody Museum, Cambridge, Mass.; **362** OHS; **363** FM; **364** SM; **365** MAI; **366–367** SM; **368–376** MAI; **377** SM; **378** MAI; **379–381** GA; **382–383** NYPL; **384** SI; **385** Kjell B. Sandved, Washington, D.C.; **387–388** NYPL; **389** U.S. Forest Service; **393** AMNH; **394** Glenbow Archives, Calgary; **395–396** AMNH; **397** Joseph Epes Brown, Missoula, Montana; **398** AMNH; **399–400** GC/NCFA; **401** AMNH; **402** GC/NCFA; **403–404** SI; **405** Nevada Nistorical Society; **406** GC/NYPL; **407** Museum of Navajo Ceremonial Art, Santa Fe; **408** Harvey Lloyd/Peter Arnold Inc.; **409** SI; **410** Southwest Museum, Los Angeles; **411** UPI; **412** Museum of New Mexico; **413–420** *Where the Two Came to Their Father: A Navaho War Ceremonial,* given by Jeff King, text and paintings recorded by Maud Oakes, edited and with commentary by Joseph Campbell, Bollingen 1 (New York: Pantheon, 1943); **421** Allan Reed; **422** UPI; **423** EC; **424** EC/PMA; **425** EC; **426** Bette Andresen; **427** MG; **428–430** ABM; **431–432** MG; **433–435** ABM; **436–440** MG.

PICTURES

ABM = Armando Braun Menendez, Buenos Aires; **AIS** = Australian Information Service, New York; **AL** = Andreas Lommel; **AMNH** = American Museum of Natural History, New York; **BM** = British Museum, London; **BNM** = Brooklyn Museum, New York; **EC** = Edward Curtis; **FM** = Field Museum of Natural History, Chicago; **GA** = George Armstrong; **GC** = George Catlin; **HL** = Hermitage Museum, Leningrad; **JV** = Jean Vertut, Issy-Les-Moulineaux, France; **KR** = Knud Rasmussen, *Across Arctic America* (New York: G. P. Putnam's Sons, 1927); **LB** = Lee Boltin, New York; **MAI** = Museum of the American Indian/Heye Foundation, New York; **MG** = Martin Gusinde, *Die Feuerland Indianer*, 2 vols. (Mödling bei Wien, Austria: Verlag der Internationalen Zeitschrift ''Anthropos''— vol. 1, 1931; vol. 2, 1932); **MSGL** = Musée de St. Germaine en Laye; **MV** = Museum für Völkerkunde, Munich; **NCFA** = National Collection of Fine Arts, Washington, D.C.; **NYPL** = New York Public Library; **OHS** = Ohio Historical Society, Columbus; **PF** = Peter Furst, Albany, New York; **PMA** = Philadelphia Museum of Art; **SI** = Smithsonian Institution, Washington, D.C.; **SM** = Stovall Museum of Science and History, Norman, Oklahoma; **UPI** = United Press International.

MAPS

Map 31. Based on information adapted from Andreas Lommel, *Prehistoric and Primitive Man* (Feltham, Middlesex: Hamlyn Publishing Group, 1967).

Map 32. Based on information adapted from Dacre Stubbs, *Prehistoric Art of Australia* (New York: Charles Scribner's Sons, 1974; copyright © 1974 Dacre Stubbs), adapted with the permission of Charles Scribner's Sons.

Map 33. Based on information adapted from H. Baumann, *Das Doppelte Geschlecht: Ethnologische Studien zur Bisexualität in Ritus und Mythos* (Berlin: Dietrich Reimer, 1955).

Map 36. Based on information adapted from Timothy Severin, *The Horizon Book of Vanishing Primitive Man* (copyright © 1973 American Heritage, New York).

Map 37. Based on information adapted from R. Gordon Wasson, *Soma: Divine Mushroom of Immortality* (New York: Harcourt Brace Jovanovich, 1972).

Map 38. Based on information adapted from H. Baumann, *Das Doppelte Geschlecht: Ethnologische Studien zur Bisexualität in Ritus und Mythos* (Berlin: Dietrich Reimer, 1955).

Map 41. Based on information adapted from Miguel Covarrubias, *The Eagle, the Jaguar and the Serpent: Indian Art in the Americas* (New York: Alfred A. Knopf, 1967); Thor Heyerdahl, *Aku-Aku* (New York: Rand McNally, 1958; copyright © 1958 by Thor Heyerdahl; used by permission of Rand McNally); Carl O. Sauer, ''A Geographic Sketch of Early Man in America,'' *Geographical Review*, vol. 34 (1944), p. 555; and Clifford J. Jolly and Fred Plog, *Physical Anthropology and Archaeology*, 2d ed. (New York: Alfred A. Knopf, 1979).

Map 42. Based on information adapted from *Encyclopaedia Britannica*, 15th ed. (Chicago: Encyclopaedia Britannica, 1982); Robert Spencer, *The Native Americans* (New York: Harper & Row, 1977); R. Underhill, *Red Man's America* (Chicago: University of Chicago Press, 1953); and W. C. Sturtevant and B. C. Trigger (eds.), *Handbook of North American Indians*, vol. 8, ''California'' (Washington, D.C.: Smithsonian Institution, 1981) and vol. 15, ''Northeast'' (1978).

Map 43. Based on information adapted from Miguel Covarrubias, *The Eagle, the Jaguar and the Serpent: Indian Art of the Americas* (New York: Alfred A. Knopf, 1967); W. C. Sturtevant and J. Helms (eds.), *Handbook of North American Indians*, vol. 6, ''Subarctic'' (Washington, D.C.: Smithsonian Institution, 1981); and Allen Wardwell, *Objects of Bright Pride* (New York: Center for Inter-American Relations and American Federation of Arts, 1978).

Map 47. Based on information adapted from John A. Eddy, ''Medicine Wheels and Plains Indian Astronomy,'' in Anthony F. Aveni (ed.), *Native American Astronomy* (Austin: University of Texas Press, 1977, all rights reserved), and Miguel Covarrubias, *The Eagle, the Jaguar and the Serpent: Indian Art of the Americas* (New York: Alfred A. Knopf, 1967).

Map 48. Based on information adapted from J. M. Goodman, *The Navaho Atlas* (copyright © 1982 University of Oklahoma Press, Norman, Oklahoma).

Map 49. Based on information adapted from J. Engel, *Grosser Historischer Weltatlas*, vol. 2 (Munich: Bayerischer Schulbuch Verlag, 1979); E. García de Miranda and Z. Falcón de Gyves, *Nuevo Atlas Porrúa de la República Mexicana* (Mexico City: Editorial Porrúa, SA, 1974); *Academic American Encyclopaedia*, vol. 11 (Danbury, Conn.: Grolier, 1982); and *Westermann's Grosser Atlas zur Weltgeschichte* (Braunschweig: Georg Westermann Verlag, 1969).

Map 50. Based in part on information from Martin Gusinde, *Die Feuerland Indianer*, vol. 1, *Die Selk'nam*, translated with commentary and analyses by Johannes Wilbert, *Folk Literature of the Selknam Indians*, U.C.L.A. Latin American Studies Series, vol. 32 (Los Angeles: University of California Press, 1975).

EXTRACTS

From T. G. H. Strehlow, *Aranda Traditions* (Carlton, Australia: Melbourne University Press, 1947), used with permission of Mrs. T. G. H. Strehlow, Prospect, South Australia.

From Elias Lonnrot, *Kalevala, the Land of the Heroes*, translated by W. F. Kirby, Everyman's Library, no. 260, 2 vols. (New York: E. P. Dutton, 1966; reprint of 1907 ed.), used with permission of J. M. Dent & Sons, Ltd., London.

From E. Lucas Bridges, *Uttermost Ends of the Earth* (New York: E. P. Dutton, 1948), used with permission of Hodder & Stoughton, Ltd., London.

From Martin Gusinde, *Die Feuerland Indianer*, vol. 1, *Die Selk'nam: Von Leben und Denken eines Jägervolkes auf der grossen Feuerlandinsel*, vol. 2, *Die Yamana: Vom Leben und Denken der Wassernomaden am Kap Horn* (Mödling bei Wien, Austria: Verlag der Internationalen Zeitschrift "Anthropos"—vol. 1, 1931; vol. 2, 1932), used with permission of Verlag Sankt Gabriel, Mödling bei Wien, Austria.

From Knud Rasmussen, *Across Arctic America* (New York: G. P. Putnam's Sons, 1927), used with permission.

From H. Ostermann (ed.), *The Alaskan Eskimos, as Described in the Posthumous Notes of Dr. Knud Rasmussen*, Report of the Fifth Thule Expedition, 1921–1924, vol. 10, no. 3 (Copenhagen: Nordisk Forlag, 1952), used with permission of Rudolph Sand for the heirs of Knud Rasmussen.

From G. V. Ksenofontov, *Legendy i rasskazy o shamanach u. yakutov, buryat i tungusov* (Moscow: Izdatel stvo Besbozhnik, 1930); translated into German by A. Friedrich and G. Budruss, *Schamanengeschichten aus Sibirien* (Bern and Munich: Otto Wilhelm Barth Verlag, 1955), used with permission.

From John R. Swanton, *Tlingit Myths and Texts*, Smithsonian Institution, Bureau of American Ethnology, bulletin 39 (Washington, D.C.: Government Printing Office, 1909), and *Myths and Tales of the Southeastern Indians*, Smithsonian Institution, Bureau of American Ethnology, bulletin 88 (Washington, D.C.: Government Printing Office, 1929), used with permission.

From Franz Boas, ''Tsimshian Mythology,'' *31st Annual Report of the Bureau of American Ethnology*, 1909–1910, Smithsonian Institution (Washington, D.C.: Government Printing Office, 1916), used with permission.

From Franz Boas, *Kwakiutl Tales*, vol. 2 (New York: Columbia University Press, 1910), used with permission.

From Mentor L. Williams (ed.), *Schoolcraft's Indian Legends* (East Lansing: Michigan State University Press, 1956), used with permission.

From Jeremiah Curtin, *Seneca Indian Myths* (New York: E. P. Dutton, 1923), used with permission of Jeremiah C. Cardell.

From Joseph Epes Brown, *The Sacred Pipe: Black Elk's Account of the Seven Rites of the Oglala Sioux* (copyright © 1953 by the University of Oklahoma Press, Norman), used with permission.

From George Bird Grinnell, *Blackfoot Lodge Tales* (New York: Charles Scribner's Sons, 1916; copyright © under the Berne Convention), reprinted with permission.

From Morris Edward Opler, *Myths and Tales of the Jicarilla Apache Indians*, The American Folklore Society, Memoirs of the American Folk-Lore Society, vol. 31 (New York: G. E. Stechert, 1938), used with permission.

From *Where the Two Came to Their Father: A Navaho War Ceremonial*, given by Jeff King, text and paintings recorded by Maud Oakes, edited and with commentary by Joseph Campbell, Bollingen 1 (New York: Pantheon, 1943; 2d ed., Princeton, N.J.: Princeton University Press, 1969), used with permission.

From Johannes Wilbert, *Folk Literature of the Selknam Indians, Martin Gusinde's Collection of Selknam Narratives*, U.C.L.A. Latin American Studies Series, vol. 32 (Los Angeles: University of California Press, 1975), and *Folk Literature of the Yamana Indians, Martin Gusinde's Collection of Yamana Narratives*, U.C.L.A. Latin American Studies Series, vol. 40 (Los Angeles: University of California Press, 1977), used with permission.

Grateful acknowledgment is made to the following for their noted contributions to this volume: Martha Otto, the Ohio Historical Society, for assuring the accuracy of data relating to prehistoric societies in the American Middle West; Jamake Highwater, and Terry Tafoya, for sharing their scholarly research.

Editorial Director: *Robert Walter*

Associate Editor: *Hugh Haggerty*

Designer: *Jos. Trautwein/Bentwood Studio*

Picture Editor: *Rosemary O'Connell*

Permissions Editor: *Cynthia Beckett Ortega*

Copyeditor/Indexer: *Leonard Neufeld*

Illustrator: *George Armstrong*

Maps and Charts: *Cartographic Services Center of R. R. Donnelley & Sons Company:*
Map Design: *Sidney P. Marland III*
Map Research, Compilation, and Project Coordination: *Luis Freile*
Map Drafting and Production: *David F. Stong*
Design, Drafting, and Production of the Two Evolution Charts: *Jeannine M. Schonta*

Type Composition by *Typographic Art, Inc.*

Printing and Binding by *Royal Smeets Offset B.V., The Netherlands*